TEN LECTURES ON THEORIES OF THE DANCE

by
Drid Williams

The Scarecrow Press, Inc.
Metuchen, N.J., & London
1991

British Library Cataloguing-in-Publication data available

Library of Congress Cataloging-in-Publication Data

Williams, Drid, 1928–
  Ten Lectures on theories of the dance / by Drid Williams
    p.   cm.
  Includes bibliographical references.
  ISBN 0-8108-2219-9 (alk. paper)
    1. Dancing—Anthropological aspects.   2. Dancing.   I. Title.
  GV1588.6.W55   1991
  306.4'84—dc20   89-27028

To the memory of Professor Sir E.E. Evans-Pritchard, who encouraged me to study social anthropology in the first place, and to whose good will and guidance I owe so much, and to the New York "group," for whom the lectures were originally devised.

7

CONTENTS

PREFACE

THE TEN CORE LECTURES WHICH comprise this book have all been given in several University contexts in connection with a variety of departments or programs that attempt to combine studies of social and/or cultural anthropology, the dance, and other systems of human movement (ritual, ceremonies, the martial arts, sign languages) in their curricula for degree-granting purposes. This means that this book is a teaching book meant for use by those who may, for a variety of reasons, be interested in a trained anthropologist's view of standard theories and explanations of the dance.

The chapters are presented almost entirely as written for graduate lectures, although some material included in Chapter VII to the end has been added for publication. Their source is to be found in a lengthy section of a B. Litt. thesis, written at Oxford between 1971–1972, entitled "Social Anthropology and Dance" in which I undertook an extensive critical survey of past writings on the subject (roughly beginning with the latter third of the 19th c., culminating with the late 1950's and 1960's). Other sections of that thesis contain an exegesis of a more contemporary social anthropological approach to the subject which has become known as "semasiology," which is one among several modern approaches to the study of human movement that has originated in anthropology during the last three decades. Some of these are outlined in Lecture (now Chapter) IX. An Appendix II on recently completed work in Australia has been added for students of Aboriginal dancing.

So far as I am aware, no such survey of literature has been undertaken before 1971 or since then, thus there were no models for me to follow, excepting that of E.E. Evans-Pritchard's *Theories of Primitive Religion*, and I discuss this choice and its relevance to the book in Chapter I (See *infra*, pp. 12–13). There are no comparable treatments of the subject of theories of the dance (or, theories *about* the dance) with which readers might compare, but the lectures are offered in the hope that serious discussion and treatment of the dance, especially, will be stimulated by a frankly provocative, iconoclastic treatment of the subject.

Because the chapters consist of a grouping of more or less self-contained lectures, there is nothing to prevent readers from starting with any chapter that seems to take his or her fancy. For those who prefer to have some idea of my own theoretical standpoint before reading critical assessments of theories which have preceded it, I suggest beginning with Chapter VIII "Body Languages" followed by a reading through the conclusion. This choice of reading will present a more "positive" view of the subject, so to speak, seen from the standpoint of some of the theoretical advances which have been made. On the other hand, some readers may prefer to begin with Chapter I. This choice would treat the series like a standard course in the subject, following a more traditional format of critical assessments of historical materials first, laying the groundwork for modern approaches to the subject and for issues that are of contemporary interest to many anthropologists which appear later. This is the order in which they would be heard in a lecture series, but either choice is meant to lead to the same levels of comprehension of the many complexities and problems that are involved when one contemplates a systematic and explicitly articulated study of an intriguing, novel, and many-facetted subject. Readers are invited to read as they please: sometimes it is profitable to read a book like this starting from the conclusion and reading backwards. Other readings, e.g., Chapter I followed by Chapter X, then Chapter II followed by IX and so on, give an interesting view of the material—or so I have been told.

However the book is approached, I would appreciate all readers' assistance in realizing that lectures are commonly meant to be heard and not read, and that these lectures were designed mainly for highly intelligent, but non-specialist audiences; that is, non-anthropologically trained audiences such as one encounters in the fields of music, dance and dance education, physical education, library science, psychology and to a lesser extent, linguistics. Much of what I say here, had I been speaking only to anthropologists or to students of social and cultural anthropology, would have been differently expressed, although it would have carried the same import. Some of what I have said would not have been said at all, because I could have assumed some of the kinds of epistemological knowledges to which I refer to be shared.

When I teach a course like this, whether in a graduate or undergraduate context—or when I lecture to librarians or musicians, for instance, on reference works in the subject of the dance, "dance ethnology," and the like, I always include a glossary of terms for the benefit of those who may not be familiar with some of the philosophical, linguistic, or anthropological terms which are common currency in the discipline. This glossary (not intended as an insult to colleagues or to more sophisticated readers) is to be found at the end of the book, after the Appendix and before the Bibliography. Notes for each chapter, where they exist, are placed at the end of each chapter.

Some further comments: I was asked by some of the readers of the draft manuscript to acknowledge the fact that this is, in some sense, a "difficult" book. Specifically, they said, for dancers who might happen upon the volume. I found the observation especially interesting since I was a dancer, choreographer, and teacher of dancing for many years before I became an anthropologist and librarian. Further enquiries into the reasons for such a forewarning, however, convinced me of the validity of the advice. Why?

Apparently it is the case that much of what I say in these pages about dancing (or "the dance," or "a" dance, or dancers) is considered *by* dancers to belong to the realm of *tacit* knowledge that they seem to believe to be *common* knowledge of the activity in whatever form. I was told that it seems strange to dancers, steeped as they are in kinesthetic awarenesses, spatial orientations, controls over their bodily environments, for example, to find such knowledges used as the basis for articulated knowledge about the subject and criticisms of writings which do not have these kinds of things as their foundations. The problem is that on the whole, these tacit, implicit knowledges regarding the vast field of human actions, whether danced or not, are a-critical. That's to say that all the majority of people ever know about movement is *that* they have moved—they have not inquired into "how" or "why" they move, or what significance the actions may have on other areas of their lives—their "world-views."

The same might be said of speaking. In general, we are aware of our reactions to others and to their reactions to us, whether we are speaking, moving, or both, but we tend to be unaware of the reasons for these reactions; all of this tends to function out of awareness. The study of a danced form (or forms) can begin to bring the powers of critical thought to bear upon what had been an un-critical acceptance of the conditions and circumstances of one's physically performed actions. At least, I found this to be true, and it is this kind of awareness that (a) it is impossible for me to eradicate from my persona, and (b) I have therefore tried to bring to bear consciously upon the discussions to follow. Throughout, I maintain a dancerly point of view on the issues, problems, and paradoxes that arise when the dance is approached, not as an activity, *per se,* but as a subject of scholarly investigation. There are, of course, further levels of comprehension open to examination beyond this more or less individualistic level of understanding, and what I have tried to do is to open the door to these levels. No hard and fast "conclusions" are reached, because this is a *beginning* graduate course, not a pro-seminar. However, there is a sense in which my representations of theories of the dance intends to bring some of the shared features of our received ideas about the human activity of dancing into consciousness—features that are usually "hidden" with regard to movement, no matter what kind of movement it is—and features that to some of my audience are bound to be somewhat disquieting if they have strong investments in certain kinds of explanations of dancing.

To bring out some of the theoretical implications and logical consequences of such tacit knowledges as dancers possess and critically to reflect upon them seems somewhat strange to dancers because they do not often pause to reflect on the awarenesses which are produced by their danced experiences. Moreover, I have had some people say to me that it is a "shame" to *write* about the dance, or to investigate it, or even to preoccupy oneself so closely as I have done with what has been written about it by others. All the "reality," according to these critics, is in the performance, and nothing that one can produce in another medium of expression or in another mode of scholarly study can even come close. Surprisingly, perhaps, I agree.

I would hasten to add, however, that this kind of argument is based, in my view, on a serious misunderstanding: one is not trying to reproduce the *experience of dancing* in an anthropological examination of it, nor in the pages to follow is there any attempt on my part to teach people how to dance or anything of the kind. The fact that "to move," whether one is dancing, walking, or engaged in the myriad activities of everyday, or signing a conversation or performing a ritual of some kind is to engage in the expression of tacit knowledges of a specific and fundamental kind does not bother me, and I hope that it will not bother my readers, either.

All my life, I have wanted to talk about dancing and moving as well as I once danced and moved. There would be no need for this series of lectures if people spoke and wrote as well about the dance as many dancers perform in their various idioms. The point is that a lifetime of thought about moving has gone into the examination of literature included in the chapters to follow; thought that has taken place whilst sweating over a ballet barre, or attempting to master a calypso dance in a New York studio, or a north Indian Kathak *tukra, paran,* or *ghat* in a similar context—and so on, including the years spent in West Africa, and now, Australia. While I am aware that for many people "moving" is an entirely unconscious, unreflective matter, for those of us who have had different experiences, even the acts and actions of everyday life are seen in a different light. For many readers, acts and actions themselves are not usually in their focal, but in their subsidiary levels of consciousness. Long experience has taught me that this fact creates special difficulties of communication, but that is the reason for bringing the matter to readers' attention in this Preface.

In my own cultural experiences, the act of dancing itself and the processes of education connected with it constituted a link between tacit and explicit knowledges, forming a bridge between two domains of reality that exist with regard to "knowledge" generally. Such linkages produce talk that is "different," and this, together with any effort to regard anything other than accepted domains of articulated knowledge as "factual" and integral to our common socio-linguistic heritage can be seen as vague—or at best, somewhat confusing. I do not apologize. I merely note the difference and ask the reader's understanding of the intent of the writing. It may be strange, indeed, to think of a dancer talking like this at all.

I am asked, sometimes, why I do not simply *describe* dances in these lectures, for I do so only briefly in Chapter II. There are those who wish all the lectures followed that model; they want to hear about the "real stuff" on the ground—not about how it is explained, analyzed, and such. Then, too, readers have wondered why I do not offer explanations of the "facts" of human movement that are more familiar, say, "facts" as they might be understood by kinesiologists, physiologists and movement educators. Primarily, it is because I wish to draw my audiences' attention elsewhere, and because I have tried to avoid cliché phrases, buzz words, and "bottom lines." My purpose is to encourage people to *think* about the subject of dancing and to make choices regarding their own approaches to it in future. In the end, it is independent, critical thinking that counts anyway, nor would I hesitate to assert that the future of dance and movement research depends upon this—not upon the repetition of what "everyone" knows, or thinks that they know.

In an age of impending environmental crises, threats of nuclear war, inflation, and all the rest of the problems that beset our times, it could seem irresponsible for an anthropologist to preoccupy herself with a study of something so frivolous as dancing, the study of which surely can have no bearing, now or in future, on the world's problems. Isn't the study itself a mere luxury that all but a few can ill afford? I think not, and for these reasons: anthropologists have always studied subjects judged to be "esoteric," "remote," and "exotic." They believe, as I believe, that such subjects and peoples are intimately bound up with the human condition, even though it may be convenient for critics to believe otherwise. Given that dances, ceremonies, signing, and all human structured systems of meanings exist for the purpose of communication, I would be prepared to assume a radical position: in one way of looking at things, we have no other "problems" today than that of communication. I think that we need to know a great deal more about how and why we "communicate" (and why we do not), especially in non-vocalized systems of movement, and I believe that a survey of theories and explanations of dancing can provide a fresh approach to the problems of communication. A reasonable place to begin is with an examination of our received ideas about the variety of systems that exist. In other words, I attempt none too subtly to direct attention to an area of self-reflexive understanding that has long suffered from neglect.

There are other more mundane problems connected with this book as well: no attempt has been made to simplify the accounts of the nature of body languages or behavior in the final chapters or in Appendix II and no attempts have been made to simplify and adorn other writers' accounts of what dancing consists. I do not try to compensate for that which any individual reader may or may not have read from the bibliography which emerges from the lectures. These readings are available to everyone and to those who might say (as some undergraduate students have) that they feel "intimidated" because of many unfamiliar references, I am at a loss to respond, really, because I cannot be responsible for that kind of thing. It does seem necessary to add, however, that readers who expect a kind of pre-digested formula which might be used as a guide for analyzing dances in the field, or as a basis for their subsequent interpretation and explanation are bound to be disappointed.

The accurate determination of units of human movement in any system of structured, meaningful human actions, danced or non-danced, is such a delicate affair, requiring such great care on the part of a serious investigator, that I do not believe that a formulaic approach is fruitful. Indeed, I consider it positively dangerous, thus a further word of caution is appropriate: those who approach these lectures as if they were a "how-to" book are advised to put the volume down immediately and search elsewhere.

However rash, my aim in teaching an anthropology of human movement, which, among others, includes courses of lectures and readings like these, is to promote a more comprehensive understanding of what combined studies of social anthropology and the dance might look like. The processes of understanding, as Polanyi (1959) has reminded us, lead far beyond that which empiricism or the Behavioural sciences have declared to be the domain of legitimate knowledge regarding movement, and I have resisted the boundaries of these domains, as defined, for most of my life. I trust that I have not fallen prey to the opposite fallacy from the many to be found in nearly all forms of Behaviourism: that of the belief that studies of the dance are both boundless and unboundable and can, as it were, include *everything*. I also want to raise issues of contemporary interest regarding how dances have been studied and thought about in the past, opening other and different doors to future lines of inquiry because I am convinced that we scarcely know what the "facts" of dances and other forms of non-vocalized human actions really are.

If I have learned nothing else from the study of social anthropology, I have learned that "facts" are greatly influenced, if not determined by, the theories and explanatory paradigms upon which they depend (See *infra,* pp. 125–126). Throughout the many attempts made over the past forty years to understand what has been said and written about dances, dancers, dancing, and "the" dance, I have been fascinated by the complexities, not only of dances, but of the entire array of gestural forms of human communication; by the notion of the *literacy* of human movement, and by the matrix of epistemological and ontological problems that these kinds of sign systems represent.

My first encounter with fieldwork taught me a valuable lesson, articulated by Saussure about spoken languages and equally true of body languages. He said, " …if we hear people speaking a language we do not know, we perceive the sounds but still remain outside the social facts because we do not understand the language" (1966:13). In West Africa, during the three and one-half years I spent there, I saw and participated in many dances, greeting ceremonies, games, and other systems of bodily communication. Although I perceived the *movements,* and for the most part could perform them, I remained outside the social facts of those systems because (a) I did not understand the spoken languages with which they were connected, and (b) lacking knowledge of the connections, in those cultures, between spoken language and the actions which were being performed, I could not arrive at an adequate understanding of the body languages.

The relationship between these experiences and the study of formal anthropology is dealt with in the Appendix to Chapter Four and included at the end of the book. If I had any choice regarding the many possible readings of this book, I would want readers to begin with Appendix I (on applied personal anthropology) because there they would discover the intellectual context for the rest of the lectures and for the Australian material, and they would realize too, that the criticisms which are made of other writers in the first six chapters are, on the whole no more severe than the criticisms I make of my own pre-anthropological writings. They would also en-counter the notion of a "personal anthropology," an idea originally set forth in Pocock (1973), which ranks in my understanding of social anthropology among the foremost ideas to have been offered to the profession during the decade of the 'seventies.

Like Pocock, in his illuminating introductory essay to the third edition of *Social Anthropology* (1977), I do not claim that this series of lectures constitutes a "textbook." It is a collection of biblio-graphic essays, fashioned into lectures, which expresses what is (and is not) authoritative for me in the literature on dancing, which leads in Chapter VII to an examination of the problem of biblio-graphic controls in the field of "dance ethnology," and because of this, I would hope that librarians, especially, will be interested—in particular those who have to deal with questions from master's and doctoral level students on subjects pertaining to anthropology and the dance.

Because I use a vaguely historical mode of presentation, I would not want readers to imagine that I think I have written a "history" of the dance—or a history of any kind. What I had to do, when faced with the task of constructing a master's level course in the anthropology of human movement at New York University, was to construct a kind of intellectual genealogy for graduate

students according to *their* present circumstances in combined
studies of the dance and anthropology at the beginning of the
'eighties. Very few of the students whom I taught in that program
came into it as graduate anthropology students, although a significant number of them are going on to do doctoral work in the
discipline, having completed their master's work in the subject. For
these students, these lectures were supplementary to their first
introductory courses in social anthropology.

There is an important sense, therefore, in which these lectures
constitute an idiosyncratic piece of writing but, as Pocock points
out, such writing can be useful to a student " ...if it reminds him of
the inescapably personal quality of his (or her) own anthropology"
(1977:viii). This means that students come to anthropology with an
"anthropology" already formed by virtue of the fact that they are
social beings and *language-users*. They come to the subject already
in possession of a mass of myths, concepts, judgments of value and
reality, expectations and such, not only about anthropology, but
about the dance as well.

> One of the first, certainly one of the most important, duties of his
> (or her) tutor is to help him to see that this is so and to encourage
> him to examine the nature of this, still largely inarticulate, private
> social world. It is because he [or she] becomes an anthropologist
> not by sacrificing his [or her] personal anthropology to any "official
> view" nor by the romantic assertion of his [or her] individuality but
> by developing the capacity to put the two in permanent relation. It
> is probably true of all students of the social sciences that unless they
> become conscious of what I have called their personal anthropolog-
> ies, they run the risk of reinforcing a split between the "received
> ideas" and their private sense of the matter; they are all set, in other
> words, for the posture of "alienation" [Pocock, 1977:viii–ix].

Dancers, in particular, tend to arrive at the study of an academic
discipline with a sense of alienation already built in by virtue of
their choice of profession in the first instance. There seemed no
point in compounding the problem for them, thus the pedagogical
strategies I chose (and would choose for any aspiring students

whether dancers or non-dancers) includes from the beginning the notions of a personal anthropology, the conditions of linguistic reflexivity, semantics, and such.

Unlike Pocock, however, I cannot say that students encountering these lectures have "weighty correctives" available to them. The notion of combined studies of anthropology and human movement is still too new (See *infra*, p. 15ff). This is both an advantage and a disadvantage, as I discovered to my cost during the years at New York University. The expectation that *any* subject offered in an American university can be reduced to "textbooks," set courses, exams, grades, and select, authoritative bibliographies is fairly firmly entrenched, and I agree with Pocock that when this happens, it is the subject that is done for, regardless of how many people might want to "do" anthropology of the dance or human movement.

The students who successfully completed their M.A. degress had to *live* their subject at the same time as they were *learning* it (the advantage) but in so doing, they could never enjoy the illusion of security held by their peers in other subjects that were traditionally more "acceptable" (the disadvantage). Clearly, we all believed that the advantages outweighed the disadvantages, because the circumstances of the novelty of the subject prevented them from developing what Pocock calls a kind of intellectual "bilingualism" which " ...effectively and affectively cuts off the chosen specialization from the rest of life" (1977:x). Nor was I encouraged during my student days at the Institute of Social Anthropology to develop this kind of posture towards the discipline, a feature of my education in formal anthropology for which I shall always be grateful.

Many thanks are owed many people for the advice and encouragement I received during the time that I spent at Oxford, and many thanks are also owed for the demands made on me in a different context to write these lectures so that they can be used as a "teaching book" by those who have had and will continue to sustain an interest in this relatively tiny field of interest in social and cultural anthropology.

Among them, I particularly want to acknowledge the helpful remarks and criticisms offered by Patricia Rovic, Jo Ward, Ronne Arnold and Jo Anne Page in Australia, but most of all to Rajika

Puri, Brenda Farnell, Dixie Durr, Diana Hart-Johnson, Holly Fairbank, Dolores Vanison-Blakeley, Gail Reese, Ed Myers, Joan
Burroughs, Roselle Warshaw and Lynn Martin, because their
needs, questions, and knowledge of existing literature helped to
form the lectures, and finally, I wish to thank three colleagues who
have patiently read the entire manuscript, offering valuable feedback, criticism and encouragement: Dr. Adrienne Kaeppler
(Curator, Oceanic Ethnography, Smithsonian Institution), Dr.
Charles Varela (Sociology, Union College, New Jersey) and Robert
Fleshman (Loyola University, New Orleans). They are not responsible for the results of their comments; suffice it to say that they
tried.

Drid Williams
The University of Sydney
Sydney, Australia

Note: References cited in this Preface are to be found in the
general bibliography. There is one phonetic symbol which appears
in some African terms used in the text, that of "ɔ." It is meant to be
pronounced more or less like the English word "awe." See pages
302, 305, and 307 for examples.

I. INTRODUCTION

THE FACT IS THAT LITERATURE ON the dance is very far from being in any way cumulative. It is a literature that consists mainly of biographies, technical books (unfortunately often, although not always, of a "how to..." nature), picture books, or narrowly focussed, quasi-theoretical works that emphasize only one idiom of dance, with the result that a serious student is at a loss to know even where to start, far less how it is that he or she might commence building on the work that has gone before. Moreover, writing about dances, dancing, or "the dance" typically focusses on one idiom (e.g., ballet or Graham technique, Flamenco, ballroom dancing or some "ethnic" form like "Aboriginal" dancing and such) which seems only to establish a narrow parochialism that is moribund. Yet, it is all of this kind of thing and the many unsubstantiated generalizations that arise from it that is vaguely referred to as "dance theory" or "theories of the dance."

Instead of seeing what amounts to a written collection of theoretical parochialisms as alternative and competing conceptions of the substantive nature and human usage of the activity of dancing, which might provide illumination—fostering healthy and discriminating critical attitudes towards theorizing and generalization—an awkward, wholly unsatisfactory taxonomic structure has emerged that divides "folk" dancing from "art," "ethnic" dancing from ballet, "western" dancing from "non-western" dancing, "ritual" dancing from entertainment—the list is as long as years of torment. Consequently, very little of that which early authors wrote remains pertinent to the field of study today in any real way.

Coupled with this and other serious problems is the fact that members of one tribe of dancers (and their followers, managers, apologists, critics and teachers) usually see themselves as a strongly differentiated group possessing strongly differentiated modes of behavior among other groups possessing relatively undifferentiated behaviors, such that each group argues ultimately for the irrelevance of all the others and for the "universal," "global" applicability of its own techniques, practices, and customs, with the result that the literature is a polyglot mass of reflections that seem to a disinterested observer to be repetitious, tedious, and decidedly unilluminating.

I contend that the lack of growth of knowledge about the dance and the lack of growth of cumulative theory pertaining to it stems from a lack of knowledge of past writers plus the lack of systematic examination of what their "theorizing" consisted. Furthermore, the seeming dedicated refusal on the part of dance educators and other academics interested in the dance to recognize that their consistent emphasis on re-discovery (as if the dance exists in a vacuum and not as an integrated part of the wider social structure) further vitiates attempts to deal with a fragmented and often dubious set of theoretical materials that, through neglect, simply continues to grow in the manner of crab grass in the more cultivated fields of western scholarship.

The social organization of theories of the dance most nearly resembles (to a social or cultural anthropologist, at least) those segmentary societies—usually of a politically acephalous nature—where members of one segment of a group classify other segments of the group and the individuals in it only in terms of its own "segmental" viewpoint, never from the viewpoint of the outside "other." The approach I suggest, as it were from a standpoint of complementary opposition, is thought to be capable of drawing out theoretical and taxonomic contrasts and similarities from a different, and perhaps higher level of organization.

These lectures are meant to examine the manner in which various writers (who can be regarded as writing in the "anthropological" field in its widest and oldest definition) have attempted to understand and account for danced behavior and for the beliefs and practices of those who dance. Not all of the writers are, or ever have been, anthropologists, and perhaps I should make it clear at the outset that I shall be primarily concerned in these discussions only with what these authors say about the dance. For example, Robert Lowie (an American cultural anthropologist) and R.R. Marett (a British social anthropologist), both of whom are rightly revered in the discipline for their contributions to theories of social organization and religion, respectively, had little to say about the dance that was of the same calibre. More general discussions about each author, their contributions to knowledge outside of their interest in the dance, are peripheral to my main preoccupation, which is to summarize in broad outline those explanations of human dancing which are offered to us from the past, whether the writers are anthropologists or not.

I shall keep to that literature, written mainly in English, that constitutes the bibliographies that are offered students of the dance in widely varying disciplinary contexts throughout England, Canada, the United States, and Australia. If it is wondered why I include the writings of literary critics, theologians, psychologists, physical educators, philosophers, anthropologists, linguists, dance educators, and others, whose fields of study connote areas of expertise outside of my own, readers will simply have to understand that this is a clear indication of the present state of the art.

If anyone were to ask what interest the activity of dancing in its many manifestations can have for us, I would reply in the first place, that dancing is a species of the genus "human action" and that all who have any interest in human movement, human behavior or human action might usefully acknowledge that a study of the practices, theories, and ideas of those who devote much, if not all, of their time to dancing in our own and other cultures (and this includes an immense variety of activities) may help us to reach conclusions about the nature of human actions in general.

In the second place, I would advocate the study of dances, of dance companies, of repertoires, and the like, because I believe that until we understand how movement and actions are utilized in their more complex and conscious manifestations, we are going to understand very little about the subject of movement in general. Dancing is only one of the many forms of expression of human structured systems of actions. It is true that it is a potent form, because dances are among the most complex systems of human actions, but the field of "dance" *per se* is limited, as everything else is limited. Something like an "anthropology of dance" might be able to persist for twenty to fifty years at the outside, but I doubt that it could sustain able research students and sufficiently sophisticated questions for much longer than that.

Often, past literature only reveals a desire to be heard: a courageous effort on the part of an author (as, for example, Scott, in the late 19th century) intellectually to justify the very existence of his art. In our own times, judging from the growth of dance departments and given that popular interest has been aroused in serious professional dancing, owing mainly to the influence of television, some of the battles, like Scott's, to be heard—to achieve a certain recognition—have been won. Those educators, aestheticians, anthropologists, linguists, and other scholars who have an interest in dances now have different problems confronting them than did their forerunners. Another of the major points made in these lectures, however, is that many of the basic questions about the nature of dancing (and of human action generally) still remain unexamined and unanswered, while field ethnographies (some done by anthropologists, but many of them not) seem to proliferate.

I, and my colleagues, am aware that many anthropologists and other students of human movement often ignore the dance, considering it to be of little account, thereby revealing their own cultural biases, but I also take much of this as a function of a necessary scholarly activity—delimitation of one's field of interest—so that when an author divides movement, as it were, into, say, the "meat and potatoes" field of gestures and body language in everyday life, considering the dance to be little more than an expensive and luxurious "dessert" (as in the case of Ray Birdwhistell and many others), or when an author has chosen to emphasize an area of majority interest, say, sports, excluding from consideration the minority interest in the poetry of human motion, as in the case of many writers in the field of physical education, it is easy to see how the academic neglect happens.

Thus, although it may appear that much of the literature that is dealt with in these lectures seems to have been composed in an historical and intellectual vacuum (mainly because no one, to my knowledge has tried to look at it all together before), it is to be hoped that readers will keep the nature of the enterprise in mind, for nowhere can I point to thoughtful, critical assessments of it that might help future or present generations of students to begin some kind of cumulative work. I can only hope that a series of lectures like this might provoke enough thought, debate, and discussion about the theoretical and analytical aspects of the subject so that something like a "field of interest" might emerge in anthropology, history, linguistics, psychology, and other disciplines some of whose proponents have, at one time or another, written things about dancing. To date, only a few of them, notably philosophers and anthropologists, have contributed anything like comprehensive, well-thought-out, systematic approaches. The "dance world" is still dominated by a philosophy of activism—understandable in a conservatory setting, perhaps, but less justifiable in a university setting, where one might reasonably expect more intellectual activity.

I would want to say that fully to understand the nature of human movement or human action, we have to understand the nature of danced actions in our own culture, and we have to examine what is thought to be "dance" in other cultures. We need to recognize that what we might refer to as "dance" in other cultures is not thought to be "dance" at all by those who generated and practice the system (see Kaeppler, 1978). Perhaps I should say that to create a *dichotomy* between "dance" and "non-dance" is basically false and makes, in the end, for obscurity, for there is a sense in which "the dance" possesses values, practices, and beliefs that are not all that different from those connected with "ordinary" movements in the human realm. In fact, one of the most tedious generalizations that is made about the dance is that pertaining to the "dance of life." Yet, we cannot understand why such sentimental truisms and metaphorical usages exist if we do not comprehend how and in what ways they arose and why there is such a desperate need for comparative studies of an informed, sophisticated, and serious kind.

I will further have no hesitation in claiming that although other disciplines, in particular the humanities, aesthetics, and literature, might look down their noses at those of us in anthropology who claim to have devoted more time and thought to this "orphan child" of human movement studies (see Williams, 1982), it is we, more than anyone, who for the past three decades have tried to bring together the vast materials on the dance, and although we cannot yet arrive at a consensus as to the best theoretical and methodological approaches to take to the study of this most complex of all human activities, we possess among us a growing body of defined and definable subject matter that however inadequate, has served since the mid-'sixties to stimulate further study and examination at a graduate level of intellectual thought—and beyond. I have in mind here the impact of the works of Adrienne Kaeppler, Joann Keali'inohomoku, Anya Royce, Judith Lynne Hanna, Diane Freedman, Jill Sweet, Suzanne Youngerman, Najwa Adra, Lee Ellen Friedland, and myself. It may be that in future, our contributions will be found wanting, but they are currently playing their parts in the history of thought about the subject of dance and human movement, as are the works of three philosophers: Susanne Langer, Maxine Sheets-Johnstone, and David Best.

It is not easy to define what it is that we are to understand by "the dance" for the purposes of these lectures. Were the emphasis to be on the question "why do people dance?"[9] then we might accept some of the minimal answers that have been given in the past: 1) they dance because they want to have fun and relax—"the dance" is basically a vehicle for leisure and entertainment; 2) they dance because of biological, organic, or instinctive needs of some kind—"the dance" as a precursor to spoken language, perhaps; 3) they dance because they want to express themselves—"the dance" as a "symbolic" activity divorced from "real" life; 4) they dance because they feel sexy, happy or sad, or something—"the dance" as a prime repository of emotions; 5) they dance because a spirit has possessed them, whether good or evil—"the dance" as an hysterical, neurotic or quasi-religious manifestation; 6) they dance to show off or to relieve their overburdened feelings—"the dance" as "catharsis" or as one of the governors on a "steam valve" theory of human emotion, which I shall explain more fully later.

All of the above answers are inadequate. They all connote theories of human actions and, indeed, theories of the nature of human be-ing, but since the emphasis here is rather on theories of the dance, I am not free to choose one of these answers over another, nor am I free to choose one of the definitions of dancing that they imply, since I shall have to discuss not only these, but a number of other hypotheses which go beyond these and other minimal definitions. Moreover, it is well to remember that the term "dance" in our culture alone includes an extraordinary variety of activities; disco-dancing, classical ballet, ballroom dancing, "ethnic" dancing, the New York City Rockettes, "folk" dancing— the lot. Just about anything that cannot be classified as "ordinary" movement can be, and has been, called "dancing." I shall be obliged to make references to all of these forms of dancing.

Furthermore, I shall have to try to untangle the often confused statements about dancing, *per se*, that were made in the larger contexts of arguments about evolutionary or developmental theories of humankind, theories of human nature, cross-cultural surveys, and the like. Victorian scholars were intensely interested, for example, in the origins of dance, largely because, one might imagine, they were preoccupied with the origins of nearly everything. Many books and articles have been written on the subject and were I to refer to all of them, these lectures would be cluttered up with little more than a recitation of names and book titles, because we can read that the dance has its origins in sex (Ellis, 1920), or in play (Huizinga and Jenson, 1949); in animal behavior (Sachs, 1937), in magic (Frazer, 1911), or that it represents the "childhood of man" (Frobenius, 1908). We can read that its most vital expression and its "essence" is to be found in ancient Greek culture (Flitch, 1912), in religion (van der Leeuw, 1963), or that it exists largely as a function of an inability to speak (Kris, 1952). In short, the dance could have begun in nearly any primordium that anyone cares to postulate and its essence has been located nearly everywhere.

None of the above-mentioned explanations are adequate. There is no way of telling whether they are right or wrong because some of what is said by each author might apply to some forms of dancing, but not to others. About the best that we can do is to ask if the explanations are plausible, then try to see their limitations, and find out upon what grounds such claims are being made. Since it is still possible to read most of what has been written in English on the dance in one lifetime, although few have undertaken the task, I have chosen several alternatives to the kind of simple quasi-bibliographical listing given above. I have selected those writers whom I know to be the most influential or who are characteristic of one or another way of talking about the activity and discuss their theories and modes of presentation as representative of widespread thinking on the subject, whether in anthropology or some other discipline, or in popular thinking. While I risk losing detailed treatments of any given author's theory, I believe I gain in clarity and the presentation of a wide range of explanations that have been given about the dance. These theories may conveniently be considered under the following headings: emotional and psychological explanations, intellectual and sociological explanations, religious and quasi-religious explanations, and functional explanations, including cross-cultural surveys. More will be said about these classifications later.

It is a remarkable fact that many of the explanations of the dance were expounded by people who knew relatively little about the activity in any of its manifestations, and who had to depend, as did Sir James Frazer's wife (pen-name, Lilly Grove) for her information on accounts given by missionaries, travellers, and others, thereby rendering her evidence highly suspect. We simply have no way of knowing how much of it was fabricated and how much was not.

The same might be said of many early accounts of American Indian dancing, for even though officers in the American army or missionaries might have reported other aspects of social life with care, we have reason to believe that much of what was said about dances and ritual practices was unreliable. By modern anthropological standards of professional research, it was casual, out-of-context, superficial and ethnocentric. Statements made about the dances of any so-called "aboriginal" or "simpler" peoples usually cannot be taken at face value, and they should never be accepted without a critical examination of sources and heavy corroborative evidence.

Because so much of what goes on in a dance *cannot be observed*, it is especially the case that great care must be taken by the investigator to represent the beliefs, values, and ideologies of the peoples concerned as truthfully and accurately as is possible. Even professional anthropologists have had trouble with "gesture," although most of them recognize the problems and some have provided us with valuable insights because of their difficulties.

I have in mind here a Dutch anthropologist, Jan Pouwer, who was puzzled by a set of ordinary gestures with which he was confronted every day. A part of the puzzling set was a gesture that he thought of as "beckoning":

> If one were to travel through various parts of West New Guinea, one might observe the following gestures by Papuans who notice you. They might put a hand to their navel, their breasts, or their armpit; they might also beckon you. If you are lured into approaching the beckoner, he will be quite surprised for his hand simply said 'hello,' and so did the navel and the breasts and the armpit and so on. All of them are visible, observable signs of an invisible message which has to be inferred [Pouwer, 1973:4].

We are told that "To these Papuans each individual person has a number of substantive *ipu*. English equivalents such as spirit or principle of life or for that matter "mana" hardly convey the meaning of *ipu*. Small wonder so many anthropological monographs are littered with native terms" (1973:3).

Pouwer refers to the visible and *invisible* characteristics of human actions, and it cannot be overstressed that while we may indeed see the *movement* that is made, it does not follow that we have an understanding of those movements as human *actions* until we possess an understanding of subtleties like *ipu* (in the above case). And the word alone is not enough either, as any graduate student who is a dancer will testify, whether it is one word or one gesture.

Let us suppose for a moment, that an investigator interested in the dances or rituals of West New Guinea goes into the field armed at least with Pouwer's insights: does that mean that it is not necessary for him or her to have learned to speak the language of the Papuans, or that one could merely mention the concept of *ipu* in passing and then get on with the "real" business of documenting the dances? Of course, it does not, but too often, it is the case that movement investigators proceed from the notion that because of the *visible* nature of the dance, they can ignore or neglect the importance of spoken language and the many *invisible* aspects of the event with impunity.

It is also the case that to focus on dances to the exclusion of the rest of the society leaves us with a distorted picture of the peoples concerned, as we are frequently led to believe that the dance and ritual behavior assumes an importance in the lives of a people that it really does not have. This is as true for the study of dances in our own culture as it is for the study of dances in other cultures. Worse yet, when scholars get to work on pieces of information provided for them haphazardly and from all over the world, building them into books with titles like *Dancing, The World History of Dance, Dancing Throughout the Ages* and such, we are presented with a composite image—or is it a caricature—of what dancing (or dances and *the* dance) is really like. Examples of this type of procedure and the accompanying promiscuous use of evidence can be culled from nearly every period of dance literature from the Victorians to present-day:

> From a comparison with the tribal dances of other races, past and present, it is possible to conjecture why the cave-dweller may have pretended to be an animal when he danced at the dawn of the world. The dances of primitive man are generally mimetic. He has not learnt to express himself in any other way, and he is therefore driven to do in pantomime the things he wishes brought about. In some savage tribes, the women dance while the men are on the war-path, imitating the acts of war they suppose their warriors to be committing; and among many instances of mimetic dancing in order to promote the growth of crops by imitation magic, Sir James Frazer mentions the old Mexican festival at which the women danced with their hair loose, shaking and tossing it in order that the maize might grow in similar profusion; while in some countries of Europe, dancing and leaping high in the air are still practised, as in Franche Comte where dancing during the Carnival is popularly supposed to make the hemp grow tall [Sharp, 1928:15].

More modern publications tend to continue in this vein, with only a few terminological changes. No one speaks of "savages" any more, and it is not considered good form to talk of "primitives" this way either.

These kinds of formulations have been beautifully satirized by Keali'inohomoku in an article first published in 1969 and reprinted in 1980, as we shall see later on. It is to Keali'inohomoku's credit that she tried to make such locutions outmoded through ridicule and example, and by drawing attention to the fact that the ballet, too, is an ethnic form of dancing.

We learn from Pouwer that a level of bare observation of movement hardly suffices to produce accurate or truthful accounts of greetings, far less whole dances. We learn, too, from the negative example above that scissors and paste compilations of the world's dances by amateur anthropologists and armchair scholars writing from a distance lead to conjecture, distortions and nonsense because it is clear that these writers lacked any real knowledge of anthropological theory or any experience of alternative ways of looking at the world. They seem also to lack any sense of historical criticism or the rules that an historian applies when evaluating documentary evidence.

It is not the case that I argue for everyone becoming an anthropologist or an historian, in case the inference has been made—far from it—what I do argue for is the application of *some* disciplinary boundaries with reference to the use of evidence, epistemological relations, logical (or at least reasonable) argument, conceptual clarity, and such things. I do not expect this to be a popular view because for at least three decades in the United States and England, students have been allowed to bring together a large number of miscellaneous examples of dancing in order that they might illustrate some general idea about the dance that they have picked up or to put forward some thesis about the *importance* of the activity. They seem to have been encouraged to believe that their efforts—innocent of nearly any of the canons of western academic discipline—are valuable because the area of interest is so new.

How new is new? And how much unschooled, untutored writing about the dance must we endure before it is realized that merely having a data-base is not enough, even if it is supported by grants for travel to exotic countries and/or the most dedicated belief that any and all reportage is automatically a good thing? In the absence of historical records, it cannot be said with any conviction that studies purporting to provide an overview of a world history of the dance are in any real sense possible anyway. Our world may be shrinking in some ways owing to telecommunications, jet aircraft, and modern technology, but when the same world is viewed from the standpoint of the richness and variety of its dances and the many peoples that are represented by them, it becomes a very large world indeed. This is why I choose to emphasize, not the dances themselves, but *theories of* and *explanations of* the dance, because it represents another gross error, anthropologically anyway, to talk about dances in terms of monolithic wholes.

I do not know, nor does anyone know, of what "African dance" consists, yet this term is toted around with great assurance in several authors' contributions and by modern students as well. I do not think we have any real idea what dancing looked like "at the dawn of the world," nor do I think that anyone knows. We do not even know what dancing looked like in ancient Greece, and we only possess one volume on the subject that has any real worth, because the author begins by telling us of what archaeological evidence and epistemological relations consist. I here refer to Lawler's excellent volume (1964) on dancing in ancient Greece.

The mode of classification that I use in these lectures follows very roughly a style of classification that Evans-Pritchard used in his *Theories of Primitive Religion*. I discussed a proposed work like this concerning the dance with him about eighteen months before he died in 1973. He approved of my ideas, saying that he could not see, given the general intractability of the material and the confused state of the literature, plus the low status of the subject in social anthropology, any other way I could go. And I must also say that my treatment of many of these authors on the dance is, like Evans-Pritchard's treatment of authors on the subject of primitive religions, "...severe and negative" (1965:4). Following him, I believe readers will not regard my criticisms as too severe when they see how inadequate, ludicrous, and just plain silly is much of what has been written about the dance, yet all of it is still trotted out in colleges and universities with blind assurance (if it is in print, then it must be true) that such theorizing is informative and useful.

It *would* be useful if sufficient critical judgment and a concern with the *weltanshauung* of the times were brought to bear upon the readings. After all, an exhausted question, or a misguided question and its development can be instructive—and knowledge of them would be especially helpful in the study of the dance, because it might relieve us of the burden of constantly re-discovering the wheel. The importance of independent, critical thinking with reference to this field can hardly be overstressed. A writer who has emphasized this point is Best, who says,

> Education, and especially higher education, should not, in my view, consist primarily in accumulating a stockpile of other people's thoughts and ideas, but rather in developing the ability for clear, critical, independent thought, and the demand, from oneself and others, for rational justification. As a result of the traditional conception of education, which might be stigmatised as the tyranny of the fact, it is still unfortunately true that too many students leave college or university supermarket with carrier-bag minds filled with pre-packed ideas. This, in my opinion, is a travesty of what education should be [Best, 1978:22].

Neither Best, nor I, mean to infer that students should ignore what has been written and said about the subject of dancing in the past—or in the present—by those who have spent years researching the subjects of dance, "gesture" and human movement. As he so succinctly says,

> The point concerns the emphasis on the way in which students should be encouraged to approach what those with greater knowledge have to offer...the critical and independent thinking which is such an important characteristic of philosophy, as of other academic disciplines, is not only *not* negative and destructive but, on the contrary, is directly related to the constructive ability to be fully sincere, in thought and feeling, since there is an intimate relationship between rationality and the capacity for emotional depth [Best, 1978:23].

My colleagues and the upcoming generation of anthropologists of human movement, plus the philosophers who were mentioned above, have shown much of this past literature to be dubious or erroneous. My task, then, in these lectures, is conceived along exactly the same lines as Evans-Pritchard's: to be critical rather than "constructive," with the proviso that such criticism is in the long run constructive, if it leads to more serious and thoughtful reflections on the part of all concerned as to what this phenomenon "the dance" amounts to. Then too, I will make many constructive suggestions as I go along and will devote the final few lectures to those authors of whom I can speak with assent and approval. I will also indicate (although only in summary form) what some of the more modern approaches to the study of dances suggest, given the rejection of much of what has been said in the past.

Mainly, I attempt to indicate that most of what has been said about the dance up to now is both uncertain and obscure and I attempt to show how theories that are acceptable in one historical context are unsupportable now and would have to be rejected— by anthropologists at least. I do not assume responsibility for the many possible ways in which other disciplines might incorporate these writings into their on-going researches, nor do I assume any responsibility for what is loosely called "theory" in departments of dance and dance education.

Indeed, looking at the total collection of writings with which these lectures deal, it is difficult to see how many of the theories put forward to account for human dancing and "human behavior" could have been accepted. We cannot, I think, conveniently explain them away by saying that these authors did not have the benefits of sophisticated technologies, or more highly developed "research tools," because the puzzling fact is that many of these theories persist, e.g., the modern re-statement of Sachs's unilinear evolutionary theories espoused in *World History of the Dance* (1937), by Langer (1953:188-207) and by Lange (1975), to the extent that they seem to have become reified and possess an existence of their own.

Such efforts might be seen as attempts to produce a cumulative body of research, but one is hard put, even with the best will in the world, to see how this is the case. Rather, efforts like Langer's perpetuate myths about "primitive" dance and Lange's seem only to update theorizing that has remained essentially unquestioned, unchallenged, and unchanged for over forty years. Then too, there are still many who believe that the question *"why* do people dance?" is a good question, mainly because they have never taken the trouble to examine where the question might lead and the many consequences and problems that are its inevitable entailments, so that is where we shall start in the second lecture.

The recurrence of the matter of the *kinds of questions that we can ask* is one that will be seen to be a repeated theme throughout these lectures, simply underlining my increasingly confirmed conviction that confusion about the kinds of questions that are asked is the single source of misconception about modern anthropological, and other, approaches to the study of movement, hence the dance. Students might also usefully spend some time reflecting on the fact that "description," "interpretation," and "explanation" vary widely as one moves from, say, social anthropology, to philosophy, to theoretical physics or kinesiology: my point being that to ask "why do people dance?" is not a question that many social anthropologists would tend to ask in any case.

There are two fundamental notions in social scientific theory that are of great importance and they are difficult to bring home to students in anthropology itself, far less to those who lack acquaintance with the discipline: those of "models" (either of data, interpretation, or explanation) and the great complexity of criteria used in judging the effectiveness and the veracity of anthropological reports, principles and what-have-you. I will therefore begin by systematically showing how we might more usefully ask, "what are people doing when they dance?"; a question that can lead to more productive ends, and one which a modern social anthropologist might start with.

I should like to say, too, that if some of these theories seem hopelessly simplistic and naïve, I would want readers to bear in mind the fact that the anthropology of human movement is not yet a sub-field of social or cultural anthropology. The study of dances, martial arts, manual counting systems, sign languages, and the like is still in its infancy. Perhaps to say that the field is still in embryonic or "foetal" form would be more accurate. "Anthropology" interpreted as "dance anthropology" or "dance ethnology" (terms my readers will notice that I do not use in relation to my own work) is little more at present than a convenient excuse for "field studies" carried out by students who, although they receive degrees in dance education, are innocent of any anthropological or ethnological training, such that the additional problem now exists of incursions into the field of interest by researchers who have learned a little of the jargon of social and cultural anthropology, but whose writings really return social and cultural anthropology to the state it was in before it became a professional discipline *circa* 1900. On this genre of writings—some of the more modern of those in the literature, I will have very little to say in this series of talks, and in any case, I have already dealt with them elsewhere (See Williams, 1983 and 1986).

Permit me to say, as I now try to move towards a conclusion, that I have read all of the books, articles, and treatises on the dance that I criticize. One finds all too often that students simply accept what others have written about what an author wrote instead of reading the author him or herself. This is why we have, I suspect, so many collections and annotated bibliographies of the dance and human movement (as e.g., Davis, 1972 and 1982), which are not really "bibliographies" in a scholarly sense, but "book lists" which do not really aid in helping us develop adequate bibliographical controls over the literature.

Also, I know of more than one dance department that hands out to beginning master's students bibliographies which have been made up, usually, simply by consulting a card catalog or a union list of some kind by persons who have no real knowledge about the contents of the works. These "bibliographies" (to use the term loosely) usually consist of roughly seventy-five or one hundred titles that include everything from Darwin to Ernst Cassirer, and from Isadora Duncan's biography (1933) to Adrienne Kaeppler's admirable anthropological studies of Tongan dance, with kinesiological, anatomical, psychological, historical, and literary critics' contributions thrown into the bargain.

The task of sorting out the welter of theory, methodological devices, explanatory models and beliefs, values, and ideologies that this kind of "bibliography" represents is enormous. No master's student should ever be expected to undertake it, yet it is implied that they can, from nothing more than a basis of general interest in some form of dancing, cope with such monumental intellectual task. I have spent the better part of a lifetime trying to sort out the materials in these lectures and I still find the task daunting, however, an example of such efforts is to be found in Lecture VII where the problem of bibliographical control in "dance ethnology" is directly addressed. Suffice it to say here that I can only hope that students will benefit from *not* having to begin their graduate study with such a thankless enterprise, and that they can see their ways clear, from a basis of these lectures, to focus on those theories which best serve their own interests and the general interests of good scholarship.

And this assertion raises an important issue: we would all be far better off if novice writers confined themselves to fewer authors, studying them in depth, perhaps. Tylor's writings on the dance and movement generally provide a good example of what I mean: he is probably one of the most fruitful writers for an anthropologist of human movement to study, even though he does not say much of value about the dance. Darwin's theories, like Tylor's, are often grossly misrepresented, distorted, and misused by "dance scholars," just as they have been by many others since he wrote, because his has become a "name" to have on a thesis or dissertation bibliography whether the writer has read him at all, or if they have, whether they have read him with any diligence.

Lest these remarks be misconstrued, it seems necessary to point out that anthropologists (physical anthropologists, social anthropologists, cultural anthropologists or what-you-will) are often appealed to as authorities in writings on the dance, whether the student has read any of them or not, or whether the context in which they made their statements is considered at all. The upshot of this is that over and over (for example), we encounter an appeal to Köhler's study of apes on Teneriffe, just as we encounter latter-day appeals to Tylor's theory of animism to explain "African" dance, and other such anthropological anomalies.

My task will not have been in vain, however, if it is in any way an aid to serious scholars, whatever their disciplinary persuasion, and if I manage to drive home the point that if one begins with, say, Darwin's theory of what the dance consists, then we are going to land up with quite different interpretations and explanations than a beginning from a linguistic and semiotic approach would do.

I would like to think that readers will begin to conceive of the field of human movement studies as an intellectual territory that has many "places," and many metaphorical mountains and plains, streams and tributaries in it. Some of the terrain is charted, but much of it is not. Some places on the map of this imagined territory are like villages—small groups of scholars who practice "kinesics" or "proxemics" or "semasiology," but the communities are at best outposts in a little known and less understood area, made the more difficult because there is very little communication between the settlements and a lot of claim-jumping and sharp practices go on, as is always the case when new areas of investigation are opened up. New "homesteaders" are often surprised, when they dog-sled into a territory to discover a mountaineer who has been there for years, whom they have never heard of.

But, as we take stock of what it is that we really know about human actions, including the dance, whether it pertains to ourselves or others, we need not be wholly despondent or discouraged about the minuscule nature of our apperceptions, for given a view, however narrow, of the vistas we may have of the history of ideas and their influence on our own thinking, we may consider ourselves fortunate to be where we are. We do not, for a start, lack information, and we possess, perhaps for the first time in history, the resources to use it, if we can rouse ourselves from our technological complacency and our intellectual apathy long enough to use it.

With that in mind, and with the notion of a "map" of a territory to be explored together, we might profitably reflect on an anonymous, but relevant, Sufi saying: "Pilgrim, you tell me that you want to go to Budapest, but I fear that you are on the road to Turkestan."

II. WHY DO PEOPLE DANCE?

IT IS WORTHWHILE MAKING CLEAR from the start that although these lectures are primarily about theories of the dance, the term " human movement" is used as a generic one, meant to include a wide variety of structured systems of human actions (dances, signing, sports, the martial arts, rituals of various kinds, manual counting systems, etc.). I have not found it useful in the past, nor do I think it useful now to engage in sterile debate over the "definitions" of these activities, although a lot of ink has been used over the years in attempts to do so.

However, should the keen reader already have noticed an interplay between my usages of the words " movement" and "action," it is appropriate to sort out some superficial problems by offering a minimal distinction between them that will permit us to get on with the discussion. Susanne Langer made very succinctly several points that underlie my usage of these words when, in 1942, she said that "gesture" and "movement" as they are conceived of and used in western theatrical dancing *do not complete the natural histories of feelings,* in contrast to the majority of movements in everyday life.

> Ritual, like art, is essentially the active termination of a *symbolic transformation* of experience [1942/1951:49—italics added].

She tells us that as soon as an expressive act is performed *without inner momentary compulsion,* it is no longer self-expressive; it is expressive in a logical sense (see Langer, 1951:54–74).

Her theories about danced movement juxtapose rather nicely with a later Wittgensteinian position, summarized by David Best: "...an intentional action is not the same as a physical movement since the latter can be described in various ways according to one's point of view and one's beliefs about the person performing it.

One cannot specify an action, as opposed to a purely physical movement without taking into account what the agent intended" (1974:193).

Whatever else may be said about danced movements, it is generally true to say that they are *intentional* movements and that they are therefore best understood as " actions." Thus it follows that when someone says that people dance because they want to "express" themselves, the proposition at least points to a human intention of some kind, although many authors do not distinguish between "expression" in a self-expressive, as against a logical sense with reference to symbolic actions. If the answer is offered in reply to the question "why do people dance?", then the answer "to express themselves" becomes a trivial answer, omitting as it does any consideration of dancing that is done, not as a momentary expression of "self," but as a profession, or dancing that is conceived of as *attainment,* not as "expression" or entertainment, or dancing that is in any way expository or exegetical.

In brief, we find ourselves flat up against the philosophical problems of the connotative and denotative relations between signs, symbols, and their objects. There are several choices available to movement investigators, of course, but these choices are not so much to be found in the dance forms themselves. Rather, they must be sought in our ways of seeing dances and thinking about the dance. The standpoint from which I view all dancing (however trivial or profound its content may be) is basically Langerian, regarding the relation between signs, symbols, and objects, and Saussurian, insofar as I have developed in considerable detail the notion of the human "action sign" (see Williams, 1979), but a thorough discussion of these matters cannot detain us here. Suffice it to say that danced movements are seen as "symbolic" in a hard logical sense, as the assumption behind these lectures (see, for more discussion, Chapter VIII, *infra,* p. 200ff).

While it is true that people "express themselves" when they dance, we are not usually told anything about *what* is expressed, nor *how* it is expressed. In fact, professional dancers rarely " express themselves" in the commonly understood sense of the phrase. For a start, they are usually enacting roles, just as dramatic actors do.[1] Idioms of dancing are highly complex sets of roles and rules. They are, because of this, both very different from, and at the same time similar to, "ordinary" actions, because the latter are governed by social rules and people enact roles in ordinary life too.

If we must use the term "expression" in relation to the dance, then we might better say that when we see a dance anywhere in the world, what we are seeing is an expression of the choreographer's (in general, the composer's) *knowledge* of human feelings, ideas, life, and the universe; a point made by Langer as well. We are not seeing *symptoms* of the composer's and dancers' own personal feelings. Along with this, we must keep in mind the anthropological proviso that we satisfactorily determine beforehand that what we are seeing *is* a "dance" and that we can legitimately translate the set of actions as if it was truly comparable to our understanding of that word.

Given that what we see *is* a dance, then it is easy to understand how the distinction between "symptoms" and "symbols" is useful, even at a simple level, because if it is true that dances are symptoms of the personal feelings of the dancers, then we might expect that a ballerina who dances Giselle will go mad and actually kill herself at the end of the ballet. But a dancer who dances Giselle is not completing the natural history of her own feelings. Likewise, if it were true that actors were completing the natural histories of their own feelings in Hamlet, for example, then most of them would be dead at the end of the play.

Sioux and Arapaho Indian men did not kill each other in a war dance. What they were doing in such dances was going through a disciplined rehearsal of what their society had taught them were "right" attitudes towards their own fears, towards killing enemies, towards courage and other ethical and social values. Similarly, young boys and girls who go through initiation and puberty dances and rituals in many parts of Africa and Melanesia and other parts of the world are going through disciplined rehearsals of socially sanctioned attitudes towards sexual maturity and adult responsibility. The stable dance traditions of the world are very highly elaborate, complex, rule-based systems, whether they are African, Siberian, Tongan, Chinese, American Indian, Balinese, or what-you-will.

To ask "why do people dance?" assumes, first, that all people everywhere are going to dance for the same reasons and that some vaguely conceived " human nature" is in essence the same, but we do not know that about the phenomenon of dancing, at least. Nor can we, with impunity, commit ourselves to a line of enquiry that presupposes, as this question does, that there can be only one sort of general statement made about the social phenomena of human dances and that other general statements are "wrong," if, say, the answer of "expression" is " right."

There is no *a priori* reason why theories purporting to explain dances in terms respectively of "expression," "relaxation," "in-stinctive needs," "sex," "catharsis," and "social function" should not all be correct, each supplementing the other, although I do not believe that they are. While it is true that interpretation can occur on different levels and there is no reason why several different explanations of the same type, or on the same level, should not all be "right," as long as they do not contradict one another, it is equally true to say that theories and explanation can be entirely incompati-ble, belonging to different worlds of ontological and epistemolog-ical explanation. And, theories can simply contradict one another.

In point of fact, I find most of the theories that we shall examine together no more than plausible, and even, as they are expounded, unacceptable or false, both because, as stated, they cannot be proved either true or false, or because ethnographic evidence invalidates them. It would make our task much easier if we could simply rely on ethnographic validation or invalidation in every case, but we cannot, because many times the implausibility of an author's explanation of the dance lies, not in the evidence that is adduced to support it, but in the theory of human nature or human culture, or both, in the context of which the evidence is offered. For example, when Hambly says,

> ...in more technical language there is a theory of culture epochs, which suggests that the history of juvenile development recapitu-

lates the phases of mental progress through which the human race
has toiled. The emotional life and want of foresight in children have
a parallel in the career of primitive man [1926:39],

telling us later, after a discussion of the dances of the Sudan that

> ...if such comparative study could be made (i.e. that of detailed
> analysis of records taken on the rhythmograph and phonograph)
> there is a probability that the identity of terpsichorean technique
> would, if accompanied by notes on the meaning and legendary
> origin, provide the clue to migratory lines of such practices as
> initiation, human sacrifice, animal cults and other complex social
> events which have, undoubtedly, had a long history [Hambly,
> 1926:276],

what are we to make of it all?

He suggests that through the study of the dances of primitive
peoples, we shall discover something about these "juvenile developments" of "mental progress" and such practices as have led, in
his opinion, to rational, " developed" civilizations, but to a sophisticated reader Hambly's typology of dances is nothing more than
an interesting example of a naturalist's or natural history approach
to the study of social phenomena—a kind of "butterfly collecting"
and classification that may be of great use to naturalists, but is of
little use to social anthropologists or movement investigators.

An anthropologically trained reader will usually not, either,
buy into a social evolutionistic "theory of culture epochs" that
makes of human dances merely events that are of a pre-rationative
and pre-rational kind. These readers will view Hambly's talk about
the value of studying "primitive" dances and their status in the
general scheme of things with extreme skepticism. The typical
dance researcher, I am sorry to report, does not. It has been my
experience that they see in Hambly someone who has written about
the dance, someone who was a member of an expedition to the
Sudan, and someone who has published; therefore, his typology and
classifications, as well as his theories of culture, are to be swallowed
whole—book, line, and thinker.

Sometimes an attempt is made to excise the dance materials
away from the theory of culture and the intellectual context in which

it is embedded, but usually, in spite of vaguely perceived meta-physical discomforts about such a theory, it is given assent, with special pleadings that it would take too much time in any case to find out about such theories or to check out their present-day status in anthropology, and so Hambly's ideas are perpetuated. This is a pity, for Hambly's work neither enhances nor aids the arguments in Frances Rust's more modern contribution, published in 1969, which, in its socio-historical aspects is excellent, but which, in its anthropological aspects is severely marred and outdated because of the author's reliance on Hambly's classificatory system and Sachs's evolutionism (see Williams, 1974, for full review, also see *infra,* pp. 132–136 for further discussion).

One of the questions that has been raised about Hambly's 279-page volume is, "should we not merely consign such writing to a merciful oblivion and get on with the job? " I say "no" to that, partly because "getting on with it" since 1926 has produced no refutations of the theories involved and because critical reading of a volume like Hambly's is salutary, in that he provides such a splendid example of how *not* to approach the study of dances. Then too, the language in which Hambly's book is written is instructive to beginning students as well, for many find it embarrassing today to hear peoples described as " primitives," "natives," or "savages," and novices in the field of anthropology need to become aware of the changing uses of language in the descriptive terminology of their discipline and its broad relation to theorizing about the human condition.

Hardly anyone would disagree with what I have said so far, but in practice, what actually happens is something else: dances are wrenched out of the first-hand records of ethnographers (even the best of them, like Buck Schieffelin) and torn from their contexts, then pieced together in collages of alleged "research" papers that represent distortions, not only of the peoples to whom the dances belong, but of the minds, integrities, and cultures of the investigators.

Clearly, it is the case that when Lady Frazer remarked that some Dakota dances are "...rare, for they denote a foresight which the savage seldom possesses" (Grove, 1895:68), it is not an unexpected conclusion, given her historical context and the intellectual climate in which she lived, but we may well wonder how Hambly could espouse such naïve social evolutionism, given that social anthropology had already had the benefits of several years of functionalism and more rigorous fieldwork approaches.

Presumably, Hambly had had the opportunity to test in the field his theory of culture epochs, but it would seem that whatever field experience he had was used to support, rather than to test, his hypotheses. Thus, we are indebted to the man for all of the negative examples that he provides. Remember, too, that he did not conduct his investigations in the light of the question, "what are people doing when they dance?"; he gives us answers to the question "why do people dance?" His answer? They dance because of their culture and their society represents the " childhood" of humankind. One wonders what Hambly thought of people who danced in his own society at the time and one wonders if he did any dancing himself.

Many people who have written about dancing have never danced themselves, except in a frivolous or cursory way at a party, when they think that they are " releasing their inhibitions" in some way or other. Often, even if they have had some sort of training or experience through which they might claim the title " dancer," they have never tried to dance outside of their own socially prescribed forms, thus they are prone to think that the habits they have formed that allow them to perform, say, the ballet or aerobics will enable them to perform a West African dance, or Bharatanatyam, perhaps, or Javanese or Yap dancing.

The differences in neuro-muscular habit patterns established in the tongue, throat, and vocal apparatus sometimes must change drastically to accommodate a foreign spoken language, or the discipline of operatic singing. Everyone knows how difficult it is to remove dialectical overtones in the speech of someone who wants to become a Shakespearian actor, perhaps, or to occupy a different social stratum in society—we even have plays which have been written about that—but when we consider body languages, where the same rules of habit formation and patterning apply to the entire body, not merely to the vocal apparatus, we seem to develop acute myopia, even with reference to that which we know about kinesiology, phonetics, and phonology. This kind of thing raises interesting questions: does the study and mastery of one idiom of body language provide the executant with the means to perform well in another idiom? Should performance ability be a requirement for qualification as an anthropologist of human movement? In future, we may develop some definite answers to this kind of question. For now, we will examine Edward Scott's none-too-subtle claims to authority based on his professional status as a dancer, made in 1899.

Scott's work was the precursor of many more modern publications, but it is his theories of what the dance consisted and the fact that he was a contemporary of Lady Frazer that will preoccupy us here for a short time. He thought that the "natural dancing of paleolithic man" was the origin of all dancing, and he actually describes this form of dancing as if he had been there (1899:1–2). He lived in England at a time when strong distinctions between academic and aesthetic institutions were even more pronounced than they are now. His attempts to elevate the activity of dancing to a more prestigious status in his society is the dominant theme of his work: "It is," he says, "a gross libel on the votaries of Terpsichore to aver, as some do, that 'the biggest fools make the best dancers.' Teachers of the art know by experience that such is not the case" (1899:5).

He was obviously, and rightly, proud of his literary accomplishments and his position as a dancing master. He criticized Lady Frazer's work both because it covered "a somewhat wide geographical range" and because little attention was paid by her to the dances of ancient Greece and Rome. He also remarked that

> …when writers on this subject (dancing) frankly confess to having no practical knowledge thereof, it would seem that there is sufficient room for the critical and descriptive efforts of those who, in addition to literary research, have made a conscientious study of the art in theory and in practice [1899:v–vi].

Lady Frazer, writing under the name of Lilly Grove (1895), had a much less narrow view than Scott's about the dances of non-western peoples, whom he hardly mentions. She had access to, and freely used, the accounts of dances given her by adventurers, missionaries, and early anthropologists: Haddon, of the Torres Straits expedition, Andrew Lang, Catlin, Molina, Captain Cook, and Chateaubriand find their way into her book. She was concerned that "picturesque aspect of life was going to be weakened by the advance of civilization, reducing everything to smooth uniformity." Old rites were fast vanishing and when this applied to the "dance forms of savage peoples," she thought that their disappearance was greatly to be deplored. She was mainly concerned because these dances, in her view, were all connected with religion (Grove, 1895:65–66).

Her work provides little reliable evidence about what the dances she mentions were really like at the time, but it does provide us with insights into a mode of thinking predominant in her time:

> Mr. J.G. Frazer, the author of the Golden Bough, tells me he believes that the more closely savage dances are looked into, the more prominent will appear their magical character. He thinks that a great many are pantomimes, intended to produce by 'sympathetic magic' the events which they imitate. What the savage mostly cares about are love, success in the chase, and prowess in war, and all these he thinks procurable by mimetic dancing. The representation of his wishes or of certain events will, in his belief, result in the realization of such wishes and events [1895:67].

In Chapter IV, we will examine "substitution," "imitation," and "magical" theories of dancing more closely. For now, it is well to recognize that although their approaches to the subject of dancing were very different, Edward Scott and Lady Frazer were both true to the general intellectual atmosphere of their times. They were both highly educated and although they diverge radically in their treatment of the dance, they were both clearly influenced in their attitudes towards it all by Jean George Noverre, a writer who, perhaps more than any of his illustrious contemporaries, shaped the particular climate and attitudes towards dancing then held by educated, upper-class English people and Europeans.

Scott points out that Noverre, who was called by Garrick "the Shakespeare of dance," was an expert dancer, composer of ballets, and writer of books (Scott:119). The model of a dancing master that

Scott had in mind was derived from Noverre and others, notably Blasis (1830), Beauchamp, Vestris, and their famous predecessor, Arbeau, who wrote in 1588 (See Beaumont, 1955 for further information). The bulk of Scott's book, as a matter of fact, follows closely the model of a treatise on deportment, manners, and etiquette, plus lengthy verbal accounts of the "modern" social dancing of the time.

Lady Frazer also regarded Noverre as a genius, saying that he did much for the ballet and the preservation of its history (1895:363). The period to which she refers as the "golden period" of ballet in England was from 1820 to 1850, a period of development that largely resulted from Noverre's writings, influence and choreography, thus, in assessing "primitive" dancing, it is easy to see how Scott's description of paleolithic dancing amounted to little more than an account of what the ballet (and his own forms of ballroom or social dancing) were not. In Lady Frazer's case, we can see, too, how she was influenced by the stereotypes of peoples of other cultures that were produced on the ballet stage.

For, writers like Noverre, of course, do not mention the dances of other cultures, yet we know that representations of other peoples appeared as characters in the dances of his times, some of which still persist to this day. Although I know of no current studies, there exists a rich, untapped source of materials that could be exploited by students in anthropology who are preoccupied with the notion of "collective representations" that has its origins in Durkheimian sociology. That is to say that theatrical representations of ourselves and others, like other forms of artistic representation, i.e., sculpture and paintings, are collective representations in the full sense of the term. They often reveal the extent to which we are prone to change the natures and characters of others to fit our own categories and conceptions. Such representations in the graphic arts are dealt with admirably in a study entitled *The Savage Hits Back,* by Julius Lips (1937) and in literature (more recently) by a British anthropologist, Brian Street, who has produced an excellent analysis of the Tarzan myths and legends and their impact on modern thinking, cf. Street (1975). One does not, unfortunately, see these lines of inquiry pursued with reference to dances. Perhaps the inclusion of two plates, the study of which I have found useful in my own research will illustrate my point more dramatically: Plate I is a photograph of a West African carving of Queen Victoria, now in the Pitt Rivers Museum in Oxford, and Plate II is a reproduction of a page from Frobenius *Childhood of Man,* used by Ananda Coomeraswamy to illustrate an essay on the nature of traditional art and by contrast, that of western art during the same period (Coomeraswamy, 1956: facing p. 137).

The point is that (often unknowingly) we speak and write about other peoples as if we did not realize that they are talking about us at the same time. That is, *we* are being categorized, classified, and stereotyped in *their* world-views as well; this inter-change, a peculiarly pan-human one, is of great interest to modern anthropologists, and it is well to note further that some early anthropological accounts provide ample evidence that human, inter-cultural encounters are in fact *encounters of different modes of conceptualization.* Andrew Lang remarked, for example, that savages and civilized men have different standards of credulity, after drawing attention to the derision with which many European concepts were met with by Africans, whose symbolic modes of conceptualization and expression appeared equally farcical from the standpoint of prevailing western rationalist views (Lang, 1887-I:91).

There is little doubt that through hindsight, it is easy to criticize, for example, Frobenius, and his interpretation of a "dog dance" in New South Wales (1908:41), for not pursuing what now seem to be obvious lines of research. We may also wonder, with Scott, why Lady Frazer brought no direct experience of dancing to her writing and how she could imagine that she could speak authoritatively about so many peoples whom she had never met face-to-face. On the other hand, we might wonder how Scott justified the involved and lengthy description he produced of pale-olithic man dancing and why he was so severely critical of Lady Frazer's omission of the dances of ancient Greece and Rome.

Frobenius's account of the dances he actually saw in Australia leaves just as much to be desired as do the results of Hambly's accounts—the culmination of observations during a trip made to

Plate I. Queen Victoria, by a West African artist. Pitt Rivers Museum, Univ. of Oxford. Photo by Narricot.

Plate II. Two portraits of the Maori chieftain, Tupa Kupa: above, by an English artist; below, by himself. After Frobenius, *The Childhood of Man*, 1909, p. 35. Pitt Rivers Museum, Univ. of Oxford. Photo by Narricot.

the Sudan. All four writers, despite their differences, seemed to have implied that the origins of modern European dancing—and civilization—could be found by examining "primitive" humankind, whether these were Australian aborigines, groups of Africans, paleolithic humanity, or some other human group.

The point is this: a theorist who believes in any one of the doctrines of evolution or "origins" that we will examine in the next chapter, is going to tend to see those origins regardless of any arguments or evidence to the contrary. The movement theorist who believes in the commonality of "dancing" among chimpanzees, gorillas and apes, and human beings as the key to all dance forms in all countries in all times is only going to see in Swan Lake a more complex form of "display behavior," or in ballroom dancing a developmentally more complex form of "mating behavior." The admirer of social evolutionism of the kind to which Hambly sub-scribed will see noting in any dance form but pre-logical, pre-ra-tional behaviors that, as they exist in our own times, are "throwbacks" of some kind to our own primitive past.

Scott, the only one of these writers who intimately knew the dance forms of his own society, makes no attempt to compare these forms or to contrast them with similar forms in Europe. Lady Frazer evidently was aware of "civilized dancing," but as she was con-cerned mainly to establish the origins of it, she concentrated on "primitive" dancing. Frobenius may have protested, could we but ask him, that he did not mean by "origin" that which was *earlier in time*, but that he was concerned only to show that it was from simple structures that more "developed" forms evolved, whether of danc-ing, or whole ethnicities and their social structures.

We shall encounter this ambiguity in the notion of origins over and over again, so I will say no more about it now, as I shall revert to the subject later on, and to other matters that have so far only briefly been mentioned. It is relevant to the present discussion, however, to note that these authors attempted to answer the ques-tion, "why do people dance?" It did not occur to any of them to ask what people were doing when they dance, nor did it occur to them to question their assumptions about the basic similarity of human nature. They were not dancers, except for Scott, and his knowledge of dancing did not seem to provide him with any extra or different insights. In his book, we are treated to an earlier version of a genre of "how to…" books that are still popular today, but these, on the whole, tend to avoid theoretical discussion of any kind.

It is necessary, therefore, to say that there is no present requirement for an anthropologist of human movement to be a dancer, although some of them are—or have been—dancers. The reason for this is that the social or cultural anthropologist is not concerned, as anthropologist, with writing only about that which reflects his or her own experiences. As I understand the matter regarding movement and dances, this is the case because there is no requirement in the discipline for him or her to justify or defend the truth or falsity of what he or she writes about, or to become an apologist for the beliefs, practices, and ideologies of others. For an anthropologist, the social facts of danced forms are of primary importance, and the relationship of those facts to other social facts. Were the truth known, it is often more difficult for someone who *has* danced to write anthropologically about it because it is so easy for them to concentrate on the ontology of any given idiom, rather than to focus on the anthropology of it.

Evans-Pritchard could make no claim to being a dancer, yet he possessed considerable understanding of its importance to social life: "In ethnological accounts the dance is usually given a place quite unworthy of its social importance. It is often viewed as an independent activity and is described without reference to its con-textual setting…such treatment leaves out many problems as to the composition and organization of the dance and hides from view its sociological function (1928:446). Edward ("Buck") Schieffelin has contributed probably the single most brilliant exegesis that we possess of a danced ceremony, the Gisaro, found among the Kaluli people of Papua, New Guinea (1976), but he is not now, nor has he ever been, a dancer. The simple fact of the matter is that one can find good and bad anthropology written by both dancers and non-dancers.

It is only in the final lectures in this book that I will take up the threads of this discussion once again when we consider the questions about language and the fluency of the anthropologist as a speaker of the language native to the people who are the subjects of our investigations. There, I will make a case for the native "speaker" (*qua* "performer") of the body language. For now, we shall briefly consider some aspects of the putative "universality" of the dance.

Dancing is generally thought to be universal among peoples of the world because movement itself is a universally used medium of communication by all peoples of the world. Mov*ing*, like speak*ing*, is associated with every human institution, every human activity and every human feeling. Because movement is a universally used medium of communication among humanity, the shift is easily made to the proposition that danc*ing* is universal. More often than not, the disguised syllogisms in such arguments are ignored: "All human beings move. All dance is movement. Therefore, all human beings dance."[2] Subjected even to the simplest rules of logic, many of the arguments put forward to support conclusions about the universality of dancing can be shown to be invalid.

Like the question, "why do people dance?", statements about the universality of dancing are problematical and these statements nearly always proceed from generalizations about the universality of movement: Laban wrote that "the whole world is filled with unceasing movement. An unsophisticated mind has no difficulty in comprehending movement as life" (1966). Ellis's book *The Dance of Life* (1923) proceeds from a similarly misleading cosmological statement about the universality of movement, hence, the dance.

To his everlasting credit, David Best has examined such claims about movement from a philosophical standpoint (cf. "The Slipperiness of Movement" and "Rhythm in Movement" in Best, 1978:26–49), so that his arguments need not be repeated here. Suffice it to say that writings about the dance that begin with arguments about the universality of movement are seriously flawed from the outset and that they make no more anthropological, than they do philosophical or logical, sense.

A modern anthropologist would have great difficulty in assessing the *significance* of such claims in any case. "Kinship" (and kin relations) is a universal phenomenon among human beings;

everyone is related in some way to everyone else, but anthropologists do not, because of this, begin studies of kinship relations among a people with grandiose claims about its universality, as if to justify the study of kinship in the first place, or as if we might validate our claims about monogamous, polygamous, and other types of human relationship by appealing to the ineluctable, all-embracing presence of "human relations." Nor does the putative relationship of everything in the universe lead us to postulate, as a result, that all kinship systems are the same, yet such claims are frequently made by writers on the dance; cf. Meerloo (1961), Haskell (1960), North (1971), and Gates (1968) for examples.

When we ask the question "why do people dance?" we are likely to get any of the answers that we have so far examined and the difficulty is, what are we to make of these answers and claims once we have them? If it is true, for example, that dancing is primarily an expression of emotion, then two men engaged in a barroom brawl, or a hysterical patient in a sanatorium, or two children hopping about and squabbling over possession of a toy are doing some kind of "dance." Are we to understand, in any other than metaphorical terms, the television sports announcer's insistence that when we see a slow-motion re-play of a double play, or some other team strategy in baseball, that he is analyzing a "dance"?

There are two issues at stake here: one related to "emotion," the other related to a muddle in the models of events. To present a slow-motion re-play of a segment of a football game as if it were a "dance" that is being analyzed constitutes a profound misrepresentation of the realities of football and an agonistic model of events, where the upshot is winning or losing (see Harré and Secord, 1972a:193ff). The slow-motion segment of film is *not* a representation of what footballers actually do on the field. The filmed version of their movements is solely the result of mechanical gimmicks. The footballers could never move like that in real life, and even if they did, they would not be making their moves for the same ends nor serving the same purposes, as dancers.

The second issue concerns "emotion": how do we know that dances do not *produce* emotions rather than being impelled or *compelled* by them? Anthropologists do not make such claims, nor have we done so for some time now, as Paul Radin has rightly observed:

> ...in an individual's experience, the acquisition of rites and beliefs preceded the emotions which are said to accompany them before he experiences any emotion at all, so the emotional state, whatever it may be, and if there is one, can hardly be the genesis and explanation of them. A rite is part of the culture the individual is born into, and it imposes itself on him from the outside like the rest of his culture [1932:247].

All these (and many more that I have not so far mentioned) are reasons why we sorely need to ask different questions about dancing, dances and "the dance." To explore the alternative I have suggested to ask, "what are people doing when they dance?" imposes certain safeguards: (1) asking the people concerned what their intentions are, (2) keeping the investigation within the boundaries of a specific ethnicity, both in terms of language and of the value system involved and (3) proceeding from a general answer that might go something like this: when people dance, they are organizing, attaining, experiencing, communicating, or representing knowledge and belief. This kind of question—and answer—permits us to proceed on an assumption that these dances can be learned, as anything else in the culture is learned, and we can further assume that human dances do not consist of random "behaviors," and—above all—that they *mean* something.

Great wisdom and meaning is often apparent in the dances of a people, and I invite readers to examine a few brief ethnographic sketches of widely differing dance traditions to further illustrate the point. The dance of the Bedu Moon of the Nafana (central eastern Ivory Coast) turns around two main ideas: (1) the dance is about the society's conceptions of male/female relations and (2) it is about how the society deals with evil, adverse happenings that have accumulated during the year. The Bedu masks are a pair. They represent what we would call "archetypal" figures of male and female principles in Nafana cosmology. The masks dance during the last month of the Nafana year (Zɔrɔnyepɔ), which roughly corresponds to Ramadan of the Muslim year.

The masks visit each compound in the village during that period and they symbolically absorb all the evils that have accrued during the past year, so that everyone starts the new cycle with a clean slate. Late in the evening, when the masks dance in a central meeting place in the village, groups of men may challenge the female mask, and groups of women challenge the male mask. These same groups challenge each other as well, in contexts of humor and socially sanctioned ritual abuse. In this way, people are thought to be cleansed of bad thoughts and feelings, particularly those held against the opposite sex, through teasing and ridicule.

In another dance of the Nafana which is only for men, a helmet style of mask is worn, called the "Gbain." The mask is worn only by one dancer and is carved in the shape of a crocodile maw or the head of a bush cow. Some Gbain masks are fire-breathing masks. They are meant to denote a wild, renegade tendency that the Nafana believe to reside in every male, and which must be purified and/or recognized periodically, otherwise the men, individually or collectively, may do great harm to themselves and others. The Gbain dance is performed, in the village where I studied it, every six weeks or two months.

Many dance idioms are centrally concerned with the relation between humanity and divinity and are devotional in nature. Although not a prerequisite, many Kathak dancers of north India, are, for instance, Bhakti yogis. "Bhakti" is the yoga (the way towards union with the divine) of devotion or love. The exact origins of the Kathak form are unknown. Its hand gestures can be seen to be modified forms of the *hasta mudra* of south Indian Bharatanatyam, and its costumes and characters closely resemble those depicted in Rajput and Moghul paintings and miniatures. The main characters that appear in the dance in the *amad* and *ghat* sections are Radha and Krishna. The *tukra* and *paran* sections do not concern such representations, nor does the bell-work section, the *tatkar*. Radha and Krishna can be understood on one level as human lovers, or, on another level, as divine, for Radha symbolizes the individual human soul and Krishna, the divine creative force in the universe. The stories of Radha and Krishna are set out in the Bhagavad Purana, which is about the *rasa-lila*, the stories of Krishna and the Gopis.

Many, although by no means all, western contemporary theatrical dances are social or political commentaries. A dance, for example, like Daniel Nagrin's "Indeterminate Figure" is a comment on the plight of modern organization man, seen to be at the mercy of the machine and gadgets that he has produced which makes him lose his human identity and dignity, becoming figure totally at the mercy of a non-human network; a "rat-race" of his own creation. Martha Graham's "Letter to the World" is about the American poet, Emily Dickinson. José Limon's masterpiece, "The Moor's Pavanne" deals with the interacting forces between the four leading characters of Othello. One of the most famous dances which deals with the subject of politics is Kurt Joos's "The Green Table"—the table of negotiation and diplomacy—recently revived by the Joffrey company of New York City.

It would require at least one or two volumes just to enumerate the meanings and subject matters of all the dances there are, my point being that to ascribe "self-expression," or "sexual urges," or "instinctive behaviors," "mimetic characteristics" and the like even to the set of dances I have just mentioned is a nonsense, yet, in many "scientific" explanations of the dance, the *only* identity that the dancer is seen to possess is a biological one. The demands, moreover, of an experimental model, or the demands for a pre-defined set of empirically measurable "data" rule out discussions of semantics—and much else, but more of that later.

For now, I should like to draw attention to the fact that physiology, kinesiology, or anatomy, for example, are not sciences which are concerned with the *social* identities of dancers, nor the role/rule relations of the characters they depict on stage, nor do they pretend to be, yet, guided by the ideal (or is it the illusion) that "scientific" explanation is the only "true" explanation of the world, we shall find many attempts in the past by aestheticians (Hirn, 1900), theologians (Oesterley, 1923), and others to bring their concerns with the conceptual, semantic, and aesthetic features of dancing into alignment with a limited number of scientific procedures that were precisely designed to ignore them, with the result that neither science nor art were adequately or satisfactorily served. A curious brand of *scientism,* in other words, seems to have emerged in writings about the dance, mainly, one suspects, through the considerable influence of positivism, either in its logical or its Comtean guise.

In its extreme forms, logical positivism was damaging to studies of dances, and indeed, of all the "arts" because it was not thought possible to make statements about the existence of external minds independent of our own minds, nor was it acceptable to make such statements because they were simply considered to be meaningless—meaningless because there are no empirically acceptable ways of verifying them. Furthermore, any talk of "values" in positivism was nearly always ruled out because values are not "objects in the world" nor can they be "found" through experimentation, testing, or experiencing them as we can verify or experience the existence of objects. It is not necessary, perhaps, for me to produce any further exegesis of the tenets of positivism.

My purpose in mentioning them at all is simply to point out that to attempt discussions of the dance, or signing, or any of the structured systems of human actions that an anthropologist of human movement might be concerned with is virtually impossible in a positivistic intellectual universe, unless one is prepared to accept the reduced status of semantics, of human values (or that to which Saussure referred as "valeur") or of anything concerning the linguistically-tied, semantically laden nature of human actions. It is not an exaggeration to remark that the dance can only be studied, in a positivistic frame of reference, as a kinesiological, or anatomical phenomenon; as a "complex joint motor activity" (to use Alan Lomax's phrase), perhaps, that is usually also described as "repetitious" and "redundant."

> Looking within the human mind has been unfashionable, at least among research psychologists, during much of this century. In the five decades during which behaviorism dominated experimental and theoretical psychology, the study of inner mental processes—sometimes derisively referred to as 'mentalism'—was considered old-fashioned and even benighted; rather akin, indeed, to feckless mystical and religious speculations about the soul. All such studies, behaviorists held, were purely conjectural; moreover, they were simply unnecessary. Human behaviour could be explained in the same concrete, nonmentalistic terms as those by which we explain the behaviour of a dog, a pigeon, a rat, or a sheep—the very animals used in a number of psychological experiments from which analogies to human behaviour were drawn, profoundly influencing childrearing, psychotherapy, and many other areas of daily life [Hunt, 1982:42].

The influence of Behaviorism and positivism on studies of the dance and human movement has been profound, and we have by no means rid ourselves of the negative effects of the older paradigms of explanation of human behaviour that were propounded through research psychology that were, and still are, heavily influenced by positivism. The fact that there has finally been a paradigm shift in this sister social science, to "cognitive" psychology, has not yet had much effect on research techniques or measuring devices commonly required for graduate theses and dissertations on the dance, especially in schools of education, thus it is to these types of explanation that we will now turn, under the general rubric of "emotional" types of explanation of the dance, dances and dancers.

Notes

1. While both dancers and actors enact roles, they approach the task very differently. An over-sophisticated reaction to this statement is possible here, but an in-depth examination of role-playing in dancing and dramatic acting would lead us far from the intent of the lecture.

2. Another common form of disguised syllogism is this: "All dancing is movement. All human beings move. Therefore, all human beings dance." Although it sounds better, perhaps, than its companion, it is still invalid.

III. EMOTIONAL, PSYCHOLOGISTIC, AND BIOLOGICAL EXPLANATIONS

WE WILL BEGIN THIS LECTURE with the conclusion of an article on "African Tarantula or Dancing Mania" because the author's theory is that dancing, together with hiking, tennis, Rugby and "...running round and round in a revolving cage..." are the results of an over-accumulation of sex hormones, for which he adduces experimental evidence collected in 1932 by a research psychologist working with rats. The evidence is offered as "proof" of the theory of dancing.

The author tells us that "In the same order of activity sponsored by the presence of excessive sex hormone would appear to be outbreaks of dancing mania. Young women, as in the Tarantella, are the most often affected, and Alas! another visitation from on high is found to be due to earthbound ties" (Jeffreys, 1953:105). As far as one can make out, the actual dancing that inspired the article was that of a religious movement started in Uyo in the Calabar province of Nigeria in 1927, some examples of which were observed by the writer:

> ...the outward manifestations so far as I myself saw them were that of the shaking of the body, so that at times they were called 'the shakers.' With these body convulsions were associated a religious fervour and a monotonous dancing. The dancing continues for hours until the dancer fell exhausted [1952:101].

The connection with tarantulas, indicated in the title of the piece, is exceedingly tenuous, for we are told at the outset that the myth of a connection between the bite of a tarantula and frenzied dancing, which originated in Taranto, Italy, has been exploded. Italians now only do the Tarantella for commercial gain. In Nigeria, there is no connection with "frenzied dancing" and a species of this spider either, as it is not native to that part of the world. In fact, after the first three paragraphs, tarantulas leave the story altogether, but they are replaced by a mind-boggling list of accounts of alleged "dancing mania" that ranges from Sibree's (from Madagascar in 1870) to Hobley's (from Akamba in 1910), to Burton's comments, made in 1864 about Sufi Dervishes, all of which proved, to Jeffreys, at least, that the dancing that he had seen in the Calabar province was an "ecstasy" and that

> This ecstasy is the Hal of Arabia, the demonical possession of the Days of Ignorance, the 'spirit of prophecy' among the Camsaids or Shakers, the 'spirit' in Methodism, and the 'jerks' and 'holy laughs' of the camp meeting…all of these manifestations, including those of the European Shakers spring from common causes, namely, discontent with present conditions, repressions, then sublimation of the psyche by the claim to a new revelation of the old, and finally a physical catharsis of nervous tension by dancing [1952:101 & 104].

Apart from the fact that the above passage represents a subordination of cultural differences to physical properties of the organism, the author includes the phrase "dancing mania." Should anyone think that this is merely a personal locution of the author's, let me point out that there were two kinds of dance peculiar to the period of the Middle Ages in Europe that attracted a great deal of literary and historical scholarly attention: the "dance of death" (danse macabre), and the "dancing mania," known also as St. Vitus's dance.

It was the latter that seems to have inspired the title of Jeffreys's article. The dancing mania, as far as we know, did become a public menace at the time, spreading from city to city, mainly in the Low Countries, in Germany and Italy during the 14th and 15th centuries. According to surviving reports, the phenomenon amounted to a form of mass hysteria in the grip of which people leapt about and foamed at the mouth. It is possible that the convulsive, frantic, and jerky movements that were characteristic of this phenomenon were the results of the epileptic-like seizures of persons suffering from the Black Death. Italy was afflicted with what seemed to be a similar phenomenon; an epidemic resulting, it was believed, by the bite of venomous spiders, the effects of which were counteracted by distributing the poison over the whole body and "sweating it out," which was accomplished by dancing to a special kind of music, the Tarentella.

Just what any of this had to do with a group of Nigerians living in the Calabar Province in 1927 is difficult to comprehend. Themes inspired by the mediaeval phenomena lost their grip as a major subject during and after the renaissance, for a start. In any case, the gap of years, the lack of evidence and the superficiality with which the allusions to dancing mania are made should serve as warnings to readers that here is yet another example of how *not* to handle the subject of dancing.

Through associations with a period of European history, the author constructed a theory which attempts to account for many forms of religious dancing in various parts of the world. He invoked one kind of scientific evidence to "prove" that dancing springs from emotional and sexual origins and concludes that religion is itself a nonsense. He advances a theory of "catharsis" to explain religious dancing nearly anywhere in the world and his is not the only theory of its kind to be found in the literature.

Jeffreys's conclusions, like so many others of the same genre, can neither be proved nor disproved by his own empiricist, behavioralist criteria. There is no way of "proving" the existence of a psyche any more than there is of proving the existence of a soul or of the Transcendental Reality by virtue of which so many have attempted to explain art in the spirit of post-Kantian metaphysics. Even if we possessed such "proofs," how would we then be able to classify or analyze dances in terms of them?

What real evidence is there that all dancers are frustrated, neurotic people who must periodically release their tensions through the catharsis of a dance? What real evidence is there that Tarentella dancers, the Shakers, a West African *vudu* elder, a Buryat shaman, Martha Graham, or Rudolph Nuryev dance because of an over-accumulation of sex hormones? How do we know that emotions (or hormones) *impel* dance, and how do we know that complex forms of body languages are invariably symptomatic of the feelings of the dancers, as Jeffreys seems to want us to believe?

Assuming for a moment that he knows that the hormones generate dancing, how does he know that the reverse relation between hormones and dancing is not the case; i.e., that the hormones are not, perhaps, generated by the dancing? He postulates a naïve cause-effect relation, in other words, that is just dead wrong. "Catharsis" is, however, a very popular underlying theory of the dance, although I have never read an authoritative examination of why this should be so. The invidious thing about such theories is, of course, that they are not real theories at all; they are merely presuppositions which have not had the benefit of prior examination, and this is, I fear, a characteristic of more popular writing about the dance.

Anyone who has done research in West Africa, for example, knows that there is a considerable literature consisting of reports written by explorers, missionaries, tourists, and others whose accounts are generally unreliable, even about matters which can be noted through simple observation, while statements that are made about the invisible side of dancing may be quite untrue. The ubiquity of dances throughout the world, their occasional bursts of popularity as a fashionable area of interest in the western art worlds, the way they now lend themselves to exploitation by the media, and the comparative novelty of serious academic approaches to them still produces a great amount of shabby work in a field that also claims the attention of conscientious scholars. We often assume that the one is irrelevant to the other, but they are not, because it is often through acquaintance with the works of popularizers that students are attracted to a field of study in the first instance. Consequently, many of them are disappointed when they find out that two distinct levels of scholarship and literature exist and that both are usually severely critical of one another. One might say that an informal recruitment mechanism is at work in this regard that puts especially graduate students of anthropology and the dance at a serious disadvantage. The disadvantage consists in the fact that popularizers of a field always seem to imagine that superficial interpretations of complex subjects will be illuminating. The implied criticism of more knowledgeable, hence more cautious and difficult writers is clear.

The naïveté with which another writer, Ladislas Segy, handles so vast a subject as "The Mask in African Dance" is therefore also negatively instructive, for his article is a pristine example of a theoretical mixed bag of re-construction, misrepresentation, common-sense errors and plain rubbish. It will come as no surprise that the main question posed in a seven-page article is "what is the basic impetus behind the act of dancing?" In other words, "why do people dance?"

Segy begins with Köhler's apes, "...which most closely resemble man" (1953:1). Because Köhler had noted that when men approached apes, they began to jump from one leg to another, Segy tells us that "This was the expression of a strong excitement—anxiety—which was released in this physical movement" (1953:1). We are to note that our children do the same type of jumping as the apes on Teneriffe when they are excited by an expectation, and, the author says that

> Further studies, which include the role of the dance in Africa [*N.B.:* the *whole* of Africa, mind, not even "West Africa" or "South Africa"] have conclusively proven that dance is a deep, organic function of man, an important vehicle of achieving physical release of emotional tension. As mankind developed, the dance, from *its origins of jumps from one foot to another,* began to be formalized [Segy, 1953:1–italics supplied].

This author is convinced that although we cannot witness authentic African dance today, we still have the opportunity of seeing the masks once used in the dances (1953:2). In a few comments relating to the function of the mask in African dance, he says that the reason why the whole dancer's body is frequently disguised by the mask and raffia-bark coverings is that "...as soon as he began to dance, he underwent transfiguration; he was no longer an individual with a definite identity, but a spirit (1953:3).

We are not told what evidence there is for this, nor does Segy tell us how he knows what happened to the dancer. If he actually saw any of these dances, it is difficult to imagine how he knew what the dancer was doing, for they are in these cases, completely covered up, yet we are informed that in order to understand this "process," we must

...bear in mind that the African believes in animism. Animism is a faith according to which an inanimate object has animation, thus life. In the case of the dance, it is believed that the mask is the abode of the spirit. When a dancer uses the mask, he becomes the spirit and thus loses his own identity. In the dance he gains communion with the world of the spirits [Segy, 1953:3].

Not only does the dancer lose his own identity, undergo transfiguration and become a spirit, he is stimulated by the audience, who are projecting their feelings onto what the dancer is doing, thus, "This communal participation is also an act of acceptance, a confirmation of his act, and he is not only the spirit, a member of his dancing group, but also he has established a psychological relationship with a great multitude of people, his own community" (1953:5). One wonders, if the dancer "loses his identity," as we have been told, then how does he establish *any* relationship? It is also to be wondered what sort of relationship the dancer had with his community before and after the dance? Surely, there was a "psychological relationship" established there as well. But, as if all of this is not enough to daunt any mere specimen of the human race, we are told that

...these excited movements become the complete catharsis of all the psychological experiences to which the dancer was subjected. Not only feet and arms had violent movements, but often the head—sometimes carrying heavy wooden masks—the hips and fingers played an integral part in the dance. When great jumps were required, an acrobatic ability of the dancer was also demanded [Segy, 1953:6].

The apotheosis of this creature, a dancer, is finally reached when we are told that "African dance enabled the dancer to give everything he had, to undergo every possible emotional experience and then collapse from sheer mental, emotional and physical exhaustion" (1953:6). Small wonder. One could easily collapse just at the thought of such an improbable ordeal.

There are several possible courses of action open to an investigator who wants to know something about the experience of dancing in an African mask. They can, as I did on one of several trips into Nafana territory to see the Bedu dance, simply *ask the dancers*. "Hard work," was the first answer they gave me, which was undeniably true, as one of the masks in question was 70 inches tall and carved out of a thick slab of silk-cottonwood. From there on, of course, one might get into more complicated subjects such as the pride involved in the technical tour de force that the dance requires and their specific knowledges regarding symbolic features of the dancing mask and the like, but in any case, one does not rightly try to reduce the dancing they do to psychological states: tensions, frustrations, loss of identity, delusions and such.

In my opinion, all such explanations of dancing, especially those which purport to theorize about "primitives" or primates— and other organized behaviors observable in the animal kingdom— are sheer guesswork. It seems to me that we are being told by this author that *if he were an ape*, then *he* would have "hopped from one foot to another." If *he* were an "African dancer" dancing with a mask, then he imagines that he would "gain communion with the world of spirits," "believe in animism," and "undergo catharsis." In order to write about masked dancing, in other words, we are meant first to try to imagine ourselves as that dancer. If we were to perform such actions as "primitives" do, then we must further imagine that we would be in some non-rational or pre-rationative state, for otherwise, our more highly developed reason would tell us that dances of this kind are "objectively" useless.

Evans-Pritchard referred to many theories of primitive religion as "if I were a horse" theories. I long ago succumbed to the temptation to refer to many theories of the dance as "if I were an ape" theories because it seems to me that very little evidence is brought forward in support of such theorizing, either by those who offer the theories or by those who are in a position to test such theorizing in the field. And here, we must ask some further questions.

What, exactly, is this "catharsis" to which Segy, Jeffreys, and others refer? If it is indeed catharsis based on tension reduction models of motivation in psychology, then it behooves us to find out what the status of these models is in that discipline. Although simplistic versions of this model have virtually been ruled out in modern psychology, we still continue to be treated to them in writings about the dance. Moreover, how can we justify the imposition of our own models of sickness, health, neurosis and the like onto other peoples in any case?

In *Religion and Medicine of the Ga People* (Field, 1937), for example, the author repeatedly refers to the dances of the Ga Wɔyei (only inadequately translated as "priests") as "fits" or "hysterical fits." The meanings of these words are highly ambiguous in our own culture, far less that of another, and it is because of this that an odd sense of disjunction pervades the experience of reading Field's accounts of a relatively small segment of Ga dances. Underneath, as it were, we can sense some important facts that are treated by this author as "throw-aways": the relation between types of dancing and the types of language spoken during possession, for instance, or the comment made about the *lack* of any "...unbalance or hysteria in their everyday behavior." We are led to believe, on the one hand, that there may be something more to these phenomena than we are told, while on the other hand, our apperceptions are strongly biased throughout by the heavy semantic and associational weight of the words "hysteria" and "fit."

Following a description of a possession dance of the Kplekemɔ of Ogbame, a war-divinity of the Alata group of the Ga, we are told, "This goes on and on till the ethnographer, bored with understanding nothing of the Fanti, limp with the atmosphere of the room, and deaf with the noise, has gone home" (Field, 1937:67). Obviously, if the ethnographer understood nothing either of the spoken, far less the unspoken, languages that such a dance represents, her reaction was probably the only possible one. But her conclusions are thereby rendered unconvincing: "The wɔyo system is probably satisfactory from the western medical point of view, as well as having the social satisfactoriness of providing a dignified niche for the type of person who in Europe would be the misfit and plague of society" (Field, 1937:109). While there is little doubt about Field's sincerity and one can only admire her honesty, we can justifiably reject most of the evidence as unreliable, even though it was a result of field observation and participation, in contrast to Segy's account of masked dancing.

Irresistibly, Evans-Pritchard's criticisms of the Frazerian style of analysis of magic is brought to mind: that is, much more would have been known if Field had compared, *in their completeness*, the (or "or") state of possession among the Ga Wɔyei and hysterical fits which might occur in a New York, London, or Sydney hospital. At least this procedure might have determined whether the category "hysterical fit" is able to subsume both systems of movements, while at the same time doing justice to possession dances. No amount of raw ethnographic data can make acceptable the kinds of crude categorization and classifications that are offered us here, nor can we, I think, be quite so hasty in assuming that legitimate discoveries about ourselves, perhaps, in so abstract a field as psychology, can be transferred "carte blanche" to others. It is because of this that however brilliant Robert Lowie's contributions may have been to other areas of anthropological enquiry, his handling of the dances of North American Indians leaves much to be desired.

He used these dances mainly as evidence to support western psychological theory. We are, for example, given to understand that the Peyote and Ghost Dance cults merely illustrate the importance of psychological processes such as "rationalization" and "secondary associations." Since the associations necessarily "...go back to processes in a single mind," it must follow that the mental operations observed (presumably through behavior) will "naturally" be those described in textbooks of psychology (1925:300). We were told that it represents naïve interpretive method to accept the the explanations of ritual participants as authentic (1925:274).

The diverse peoples and dances Lowie describes cover a wide range of Plains Indian and Pueblo peoples, with a few West African and Polynesian peoples dances thrown into the bargain. It is difficult, if not impossible to believe that all of these can really be explained by "mental operations" outlined in textbooks of psychology, which in 1920 were necessarily greatly influenced by theories developed with regard to late nineteenth century upper-class Viennese people. Great though these contributions may have been, it is inconceivable that they would have applied to the peoples that Lowie concerns himself with when he talks of dancing. It is simply a nonsense, in other words, to lump together dances from three different areas in the world and then declare that they are all the same because they all stem from emotions of one sort or another, whatever those emotions are though to be. But, Lowie postulated an "aesthetic impulse" as one of the irreducible components of the human mind, a "…potent agency from the very beginning of human existence" (1925:260). With reference to the dance, Lowie thought that aetiological or teleological justifications, given for such things as thanksgiving rituals or prayers for public welfare to rationalizations having "…nothing to the with the real case" (1925:291).

Lowie aligned himself with R.R. Marett, mainly because Marett also professed an emotionalist and psychologistic view of primitive religion and dance. He was quite clear about this, saying that "To recognize the false intellectualistic psychologizing behind ths specious reasoning (mainly that of Durkheim and Frazer) is to knock it into cocked hat. Dr. Marett anticipated and clearly refuted the objections" (1925:291). Nor was Lowie wrong about what Marett was trying to do. According to Evans-Pritchard, Tylor's and Frazer's theories about primitive religion (hence primitive dancing) had remained unchallenged for a long time. Thus, like many of the emotional explanations for the dance, it would seem that Marett's formulations were partially prompted by his reaction against intellectualistic and biologistic explanations, both of the dance and religion.

In Marett's theories are to be found an elaborate metaphorical usage of "the dance of life" genre, plus an activist philosophy of the dance and primitive religion, but he says himself that "…we reach feeling or emotion as the key to the primitive in every sense" (Marett, 1932:2). His writing was the acknowledged inspiration for the writings of W.O.E. Oesterley (1923), the Vicar of St. Albans, who wrote one of the major source books in English on religious dance, whose work we will examine in the chapter on religious explanations, but for now, we will concern ourselves somewhat further with what Marett had to say.

He conceived of the activities of fine art, religion, and play as "belonging to the same family" in some psychological sense. They were "recreational forces" in the life of humanity, providing relief from the realities of everyday life and the struggle for existence. He distinguishes religion from play by the greater degree of seriousness held by the former as against the latter, and says that, "This differentia does not perhaps serve so well to mark it off from fine art, which though in common with play it is a kind of pleasure-seeking, reveals in its more refined forms a sincerity of purpose, a depth of inner meaning, a devotion to its own immanent ideal, which brings it near to the spirit of religion; so that it is not without reason that we speak, metaphorically of the 'cult' of beauty" (1932:13–14).

Fine art "softened" human life, where religion promised a mastery over "real life" that mainly consisted, in Marett's view, of "hard knocks":

> Religion thus brings to a head what is essentially the vital problem as it confronts man, the sole careerist of the animal kingdom. Born in the mud like the other beasts, man alone refuses to be a stick-in-the-mud. At all costs, he must contrive to slough off his primeval sluggishness. So he dances through his life as if he would dance until he drops, finding out however, on trial that he can develop as if it were a second wind by dancing to a measure…. Some instinct told him that he must abandon himself boldly to the dance if he would pick up the rhythm, and so dance on more strongly and more happily than ever [Marett, 1932:18–19].

For Marett, real and not metaphorical dancing performed the positive function of being a safeguard against what he conceived to be humanity's ever-present, natural lethargy and apathy. Real dancing provided this author with a foil to illustrate his contentions (where the main point of his challenge to the intellectualists lay) that primitive peoples were not trying in any way to philosophize or intellectualize their religious beliefs in the same way as western man did. Marett saw that most of the intellectualizing that was done, was done by the authors of books on primitive religion. He said, "Religion according to the savage is essentially something you do" (1914:xxxi). It is to Marett that we owe a clear statement of a still strongly prevailing notion about the dance.

Religion pipes to him [the primitive] and he dances.... So far,
however, as he achieves form in giving vent to his feelings, thereby
acquiring in like degree self-mastery and self-direction, he does it
in order, not of thoughts and words, but of sounds and gestures.
Rhythm serves him in lieu of reasoning. His moods respond to
cadences rather than to judgments. To put it somewhat broadly and
somewhat figuratively, in primitive ritual the tune counts for a great
deal more than the words [1932:6–7].

Although its credibility has been considerably reduced owing to
modern linguistic and anthropological research, Marett's writing
points to another presupposition about the dance that has existed
up to now: that humanity dances because it is either unable to be,
or is incapable of being, verbally articulate (see Kris, 1952, for a
clear psychological statement of this notion). Largely a product of
nineteenth-century rationalism, Comtean positivism, and social
evolutionism, the general idea was that people who live in societies
that are lower on an evolutionary scale are compelled to resort to
non-vocalized systems of symbolization.[1]

    Given that pre-supposition, it follows that people who are born
into those societies which are considered higher on the evolutionary
scale, whose dominant modes of expression are "non-verbal" (as
if, lacking an ability to speak, in the case of members of deaf culture,
they also lack the human *capacity* to speak) are also classified as
"primitive." In the case of dancers, who have the ability to speak,
but who choose to express themselves in another medium besides
conventional language, it is usually thought that their "responses"
are "escape mechanisms," "sublimations," or something of the
kind.

    I state these kind of pre-suppositions baldly, including those
which (1) support a theory of catharsis, (2) dichotomize words and
thought against sound and gesture and (3) begin by supposing that
people dance because they cannot speak or write very well, because
this is what emotionalists theorizing about the dance often boils
down to. The fact that we simply do not know how "primitive man"
danced, whether we mean paleolithic man or some ape-like ancestor, or both, seems irrelevant.

    Yet, Charles Darwin supposed that courtship at some stage of
lower evolution was carried out by "art." In support of his conten-

tions, he mentions the evidence of the important part that sexual selection plays in the "artistic activities" of animals, including, movements and the dance (1899:ii & 410 & 418). The anthropomorphisms in his usage of the terms "courtship" and "art" are glaringly obvious, but such usage does permit the inference to be made that there are homologies between "display behavior" and "courtship"; between "mating" and "marriage"; between, say, filial human love and "pair-bonding," thus the temptation, one supposes, to ascribe the artistic activities of human beings, especially dancing, to the function of erotic propitiation was well nigh irresistible.

Havelock Ellis's notions about the dance concurred closely with Darwin's theory (1923:30–31), and he was quoted at length by A.E. Crawley in an extended essay of his on dancing under the heading "Processions and Dances" in the Hastings *Encyclopaedia of Religion and Ethics:*

> The powerful neuro-muscular and emotional influence, leading to auto-intoxication, is the key both to the popularity of dancing in itself and to its employment for special purposes, such as the production of cerebral excitement, vertigo, and various epeleptoid results, in the case of medicine men, shamans, dervishes, prophets, oracle-givers, visionaries, and sectaries even in modern culture. The similar results attainable by the normal person indicate that the dance with its power of producing tumescence was the 'fundamental and primitive form of the orgy' [Crawley, 1911:357].

It is also thanks to Havelock Ellis that we now possess the often-repeated euphemism that life *is* a dance (1923), and the strikingly unprofound statement that "...the dance is the basis of all the arts that find their origin in the human body" (1914:184–86). And why is dancing singled out as the basis of it all—surely a doubtful privilege? Why not sports and competitive games, for instance, or eating, or walking? The majority of humanity engages in these activities much more often than they do in dancing. Is it because "games" are not classified as "art," nor is eating an "art"? Or is it that dancing is "movement" and movement is universal, therefore dancing has to be the basis for all the arts? What human activity is *not* connected with the human mind/body?

It has been suggested by Jones (1967) that Darwin's principle of natural selection has strong functional implications, which may account for the popularity of his ideas an infra-structural explanation of theories of the dance which are dealt with in the chapter on Functional Explanations of the dance. Although I agree with Callan that Darwin's thought is unquestionably "...an obvious landmark for anyone studying the development of evolutionary thought in the nineteenth century as it affected both the biological and social science of the future" (Callan, 1970:13), I have strong reservations about an application of his principles of natural selection regarding the activity of dancing. What, simply stated, might the Darwinian position look like?

Through mutation, animals acquire characteristics which enable them to deal more or less effectively with their environments. Their characteristics are then described in terms of distinctive features that contribute to the organism's perpetuation. The organism's biological system is primary. Functions, of course, maintain the system and structures, i.e. fins, paws, claws, arms and legs, perform functions. The biological, system-maintaining characteristics of movements pertaining to erotic propitiation and mating, if seen as "dancing" (or "a" dance) of some kind, are thus seen as extensions of the structures that maintain the system and perpetuate the organism.

Many claims have been made with regard to the relevance of phylogenetic histories of biological organisms to the understanding of the social history of humanity. Equally many claims have been made with reference to the relevance of a purely biological study of the behavior of animals or other kinds of organisms, emphasizing, e.g. their "species-preserving functions" and the behavior of human beings. The point at issue is, of course, a question of procedure. How valid are general conclusions about human social history or human activities like dancing when they are lifted, sometimes *en toto* from the theoretical and methodological frameworks of the non-human sciences?

These and other equally important considerations lie, as does the greater portion of the bulky mass of an iceberg, below much surface talk about human modes of behavior and actions. For some reason as yet incomprehensible to me, authors of theories of the dance seem compelled to look upon dancing as a link between humanity and beasts. They seek explanations in this vein in emotional, sexual, or broadly "instinctive" terms: in broadly psychological origins, but they rarely stop there. They also attempt to place the dance on an evolutionary scale of gradation so that we are led to believe that dance forms of diverse types, chosen, it seems, almost at random from all over the world, represent stages in human social development.

As an example, I offer a reference (merely one of a kind) with which American "folk" and square-dance enthusiasts are especially bemused: "Anthropologists report that the great apes have been observed dancing in lines and circles. If this is so, folk dancing is probably older than mankind...etc." (Damon, 1957:1). One can only wonder why a volume on the history of American square-dancing begins like this. What difference does it make whether dancing is older than mankind or not? Or, as one graduate student asked, "why do people feel insecure unless they are able to attribute their actions to apes?" To a semasiologist, or a Labanotator, the sentence above points to another problem: that of the great apes dancing in lines and circles. So what? Given the characteristics of three-dimensional space, there are certain paradigmatic limitations upon which all movement is based, but these meta-rules themselves do not permit incorrectly drawn conclusions, i.e., that the apes moving in these forms supports a conclusion about the *age* of dancing. That this kind of approach is not necessary has been ably demonstrated by Professor Gyula Ortutay, a member of the Hungarian Academy of Sciences, editor of a series of books published by Corvina Press on "folk art" (1974).

One can only suggest that, explicitly or implicitly, explanations of the dance that begin from the animal realm are meant to hold for all dancing that is ambiguously classified as "primitive." Are we then meant to believe that this is the origin of the ballet, the classical dances of the far east, and by implication the whole field of human, non-vocalized symbolic communication systems, including elaborate religious rituals and the military arts? And, if we are *not* meant to draw this conclusion, then why is the case rarely if ever made explicit? Theorists who take animal behavior as the magic "key" to all human systems or actions are justly regarded as reductionists. Doubtless this search is for a level of simplicity which is in some sense universal, and while I have great sympathy for the search, I do not assent to this kind of conclusion.

Perhaps there will always be those who see a straight one-to-one relationship between the signalling device of tail-wagging, prevalent among canines, and the symbolic device of action signs in a human dance that expresses gratitude to a divinity. In virtue of the same biologically deterministic lines of reasoning, we will be led to believe that there is a homology between a stallion mating with a herd of mares and the dance of Krishna and the Gopis, depicted in the Kathak dance (See Singha & Massey, 1967 for good material on the dance), written about in the ancient text of the Bhagavad Purana, referred to in the Gita Govinda (Mukerjee, 1957). According to many emotionalist, biological, and intellectualist theories they seem to be one. It is perhaps needless to say, therefore, that such reasoning represents an inevitable conclusion if (and only if) one accepts the premises and the limitations of such deterministic theories in the first place.

At this stage of our discussion, we should begin to take notice of a significant feature that all of the explanations so far examined have in common. So far, all of them have represented attempts to locate the *origins* of dancing, whether in vaguely historical or archaeological terms, or in the presumed "simpler structures" of human activity, or in the emotions or an "aesthetic impulse." Already we can begin to see how the *locus* of the origins of dancing seems to shift and change—and we shall continue to see these changes, as if we were mentally to follow the path of a moving spotlight, its luminous pool picking out first one, then another location for the subject. We have focussed on history, geography, the emotions, the remote reaches of time, the body, and "human nature" itself.

Should readers imagine, therefore, that we are engaged in the examination of a putative development of human thought about dancing that looks on the face of it, like a progression from ignorance to understanding, or like an emergence from darkness to light, let me disabuse him or her of this notion. An unknown writer, contributing to the second edition of the *Encyclopaedia Britannica* (1778–1783), may have been closer to the mark, although he wrote this passage before any of the writers we discussed were born:

> There is no account of the origin of the practice of dancing among mankind. It is found to exist among all nations whatever, even the most rude and barbarous, and, indeed, however much the assistance of art may be necessary to make any one perfect in the practice, the foundation must certainly lie in the mechanism of the human body itself. The connection that there is between certain sounds and those motions of the human body called dancing, hath seldom or never been enquired into by philosophers, though it is certainly a very curious speculation [press mark 737h:p.2375].

Anthropologically speaking that writer was more nearly correct than many later writers. The accounts of the origins and functions of the dance which have since arisen are on the whole deduced from the behaviors of alleged "primitives" thought to be still surviving today. It is to the conceptual inconsistencies and confusions between these theories and the ethnographic evidence that we do possess that I would now like briefly to turn.

It is not known how primitive humanity danced, but it can be *deduced,* it is thought, from surviving primitive tribes that the rhythms that spurred the dancers on came mostly from the beat sustained through the stamping of feet upon the ground. There is no more reason to believe that a deduction about rhythm can be made from the beat of "feet" or "hands," and if Polynesian, Micronesian, or Samoan dances are the "survivors" from which we make the deductions, then it is highly likely that hands, not feet, take pride of place, for the hand to body clapping dancers which are to be found in this area of the world are many.

If, however, one chooses feet, then in this mode of theory construction, one now has to assume that footwork probably would not have been intricate, and rhythms would have been simple, and here, perhaps, is where the deductions completely fall down, or better still—they could be drowned in a righteous flood of field notes, mainly from ethnomusicologists, any of whom would be quick to point out that the poly-rhythmic structures of West African music, for example, are among the most complex in the world, rendering modern "disco" rhythms totally "primitive" by comparison. And if one then tries to defend the "surviving primitives" theory by saying that one does not mean by "primitive" that which is less complex, but only that these peoples are technologically underdeveloped, then one faces another avalanche of fieldnotes, this time from anthropologists working in Indonesia, Bali, Burma, and Java where countless examples of peoples who are not technologically developed possess highly intricate, sophisticated forms of music, drama and dancing that again render, by contrast, the "complex" forms of western dancing rather simplistic by comparison. While it is true that nowadays, such theorizing is couched in far more tentative terms than it once was, we cannot simply attribute the preoccupation with origins arguments and the dance to our Victorian forebears and let it go at that.

An instructive exercise which I have sometimes resorted to when training graduate students in the anthropology of human movement consists in the demand that they read all of the definitions of "dance" and "dancing" which have been given in the *Encyclopaedia Britannica* since 1768 and in the *Encyclopedia Americana* since 1830. It is possible, through the use of this pedagogical device, for potential theorists and describers of the world's dances to comprehend not only the power and influence that such books of reference have in technologically advanced societies, but to comprehend the semantic difficulties involved in attempts to translate the body languages and conceptual structures of one people into the concepts of another people.

Considerable insights can be gained at a beginning level by trying to translate the English word "dance" (meaning movement to music) into Fr. "danse,f"; Ger. "Tanz,m"; Ital. "danza,f."; Span. "baile,m"; Swed. "dans,nn"; or Yiddish, "tants,m", and we might perform the same translations for the notion of "dance" (meaning a party) or the infinitive "to dance," but we know perfectly well that there are considerable difficulties connected with the semantics involved among the above mentioned languages, far less the difficulties that one is faced with when the language is Swahili, Japanese, Hindi, Yap, Eskimo, or Twi. Furthermore,

It is commonplace to separate dance, along with music, from other forms of human behavior and label it 'art.' Once it has been so separated, it is often felt that it need not be dealt with. This ethnocentric view does not take into consideration that possibility that dance may not be 'art' (whatever that is) to the people of the culture concerned, or that there may not even be a cultural category comparable to what Westerners call 'dance' [Kaeppler, 1978:46].

It is well-known that the Hopi, for example, have no term for "art" in their language, and this is not a "mere semantic problem" (as some would like to say, as if semantics were a "mere" problem in any case). There are no "mere" semantic problems involved in the business of cultural translation, there are only *real* semantic problems (see Williams, 1986, for further discussion). For example,

...there can be powerful and dissonant side-effects from the insistence of including art as an interface to dance. The manipulative attitudes of super-ordinate peoples can force adaptation by subordinate peoples that is not the same as an internally developed evolution. We may, for example, force the Hopi *kachinas* onto the proscenium stage and Hopi 'dance' may become an 'art.' If this happens, the world will lose at least as much as it gains [Keali'inohomoku, 1980:42].

Observations like these, made by concerned anthropologists, are not only relevant to "subordinate" peoples. Kaeppler states the case clearly with regard to a cultural context of a people who, unlike the Hopi, are not subordinate to anyone:

There is little anthropological reason for classing together the Japanese cultural form called *mikagura* performed in Shinto shrines, the cultural form called *buyo* performed within (or separated from) a Kabuki drama, and the cultural form commonly known as *bon*, performed to honor the dead. The only logical reason I can see for categorizing them together is that from an outsider's point of view, all three cultural forms use the body in ways that to Westerners would be considered dance. But from a [Japanese] cultural point of view either of movement or activity there is little reason to class them together. Indeed, as far as I have been able to discover, there is no Japanese word that will class these three cultural forms together that will not also include much of what from a Western point of view would *not* be considered 'dance' (Kaeppler, 1978:48).

I emphasize these semantic predicaments because they have great importance for the understanding of theories of the dance. One may, it is true, find some word or phase in one's own language by which to translate a concept native to another language, as Kaeppler indicated, but we are then, as she also indicates, obliged to ask what the word means to the native speaker, and what the word means to the translator and his or her readers. Always and everywhere we have to deal with double levels of meaning, even if we consider the spoken language alone. We are faced with triple and even quadruple levels of meaning if we attempt to deal sensibly with "gestures" or "the dance." At best, there is only a partial overlap of meanings and so far, we have only been able partially to overcome the difficulties.

Nor will I discuss the matter of translation further here, for it is so important to theories and research of the dance that it requires more space, so that it will be given fuller attention in later lectures. I mention translation at this stage of the argument only because we should keep in mind the fact that we must all communicates with words, even when we are talking about another medium of communication: movement. We are never free of the problems of language whether it is used in our attempt to describe, interpret, or explain the dance, or whether it is incorporated as part of our effort to understand what another author from the past might mean.

Whatever the theoretical or disciplinary context, for instance, it is *not* always clear whether an author means by the word "feelings" actual physical sensations or emotions or both. The words "desire" and "needs" put us in no better explanatory position, for when the locus of the origins of dancing are shifted *away* from historical or archaeological primordia, or geographical location, and *into* "human nature" or the human body, nearly any need or feeling could and did provide a *raison d'etre* for dancing. Sexual satisfaction or the sublimation of sexual satisfaction was merely one of them.

I am sure, although I could not swear to it, that the ambiguity inherent in the term "feelings" eventually separated into two distinct areas of study with regard to the dance and human movement: (1) those where "feelings" could be clearly interpreted as emotions and (2) those which were more truly mechanistic in the sense that they focussed on the sensory and physical aspects of movement. Considerable use was made at the turn of the century, for example, of Herbert Spencer's Sociological Tables, in particular those labelled "Aesthetic Products," for Spencer stressed the physical *discharge* of feelings, although he believed that movements were mainly generated by emotion. Evidence for this is to be found in passages like the following, from the ninth edition of the *Britannica* (and, of course, from Spencer's own writings):

> Regarded as the outlet or expression of strong feeling, dancing does not require much discussion, for the general rule applies that such demonstrations for a time at least sustain and do not exhaust the flow of feeling. The voice and the facial muscles and many of the organs are affected at the same time, and the result is a high state of vitality which among the spinning Dervishes or in the ecstatic worship of Bacchus and Cybele amounted to something like madness. Even here there is traceable an undulatory movement which, as Mr. Spencer says, is 'habitually generated by feeling in its bodily discharge.' But it is only in the advanced or volitional stage of dancing that we find developed the essential feature of *measure,* which has been said to consist in the alternation of stronger muscular contractions with weaker ones', an alternation which, except in the cases of savages and children, 'is compounded with longer rises and falls in the degree of muscular excitement caused by the excess of blood sent to the brain' [1895–1899:Vol. 6, press mark 122140.1, page 801].

Just after the turn of the century, the era in dance research of electromylograph studies, of one-hundred page analyses of steps, hops and jumps, of centrifuges, foot-pounds of effort and minute kinesiological studies had been laid out, for it seemed obvious that the sciences of Anatomy, Physiology, and Kinesiology could provide the more nearly solid scientific approach to the study of movement and dancing.

There is little doubt that these sciences have proved themselves of great value in the teaching of educational dance because they developed an awareness of the mechanical and technical difficulties involved in dance training in the west. Probably one of the most distinguished exponents of the anatomical approach was Dr. L. Sweigard (1974), whose work will ever stand as a monument to the kind of productive relationship that can obtain between movement (including the dance) and the sciences of anatomy and neuro-anatomy.

It is the case, however, that while great insights into the anatomical mechanisms of the human organism have been achieved by her kind of research, great insights into the nature of dancing itself, and collective representations of which dances are a part have *not* been achieved through these sciences. Insights of the latter kind will never be gained through dissecting cadavers in an anatomy laboratory, nor is there any reason why they should.

The sciences of kinesiology and physiology and their many branches are not concerned with the social identities of dancers or with the dispositions of whole constellations of movements, gestures, internal states and such that every role they dance evokes and requires them to enact. Nor are these sciences concerned with syntactical or grammatical elements of dance idioms, nor with the structured spaces in which dancers, priests, T'ai Chi masters, football players, and many others, move. The tranformational aspects of dancing as a symbolic mode of communication are totally irrelevant in that kind of scientific explanatory paradigm.

We should probably think it absurd to imagine explaining a sculptor's or a pianist's artistry in terms of an anatomically functional analysis of his or her shoulders, arms, and hands, but we evidently do not think it is absurd with regard to dancers, for countless students have had to undertake studies of this kind in order to legitimate degrees in Dance Education, possibly because the woman who, in 1918, established the first dance program in the United States, as a part of the department of physical education at the University of Wisconsin, Madison, was a biologist, who had been deeply inspired by Isadora Duncan: Margaret H'Doubler (1962). I raise the matter here simply to underline a point made some time ago: to have a data-base does not mean that one has theoretical structure with which to approach it. And by now, it should be abundantly clear that "theories of the dance" consist of theories of human be-ing in an extraordinary array.

Before going on, it seems necessary to say that I do not attempt here to make some kind of "straw dog" out of the anatomical sciences. There is no objection stated or implied in their study and use in relation to the dance, if they are used in an honest, sensible way, and if their style of descriptive, technical language is used in context—a point which is elaborated at the beginning of Chapter VI, so that no more need be said about it here. The point I wish to make is that many theories of the *dance* are not theories of the dance at all, e.g., a theory about energy expenditure and muscle-work, however valid it may be, does not constitute a theory of *dancing,* or "a" dance or "the" dance.

As we have seen, many alleged "theories" of the dance amount to little more than a set of presuppositions, claims and observations about the human condition, and many consist quite simply of justfications for using or teaching the dance in certain situations in lieu of sports, perhaps, or something else. The general idea from an emotional or psychologistic standpoint regarding the latter is quickly stated: the dance is really a harmless, socially acceptable means by which feelings are expressed which otherwise might lead to harmful, socially unacceptable consequences. I refer to these justifications and their many variations as "steam-valve" theories of dancing, although I believe that the term used in psychology is "tension management."

The confusions over whether or not the word "feelings" is meant to denote emotion or sensation can be extreme. When, for example, religious and devotional types of dancing are explained as the satisfaction of a need to placate a deity, we can reasonably assume that the underlying emotion is likely to be fear. At the same time, fear is known to produce certain physiological changes and muscular tension, consequently it is unclear whether we are meant to understand that the dancers are performing the movements in order to relieve their possibly unpleasant physical sensations or whether the physical sensations prompt the movements to relieve an internalized emotional condition of fear, perhaps guilt, frustration or some other "feeling" (i.e., emotion).

As in the case of the genre of "if I were an ape" theories of the dance, there is a lot of very basic guesswork involved in steam-valve theorizing too. Investigators who begin by assigning the origins of dancing to needs and feelings generally find themselves in trouble fairly early on because they are obliged to organize the feelings (or sensations) into some kind of pyramidal set-up, committing themselves to single out one or the other of them as the most basic need or feeling of all.

Probably one of the most interesting writers who tried to make sense out of all of this from an aesthetician's point of view was a Finn, Yrjö Hirn, who documented his sources and his thought rather better than most with reference to theories of the arts. His work will conclude this lecture on emotional explanations and form a bridge into the next, because he relied heavily for some of his ideas on the Frazerian doctrine of sympathetic magic and its accompanying substitution theory of the dance.

"In none of the modern systems of aesthetics," Hirn says, "has sufficient room been made for certain forms of art which, from the evolutionists' standpoint, are of the highest importance such as acting, dancing, and decoration" (1900:278), citing Frazer, Hartland, and Béranger Féraud as leading scholars expounding the subject. Hirn found the notion attractive, lacking only a psychological interpretation of all the facts which had been brought together by these writers to establish it as a fundamental principle, closely related to two forms of associationalist psychology. He thought sympathetic magic was in one of its forms, to be understood as mistaken beliefs based on *pars pro toto* fallacy of a material connection between things; in other words, it was to be understood as imitation or substitution, but we will examine these theories themselves later.

Hirn addresses himself to the problem of changing conditions in the intellectual life contemporaneous with his times by trying to bring the methods of aesthetic inquiry into line with general scienctific development. "Art can no longer be deduced from general philosophical and metaphysical principles; it must be studied by methods of inductive psychology as a human activity" (1900:93), saying that

Metaphysicians as well as psychologists, Hegelians as well as
Darwinians, all agree that a work, or performance which can be
proved to serve any utilitarian, non-aesthetic object must not be
considered a genuine work of art. True art has its one end in itself,
and rejects every extraneous purpose: that is the doctrine, which,
with more or less explicitness, has been stated by Kant, Schiller,
Spencer, Hennequin, Grosse, Grant, Allen and others [1900:7–8].

Hirn argued against the fine art/folk art distinction, illustrating
how such negative criteria as the rejection of purpose are ultimately
useless, even in connection with "civilized" art and artists. He was
aware that it was impossible to apply the criterion of aesthetic
independence to the productions of non-western peoples. Even
though these dances might appear to the uninitiated as "aesthetic"
according to the prevailing definition of the time, authoritative
observers (Reade, Catlin, Lichtenstein) said that they were better
understood as forms of sympathetic magic. Hirn was simply to
remain uneasy with the imposition of western artistic criteria onto
non-western art. He could not do away with the distinctions implied, nor with the practice of subsuming other cultures' activities
into our own categorical sets.

He argued that the sheer quantity of theory about independent
aesthetic activity must mean that it corresponds to some psychological reality, citing a French writer, Guyau (1884:15 & 24) who
did suggest that the distinction between art and other manifestations
of human energy use be abolished. Other writers of the period
agreed that a "fine art" category was awkward, saying, for example,
that art was simply "...a creative operation of the intelligence, the
making of something either with a view to utility or pleasure"
(Collier, 1882:2), but that, apparently, would not do. How could
intelligence be attributed to the imitative representations of "savages" or to those western artists who were compelled, "driven" by
their instincts or their emotions to create?

It is impossible to do full justice to Hirn's beautifully constructed, although somewhat tortuous arguments as he tries to make
sense of these disparate views. Ultimately, he concludes: "...the
instinctive tendency to express overmastering feeling, to enhance
pleasure and to seek relief from pain forms the most deep-seated

motive of all human activity" (1900:49). This proposition, then, contained the fundamental hypothesis of his book. He realized that it was invalid so long as it was treated solely in terms of the psychic life of individuals and because of this, suggests looking to the social relations of mankind for an answer, attempting to show a connection between an "art impulse" (biologically determined and evolutionist-based) and emotional activites (socially based). He believed that the same laws could apply to sical groups as are found to be valid for the emotional life of individuals.

In fairness to Hirn, he knew this position required special pleading. His idea was that "In the motor concomitants of physical as well as mental feeling, we have to do with a form of activity which, taken by itself, is independent of all external motives" (1900:73). The results of all this for dancing were as follows:

> In these three logically most primordial arts, viz. gymnastic dance, geometric ornament and unmelodic simply rhythmic music or singing, the unmotived 'objectless feeling' is expressed in a medium which directly conveys to us its accompanying modifications of activity. Notwithstanding the meagre intellectual content, these purely lyrical forms, if we may so call them, are therefore emotionally suggestive to a high degree...their expressive power is also confined to such purely hedonic states [Hirn, 1900:93].

Once Hirn had established the art impulse, not *in* the biological mechanisms of the human body, but in the emotional nature of humanity; once emotional expression became the reason for dancing, it was assumed that the activity was an emotional "response" to external stimuli. In the light of this idea, the rest of Hirn's arguments become clear: "howling choirs of macaws" and "drum concerts of chimpanzees" are unmistakable instances also of "collective emotional expression" (1900:87).

But Hirn's theory of the dance was not just another elaborated version of a simplistic "if I were an ape" theory; his was a far more sophisticated and subtle mind than that, and in any case, his cogitations produced a theory of art, in which dance, along with other manifestations of human expression, found its place. At least, Hirn's book is well-argued. If my interpretation of his position is accurate, the over-arching aim of his book was to establish for the arts, a kind of hierarchical order of dependency that was reached by describing relationships among artistic phenomena mainly in terms of their coexistence and putative resemblances in a form that was more than faintly reminiscent of Comtean positivism.

Note

1. This is, sad to say, an explanation of dancing that is still popularly held, and it is no good, when one is teaching dancers, to try to gloss over the fact.

IV. INTELLECTUALISTIC AND LITERARY EXPLANATIONS

SOME OF THE MAIN TENETS OF COMTEAN positivism that are well known are those of the "three stages" and his notion of "Progress," but I shall ask readers to bear with me through the presentation of a general précis of these ideas, because they have had—and still tend to have—great influence on thinking that includes the dance. To Comte, the history of thought can be seen as an unavoidable evolution composed of three main stages: (1) the theological stage, during which anthropomorphic and animistic explanations of reality in terms of human wills (egos, spirits, souls) possessing drives, desires, needs, predominate; (2) the metaphysical stage, during which the "wills" of the first stage are depersonalized, made into abstractions, and reified as entities such as "forces," "causes," and "essences"; and (3) the positive stage, in which the highest form of knowledge is reached by describing relationships among phenomena in such terms as succession, resemblance, coexistence. The positive stage is characterized in its explanation by the use of mathematics, logic, observation, experimentation, and control.

Each of these stages of mental development is thought to have corresponding cultural correlates. The theological stage is basically authoritarian and militaristic. The metaphysical stage is basically legal and ecclesiastical and the positive stage is one characterized by technology, industry, and science. The evolutionary fulfillment of these three stages of the history of thought is "Progress" and that, too, is thought to be inevitable.

The sciences, in Comte's schema, are conceived of as one unified whole, but they, too, are in differing stages of development and are related in a hierarchical order of dependency; for example, Comte thought that astronomy must develop before physics could become a field in its own right, just as biology must reach a given point of sophistication before chemistry could begin its development. "Reality" could be understood by means of basic concepts such as "organic unity," "order," "progression," "succession," "resemblance," "relation", "utility," "movement," and "direction." The highest form of religion in this intellectual context (for religion itself would also inevitably evolve) would be a universal religion of a universal humanity, based on reason, which would be devoid of references to God.

Auguste Comte was born 19 January 1798, in Montpellier, France, and is considered by many to be the founder, not only of sociology, but of positivism in any of its forms. He is important to our examination of theories of the dance not only because his ideas have become part of the received ideas of many people who have never heard of him, but mainly through the influence of his ideas on Sir James Frazer in particular.

For Frazer, dancing fitted into a scheme of stages of human intellectual development; stages which were constructed after the ideas of Comte. Frazer's stages included a progression from magic to religion and from religion to science. With specific reference to the dance, Frazer's emphasis was on the magic to science connection. On one of the points of this triangle of evolutionary stages of thought, the dance was placed as an exemplar of magic. Frazer thought that "primitives" called on magic when their capacity to deal with situations realistically was exhausted. Magic thus provided a *substitute* reality: if a tribe could not really make war on a neighboring village, then it could at least do a dance about it. Through imitating the actions of war, love, or hunting, people were thought vicariously to satisfy what was beyond their powers to do at the present moment. In the Frazerian scheme, dancing was classified as a form of sympathetic magic.

The doctrine of sympathetic magic maintained that a copy of a thing may influence a thing itself at a distance (1911:54). The clearest examples he gives are those of rain-making and sun dance rituals (1912:13–18 & 22–23). A dance, besides providing an imitation of reality, might compel game to come nearer (the famous example of this, used also by Tylor, was Catlin's account of a Mandan buffalo dance). Dancing is therefore accounted for in two major ways: 1). it is an *imitative substitute* for anything which cannot be dealt with practically or realistically, and 2). it is a *naïve application of causality*.

Although no one that I know in social anthropology accepts Comte's or Frazer's theory of stages or the latter's assessments of the dance today, and one doubts if many anthropologists ever regarded Frazer's arguments about the dance (together with many other things) as other than speculation, it would be a mistake to underestimate the influence of his ideas on other writers in diverse areas of study. Godfrey Lienhardt has pointed to the possible reasons for this in a lively and informative essay on Frazer and Tylor that is now, unfortunately, out of print (1969).

In spite of the fact that Frazer was a classical example of an "armchair anthropologist" and the fact that there are many flaws to which one might point in Frazerian theory and methodology, there is a sense in which he did see dances as if they included some *cognitive* content. That is, the dances about which he speaks were characterized as embodying concepts by which people try to make sense of their lives and the world, otherwise he could not have thought that magic, hence magical dances, amounted to wrong-headed science. He seemed to assume that the science of his time was in a highly evolved state and that it should provide a model from which magical practices were merely deviants, or at best poor reflections. Frazer thus interpreted causality with regard to dances by seeing them as activities that were meant to produce happenings in the world, but which did not produce the desired effects.

If they *did* produce the desired effects (say, it did rain), then it was really a result of other things which would have happened anyway, whose real ordering, couched in his understanding in terms of Human causality and its attendant theory of regularities, were beyond the comprehension of a primitive mentality.[1] (One wonders, on a somewhat more mundane level, how Frazer would have dealt with the fact of so many "primitives" studying, not only anthropology, but law, physics, chemistry, etc., in the universities of today?) Frazer saw, or thought that he saw, for example, a rain-dance as an expression of what people thought *ought* to be the case in a given situation—a drought—of what was *actually* the case. Oddly enough, in Frazer's whole scheme of things, dancing is characterized as a misguided form of science, for in the intellectual battles that he was really interested in fighting, he opposed *both* magic *and* science to religion. Seen as exemplars of sympathetic magic, dances were nonetheless expressive of humanity's desire to inhabit a world ordered by natural law, however mistaken their perceptions might be of the ordering.

E.B. Tylor, Frazer's senior by several years, was not very optimistic about the future of dancing in the then modern civilization, as well he might not have been, for if it was true that "civilization" was in any way to be equated with verbalization and the subsequent minimization of "non-verbal" forms of expression, then eventually such phenomena as dancing would undoubtedly disappear altogether. Tylor thought that what remnants there were in England of folk dancing were dying out, that "sportive dancing" was falling off, and although sacred music was flourishing, civilization had mostly cast off sacred dance (1895/1930:53). "At low levels in civilization," he said, "dancing and play-acting are one".

He based this assertion on evidence of historians, " ... who trace from the sacred dances of ancient Greece the dramatic art of the civilised world" (1895:53). To many of these writers, as we shall soon see, the dance was the inarticulate origin of both drama and religion. The specific idea that Tylor had about dancing—that it was basically "playacting"; a kind of dumb-show—was a type of intellectualist theory that had a few different consequences for the dance over the years, although there is a close relation between Frazer's substitution theory and Tylor's "pantomimic" theory because both tended towards the notion of imitation. In substitution theories of the dance, people imitate happenings that they wish to come about or they imitate events as they would desire them to exist. In pantomimic theories, basically, the dancers are enacting, in pantomime, what they are unable to express otherwise, or they are copying nature in some fashion.

Thus it would seem that although Tylor leaned more overtly, perhaps, towards emotionalist types of theories of dancing, his writings, like Frazer's, present a mixture of ideas: "Dancing may seem to us moderns a frivolous amusement," he said, "but in the

infancy of civilization it was full of passionate and sober meaning."
To his sober Quaker upbringing, it must have seemed even more
frivolous than to many others of his time, but one's admiration for
Tylor's views on dancing stems from the fact that he did not allow
his religious persuasion to affect his views on dancing in the ways
one might have expected. He seemed really to possess a culturally
neutral view of the activity, but this is not strange, coming from a
man who managed to place a neutral, anthropological definition
onto the term "culture" that still holds to this day. His capacity to
withhold moral judgments about dancing at a time when others of
Protestant and Catholic persuasions were damning it as "sin" in one
form or another was extraordinary. Moreover, he travelled, and it
is likely that he had seen some dancing in other cultures.

Tylor's real interest in symbolic movement did not lie in its
manifestations in dancing but rather in the language of gestures
used by those having a handicap of impaired hearing. It is regrettable that he could not see dances as he saw gesture language: as
" ... dependent on Man's powers of symbolization and abstraction
... ." (Henson, 1974:10), and it is not within my powers to produce
reasons for what seems, from a distance, to be a severe case of
intellectual myopia, but I would argue that it is possible in cases
like this, to understand something about the power of conceptual
categories and how they can prevent us from seeing what is apparently under our very noses.

We now understand that both dancing and deaf-signing are
simply different categories of non-vocalized communication systems, and that dances, no less than sign languages, are " ... closed
systems of mutually agreed, and therefore artificial signs" (Henson,
1974:10). Tylor's work on gesture language is a rich and original
source of linguistically-based movement theory in social and cultural anthropology. It is therefore a gross error to underestimate his
relevance to modern anthropological theories of human movement,
the dance and actions because of his comparatively short-sighted
views on dancing, *per se*.

Dancers, at least, have just cause to be grateful that social and
cultural anthropology trace their patrimony, in part, to a man who
started the discipline "aboard a Cuban omnibus," as Lienhardt put
it. And there are other reasons why Tylor's more cosmopolitan

views and use of language, in sharp contrast with Frazer's lack of contact with any of the peoples about whom he wrote so much, are to be commended: much speculative sociologism is constructed without the benefit of contact with or recognition of cultural settings, as we shall later see when we examine a modern cross-cultural survey of dances.

Tylor certainly adhered to an evolutionist's point of view: his thinking was in many ways a true reflection of the general evolutionary bias of nineteenth-century anthropology, and much of the writing that we have yet to examine began with sections or whole chapters on early Greek, Roman or Egyptian dancing, yet, it was Tylor who remained critical of "instinctive" theories of gesture language such as those held by Mallery (1880 and 1893), and he voiced his criticisms (Tylor, 1878:15–16). He was also not in agreement with Sayce (1880), who expounded earlier linguistic theory.

It was also Tylor who pointed out the doubtful character of stories about tribes who supposedly could not make themselves understood in the dark, because, it was said, they could only communicate by gesture and movement and were therefore forced to silence at nightfall or in the absence of a light-source. Tylor objected strongly to writings like those of Mary Kingsley (1897 & 1899) who believed that many of the peoples she observed in West Africa (e.g., the Bubi) could not speak to one another in the dark. In agreement with modern language-oriented anthropologists, Tylor's interest in gesture languages can be seen to pre-figure some of the proposed semiology of Saussure, but even here, we are reminded that " ... he held firmly to an evolutionist view that early linguistic signs were 'motivated' " (Ardener, 1971:1xix). He is therefore placed in these lectures in an intellectualist context even though, with reference to dancing, it might be said that he shifted his emphasis to emotional motivations. More important, perhaps, was his use of Catlin's example of a Mandan buffalo dance to show how, in the "lower levels of culture," men dance to express their feelings and wishes, leading him to state that

> All this explains how, in ancient religion dancing came to be one of
> the chief acts of worship. Religious processions went with song and

dance to the Egyptian temples and Plato said that all dancing ought to be an act of religion [Tylor, 1878:52–53].

Tylor appreciated what he thought of as a use of pantomimic action as a means of conveying religious sentiments and he seems to have given some credence to specifically "religious emotions," as they manifested themselves in movement and gesture, which might account for the connection that he made between Mandan dancing and Egyptian dancing.

I have drawn out the above discussion of Tylor because I think that his relation to the dance, benevolent though it may be, is a rather obvious cautionary tale in several ways. His section on the dance in *Anthropology* (1895:Vol.II) places the origins of dancing in classical Greece. As I have noted earlier, there was no more evidence then than there is now of what Greek forms of dancing actually were and there are no analytical accounts of them. This is why the modern scholar interested in the dance can so easily arrive at the conclusion that past writers really make no sense at all—or very little sense: the invocation of dance forms from such remote times and places as virtually the immediate predecessors of the dancing in Europe, England, and the Americas is difficult to justify. While it is true that writers like Scott, Grove, Pater (1892) and their contemporaries felt strong *cultural* affinities with ancient Greece and Rome—an affinity that was reasonable then and is equally reasonable from a philosophical, linguistic, and literary standpoint today—the general cultural relation seems hardly strong enough to bear the heavy weight of ethnographic comparison. Nor are we, I think, prone to accept such widely drawn canvases of "human culture." As Beattie has pointed out:

> It is only quite recently in human history that it has come to be fairly widely—though by no means universally—accepted that all human beings are fundamentally alike; that they share the same basic interests, and so have certain common obligations to one another simply as people. This belief is either explicit or implicit in most of the great world religions, but it is by no means acceptable today to many people even in 'advanced' societies, and it would make no sense at all in many of the less developed cultures [Beattie, 1964:1].

Thus, although we may account for the general philosophical and linguistic affinities that English-speaking peoples have for ancient Greek culture, and we may see these affinities reinforced time and again through language, art, and literature, we are permitted to question some of the relations that modern exponents of "Greek dancing" believe to exist between ourselves and classical Greece. We can also challenge theories of the origins of the dance which designate, e.g., the ritual forms of American Plains' Indian religions or Asian forms of drama and dance as the precursors of Greek tragedy. Forms of dancing and ritual behaviors do not lend themselves to arrangement on a simple unilinear evolutionary continuum. They are better and more accurately conceived of as independent developments having their own internal evolutions and separate histories.

Isadora Duncan was the most famous exponent of a type of reconstructed "Greek" dancing, variously referred to throughout Europe, the United States, and England as "free," "interpretive," or "artistic" dancing in order to distinguish it from classical ballet. Her art was based on creative and imaginative reconstructions after paintings, bas-reliefs, and pots and sculptures of the classical period. Some day, we may be treated to a sophisticated examination by an anthropologist of human movement of the significant social and political statements which her dances represented during the period 1900–1918 in the United States (where she was, initially, a failure) and elsewhere. Her work represented an artistic, political, and ideological rebellion against the strictures of the ballet, which dance form she deplored, especially with regard to the position of women.

In no sense does it detract from Duncan's artistic contribution to say that similar results might be obtained, on one level, if two-and-a-half thousand years from now, someone attempted to reconstruct, say, the ballet from a few of Degas's paintings and sculptures, some photographs, a few descriptive accounts of ballets and the biographies of Baryshnikov and Maria Tallchief, with the odd comments about the art by a few philosophers thrown in. Yet, to the unsophisticated mind, the dancing that Duncan did really *was*

"Greek dancing," or if it was not *really* Greek, than the research that stimulated it must have been of sufficient scholarly calibre to warrant its name.

By now, it should be very clear that the ambiguity surrounding usages of the terms "cause" and "origin" is the source of much of the confusion surrounding theories of the dance, regardless of the historical period in which we find their authors, or the intellectual context from which they were speaking. After many years of experience and reading, I still find it perplexing that anyone thinks it worthwhile to spend such an extraordinary amount of time and effort speculating about what might have been the origin of the act of dancing, because in many cases, we cannot even know what might have been the origins of some of the dance forms we know to exist, simply because of the absence of historical evidence. When this search for origins is extended so that we are not simply asked to consider speculations about the origins of single dance idioms or single dances, but we are asked to look into the origins of speech or drama, sculpture, painting and other western art forms, only to be told that *their* origins are to be found in dancing, our credulity is, to my mind, stretched beyond any reasonable limits.

I invite readers to pause for a moment and reflect upon these things, for, even modern science, with its formidable array of models, technologies, methodologies, and all the rest, cannot deal with the mixture of conceptions of "causality" that are implicit in the works we have so far examined. Frazer had in mind "cause" in a fairly strict Humean sense when he spoke of dances as the producers of effects in the world. It is even possible to understand the notion of "cause" phylogenetically in the context of a simple-to-complex continuum of biological organisms, but to postulate that the dance represents some hazy "cause" in the sense of a primordium for everything else that follows is simply ridiculous.

Here, we are asked to believe that dancing "causes" the allegedly more coherent art forms:

> But historically and also genetically or logically the dance in its inchoateness, its undifferentiatedness, comes first. It has in it a larger element of emotion, and less of presentation. it is this in-

choateness, this undifferentiatedness, that apart from historical fact, makes us feel sure that logically the dance is primitive [Harrison, 1913:171].

In the interests of clarity and accuracy, we will take the time to analyze Harrison's intellectual constructions and to examine her claims. We will do so because they are somewhat more complex than those of Frazer and Hirn. That is, she assigns not *one*, but *three* types of priority to the dance, and because her views have been repeated, with elaborations by many others since then. Indeed, Harrison, Havemeyer (1916), and Ridgeway (1915) form a kind of "troika" of dance theorists who were all classical scholars contemporaneous with one another and no keen student of theories of the dance can really avoid them. It is to be hoped, however, that these theories are not accepted as "the last word" on the subject of dancing from scholars of this kind or calibre today. I suspect that they might have been abandoned in favor of more semiological approaches, but I could be wrong. However, we will now get on with a closer look at Harrison's assertions and declarations.

The two sentences cited immediately above are preceded, in context, by roughly two paragraphs which indicate Harrison's conclusions and represent a précis of her theory. In the first of these, Harrison sets forth her basic difference between dancing and sculpture. In more modern language, she sets them up as a difference between "events ontology" and a "things ontology," i.e.,

> In passing from the drama to Sculpture we make a great leap. We pass from the living thing, the dance or the play acted by real people, the thing *done,* whether as ritual or art, whether *dromenon* or drama, to the thing *made,* cast in outside material rigid form, a thing that can be looked at again and again, but the making of which can never actually be relived whether by artist or spectator [1913:170].

If we understand her, she indicates that the thing *done,* the event, is impermanent—gone forever, while the thing *made,* the sculpture, is permanent (or relatively so). The contrast, as expressed, depends entirely on *time elements* and *an assumption that there is no thing made in the event of a dance.* We are thus led to believe that every "primitive choral dance" was a once in a lifetime event, that does not possess the form of any *thing* which could be repeated. Next, she postulates a *fusion* of artist, work of art and spectator:

> we come to a clear three-fold distinction and division hitherto neglected. We must at last sharply differentiate the artist, the work of art, and the spectator. The artist may, and usually indeed does, become the spectator of his own work, but the spectator is not the artist. The work of art is, once executed, forever distinct both from the artist and spectator. In the primitive choral dance all three—artist, work of art, spectator—were fused or rather not yet differentiated. Handbooks on art are apt to begin with the discussion of rude decorative patterns, and after leading up through sculpture and painting, something vague is said about the primitiveness of dancing [1913:170–171].

We must notice that in the case of sculpture, she bases the differentiation of artist, art work and spectator solely on the presence of a material object. Since ritual, dance and drama are included equally in her events ontology, we may suppose that the speech in drama, for example, is also "a unique event" which is impermanent and cannot be repeated like the choral dance. The "fusion," then, which characterizes the dance *also characterizes the drama*. But, she goes on to designate the dance, but *not* the drama, as "first," meaning, we suppose, that it is "logically prior" to the art of sculpture. Most, if not all philosophers would agree, I think, that to assign the logical priority to either things or events is meaningless.

Harrison could have argued with considerable force that speak*ers*, act*ors*, danc*ers*, and sculpt*ors* are ontologically prior to dramas, dances and sculptures, but that was obviously not her intention. She wanted to establish the primitiveness of the dance. Then, too, we are asked to accept that the dance had historical priority as well. As for that, we can only ask, lacking recent or intimate knowledge of relevant archaeological research, "*what historical fact?*" Presumably, she refers to evidence which could be brought forward in the form of cave paintings depicting dances or "events" of some kind that would convincingly demonstrate that either the dance (an event) or the things that are also depicted in such contexts, were historically prior to each other or to something else. This evidence would necessarily have to be combined with authoritative statements about the intentions of its creators, for it to possess social anthropological veracity at any rate. If such evidence is available, then Harrison's historical argument for the primitiveness of the dance could be conceded, but it would still not alter the speciousness of the argument from logic.

Dances do not simply spring up like mushrooms on the occasion of performance in our own society, nor in West Africa or any place else that I have ever heard of, and there is no just cause either for us to label the odd bit of spontaneous cavorting or gambolling about as "a dance." A ritual does not simply appear as if through spontaneous combustion either, although it has pleased many writers to imagine that this is the case, especially with dances. Harrison's contribution has null value with reference to her arguments for priority, but it has great value in terms of the questions it raises.

For example, there has long been a problem in the minds of many as to the *existence* of a dance, except, of course, during the period when an actual performance is taking place. The ontological status of the same dance when it is *not* being performed is, to some thinkers, nil. It is as if we are being asked, "*where* is, e.g., *Swan Lake,* when no one is performing it?" Otherwise sensible, rational persons who would hoot at the question, "*where* is spoken language when it is not being spoken?", ask the question about dancing in all seriousness. In fact, there is a school of philosophy which emphasizes the immediate, existential character of any event whatsoever, including the dance. The kind of philosophical approach to which I refer is ably set forth in Sheets-Johnstone (1966) and consists of a phenomenology of the dance.

This approach to the study of dancing, and to many other activities as well, has the advantage of being a well-thought-out and systematic approach to the dance. Phenomenology has the additional advantage of providing an alternative explanatory paradigm to that of hard-core empiricists and logical positivists, which may account for its popularity among so many scholars of good repute, but those of us who reject certain elements of a phenomenological approach to the study of dances do so because it tends to preclude any notion of pre-conceptions; that is, a phenomenological approach to the dance seems to deny the dance any duration in time. This is an idea worth thinking about.

Empirically, no dance, whether it is *Swan Lake,* the Bugaloo or Bharatanatyam, exists as a virtual, or visible, entity, except when it is being performed. Apart from clichés about its universality, the most commonly repeated platitudes about dancing are those which stress its ephemeral nature: such statements often take the form of Yeats's often-repeated question at the end of his poem "Among Schoolchildren": "how can we know the dancer from the dance?"

We may as well ask how can we know the speaker from the language or the music from the flute-player? I am well aware that I now risk having the epithet "philistine" thrown at me from offended poetry buffs, but I would want to mitigate this impression by reminding them of the enterprise I have undertaken: an examination of theories and explanations of the dance that is un-sentimental, un-emotional and (if they like) un-poetic as well. Surely there is a place for that kind of thing—and I do not dislike poetry, especially Yeats, but that is not the point.

The point I wish to make is that a danc*er* is logically prior to "a dance," or to "the" dance, just as a speaker is logically prior to "a speech" or to the act of speaking or the notion of "language." But Harrison has said that there is no *thing* made in the case of a dance. One wonders if she would have defended the point of view that in conventional language, or in drama, there is no *thing* made, either? If "thing" in the above cases is defined as a material object, then she is correct in making the statement. If "thing" is defined as a virtual entity (Langer, 1957:6), or, if "thing" is defined as manuscripts consisting of kinetographic scores of dances such as those existing in dance archives, then what she says is incorrect.[2]

My argument is that she is incorrect in any case because she denies any ontological status to the dance except when it is being performed, and therefore, to all "events." Assent to her position commits us to the notion that events have no permanent, near-permanent or long-range character in human social life—a basically indefensible position. Events not only include dances in the human realm, but such things as the signing of declarations, court trials, wars, christenings, marriages, funerals, and so on. Few, if any, would agree that events have no permanent character. It follows that "a dance" like "a speech" or "a ritual" is simply a virtual, non-material entity or "thing." True, none of these consist of material entities like sculptures, but to deny ontological status or duration in time to them is absurd.

As many of my readers will be more familiar with examples of spoken, rather than body, languages, let me remind them that "a man's word is his bond"; only one of many commonly used sayings tied to the fact that verbal contracts are social facts in human life and they do possess duration in time. They often entail heavy consequences, as for example, any felony or misdemeanor. Both speech and actions are involved. Acts thus conceived of a sequential series of moves can be notated. They can be repeated. If they can be notated and repeated, we need have no trouble over their ontological existence. This being the case, we do not have to trouble ourselves with the philosophical status of their identities. There are, moreover, recognizable boundaries within which we can identify elements of actions that are the same and those which are not.[3]

I have now begun to speak, as is probably apparent, from conceptions and theories about the dance that are entirely different from those which generated Frazer's, Hirn's, Tylor's, or Harrison's theories of "substitution," "art impulse," "play-acting," or "primitiveness" respectively, and before going on to another theory; that of "mimetic instincts," I should like to catch up one loose end regarding Harrison's formulations: it is still a complete mystery to me what this author meant by the "genetic priority" of the activity of dancing, and with that confession of ignorance, we will turn to two writers, both of whom assigned an instinctual origin to mime and drama and who based many of their ideas on the Frazerian notion of sympathetic magic, which they thought, somewhat mistakenly, to be "religiously based."

Both authors give accounts of what they conceive to be the mimetic instinct in animals and while they attribute the mimetic ability in human beings to "desire" rather more than to "instinct," it was through imitation or substitution that the dance enters into

Havemeyer's discussion. He conceived of dances *as* primitive dramas (1916:90–91), telling us that Greek plays of the early period and such dances as an Arapaho Sun Dance were essentially the same, because both acted out legends. He tries to make a correlation between hunting and agricultural stages of evolutionary development; a "low" and "high" stage of culture, which led him to suppose that the Plains Indians who were hunters could be the predecessors of the Greeks whose early plays acted out myths about gods of vegetation (1916:90). This thesis is somewhat reminiscent of the "nature-myth" theory of dancing and religion, a product of an early German school of anthropology, the "Kulturkreislehre," about which we will hear some more later.

Havemeyer suggests that one of the major differences between these types of "low" and "high" drama was that in the drama of savages, the dance dominated the performance, while in the Greek plays, the dance was subordinate to the verbal aspect of the plays. The relationship of myth and ritual, as he conceived them, was that originally (one might almost say, "once upon a time"), both savage and Greek drama arose from "a body of worshippers"—thus he at least avoided Harrison's errors of the assignment of logical priority. "Worship" to Havemeyer must have meant that "religion" was present. The myths which these worshippers enacted were both content and context of the religion. If there was any cognitive content present at all, it was present in the myths but not in the dances.

In this theory, the dance was the "non-verbal" imitative enactment of a myth, therefore the dances of American Plains Indians preceded early Greek drama, much in the manner in which movement precedes speech in child developmental theories. Participants in dances *move,* but do not *speak*. Animals, too, it is suggested, move and do not speak in the same manner as humans who dance, therefore, the dance is the origin of all the theatrical arts requiring speech.

May I say that I do not exaggerate or misrepresent these arguments? Nor do I doubt the sincerity or the effort that these authors put into their researches on the subject of dancing, nor do I doubt the earnestness of their efforts to understand the human condition. But, it should be recognized, I think, what their intentions were if we are to understand their theoretical contructions. Many of them sought, and found in the dance, especially in its connections with primitive religions, a weapon with which they could belabor the religious beliefs of their own societies. If primitive dancing and primitive religion can be explained as intellectual aberrations, or as child's play, or as illusions that are the result of emotional stresses of some kind or another, then it is inferred that "higher" religions and practices relating to rituals and the like can also be discredited. This intention is scarcely concealed in Frazer's, Jeffrey's, and Frobenius's accounts, but, having said this, I do not wish to imply that all of the authors that we have examined had this intention.

Marett offered a different explanation of dancing: he wanted us to consider the proposition that *actions give rise to ideas* and that it is the motor side of primitive religion (chiefly to be discerned through dancing) that is so significant, not its reflective or cognitive side. And in dancing, he thought, we see proof that it is not ideas that give rise to actions, but actions that produce ideas, which derive, ultimately, from affective states. Harrison, Havemeyer, and Ridgeway, I believe, wanted to show that it was from primitive dancing that the greatness and splendor of Greek drama and philosophy came into being. They greatly revered and appreciated dancing because it provided them with the means to understand how we have arrived at our own advanced stage of civilization.

It is not my purpose to choose between these alternatives, for I see little value in belittling especially religious beliefs, whether our own or those of other cultures, nor do I hold with writers who seem to overrate western cultural accomplishments at the expense of others. It seems to me that to "prove" that dancing is really a throw-back to our animal past is to try to prove that religion is also nothing more than a primitive stage in human development. To "prove" that art or science or technology, and not religion, is to be responsible for the redemption of humanity is simply to "prove" Comte's philosophy. It does not seem to prove much else, given the lack of evidence to support his presumed stages of thought. And to prove how justifiable is our own technological and philosophical advancement seems only to prove how shaky is our own belief in it.

Ridgeway (1915) was equally convinced that drama sprang
from the dance (one is irresistibly reminded of the image of Athena
springing fully armed from the head of Zeus), and he was especially
preoccupied with proving that Greek tragedy originated in primitive rites for the dead; not a difficult exercise, surely, because all
human ethnicities seem to have some sort of rites for their dead. I
shall not, in Ridgeway's case, offer an exegesis of his thought.
Rather, I will ask that the reader gain further insight through the
remarks of another critic, Arthur Wayley, whose comments are
included in his preface to Beryl de Zöete's and Walter Spies'
comparatively competent and exhaustive research monograph on
Balinese dancing (1938):

> For example, Ridgeway ... makes only one casual mention of Bali,
> in connection with the shadow plays. His book indeed was written,
> not in order to discover the facts about oriental dance, but to prove
> a thesis about the origins of Greek Tragedy. Everywhere he assumes
> progress in a straight line from dance to relatively pure drama,
> whereas the facts in Indo-China as in Indonesia point to a circular
> process, in the course of which dance alternately links itself to and
> detaches itself from drama. Nowhere can the contrast between the
> facts and Ridgeway's theory be better seen than in Burma. Here
> Ridgeway found a drama which 'had not advanced beyond the
> lyrical stage, consisting of dancing, singing and instruments of
> music', though it had made 'distinct steps towards the true drama
> which Thespis in Greece and the forerunners of Marlowe and
> Shakespeare in England detached from the sacred shrines and lifted
> into a distinct artistic form' (p. 256). The facts, as recently shown
> by Maunting Htin Aung in his *Burmese Drama* are very different.
> The danced lyrical drama concerning which Ridgeway had infor-
> mation was the successor of a literary drama (dating from the first
> half of the nineteenth century) from which dance and song had
> almost been entirely eliminated. So far from having made 'distinct
> progress towards the true drama' the Burmese stage was in
> Ridgeway's day in full flight from drama and embarked for the
> moment on the path of ballet and opera [1938:xvii-xviii].

There is really nothing that one would want to add to that.

We may well ask why, if so many origins arguments regarding
the dance seem concerned with chronology, i.e., distance backwards on a linear reckoning of time, then why not appeal to other
sources than the Greeks or "primitives," even if we bear in mind

the cultural relationship between western civilization and ancient Greece? Much more of a specific nature is known, for example, about the origins of the classical dances of India than is known about the dances of Greece, partly because early Sanskrit scholars codified them, or elements of them. The oldest document that refers to Indian danced and dramatic forms, couched in fairly explicit terms, dates approximately to the 3rd century, B.C. (see Jairazbhoy, 1971:16 and also Puri, 1983, for more thorough discussion).

To answer that question, we will turn to a passage from another writer whose book was published twelve years after Edward Scott's in 1912:

> If Egypt was the seed-ground of the arts, it was in Greece that they flowered. As we should naturally expect, it was there that the art of rhythmic gesture achieved the most perfect expression. Thoroughly to appreciate the curious poses of the ancient dances of India and Egypt it would be necessary to understand the exact spiritual meaning of which these gestures and poses were but the symbol. But the dances of Greece, by their supreme beauty of movement and their power of rendering all the gamut of human emotion, are of universal appeal. There the dance escaped from its tutelage to religion and was made free of the kingdom of art. It had its part in that imperishable achievement of Greece—the revelation of the full glory and beauty of the 'human form divine' [Flitch, 1912:19].

Here is an author who wants to divorce the dance, not only from religion but from art as well. To appreciate dancing is to appreciate the human body in motion. The rest of his book is filled with near-rapturous accounts of such appreciations of the dancers of his day. He wants us to believe that Greek dancing was capable of rendering "all the gamut of human emotion" and that they were of "universal appeal," although just who it was (given the many peoples in the world) who occupied that universe is difficult to discern. One wonders how Flitch knew that Egypt was the "seed-ground of the arts" and upon what basis he made that choice. It is equally unclear how he knew that "the art of rhythmic gesture achieved the most perfect expression" in Greece.

How do we know that contemporary expressions are not, perhaps, far superior? Or, that other forms of dancing, such as Balinese dancing (Belo, 1970), or some form of ancient Chinese dancing did not reach heights undreamt of in Greece? We certainly possess evidence that the execution of balletic body language is today far superior to the technical execution exhibited by ballet dancers at the turn of the century (see Durr, 1984, and Beaumont's many excellent volumes on the history of ballet). It is not unreasonable to assume that contemporary expressions of "rhythmic gesture" may well be superior too, especially if "rhythmic gesture" refers to gymnastics. Of course, we have no real way of determining the matter in any case and we risk, with Flitch, reifying "the dance" into a universalistic phenomenon that we expect always and everywhere to be the same.

There is evidence throughout recorded history, of people dancing (or what we take to be dancing) but the evidence is static—in drawings, paintings, and sculpture, or in pictures of hands, for example, as is the case in the Indian examples of the *hasta mudra*. It is only possible to guess how the dancers portrayed may have moved from one pose to another, and it is here, in this feature of moving from one pose to another, that the first fundamental picture of what the phrase "body language" might point to can be seen, but that will be dealt with in a later lecture (see Chapter VIII). Not until the 15th century in the west is there any actual verbal description of actual dances, and, although scholars have attempted to reconstruct the social dances of the thirteenth and fourteenth centuries, they are, to their credit, still reluctant to say more about these reconstructions than "they *may* have danced in this manner."

One has great admiration for these scholars (for example, Brainard [1970], Wynne [1970] and others) because they know that nothing at all is known of the works of the first *western* choreographers, far less the works of composers in other cultures. Some author may have suggested the "shapes" or some of the meanings of early western "folk" and "group" dances, but only the work of those who have tried to revive and preserve them can be studied. It may be, given a more sophisticated theoretical framework and a shift of explanatory paradigm from "behavior" to "body language" that we can make fuller use of the historical materials that we do have, but that is a possibility for the future. It is not something that we can claim in 1988.

Attempts have been made to write down dance patterns, both social and theatrical, from the time of the first books on dancing. Western dance can be reconstructed from various systems of notation ever since Arbeau (a canon of Langres in France) published his *Orchesographie* in 1588. The systems, however, although they can be deciphered by experts today, leave much to conjecture.

I would ask that readers remember that human speech has had forms of graphic notation for several thousand years. Music has possessed notation systems for roughly a thousand years, but the dance and human movement has only possessed this kind of technology for a mere half-century. Because speech and music have had systems of notation, because they are *literate* mediums of human expression, they have been much more amenable to study and although we can trace a fairly distinguished line of attempts to notate human movement, it is only within the past few decades that the benefits of this technology have begun to be incorporated into the combined studies of anthropology and human movement.

Lacking the advantages of literacy, it is the case that dancing is of the same genre as any oral tradition that has been studied by social and cultural anthropologists. There is no doubt that the usage of anthropological method and theory regarding the study of oral traditions would be of great value to the study of dancing and human movement. Sir Raymond Firth's work (1936 and 1970) is sufficient testimony to that; however, that does not alter the facts that (1) the dance and human movement studies have lagged far behind music and speech in the history of the western scholarly tradition and in other traditions, say, Asian and Islamic as well, and (2) the condition of non-literacy simply means that there is a great deal that we shall never know regarding the culturally meaningful structures of the movement systems, particularly of ancient cultures. I do not mean to imply that we must resign ourselves to knowing nothing at all. I only emphasize the boundaries of our knowledge and the real constraints on the accuracy and veracity of our reports about human dancing.

It is because of all this that I am dissatisfied, and would hope that my readers are dissatisfied too, with origins arguments that read like the beloved "just so" stories of the nursery. Perhaps the genius of the writers of unilinear evolutionary theories about the dance lies in their myth-making abilities, and perhaps we are waiting for a keen anthropologist of human movement interested in the study of myths to produce a thesis that would examine these myths and the significance they have to our own thinking. In the meantime, it behooves us to separate the mythos from the logos, as it were, in writings about the dance, and we will turn to Kaeppler for an exegesis of one of the origins of the myth of origin in the dance world:

> The first publication about the dance that had any real relevance to anthropology was Curt Sachs' *Eine Weltgeschichte des Tanzes,* published in 1933 and translated into English in 1937 as *World History of the Dance.* This book has been widely used, and indeed is still used today, as a definitive anthropological study of dance. Although this book certainly has a place today in the study of the history of anthropological theory, it has no place in the study of dance in an anthropological perspective. Its theoretical stance is derived from the German *Kulturkreis* school of Schmidt and Graebner in which worldwide diffusion resulted in a form of unilineal evolution. But just as modern non-Western peoples do not represent earlier stages of Western cultural evolution, there is no reason to believe that non-Western dance represents earlier stages of Western dance. Yet some anthropologists find it possible to accept the latter without accepting the former [Kaeppler, 1978:33].

Kaeppler goes on to say that Franz Boas's work was much more important for the study of dance in an anthropological perspective, " ... although he did not really address himself to the subject," because his orientation offers scope for analyzing dance as culture, rather than using the dance to "fit theories and generalizations," which is what we have seen so many authors do so far.

> Boas felt that man had a basic need for order and rhythm—a need which Boas used to help explain the universal existence of art. By refusing to accept sweeping generalizations that did not account for

cultural variability, he laid a foundation for the possibility of examining dance and responses to it in terms of one's own culture
rather than as a universal language. In spite of Boas and others,
however, the idea that dance (or art) can be understood cross-culturally without understanding an individual dance tradition in terms
of the cultural background of which it is a part, is not yet dead,
especially among artists and dancers [Kaeppler, 1978:33].

Boas seemed convinced that on account of the intense emotional
values of music and dance, they enter into all those social situations
that imply heightened effects, and, in their turn they call forth an
intense emotional reaction. Thus, war and religion offer numerous
situations which are accompanied by music and dancing, that are
in part an expression of the excitement inherent in the situation and
in part a means of further exciting the passions that have been
aroused. He advises us, however, that it would be an error to assume
that the *sources* of music and dance must be looked for in these
situations. It seemed more likely to him that music and dancing
share with other ethnic phenomena, particularly religion, the tendency to associate themselves with all those activities that give rise
to emotional states similar to those of which they themselves are
expressions (Boas, 1938:607).

Research into the dance, ritual, and human actions has much
to thank early anthropologists for, and Boas, like Firth, is just one
of them. For the moment, however, we must return to Sachs's book,
seen as a prime example of a myth of unilineal evolution. He
established a nexus, a primordium based on a speculative evolutionary continuum for which there is no evidence whatsoever. It
begins with what he calls the "mating dances" of mountain chickens
in British Guiana, proceeds to stilt birds in Australia, thence to
Wolfgang Köhler's apes on Teneriffe. The "danceless peoples,"
whom he thinks of as the dwarfs of the Malaccan forests (the Kente
and Beteke), are the "link" between the great apes and Man, as are
the "remnants of the oldest inhabitants of Indonesia." Humanity
appears on the scene with the Redan Kebu of Sumatra and the Toala
of the Celebes. Further up the scale we find the Vedda in Ceylon
and, finally, we arrive at the Andamanese. One wonders how he
missed out the Tierra del Fuegans and the Aborigines, for they are

usually to be found at the bottom of one of these ready-made, ever-fanciful evolutionary barrels. It comes as no surprise when we discover that the second half of his book concerns western forms of dancing.

Were I to address a purely anthropological audience, I would not allude to these kinds of evolutionary, scientistic mythologizing, but one does not often have the luxury of addressing audiences who share the same disciplinary intellectual tradition, therefore I must take comfort in the fact that other of my anthropological colleagues who have strong interests in the dance have been forced to deal with the same kinds of thing in other contexts. We shall turn to the published observations of Joann Keali'inohomoku to further explain what is meant:

> Despite all [modern] anthropological evidence to the contrary, however, Western dance scholars set themselves up as authorities on the characteristics of primitive dance. Sorell (1967) combines most of these so-called characteristics of the primitive stereotype. He tells us that primitive dancers have no technique, and no artistry, but that they are 'unfailing masters of their bodies'! He states that their dances are disorganized and frenzied, but that they are able to translate all their feelings and emotions into movement. Primitive dances he tells us, are serious but social. He claims that they have "complete freedom" but that men and women can't dance together. He qualifies this statement by saying that men and women dance together after the dance degenerates into an orgy! Sorell also asserts that primitives cannot distinguish between the concrete and the symbolic, that they dance for every occasion, and that they stamp around a lot! Further, Sorell asserts that dance in primitive societies is a special prerogative of males, especially chieftains, shamans and witch doctors. Kirstein also characterizes the dances of "natural unfettered societies" (whatever that means) [Keali'inohomoku, 1980a:83–97].

There has emerged a probably largely unconscious format for books on dancing that exists even now and that apparently takes its shape from the same diffusionist theoretical sources that inspired Sachs's book (see Evans-Pritchard, 1962, for a discussion of diffusionist theory), because they are all based on a unilineal evolutionary continuum. I refer, now, to what were at one time thought to be "coffee table books" on the dance, i.e., Haskell (1960), Kirstein (1924), DeMille (1963), Terry (1956), Martin (1939 and 1963) and Lange (1975). Unfortunately, given that dance departments are now fairly common in the United States and are becoming so in Great Britain and in Australia, these books no longer repose solely on sitting-room tables. They are solemnly quoted on examination papers and cited as references for degrees. They are quoted in dance history and theory classes, as if they were something other than imaginative flights of fancy. They are all quasi-anthropological and it is regrettable that dance scholars seem unaware of the development of anthropology itself, especially if so much of what is written about the dance by this group is going to be laid, by implication or otherwise, at anthropology's door.

The interesting thing is, perhaps, that while one may find all manner of anthropological gobbledygook about the origins of the dance in the published literature on dancing, nowhere can there be found histories of the development of dance departments in the United States or historically sensitive accounts of the development of, say, American modern dance or jazz dancing and the like. And if all this sounds a bit like "overkill" or an indulgence on my part in over-emphasizing the disastrous effects of our ethnocentrisms upon ourselves and others, let me recall an experience that I had at the University of Ghana, Legon, in 1968, where I was asked to teach dance history to twenty-three young Ghanaian men at the Institute of African Studies. The reference books that I had to depend upon were the set I have mentioned above, plus a few others, including the *Dance Encyclopedia* (Chujoy and Manchester, 1967). The experience to which I refer involved, among other things, trying to explain why these books were designed the way they were. I shall never forget my ultimately futile attempts to explain what the western dance world meant by the phrase "primitive dancing."

I have had equal difficulties trying to explain to students from Asian or Middle Eastern ethnicities why their dances usually fall into the middle of this standard format of dance book, between "primitive" and "civilized" dancing. It is an impossible job, really, because I could find no more justification then than I can now for the ethnocentrisms that are so glaringly obvious in so much of western dance literature. Because of all this, and because I, too, tried to do research into other dance forms before I became an anthropologist, I append an article to these lectures, written in 1976, both because the thoughts contained therein are, I believe, directly relevant to those of my audience who are specifically interested in dance research and because this article pre-figures much of what will be said later on about semasiology (see *infra*, pp. 287-321).

But now, I should like to conclude this lecture by pointing to the strong connections that all of the theories so far examined had with religion—specifically "primitive" religion. It is time, also, to draw attention to the still unresolved conflicts that attend considerations of another question frequently asked about dancing: "*what is the dance?*" Is it "art," disguised religion or play? Is it best described scientifically or aesthetically? We shall seek a reasonable relation to some of the issues which are inherent in an examination of religious explanations of the dance. To do so, it is necessary to keep in mind that a question which was relevant about dancing at the end of the nineteenth century was this: "Is dancing a straight imitation of Man's immediately prior animal state or is it an imitation of animals only insofar as they represent deities?"

Notes

1. For the benefit of students to whom Humean causality is not something to be questioned, a reading of Harré and Secord's exegesis of the inadequacy of some of Hume's ideas may prove illuminating (1972).

2. An important question is involved here, i.e., that the dance is or is not, only dependent on the actual performance. The point is that identifying dances *only* as performances (in Saussurian terms, *only* at the level of *la parole*) is to see them only phenomenologically, simply as appearance, and therefore as something which has no real character or structure and which in any of its manifestations does not lend itself to any kind of rational, "scientific" or other forms of educated treatment.

3. Winch (1958) offers the best discussion I know about regarding the problem of whether or not especially two actions are "the same."

V. RELIGIOUS AND QUASI-RELIGIOUS EXPLANATIONS

NOT ONLY ARE DISCUSSIONS OF religion and dancing complicated by the fact that the dance became the disputed subject of argumentation between evolutionists and religionists at the end of the nineteenth century, matters were further complicated for students by those who insisted on classifying the dance in an autonomous field of "art." Complex hyphenated terms began to appear in the writings that were published during the first quarter of the twentieth century, viz., "religio-aesthetic," "magico-religious" and the like, indicating an upheaval in the scholarly establishment in Europe at the time that pointed to a breakdown of some of the walls between intellectual disciplines. The successes of existential philosophies over rival forms of positivism, the interest in and comparative success of depth psychology to explain some of the more enigmatic features of western thought and a revival of interest in western Europe in a modern "renaissance man" as an ideal scholar all contributed to the proliferation of passionate alliances, manifestos, and re-definitions.

In the foreword to *Sacred and Profane Beauty: The Holy in Art*, van der Leeuw, a Dutch theologian who took the dance very seriously indeed, summarizes part of the problem succinctly: "Whoever writes about religion and art," he says, "comes into contact with two sorts of people: Christians of the most varied stamp, and connoisseurs of art. Both are rather difficult to get along with. There are Christians who are delighted to discover that although a picture by Rembrandt may be very beautiful, it is still just as transitory as the rest of the world. In their hearts they think that something might exist which could be assumed to escape this general impermanence. The thought that this is not true pleases them. Their love of art is like resentment, and is brought forth by their ostensible grief at their own impermanence. Because they see no possibility of changing this, they make a dogma of it. If I must perish, at least I shall drag everything with me when I go." On the other hand,

> There are connoisseurs who devote themselves with equal pleasure to the blessed assurance which the enjoyment of beauty can furnish; who imagine that they have a monopoly on art; for whom the practice of art is synonymous with piety and culture and science and similar worthwhile pursuits. These are the literati and aesthetes, the melomaniacs and company managers of beauty, who do not want to join the rest of the world in perdition, but want to enter this world in its glorification of beauty [van der Leeuw, 1963:xi].

There are several dilemmas awaiting those foolhardy enough to attempt to clarify these points of view and I claim no exception. As I am not obliged, however, to become an apologist for either side of the science-religion debates or the art-religion controversies, I will ask that readers attend momentarily to the metaphor of the map of the territory of human movement studies to which I alluded at the end of the first lecture.

With that in mind, I would want to say, in agreement with Crick (1975) and others that

> Religious discourse is a map for which God is the 'integrator' (Ramsey, 1961): theology is thus 'God-talk.' From this presuppositional concept may be derived the general idea of the nature of the map, and so insights about how one could best translate landmarks on the map. As the boundary notion, God has a strange status. The non-religious do not properly use such a map, and for the religious the question of the existence of God does not arise. 'God exists,' therefore, is perhaps best treated not as a religious proposition itself, but rather as the presupposition for any religious language [Crick, 1975:132].

It follows that the proposition "God does not exist" can equally be treated, not as an atheistic proposition itself, but as the presupposition for any non-religious language concerning the map of the study of dance and human movement. The *same* ritual, ceremony, or dance, seen from the standpoint of these contrasting presuppositions, can appear to be very different indeed. Cognitive maps of this territory can appear totally unrelated, in fact, depending upon who is the cartographer, so to speak. It is necessary to keep in mind as well that two—or three or four—observers, some of whom are believers and some who are not, *can agree on a sequence of facts, yet disagree on what they all mean.* There is a sense in which, because they view events from different paradigmatic frameworks and/or different presuppositions about the nature of reality, the event is not the same for all of them. Then too, religious explanations of the dance are difficult to deal with in the context of western culture because they are frequently not really religious. They are often combined conceptions or they are only "religious" in a very restricted sense.

That is to say that much of what is called "religious" in discussions about dancing has been little more than dogmatic moral disputation—and the notion of "moral" which is involved seems usually to be limited to prurient preoccupations over sexual contact. In other words, there are writers who speak about the dance from an extremely impoverished notion of humanity's relation to divinity, assuming, for example, that if they live in an intellectual context where God is thought to be dead, then everyone else in the world must believe that too. Believers are not exempt from a like narrowness of vision. What I attempt to get at here, is the notion that it is possible to experience in a very real way the *intellectual imperialisms* that are inherent in a strictly scientific, a strictly religious or a strictly aesthetic view of dancing, for each of these intellectual domains, seen as monolithic wholes, must somehow *claim all of life*: must produce ultimate explanations for everything. The danger lies in accepting one of these domains as "true" rendering all others "false" with the result that supporters of each domain begin to display all of the same kinds of bigotry, narrow-mindedness, and fanaticisms that they generally accuse others of possessing. Instead of peaceful co-existence, "war" is declared, to the detriment of all concerned. Some try to fuse the three maps together, usually with minimal success, and Oesterley was one of these.

His treatment of the subject of sacred dancing (1923) is a valuable documentation of references to the dance in the Old

Testament and a thorough, knowledgeable, and scholarly presentation of Old Testament terminology for dancing. His book is also an
excellent source of references to the dance from the classics. The
Vicar of St. Albans was obviously a well-informed man who was
deeply concerned about religious studies of dancing. He says,

> As soon as one attempts to define what dancing is in its essence one
> realizes the difficulty of doing so. It can be defined in such a number
> of ways, all of which contain elements of truth.... The recording of
> a number of definitions would be wearisome, Voss alone gives
> dozens by different people ... they show that the term dancing
> connotes a great deal more than is attached to it nowadays [Oester-
> ley, 1923:5].

The writer to whom he refers, Rudolph Voss, was a German
royal ballet master, who wrote *circa* 1841–1869, about whose
research more will be said later. Here, we are concerned with
Oesterley who unfortunately did not allow his basically linguistic
orientation to (and understanding of) Biblical history to stand on its
own merits. Instead, he tried to interpret this material in the light of
Frazer's doctrine of sympathetic magic, and (odd though the combination may seem to a social anthropologist) he attempts a fairly
awkward, unsuccessful "splice" of these ideas to Marrett's theories
of primitive religion.

Oesterley's interpretations of the origins and purposes of the
dance reflect agreement with other writers of the same general
period on anthropological themes, as, for example, Jevons,
Crawley, de Cahusac, Robertson Smith, Ridgeway, Harrison and
others. He cites all of these writers, as does Crawley, in his article
in the *Encyclopaedia of Religion and Ethics* on "Dancing." I single
out Oesterley's work for special attention, because he, like van der
Leeuw, was a theologian, and he may be the only English-speaking
scholar of this kind who wrote specifically about the dance. Van
der Leeuw's work comes to us in translation, and we only possess
one example in English of this prolific writer's contributions. I am
convinced that the elements of linguistic and historical references
in Oesterley's work alone could provide a useful basis for contemporary examinations of the subject of sacred dancing, however, it
would be necessary first to excise these elements from the then

topical arguments concerning the dominance of either "science" or "religion."

Oesterley's arguments, like others of those who subscribed to the religious side of the evolutionary controversy, not unexpectedly shun humanity's real or putative connections with anthropoid apes or other primate groups, focussing instead on Aristotle's theories of imitation to be found in the *Poetics* (II), that offer us an explanation of the origins of sacred dancing that stemmed from the imitation of supernatural powers. Sacred dancing, in this frame of reference, was thought to have preceded all secular forms of the dance. The opposition "sacred/secular" thus dominates Oesterley's classificatory schema, and the opposition "sacred/profane" dominates those of van der Leeuw. It is not my purpose to provide an exhaustive examination of Oesterley's work. I shall merely attempt to summarize the evolutionary controversy as it affected him and the subject of sacred dancing.

In discussions about religious dance, the kernel of the argument that humankind came from the apes was as follows: imitation of animals was thought to belong to a very *early* stage of prehistoric humanity by those who aligned themselves on the "scientific" side of the question. *Symbolic* animal connections with deities were thought to belong to a *later* stage of human development. The evolutionists therefore argued that sacred dance could *not* have arisen from earlier, but arose from later stages of development. Through this argument, they meant to imply that religion itself was not fundamental to Mankind. Because they wanted to show that Man had descended from animals and that his impulses towards religion had *derived from* the dance, they took the view that the dance was originally a "straight" imitation. That is, the dance was a representation of that which had been his immediately prior state of animality. Somewhere, sometime, there had been a group of people who had danced about animals, and when they did so, it was with or without awareness that they were dancing about their "fathers" and "mothers," or "grandfathers" and "grandmothers."

Interestingly, defenders of the religious point of view *did not* reject the notion of a biological continuum, but they *did* reject the notion of humanity's straight linear descent from animals. They said that people *only* imitated animals in their dancing at *any* stage of their development *insofar as the animals represented deities*. This view established a connection with the then scientific, physical anthropological view, supported by available evidence from Frobenius, C.M. Brown and others. At the same time, it did not admit of the anti-religious primordium eschewed by the evolutionists.

If the imitative act (which they all thought was evident most clearly through the dance) could be shown to be connected with deities and the supernatural from the start, then the traditional religious explanation of the Creation could remain intact. From my own standpoint, it does not seem that the epistemological bedrock of these seemingly opposed views was all that different: underneath, the arguments seem depressingly similar because both contained the notions of imitation and of a unilineal evolutionary continuum. These ideas were coupled with subordinate questions of humanity's relationship to the animal kingdom and the question of the origins of its activities. These considerations led to preoccupations with the nature of human be-ing: that is, did people copy things from outside (a passive-receptive "organism" model of human nature that Haddon [1895] and others espoused), or was there something inside humans, something innate, perhaps (the philosophical-rationalist model), that was usually unsupported by empirical evidence? The points of view seemed to be polarized into an opposition between "inside" and "outside"; between "organism" and "environment."

Oesterley used Clarke MacMillan Brown's evidence (1923:203) to prove that "... all dancing was originally religious and performed for religious purposes" (Brown, 1907, quoted in Oesterley, 1923:21). The work of these writers and others like them yield valuable insights into the history of thought regarding dancing, and it is a pity that we possess no current examinations of evolutionary or religious views on the subject with which we might compare—perhaps these are yet to come. Clearly, it is the case that on balance, it was the scientific establishment at the time that in some sense "won" these arguments, thus it seems that it was able to hold the view that religion (and art, and women) simply had to become more sophisticated—less naïve, perhaps, both about scientific explanations themselves and about the nature of the universe.

To some extent, at least, this has happened. We now know that any claim to knowledge presupposes a claim to some kind of paradigm of explanation or to an explanatory procedure that is, in the end, supported by faith—even in the domain of science. Thus, no one anymore is exempt from the pitfalls and dangers of dogmatism, fanaticism and the like, no matter which of the domains of "art," "science," "religion," or "philosophy" that they choose.

I doubt that social anthropology can be practiced with any success without the aid of science and the aid of art, religion, and philosophy. Some of the more instructive exercises in which I have participated during my academic career have been those seminars, lectures, and discussions which promoted active dialogues between practicing anthropologists and philosophers; linguists and anthropologists; theologians, mathematicians, and anthropologists. Not much of this kind of talk ever seems to get published, but there are a few outstanding examples of works that examine the philosophy/ science relation that I believe to be of fundamental importance for modern students, namely, Winch (1958), Wittgenstein (1967), Toulmin (1953 and 1961), Harré (1972), and Diesing (1971).

From a standpoint of real interdisciplinary understanding, one can with impunity offer the idea that the crucial connection regarding any knowledge we may think we possess nowadays is that between paradigm and knowledge. This connection is composed of a combination of method, faith, and a disciplined imagination that is supported by knowledge of the intellectual history of one's chosen field. Ever since Heisenberg, Wittgenstein, Saussure, Sapir, Jakobsen, Lévi-Strauss, Polanyi, Kuhn, and others, we now see that it is the paradigm that makes any claim to knowledge viable. Perhaps our mistake is to reify these domains of study into "domains" in the first instance, treating them as if they were political territories that are mutually exclusive, but I now digress.

Not only has dancing been considered the missing link in evolutionists' arguments and as the origin of religion by theologians, dances and dancing have also been used as metaphors for a notionally complete quasi-religious or aesthetic unity. The dance and human movement have been offered to us as the grounds for a synthesis of all humankind. Moreover, an interest in dancing or preoccupations with the dance has been classified in the west as vaguely "feminine" in contrast to other human activities and capacities (notably "thinking") that are thought to be "masculine." Erich Heller reminded us that there was a "religion of art"; a kind of deification of the "artifice of eternity" or the "aesthetic phenomenon" that "for so many great and good minds of the last hundred years has taken the place once held by a different gospel of salvation" (Heller, 1969:65).

The art gospel to which he referred was supported by a sense of a condemned real world, and he says that although such rhetorical questions do not require answers, the question of what is real in the world was answered by Nietzsche long before the poet, Yeats, asked it. "'Thought,' in *Michael Robartes and the Dancer* was just powerful enough to make women ignore the wisdom of the mirror, obstruct the natural intelligence and 'uncomposite blessedness' of their beautiful bodies, frustrate their lovers, and grow perplexed at the amorously and blasphemously theological question: Did God in portioning wine and bread, give man His thought or His mere body?" (Heller, 1969:70).

In the above-mentioned poem, "thought" is characterized as wrong and erroneous. In particular it prevents women from seeing the joy, which is evidently considered to be "beyond" thought, of erotic abandonment. Heller's exegesis of these matters, is, to me, unexceptionable. He tells us that the sad story is a very old one; that the tree of *knowledge* does not stand for the good life, and that over and over in his later years, Yeats returned to this grand theme:

> That chestnut tree and great rooted blossomer has grown from the richest soil of Romantic poetry. It embodies the Romantic vision of the Tree of Life that has the power to cure the disease man has contracted through so greedily reaching for the Tree of Knowledge:
>
>> O chestnut tree, great rooted blossomer,
>> Are you the leaf, the blossom or the bole:
>> O body swayed to music, O brightening glance,
>> How can we know the dancer from the dance?
>
> [Heller, 1969:70].

Alas! Heller exclaims, "...out of the delicious light and shade of the great tree, we can know and we do know. Nietzsche has much to tell us of dancers who wear their dance like a mask of innocence and Rilke ... in the fourth of the *Duino Elegies*, angrily dismisses his dancer, the dancer who theatrically dances before the backdrop of the "well-known garden." He dismisses him because he *is* not what he *does* but disguised; "a mask half-filled with life," and will be a mediocrity as soon as the performance is over and the make-up removed.... The figure of that dancer came to Rilke from Kleist's essayistic story about the Marionette Theatre, a story of modern man: his painfully growing awareness of the lost unity between dancer and the dance" (Heller, 1969:70–71).

I quote Heller at length regarding these authors and Romantic thought in general, because I cannot write like this, and it seems to me that the very style of this author's prose admirably captures the spirit of his subject; a general disillusion with science, perhaps, that led to the elevation of a philosophy of activism (or a philosophy of eroticism) or some kind of emphasis on a "language of the body" over that of the mind or spirit. The fragmentation of faculties of the human being is extreme, but reflects a not-unexpected reaction, really, given the dominance of a philosophy of positivism in the empirical sciences and the obvious success of experimental science as a paradigm of explanation. All this, coupled with the Romantic attachment of women to corporeal and men to ethereal domains of life seem simply to have produced further permutations of the well-known Cartesian mind-body split. But, we are told,

> Later sufferers of the metaphysical discomfort—Nietzsche, D.H. Lawrence or Yeats—were more impatient. Long before D.H. Lawrence discovered the liberating powers of Priapus, Nietzsche enthroned and celebrated Dionysius, the god of intoxication and ecstasy, in whose revels the conscious and the self-conscious self vanished, merging as it does with that universal dance that is not so much danced by the dancers as it *is* the dancers "in their orgiastic self-forgetfulness" [Heller, 1969:71].

This author also points out—to my mind, rightly so—that while Hegel thought that the history of the world would be a progression from "natural" functions towards consciousness,

Yeats's very question seemed to have postulated the opposite view: "Yeats' query reads, on the contrary, like a promise given to the artist that his 'spontaneous creativity' would inherit the earth. Dance and dancer would again be one. What is in the making ... is the anachronism of an artistic eschatology. The Day of Judgment will be the Day of Art" (Heller, 1969:71). However, the author concludes (and I would agree) that there is no salvation in consciously induced spontaneities, and there is no salvation through Art, or, one might add, through science or through an impoverished view of religion either.

It is to one such impoverished view of religion—and the dance—that we will now turn, fully aware, I trust, that as we do so, we are required to turn for the moment from more sublime usages and explanations of the dance, to the ridiculous. It is well to remember also, that the author whose work we are about to examine does not offer a theory or an explanation *per se* of dancing unless we can call it a "theory" that dancing is evil. It is possible that narrow moralistic discourse has produced more impassioned and lengthy treatments of dancing than are to be found elsewhere, although upon reflection, one realizes that there are no *more* of them, they simply seem to be more well-known.

The writing we will examine is that of a French author, M. Gauthier, who wrote in 1775. I have deliberately chosen an author sufficiently removed from us in time in the hope that we can adopt a perspective of tolerance and humor towards his work and to his harangues, for that is what they were, starting with what may be one of the lengthiest titles in the history of western literature: "Traite contre les Danses et les Mauvaises Chansons, dans lequel le danger et le mal qui y sont renfermes sont demontres les Temoignages multiplies des Saintes Ecritures, des S.S. Perces, des Conceiles, de plusieurs Eveques du siecle passe et du notre, d'un nombre de Theologians moraux et de Casuistes, de Jurisconsultes, de plusiers Ministres Protestants et enfin des Paiens meme." This is the title of the second edition. I shall refer to this tome hereafter simply as the *Treatise Against Dancing and Dirty Songs*, and would want to remark as well that M. Gauthier was *not* a cleric, but a layman, who became a self-appointed spokesman for both Catholic

and Protestant theologians, for the Saints and for the French government of the time.

Many people criticized Gauthier's work; he documents his
critics with the same zeal as he documented what he conceived to
be activities that were "manifestations of the devil," thus there is
no doubt that some of them were theologians. His cavalier disregard
for Biblical history and cultural context alone would have been
enough to arouse their indignation, however, we must note that
popular demand for his book created a need for a second edition,
and there may have been more. Sensationalism and slander have
ever seemed to enjoy popularity, and Gauthier evidently felt in a
sufficiently secure position to group all of his detractors and their
impotent protestations anonymously in the body of his work, under
the general headings that dominated all of his thought: good/evil,
Christian/pagan, God/Devil, men/women, non-dancing/dancing,
non-foreign women/prostitutes. Men who danced, were, of course,
effeminate.

Some of Gauthier's critics pointed out that since dancing is
public, nothing really evil can happen, to which he replied that it is
not what actually happens, but wicked thoughts and desires that are
to be avoided. Equally fruitless arguments brought against him
were based in the enumeration of facts that nothing had ever been
proved about the dangers of dancing. These were answered by a
simple quote from John Chrysostom (p. 250). Others said that
dances, after all, had been in use in all times and all places, which
only proved to M. Gauthier that wickedness was universal. It was
pointed out that there were priests and confessors who did not object
to dancing, to which he replied that they were ignorant of their duty
and "false prophets." He devotes two chapters to reports of various
ordinances in France against dancing that were enacted between
the years 1520 and 1700, including two injunctions passed by the
Parlement of Paris forbidding public dancing under the pain of large
fines (p. 75 and Chapter IV; part one, and Chapter V).

In view of these kinds of dogmatic, moralistic ideas about
dancing, it is hardly surprising that most, if not all of the historical
material that has survived about French dancing consists of records
of the dancing done in courts, or later, as ballets. These forms of

dancing were sanctioned by nobility and it is not surprising that
Gauthier does not criticize these forms of dancing—those which
are referred to by modern scholars as "pre-classical" forms (See
Horst, 1937), for those escaped such legal and moral strictures.
They enjoyed high status, if not always high respectability among
the bourgeoisie of the time. It was the dancing of rural France and
the lower classes to which Gauthier mainly referred and he provides
us with an example of a type of figure that has throughout human
history has been with us: that of a narrow-minded, self-righteous
bigot to whom even the arguments presented by scholars of his own
religious persuasion had no meaning.

Nor did the writings of those who were the purveyors of the
culture, manners, and deportment of the times have any effect upon
M. Gauthier's attitudes (cf. Lauze, 1623) or any of the distinguished literary figures of his day, including Voltaire, whose name
was significantly absent in M. Gauthier's writings, but who gave
as one of his reasons for loving the ballet that it was both a science
and an art. One wonders if he was acquainted with the writings of
Theophile Gautier, another champion, critic, and high priest of the
ballet, whose views were the opposite of his own. Perhaps it was
influences like these which prevented Gauthier from saying much
about the ballet, but it is to one such writer, from Germany, that I
now want to draw attention: Rudolph Voss.

The contribution of this ballet master still awaits translation
into English, and because I do not read German, I depended upon
the able translations of Voss's work that were done for me by Anne
Oppenheimer (at the time at Oxford completing a thesis on Franz
Kafka). Voss's book is entitled *The Dance and Its History, A
Cultural–Historical Choreographic Study, With a Lexicon of Dances* (Der Tanz un seine Geschichte. Eine Kulturhistorisch-
choreographische Studie. Mit einem Lexicon der Tanze). Voss's
study of the dance is a pleasure, even to the mind of a modern
anthropologist, because he seemed to have worked in a true spirit
of objective enquiry in his own cultural context. I shall not do full
justice to his writing here and can only hope that in future, some
keen student of German, working together with an anthropologist,
might produce an English translation with commentaries. Just one

of the types of definitions of the dance that Voss dealt with answers a question often asked in the past and still asked today about dancing: is dancing "good" or "evil"? In true scholarly fashion, Voss simply sets out what had been said on both sides of the question, meticulously documenting his sources, so that we have little doubt that dancing was thought by some to be "good" and by others to be "evil" during the sixteenth century, as the following examples of the "evil" side of the discourse seem to indicate:

> Dancing is a lewd movement and a disgraceful spectacle by which one is annoyed.
>
> Dancing is a frivolous disgrace, wickedness and vain darkness.
>
> Dancing is a satanic pageant.
>
> Dancing is a movement of pleasure, a game that ill becomes all devout people.
>
> Dancing is a practice that came not from heaven, but from Satan himself, invented to offend God.
>
> Dancing is a heap of filth.
>
> Dancing is a rotten tree.
>
> Dancing is a hideous monstrosity, a tiresome, dishonorable, disgraceful and wanton abuse.

Some of these epithets could well have been lifted from the sermons of late eighteenth and early nineteenth century American puritan ministers, such as Cotton Mather or Jonathan Edwards. We might also reasonably suppose that such hell-fire and damnation terms were some of those which prompted a wry comment about the effects of Christianity on the dance to be found in the first edition of the *Encyclopedia Americana* of 1830:

> Its ancient character, however, of an expression of religious or patriotic feeling, gradually declined, as the progress of refinement and civilization produced its unvariable effect of restraining the full expression of the feelings and emotions. This circumstance, added to the chastened and didactic character of the Christian religion probably prevented the dance from being admitted among the rites of the Christian religion; but it has always been cultivated among

Christians, as an agreeable amusement and elegant exhibition [1830:110–111].

Dancing that was associated with the devil, however, was not of the nature of "an agreeable amusement or elegant exhibition."

Interestingly, Voss devotes a section of his book to witch dances (1869:96). He suggests that "The devil was not originally a member of the witches community. Only with the spread of Christianity is belief in the devil added to the (notion of) witch cults or witchery, making the assembly of witches of later centuries into wild goings-on" (1869:97). His work points to an item of modern anthropological interest; that is, witches, in the tradition Voss describes, were defined as people who dance. Godly people, in contrast, were defined as people who did *not* dance. In other words, the activity of dancing in this context became a categorical distinction between "good" and "bad" people and "good reality" and "bad reality." Non-witch and non-dancer were associated in the Germany of the time. I make a point of this to reveal just how easy it is hastily to assume that this categorical distinction is somehow "universal" and to point to anthropological evidence that it is not. As is well-known in anthropological circles, in some African contexts, just the opposite is the case. Witches *do not* dance and it is the people who are connected with the traditional religious hierarchy who *do* (see Rattray, 1923).

Voss's section of his book devoted to the analysis of devils is slightly longer than the section he wrote on witches, for the devils that were associated with the mythology of early and mid-nineteenth century Germany, apparently, comprised a legion. They were presided over by a grand dancing devil, "Schickt den Tanz" (Send the dance). Not only did this leading devil have a name, lesser devils did too, although I shall not enumerate them here. Voss also refers to "gesindeteufel," i.e., devils of the common people of domestic staffs, but these were not given specific names. The writer's theory about why ten of the lesser named devils came into being was that the clergy at the time felt themselves justified in exercising control over dancing manners, especially in rural areas, by emphasizing the deterrent nature of the devil (Voss, 1869-107).

Unlike M. Gauthier, Voss was extraordinarily clear-headed and fair, refusing to accept popular superstition and lack of education as a criterion for truth about these matters, whether he found these ideas offered by clerics or members of congregations. He cites such ministers as Martin Luther, for example, who was of the opinion that the evil which might take place in relation to dancing was not "...the fault of dancing alone since the same may happen at table and in church" (1869:113). Luther pointed out that it was not the fault of eating and drinking that people make gluttons of themselves and said that faith and love were likewise not dependent on standing up, sitting down, or dancing. There are many who might benefit from taking a page from Luther's book, whether they are Christians, Behaviorists or artists. Dancing in itself, however, was not a subject that Luther devoted much thought to, although many years later, van der Leeuw did.

Ultimately, van der Leeuw's map of the territory of the dance and human movement is as unsatisfying as is the "route map" that we are offered that leads almost irreversibly to an artistic eschatology or to a scientific program that would write "delete" in connection with humanity's relation to divinity. However, as a writer he asks some different questions and presents us with a clarity of thought and expression that is admirable. It is from him, too, that in the context of these lectures we get the first intimations of "structure" (although not of the more familiar Lévi-Straussian kind) and we are freed from more common interpretations of the terms "primitive" and "modern":

This is not the place to propose at length what is meant by "primitive" and "modern." I have done that in another place (See *La Structure de la mentalitie primitive*. Strasberg-Paris, 1928). From what follows, usage will become apparent automatically. One remark only should be made in this regard: "primitive" never means the intellectual situation of earlier times or other lands, and "modern" never that of here and now. Neither is a description of a stage in the evolution of the human spirit; rather, both are structures. We find them both realized today just as much as three thousand years ago, both in Amsterdam and in Tierra del Fuego. Of course, a more complete realization of the primitive intellectual structure is evidenced by the ancient and so-called un-civilized peoples than by

the West Europeans of today. But as primitive is never completely
lacking even in the most modern cities, so the modern is present in
the least-educated native in Surinam [van der Leeuw, 1963:7].

The above quotation is taken from the translation of an original
work that was written much earlier, we assume from around the
same time as his book entitled *In dem Hemel is eenen dans* (Amsterdam, 1930) and *De Primitive Mensch en de Religie* (Groningen-
Batavia, 1937). It remains for an important work in anthropology
of human movement to be done, namely, that of a comparison of
van der Leeuw's work with that of Lucien Lévy-Bruhl, out of which
we might be able to ascertain whether he, like Lévy-Bruhl, tried to
stress the differences between ourselves and "primitives," even
though by so doing, the facts of the matter are bound to be somewhat
distorted. One suspects that van der Leeuw's theological perspectives would force him to stress similarities, but one simply does not
know.

One of the main questions that is addressed by this author is
"to what degree the consciousness and the realization of the holy
can be art." He implies the possibility of a very complicated modern
art that coalesces into a unity with religion in a way that he
undertakes to examine in his book, and he advances the thesis that
primitive artistic expressions stand in just as close a connection,
although these are of a different sort. The author constructs his book
so that the different arts are treated one after the other and not
unexpectedly, the dance is first. He offers a fixed plan of discussion,
and repeats the plan with reference to the dance (1); drama and
liturgy (2); holy words (3); the pictorial arts (4); architecture (5);
and music and religion (6). One of the major themes of his work is
that of showing how and in what ways all of these manifestations
of human activity began in connection with religion, and how their
histories reflect a movement from religious to secular spheres of
life. For example, he believed that the history of drama was the
history of secularization, i.e., "One might say that the drama
emerged from the church to the church square, from the temple into
the market-place" (1963:80). As for the dance, which he conflates
with movement in a manner with which we are by now very
familiar, we are confronted by fundamental "religious acts," but

there was more to it than that. The sixty-one pages devoted to the subject are a review, from a theological standpoint, of many of the authors whose writings we have examined in previous lectures. Under the sub-heading "Dance and Culture," we begin with Huizinga ("Dance is one of the purest and most perfect forms of game"), and rapidly move on to Goethe (1906), then to Curt Sachs, who is named "the greatest expert on the history of the dance" (1963:13). Harrison, Marett, Mead, and Wolfgang Köhler are also cited, but the point of it all consists in this:

> The art of beautiful motion is far and away the oldest. Before man learned how to use any instruments at all, he moved the most perfect instrument of all, his body. He did this with such abandon that the cultural history of prehistoric and ancient man is, for the most part, nothing but the history of dance. We must understand this literally. Not only is prehistory mostly dance history, but dance history is mostly prehistory. Like a giant monolith, the dance stands in the midst of the changing forms of human expression. Not only as an art, but also as a form of life and culture, the dance has been grievously wounded by the general disappearance of culture. In the European culture of today the dance plays only a very small and often inferior role. Only in recent times have changes in its character become noticeable. Since there have existed men who write about it, like myself, for example, and who, like the "audience" at an afternoon ball, would rather look on than dance themselves, since the couple dance has pushed aside all other forms of dance and eroticism has laid claim to the dance for itself alone, the monolith seems to totter. This tottering is connected with the general and much more serious tottering of our culture [1963:13].

The calamity for the case of present-day studies of the dance that van der Leeuw's assertions and others like them represent can hardly be over-emphasized. No matter how human pre-history is written, or from what standpoint of what intellectual imperialism, whether religious, scientific, or aesthetic, the dance becomes the "unchanging monolith" of primordial beginnings. The monolith has hardly tottered at all, as we have seen, and perhaps readers can now perceive what it is that we have been up against since we began: the firmly entrenched notion that we are meant to search for meanings that we can attach to the dance *within the totality of human culture*, and meanings, moreover, which are "universal" and the same, regardless of cultural context, the historical process, creativity and innovation or what-have-you.

Although one can concur with some of van der Leeuw's notions, viz., the minimal definition of "primitive" and "modern"; the fact that dancing is not "natural movement" but specifically *human* movement created by people, and that it is both ordered and purposeful, one cannot agree with his (or anyone's) separation of dancing (or human movement) from the language-using faculties and capacities of the human mind. Nor could one agree with his notion (which he ascribes to Lévy-Bruhl) that masked dances simply teach us that "the dancers *are* animals, spirits, gods" and the like.

One would hope that contemporary social and cultural anthropologist do not try to attach meaning to the dance viewed in this manner: as a monolithic whole or as an homogeneous phenomenon within the totality of human cultures. "The dance," regarded not as a monolith, but simply as the sum of all existing dances in human cultures provides a rather different point of view from which to begin reflection. For a start, to understand the role of movement or the dance in human ethnicities, we must have some means of ascertaining their relation to speech and the language-using capacities of human beings in general, and we are a long way from knowing very much about that, although research during the past three or four decades in linguistics and anthropology have made some inroads; enough to say that we have begun, at least.

Completed research in hand includes the first study of an idiom of dancing compared to a sign language (see Hart-Johnson, 1984), the first study of American Sign Language compared to Plains' Indian Sign Language (see Farnell, 1984a) and the first definitive present-day study of the Indian *hasta mudra* system of gestures (see Puri, 1983), plus an examination, from a Chomskyan transformational standpoint, of features of the American dance form, the Foxtrot, as it exists in its cultural setting of American commercial ballroom dance studios (see Myers, 1981), and the first treatment of the ballet as an ethnic form of dance (see Durr, 1984). These accomplishments are "beginnings" that have been made at great cost, partly because, in view of "primitiveness theories" and the prevailing lack of sophisticated methodology and theory in the dance field, they seem uncommonly strange and "new" (see Williams, 1981, for further discussion), such that their authors are unfortunately obliged to spend most of their time explaining why they do not ascribe to more familiar theories and explanations of the dance.

Not only does the assignment of the dance to the status of a primordium that generates everything else mean, in the eyes of many writers and others, that the "last word" has already been said about the dance, it means that there is nothing further left to examine. The literal interpretation of prehistory as dance and dance as prehistory precludes any other treatment of it—or the necessity for any other treatment of it. I put it to my readers, however, that given the theories we have examined so far, this 'monolith' does not really exist, except as a product of our own minds. The monolith sorely needs to be tottered, indeed, shattered, but in an entirely different way from that suggested by van der Leeuw.

We can usefully start by viewing with extreme skepticism such categorical distinctions as "hunting dances," "labyrinth dances," "circle and line dances," "imitative dances," and the like, because the kind of thinking that these classifications imply will never produce more understanding of dances as the creations of societies and the individual human beings of which they are composed, nor will that kind of thinking unravel the many complexities of the subject.

Danc*es* are creations of society. Danc*ing* is a creation of human societies, not of individual reasoning and emotion, although the creation of individual dances may satisfy an individual's reason and emotion alike. The classification of danc*ing* as nothing more than "ordered movement" will never stimulate research into anything but the syntactical features of any given idiom. The pronouncement that the dance is "the father of all other arts, but its children are richer than it is" (van der Leeuw, 1963:73) simply enshrines it forever in the dim mists of time or in some hyperbole of a concept of ultimate structure that is devastating in the mundane world of grant applications or the humbler aspirations of those who seek to understand how a dance idiom is put together as a system of human body language. Such declarations and beliefs are inimical to those who would ask, "what are people doing when they dance?"

To say (and of all van der Leeuw's assertions, I find this the most bizarre) that "It is the curse of theology always to forget that God is love, that is, movement" and that "*the dance reminds theology of this*" (1963:74—italics supplied), is to my mind, to say precisely *nothing*. It says nothing because the dance is fitted into a prescribed schema that identifies it as an activity with God himself and we are thus forced to try to understand the dance as a thing-in-itself and not in its variety of cultural contexts. The dance, in my judgement, will only become intelligible when it is related to ordinary body languages, to spoken languages in a wide variety of cultural contexts, and when novice and professional writers cease trying to treat it as a monolith.

I cannot speak for anyone else at this stage of the argument, of course, but in my understanding of social and cultural anthropology, we no longer seek for "origins" and "essences," especially when so much evidence can be produced that they have not so far been found during the past seventy or eighty years of the existence of our discipline. I do not deny that there may be religious reasons for dancing, or emotional reasons, or erotic, playful, or competitive reasons for dancing, but I do deny that any of the theories that we have examined so far, taken singly or together, explain what danc*ing* is, what "a dance" is, or how "the dance" might usefully be conceived of, especially in view of the fact that it does not represent sound social scientific method to seek for origins and essences anyway, as if our scholarly task amounted to some permutation of the efforts of chemists in the perfume industry.

Modern social science deals with relations, with the forms that empirically perceivable regularities might take, and beyond this, it also offers explanatory paradigms regarding the invisible side of dancing—its "intransitive structures" as it were, that in a present-day synthesis are not imperialistic in the same sense in which older types of explanation seem to be. Contemporary students enjoy a wide range of choice of methodological techniques and paradigms of explanation (see, for examples, Diesing, 1971), although in my experience, very few of them seem to know very much about them.

Because I do, I can say that an open, structural theory of human actions like semasiology, for instance, does not begin by classifying dancers wherever they may be found with primitives, children, neurotics, apes, women, or God, making the mistake of assuming that because things resemble each other in some particular feature, they must be alike in other respects—the old *pars pro toto* fallacy. I have wondered as I have read some of the writers we have discussed who espouse primitiveness of dance theories if what they are really saying is that dancers do not think "scientifically" or "aesthetically" or "theologically"; or that they are not, at the same time that they dance, also experimental scientists, lab technicians, lawyers, government officials, medical doctors, politicians, or ministers. I have never met a dancer, primitive or otherwise, who thought that by dancing he or she could change the world—or create it. They know very well they cannot. They think that they can influence the world, "make their mark" on it through their dancing, and they know that dancing is thought, felt, and willed by individuals. "Society" at large has no "mind" to experience these things—thus as such, dancing is a phenomenon of individual psychologies, a subjective phenomenon (for those who still use such positivistic distinctions) and there is no doubt that it can be studied accordingly. In a diagnostic context, and under the aegis of a diagnostic model of events, as in dance therapy, it is studied that way all the time.

But, dances are also objective, social phenomena and they can be studied under dramaturgical, liturgical, agonistic, diagnostic, linguistic, and historical models of events as well. What gives dancing objectivity, basically, are the same things that confer objectivity on any social phenomenon: first, dancing, dances, and the beliefs and practices connected with the activity are transmitted from one generation to another, so that whatever dancing is learned (and if the ethnicity includes it) is in one sense "inside" the individual, but in another, it is "outside" him or her, in that the dance form was there before the individual was born and it may persist after death.

The form of dancing, and indeed the body languages of human individuals are acquired in the same way that their spoken languages are acquired: the people who use these mediums of communication are born into a particular ethnicity. Whatever the forms of dancing, or of body language, there are many features of them that are general: that is to say that everyone in a given ethnicity knows and understands the same structured systems of human actions and it is their very generality or collectivity that gives them an objectivity that places them over and above the individual psychological experiences of any one person. Finally, although forms of dancing are not usually themselves obligatory, the forms of body language, the deportment, "manners" (or lack of them) and the roles, rules, and conventions governing them at any level *are* obligatory. An individual has no option but to accept what everyone gives assent to regarding these features of human life, because there is very little other choice, just as there is very little choice as to the language that is spoken. In adult life, of course, choices can be made; other forms of body language, like other forms of spoken language, can be learned. Sometimes this occurs early on, although it is usually the case that even if a child learns two or more spoken languages from early childhood, because body language is generally thought to be "universal," the differences in body languages will remain unexamined and unexplored such that, with reference to English-speaking societies at any rate, bi-, or tri-lingualism in speech is merely grafted onto a mono-somatic body language, thought to be universal, and dealt with through "chance," "luck" or something.

Clearly, we have again moved into another kind of paradigm of explanation of the dance from any of those which we have encountered so far, and since I am nearly at the end of this lecture, I must restrain myself from pursuing these thoughts further, but will revert to them later on. In the meantime, we will prepare ourselves to deal with "functional" explanations of the dance in the next lecture, and in Chapter VII, with the central problem of bibliographical controls in the literature on dancing.

From the lectures so far, we can see that, with reference to theories of the dance, there seem to exist two distinctly different world-views: the "religious," characterized by the notions of moral order, purpose, and a concept of spiritual agencies that is sometimes taken over by or closely related to a "quasi-religious" view that ultimately propounds an eschatology of art if it is followed through to its logical and other consequences. This world-view is in contrast to a commonly held "naturalistic" or "scientific" view, characterized on the whole by the notion of random events, entropy and chemical agencies, perhaps, where the world is indifferent to human values of any kind and where the ultimate governance of the world can be attributed to blind physical forces.

One would want to argue that all three of these world-views in any of their permutations and combinations consist of a set of assumptions about the world. They are highly developed, sophisticated sets of assumptions that should themselves be examined. Perhaps, as I shall suggest toward the end of this book, the semanticists' insistence that we investigate *levels* of abstraction, *types* of symbolization and the nature of symbolic discourse itself is one way to free ourselves of the imperialistic demands of the science-religion, or the religion-art or the art-science debates. Whether we manage to topple these monoliths (or the monolith of the dance as the primordial beginnings of everything) remains to be seen. Changes of this magnitude do not happen quickly, but I would want to say that an anthropology of human movement would be able to shed some light on such matters, because we can make thorough-going studies of human actions and body languages these days with the same exactness as linguists study spoken language and cognitive and symbolic anthropologists study societies.

But that is still ahead of us. Post-World War I anthropological explanations of the dance provide a refreshing change because in the wider context of anthropology itself, functionalism provided an alternative to evolutionary theory and trait-diffusion analysis. With the functionalists, we will not concern ourselves with whether or not the dance is (or is not) a "proximate occasion of sin," or a "universal recreation," the "most perfect form of play" or an "art-form," both because the different questions that the functionalists asked about society and their view of societies as "organisms" led to different preoccupations and because by now, we know that we can

read that the origin of dance was in play and that it was not in play, that it was for magical purposes and that it was not for those things: that it was for courtship; that it was the first form of communication and that communication did not enter into dance until it became an 'art'. In addition we can read that it was serious and was totally spontaneous and originated in the spirit of fun. Moreover, we can read that it was only a group activity for tribal solidarity and that it was strictly for pleasure and self-expression of the one dancing. We can learn also that animals danced before man did and yet that dance is a human activity [Keali'inohomoku, 1980a:24].

Functional explanations of the dance rejected questions of origins and diffusion and concentrated on the function of dance in society. Many of these explanations are utilitarian, some are biologically or sociologically deterministic or both. Some are tautological and in some cases they are courageous if somewhat misguided attempts at validation and statistical "proofs" of such things as "dance styles" and "cultural affiliations," nevertheless, we shall inquire into their constructions, into their philosophies of human nature, and into the claims that are being made.

We shall also come to understand, I trust, why some areas of enquiry escape adequate bibliographic treatment, even when there are courses taught in universities pertaining to the subject of interest and when there are demands made on the existing reference literature that it cannot serve. We shall examine, briefly, some of the existing literature on "dance ethnology" from a user's point of view, both because it was during the period of functionalist anthropology that a field of study known as "dance ethnology" or "dance anthropology" arose, and because we need to know what kind of literature is included in these categories.

For those who are following these lectures in the series that they are presented in book form, I would want to ask that before tackling the next chapter, they remember that Malinowski's functional theory of society insisted upon the principle that in every type of civilization, every custom, material object, idea and belief, fulfills some vital function and/or has some task to accomplish and represents, moreover, an indispensable part within a working whole. This theory, as we shall see, was attractive to those who were interested in rituals and dancing mainly because it placed those activities on an equal basis with everything else and because it opened up the possibility for "dance ethnology" or "dance anthropology" as a viable field of study.

VI. FUNCTIONAL EXPLANATIONS

IN THE SOCIAL SCIENCES, the theory of the relation of parts of a society to the whole of society and of one part to another gained prominence through the works of 19th-century sociologists, in particular those who viewed societies as organisms, after the manner of biological scientists. Especially did Durkheim argue that it was necessary to understand the needs of such a social organism to which the social phenomena under investigation corresponded. For later American sociologists, functionalism provided a basis for analytical method, such as that exemplified by Talcott Parsons. For anthropologists, it provided an alternative to older paradigms of explanation. Malinowski was explicit about this: instead of

> ...vast edifices of reconstruction, diffusionist or evolutionary, it seemed better to turn to the analysis of each culture as a going concern.... This 'functionalist approach' was nothing but the vindication of a strictly empirical inspiration in theory, and, conversely, the demand that observation should be guided by knowledge of the laws and principles of culture as a dynamic reality. The general tendency of the school was to make the savage essentially human, and to find elements of the primitive in higher civilizations. In the last instance, functional analysis aimed at the establishment of a common measure of all cultures, simple and developed, Western and Oriental, arctic and tropical [Malinowski, in his Introduction to Ashley-Montagu, 1937].

Although functionalism became a school of thought in British anthropology connected with such distinguished names in the discipline as Malinowski, Radcliffe-Brown, Firth, Mair, Richards, and later, Beattie, it was not peculiar to that field alone. Franz Boas was inclined towards functionalism as well. He was the founder of the "culture-history" school of anthropology, which for much of the 20th century has dominated American cultural anthropology and

which emphasized fieldwork and firsthand observation. He inspired several famous American anthropologists—Benedict,
Kroeber, Mead and Sapir, for example—to seek evidence of human
behavior in their socio-cultural environments. While Boas and
Malinowski disagreed on many things, their shared emphasis on
fieldwork, observation, and a functional type of integration (liken-
ing societies to living organisms or machines with interdependent
parts) tended to unify British and American approaches to the study
of the cultures of humankind during the post-World War I period
of its history.

Herskovitz, a student of Boas, put matters succinctly when he
said that the functional view attempts to study the interrelation
between the various elements, small and large, in a culture. Its
object is essentially to achieve some expression of the unities in
culture by indicating how trait and complex and pattern, however
separable they may be, intermesh, as the gears of some machine, to
constitute a smoothly running, effectively functioning whole
(1943). Leach, a student of Malinowski at the beginning of his
career, was to make the distinction regarding the paramorphic
partial homologue of machines to society in this way: "Radcliffe-
Brown was concerned, as it were, to distinguish wrist watches from
grandfather clocks, whereas Malinowski was interested in the
general attributes of clockwork" (Leach, 1961/1966:6).

Boas insisted upon the method of considering any single
culture as a whole and tended to emphasize the problems posed by
connections between culture and individual personalities. Boas's
daughter, Franziska Boas, attempted to stimulate interest in, and
carry out, these views in the early 'forties in the United States by
publishing and copyrighting one of the most influential books used
by later dance ethnologists, *The Function of Dance in Human
Society* (1944), now, I believe, out of print. This work included four
essays, one by Boas himself ("Dance and Music in the Life of
Northwest Coast Indians of North American: Kwakiutl"); one by
Geoffrey Gorer ("Function of Dance Forms in Primitive African
Communities"); one by Harold Courlander ("Dance and Drama in
Haiti") and one by Claire Holt and Gregory Bateson ("Form and
Function of the Dance in Bali").[1]

If one is familiar with the many types of explanation which preceded them, functionalist explanations of the dance are refreshingly different because they concern themselves with what the investigators saw in the dances of societies observed in the field, not with what people sitting at home thought went on in those societies.[2] The first world war produced drastic changes in world viewpoint: the speed of communication began to increase and population growth increased as well. Colonialism came under serious attack and it was no longer feasible to see other cultures or their dancing in the same kinds of ways. These new concerns "...raised problems of interpretation and analysis which had not existed for earlier 'armchair' anthropologists.... So for the first time, the question arose: how are these unfamiliar social and cultural systems to be understood?" (Beattie, 1964:10–11).

Still, the emphasis with reference to dances did not change to *understanding* the dances themselves, but to understanding the "function" of any given dance in the society to which it belonged. On the whole, dancing in a functionalist theoretical context was epiphenomenal; that is, the overall aim of this type of explanatory paradigm was to describe danced and ritual behaviors in terms of social needs and social equilibrium, such that both were viewed primarily as *adaptive* or *adjustive* responses either to the social or to the physical environment. Functionalism was mainly an heuristic device: an indicator only for describing the *role* of the dance (and ritual) in society.

The result of this was that there now exists a fairly large body of writings about the dance that relates it to nearly every institution in the larger society:

> Thus Sachs points out that a dance has aided sustenance and well-being [1932:2]. Cherokee dances, like many others are prophylactic and contain "the principles that ensure individual health and welfare" [Speck & Broom, 1951:19]. The Samoan dance aids education and socialization because it "offsets the rigorous subordination of children" and "reduced the threshold of shyness" [Mead, 1949:82–83]. A statement by Mansfield about the Cocheras holds for many other peoples as well: "The dance is the most satisfying expression of their religious feelings" [1952]. Such

motivations of utility or religious feelings are confirmed by many writers [Kurath, 1960:235–236].

If a society functions adequately only if its "needs" are satisfied, and if rituals and dances satisfy these needs, then it is plain that we only affirm the logical consequent which denies the empirical facts of *conflict*, i.e., the satisfaction of the need to disrupt the society or to change it. Single dances and whole dance forms are often created to satisfy that kind of "need," but apart from that, one wonders how Mansfield knew, for instance, that the dance was the most satisfying expression of Cocheras' religious expression? She does not explain *how* she knows (nor do any of the dance ethnologists explain how they know what they say they know). Because of this, their writings tend to be suspect.

Whether the dances of a people are seen to be tied to the political system, viz. Mitchell (1956), or to the economic system (Firth, 1936/1965 and Malinowski, 1922), or as a vehicle to accomplish psychological adjustments for Samoan and other teenagers (Mead, 1931), or for tribal solidarity (Radcliffe-Brown, 1913/1964), made little difference regarding the overall theoretical frame of reference in which all of this type of description was and is made because throughout, a mechanical model of human society and, indeed, of humanity itself, is at work. That is, it is as if the actions of a person or the actions of a whole ethnicity were somehow like the behavior of a watch, where, as Winch pointed out, "…the energy contained in the tensed spring is transmitted *via* the mechanism in such a way as to bring about the regular revolution of the hands" (1958:76).

Given whatever dissatisfactions we may now have with functional explanations, there were advantages in the approach which constituted a distinct improvement over the theories and explanations of the dance which preceded them: functional explanations did not reduce dancing to a single metabolic, chemical or psychological attribute of the human organism; they tended to stay away from low-level moral and aesthetic judgments about non-western dances and other art forms. They demanded familiarity with the spoken language of the peoples concerned, and, given trained observers,[3] the dances described did not (indeed, could not) fall into naïve, all-inclusive "primitiveness" theories of the dance, treating it like a monolithic whole. These investigators did escape some of the traps that claimed their predecessors.[4]

In fact, some functionalist arguments effectively discredit origins arguments such as those of Harrison, Sachs, and others, and for this, we owe these anthropologists a great debt. The account Malinowski offers of the Gumagabu dance in the Trobriand Islands, for example, is final evidence that Harrison's and Sachs's arguments are wrong-headed:

> The other type of transaction belonging to this class is the payment for dances. Dances are "owned"; that is, the original inventor has the right of "producing" his dance and song in his village community. If another village takes a fancy to this song and dance, it has to purchase the right to perform it. This is done by handing ceremonially to the original village a substantial payment of food and valuables, after which the dance is taught to the new possessors [1922:- 186].

We recall that Harrison (1913), using a different explanatory paradigm, based her arguments for the *lack of differentiation in the dance*, hence its "primitiveness" on an events ontology and the notion that there was no "thing" made in the case of a dance. Obviously, the Trobrianders considered that there *was* something made in a dance. Moreover, something that could be purchased and in which the creator and possessors of the dance had rights. A dance, in other words, meant something, and we discover too that dances evidently had continuity and duration over long periods of time. "In 1922," we are told, "the Gumagabu dance was owned by To'oluwa, the chief of Omarkana, his ancestors having acquired it from the descendants of Tomakam by a *laga* payment" (Malinowski, 1922:291).

The significance of these observations can hardly be overstressed. While western dance forms are commonly thought of as having composers, performers, dancing masters, and the like, the dances of non-western peoples—particularly those lumped into the category "primitive"—are not usually thought of in the same way. On the contrary, as we have seen, these dances are thought of as having no rules or form. Both Malinowski's and Firth's treatment of the dance with regard to features of continuity, change, innovation, creators, and established conceptual systems for danced actions in the Trobriands and Tikopia discredit the types of theorizing that I call "steam-valve" theorizing and "if I were an ape" theorizing about dancing.

> In the field of amusement foreign contacts have had an indirect effect being responsible for additions to the content more than to changes in the manner of amusement. This applies particularly to dances, borrowed from Anuta and elsewhere and to dance songs, many of which have been composed with reference to other lands and experiences abroad. A specific dance, the *mako fakarakas*, was presented by Pa Makava recently in an adaptation of a Raga dance which he had seen in the Banks Islands.... The motives for the adoption of new cultural elements have been mainly for the desire to secure economic advantage or enhancement of the person. Mere imitation, as such, seems to have played little part; there has been in each case a set of ways of behavior into which the new item has fitted. It is the proper existence of this general pattern that has given cultural value to the items introduced by individuals, made them into objects of general desire, and not merely the unsupported whim of the introducer [Firth, 1936/1965:35].

Firth's observations about the dance in the above context (as well as those he makes with regard to dancing connected with the spirit world, dances of abuse at weddings and at initiations) reduce cherished notions of "spontaneity," "untrammelled emotional expression," and such as the prime *impetus* for dancing to nil. Firth's later approval of ethological theory for explanations of gesture and human movement (see Firth, 1970), is somewhat incongruous, and as far as I know, unchallenged, however, the importance of what he said following his field research in the early 'thirties should not be underestimated, for he draws attention to an established conceptual system for the dances of Tikopia into which innovatory materials were incorporated, which is something that rule-following, role-creating, language-users do in contrast to language-less creatures. And, he introduces the notions of innovation and change into what we have been led to believe by other authors is an *unchanging*, timeless phenomenon: dancing.

Radcliffe-Brown, whose type of functional explanation stressed the relations between a social institution and "necessary conditions of existence" of a social system, considered that a unit of social structure functioned insofar as it contributed to the maintenance of social structure, by which he meant the relationship between units. With reference to the dance, Radcliffe-Brown suggests that its chief function consists in the submission of the personality of the individual to community action. The harmonious concert of aggregative individual feelings and actions, especially apparent in dances, produces concord and unity (i.e. "tribal solidarity") which is intensely felt by every individual member who participates (see Radcliffe-Brown, 1913/1964).

There is no reason to doubt that what this anthropologist said about Andamanese dancing may have been true; the problem arises when later writers apply the "concord and unity theory" of dancing to dances of other cultures and/or to "the dance" seen as a monolithic cultural unit in a functionalist mosaic of the whole world. There are many cases of dances which are not cases of "harmony" but of disharmony at many levels. The Kalela dance of the Bisa (Mitchell, 1956) is an example, and this is by no means the only instantiation of its kind that can be found. Whole dance forms, e.g., American modern dancing (the theatrical kind) contains elements of social dissonance as its subject matter or "motivation" if you will. A specific dance might be said to have as its function the promotion of solidarity, but to say that *dancing* (inferring a conclusion about all dances everywhere) has this as its function is simply to commit a *pars pro toto* fallacy.

Examination of the often conflicting evidence provided by twenty or thirty articles written by functionally orientated authors (such as those represented on the Kurath book list in the next chapter) thus points to some important theoretical considerations. They do not, as some students seem to think, merely point to the fact that anthropologists are a rather stupid lot who cannot seem to agree on anything. When the author is not an anthropologist, but a dance ethnologist, then it is probably the case that the explanation is simply a choice among those which the investigator thinks might be palatable according to current fashion.

It becomes patently clear, for example, that the nature of functionalism itself had to give rise to some kind of "conflict theory"; that is, in cases where it was manifestly false to say that a dance or a ritual contributed to "harmony" and "solidarity," then it had to be shown that even social practices and institutions which were "dysfunctional" had to be functional in a positive sense and work towards the solidarity of the whole system. In British anthropology, Max Gluckman (1959) is probably the most well-known writer to expound this theory.

When it is assumed that a society or a culture is a functional unity as is a human body, a watch, or a computer, in which all parts work together with the same degree of internal consistency; where it is believed that all social phenomena have a positive function and that all are indispensable, distinctions have to be made between "positive functions," "latent functions," and "dysfunctional functions."[5] Something has to be said to account for phenomena that are obviously politically sensitive, divisive, and disharmonious. I believe that it is the case that because the body languages of dancing and dances are less likely to be understood as social and political *statements* than are verbal utterances about them, dissonant statements are often couched in these forms of body languages, with the result that attitudes and beliefs which might otherwise be severely punished manage to maintain a cognitive and conative reality that is denied them in the spoken and bodily languages of the dominant establishment, whatever it may be. Perhaps, although we ascribe to familiar folk aphorisms such as "actions speak louder than words," and although we give lip service to the connections between speech and behavior, we are not yet sufficiently convinced by our own assertions and we do not see what is before us. A rude gesture is, after all, just as effective as a rude remark—perhaps more so in some situations because the antagonist may not even see or recognize it.

Dances can be either dissonant or harmonious with reference to the ethnicities in which they are found, and either way, they may exert long-lasting influences and entail far-reaching consequences. Certainly one of the more famous dancing dissidents in our own culture, Isadora Duncan, managed to mother a whole host of dance forms as offspring of her rebellion against the ballet, and in South Africa, the beliefs and attitudes of anti-apartheid militants have long been expressed through the dance and body languages, largely because, one supposes, they would otherwise be ruthlessly suppressed.

Dancing can be satirical, ironic, cynical, and comic, as even cursory study of the calypso tradition of the Caribbean Islands will prove. The *merengue*, for example, started out as a satire upon the Spanish *paso doble* and there are many more examples from other traditions throughout the world.

The point is that explanations of the dance which stress its educational, moral, prophylactic, and other functions *do* stress features of the activity of dancing which are neglected or ignored in other types of explanation, which leads to the conclusion that it is just as important to understand the theory of the paradigm of explanation as it is to understand the evidence itself. In the minds of many, if not all, social scientists, *evidence cannot be understood unless the theoretical frame of reference is also understood.* A "fact" is thus a construct that is created by interpreting an event like a dance, therefore the "facts" of an event—the "what" that is being talked about—is dependent upon the theory.

In turn, the facts and the theory are to some extent dependent upon the investigator's skillful, accurate, and appropriate procedures, i.e., *methods*, but these are also governed by theory. It is the theory of a game, for example, which tells us what the facts of the empirically observable moves are. The procedures that the investigator uses, which include the terminologies selected to describe, say, the units of movement in a game, are what ensures comprehension, the possibility of cross-cultural comparison and all the rest.

Facts by no means stand alone and any conception of "method" in social sciences, as in other fields of enquiry, is historically oriented and relativistic. Theories and methods in any academic discipline change slowly and continually: they develop, combine, separate, and they may be subject to fashionable trends. They enjoy no "timeless essence"—or any essence they do possess usually does not become apparent through purely descriptive approaches. In any case,

To find out what actually happens in science, direct observation is necessary in addition to reading. This means observation of work in progress, including the study of experimental apparatus, questionnaires, field notes and diaries, uncompleted models, and particularly the comparison of different stages in the development of an apparatus, questionnaire, or model. It means talking and listening, personally and in colloquia, about a scientist's own work, experiencing at first hand the problems and the modes of solution in use, which is indispensable if one is to infer the actual performance behind published work and to interpret the meaning of methodological discussions [Diesing, 1971:19].

Although functionalism has so far been talked about in the past tense and as if it represented theory that could be put behind us, this is not the case with reference to studies of the dance. While it is safe to say that there are relatively few modern social anthropologists who are functionalist, or even "structural-functionalist" in a strict Boasian or Malinowskian sense today because of the loosened grip of a philosophy of logical positivism and the intrusion of more sophisticated approaches to language in anthropology, these generalizations do not apply to the field of dance studies or the study of ritual, ceremonies, and such that include dancing. Historical accident placed the beginnings of "dance ethnology" in the functionalist period of cultural anthropology in the United States and with a few outstanding exceptions, the theories, models, and methods used have stayed the same.

Because of this, there is a great disparity between the writings of dance ethnologists and mainstream anthropologists today. Modern anthropological approaches to ethnography are very different from those of earlier anthropologists. About the same time that major shifts in explanatory paradigm occurred in social and cultural anthropology (roughly starting in the late 'fifties and extending into the early 'seventies) serious attention was being drawn to the status of ethnological studies of the dance in the United States for the first time:

A third question on which there is published disagreement is that of the extent of a need for dance ethnology within the broader field of general ethnology. In part, the answer to this question must await further inquiry into the function of dance in culture, which in turn depends on more findings on the relative significance of dance in particular cultures. Scholars have justified their studies on dance, not only by their use to readers in search of information or of material for performances but also by the functional significance of dance in society [Kurath, 1960:235].

By the time Kurath was able to publish such statements as these, Hempel (1959) had already shown functionalism to be non-scientific, *producing explanations that were compelled to triviality* that were based on vaguely defined notions of "needs" and Nagel (1960) had presented an elegant exegesis of faulty explanatory relations in the implicit logic of functionalism. It is perhaps the case that Kurath had no way of knowing that functional explanations are a type of explanation of social phenomena that are usually *opposed to* explanations in terms of purposes, or intentional striving for goals, but the fact that she was unaware of such things not only vitiates her case for "dance ethnology," but calls the whole enterprise of studying dances into question in the wider anthropological community.

There are many dance ethnologists today who, like their distinguished predecessor, do not seem to realize the implications of the theoretical paradigm that they use for explanatory purposes. Hanna is one of these, and she is by no means alone. In functional psychology, for example, the doctrine that conscious processes or states such as willing, volition, thinking, emoting, perceiving, or sensating are the operations of an organism in physical interrelationship with its physical environment and *cannot therefore be given any hypostatized substantive existence* is primary to the theory. In that paradigmatic context, it is thought that these activities facilitate the organism's control (i.e., survival, adaptation, engagement, withdrawal, recognition, direction, etc.), but that they are not produced by "faculties," i.e., a "mind" or a "soul," or by *any differences* in the natures, powers, and capacities of human beings. Functionalism in any of its forms and variations, is really only concerned with a physical environment. In this explanatory mode, *there is no theory* that human consciousness (volition, willing, thinking, feeling, speaking, and such) is caused or explainable by faculties of the mind that correspond with the states of consciousness. Is this not an inappropriate (if not strange) paradigm of explanation to use for human dances and dancing?

In my understanding of social anthropological usages of this type of explanation, *a functional approach is one which compels indifference to the nature of the part of the whole that is under investigation.* Although it was the aim of functionalist anthropologists (and, perhaps, functionalists in other disciplines, too) to make all the peoples of the world more human, it seems that in their desire to be "scientific," they sacrificed some, if not all of this objective. I do not say that they could have done anything else, or that, like sheep, they were led astray or something of the kind. I simply offer an account of certain facts in the history of the discipline of anthropology and wish to remark that matters have changed greatly since then. I do not know how much they have changed in dance ethnology, but judging from the continued dependence on the paradigm (see Hanna, 1979), it would appear that they have not changed very much. Kurath's work certainly points to the widespread allegiance to functionalism in America and although her work compiles a list of mainly functionalist writings on the dance, she offers no critical analyses of functionalist theory or methods.

Because of this, her concerns to see a dance ethnology as an autonomous field of interest, like Hanna's, are based on an uncritical acceptance, not only of the paradigm itself, but of what "science," defined solely by these criteria amounts to. It is because of all this that one has great difficulty understanding the import of statements like these:

> ...clan totemism produces complex rituals, as in Australia (Eberle, 1955:427–453). However, the relationships between clan divisions and dance patterns have not been clarified, whether because of non-existence, or non-observance by field workers, we do not know [Kurath, 1960:237].

"Totemism" in the late 'fifties and early 'sixties was suffering its death throes regarding its value as an explanatory category in anthropology. The *coup de grace* was delivered by Lévi-Strauss in 1962. As Poole points out, "...it is only with Lévi-Strauss's book that we can say that the 'problem' of totemism has been laid to rest once and for all. If we talk about 'totemism' anymore, it will be in ignorance of Lévi-Strauss or in spite of him" (1973:9). Even if we acquiesced in the totemism game, are we to understand that "clan totemism" *produces* complex rituals? How can an abstraction like that produce anything like a complex ritual or a dance? Is it not *people* who produce both the clan totemism and the complex rituals? Talk like this falls strangely on the ears of many social anthropologists, given the sensitivity to language, semiotic and semantic concerns that have developed over the past twenty years. And, how literally are we meant to take statements like this:

> Economic specialization often creates occupationally disparate groups with special dances, dance organizations, and dance functions. Gorer distinguishes these characteristics in African communities: 'The best dancers come from the smaller hunting tribes. In the larger, agricultural tribes dance diminishes in importance and vitality' [1944:34] [Kurath, 1960:237–238].

The quoted statement of Gorer's is the last sentence of the paper he gave for Franziska Boas's seminar, from which the book, *The Function of Dance in Human Society* was published. In fairness to Gorer, although he did make such naïve observations, the opening remarks that he makes in the same paper should be reproduced:

> I am appearing here under false pretenses. I know little about West Africa and even less about dancing. All my experience consists of a four-months journey which my publishers insisted on calling "Africa Dances". Besides this book my only source of knowledge is my undoubtedly very fallible memory for all the notes which I have not incorporated in my book are somewhere in England.

If this is the case, then one wonders why this author's statements about the dances of hunting tribes and agricultural tribes are taken seriously? Why are the characteristics that Gorer distinguishes in African communities given more credence by Kurath than they were by Gorer himself?

Valuable though the influence of the contributions of functionalist authors (including Kurath) have been on the subject of dancing—suggesting more systematic ways of studying them, stressing fieldwork observations and all the rest, one has the uneasy suspicion that Kurath and her successors are mainly concerned to see that studies of the dance are "legitimized" in some way. There is a sense in which functionalism made the study of the dance in anthropology and its sub-disciplines *possible*, because an approach that compels indifference to the nature of the part of the society under investigation *does* make everything equal. The dance thus gained equal status, if not equal attention, with any other cultural manifestation, but, one wonders if dedicated functionalists who wrote about the dance could really afford to see the ideological ends that functionalism itself served because of their own needs to serve those ends in order to further the cause of dance studies?

The tendency in dance ethnology, seems to be simply to seek for methodological and explanatory *formulas*, or to seek for "research tools" without devoting any time or thought to the conceptual and philosophical elements of the resources that are available in any given discipline at any one time. Such tendencies are to be deplored in the case of dance ethnology, or any other research endeavor. The hope seemed to have been that such approaches would lead to the possibility of making cross-cultural generalizations, having universal intent, but it is precisely at the level of cross-cultural generalization that functional accounts of dances (dancing, and "the dance") fall down.

The difficulty is that if one investigator says that the chief function of dance is education (Hanna, 1965), and another says that dances are "instruments of moral edification and entertainment" and "danced faiths" (Thompson, 1966), yet another says that "they express masculine and feminine ideals" (Harper, 1966). Then we have first to ask, upon what basis are comparisons to be made? All of these explanations have some truth in them, but none are true of all dance forms, leading us to question, perhaps, the value of looking for the regularities of dance forms "on the ground" as a useful point of entry for generalizations about dances.

Might we not more usefully ask what form the regularities are likely to take prior to the field study, wherever it may be carried out? Might we not direct our attention to that which Evans-Pritchard pointed out in 1928, viz., that the many problems connected with *the composition and organization of dances* seem to be what whole that was perhaps left out? Evans-Pritchard was not indifferent to the nature of the part of the investigation, which is the reason why he was not a functionalist.

Hanna is no doubt right to assert that the Ubakala dance plays perform an educational function in Ibo society, but she cannot extend her arguments to include *Swan Lake* or Catlin's O-kee-pah. Thompson can argue, and rightly so, that many West African dances are "danced faiths," but he could not then generalize his contention to include Hungarian or Polish folk dances. Mead can show that Samoan dance provides a cathartic outlet for adolescent tensions, but cannot then generalize her explanation to include Japanese Kabuki or Gagaku dances, nor to any dance primarily performed by persons exceeding age twenty. As Leach and many others have pointed out, these kinds of assertions and the typologies and classifications which arise from them simply proliferate endlessly, for they have no logical limits. Moreover, as is well known in scientific circles, the mere stockpiling of data never has and never will produce theory that is adequate to handle it.

Functionalist explanations of dances undoubtedly emphasize features of dances which are ignored in parochial religious explanations, in aesthetic explanations—in particular those that are predicated on a doctrine of aesthetic independence. They successfully removed the activity from the realm of the unchanging monolith of prehistorical explanations. Nor are tautologous functional explanations to be underrated either, for all their circularity. After all, if saying that "X is X" in this context illuminates some feature about X that is not taken into account in other explanations of X, then saying that "X is X" has minimal explanatory value.

But, by far the most puzzling feature of functionalist explanations of the dance is to be found in statements like these:

> In the study of primitive folk-lore and native decorative art, of dancing and music, we shall find elements which may prove almost completely refractory to scientific analysis and yet will have to be recorded. Here, the anthropologist may have to cease to be a mere

analytic man of science. He may have to become almost an artist
[Malinowski, in the introduction to Ashley-Montagu, 1937:xxxiv].

In contrast, Irmgard Bartenieff has said that "Dance cannot
profitably stretch its concepts to fit the mold of existing scientific
models" (1967:68)

I juxtapose these two statements to draw attention to the
ideological predicament that anyone will encounter who tries to
replace the activities and neurological sophistication of the human
mind with the self-regulatory features that govern non-language-
using creatures or self- regulatory automata. If "scientific analysis"
is conceived of as a type of reductive materialism which attempts
to explain human consciousness in terms of overt behavioral
responses or covert dispositional states, excluding reference to the
unique nature, powers and capacities of human beings, then Bartenieff is right because this "mold" cannot handle the volitional,
intentional, goal-oriented features of any human dance tradition.

But, Malinowski is right too, because if, as he says, being an
"analytic man of science" means that one is obliged to live out one's
intellectual life within the confines of the conceptual imperialisms
of cybernetics, behaviorism, or, say, Freud's analysis of humanity,
based on concepts of complexes, censorship and repressions, or
Marx's emphasis on economic production as the sole and universal
key to intelligibility regarding what goes in human societies, then
anthropologists must—perhaps they had better—become "almost
artists."

Dedicated functionalists in dance ethnology claim that the
methods and theory connected with various schools of
functionalism are "objective" and "value-free," although these
claims have been challenged by many. Nevertheless, there are those
who are convinced that functionalism

> …is not, in the strict sense of the word, a social theory; but rather a
> systematic mode of analysis, which makes possible the clear enun-
> ciation of, the pursuit of, and the elaboration of social theories [Rust,
> 1969:2].

The insistence that functionalism is not a theory but a useful methodological tool is used as justification for a published doctoral thesis entitled *Dance in Society* that was

> ...conceived within the broad framework or conceptual scheme, provided by a 'structural-functionalist' analysis of society. The functionalist 'school' if it may be so termed, has never lacked critics and detractors but, in spite of opposition, it continues, in my view, to offer the most useful approach to a systematic analysis of social structure, or any element of social structure [Rust, 1969:6].

Rust's study is specifically about the dance and was completed two years after Adrienne Kaeppler, halfway around the world in Hawaii, had completed her doctoral thesis on Tongan dance.[6] Rust invoked Radcliffe-Brown's theories of structural continuity, although none of what he said about the dance is cited. Perhaps it is because what he said about how society turned "a jump into a dance and a shout into a song" has been criticized as unsatisfactory, that this author disregards or ignores such signals and cites no work beyond the Andaman Islanders in her section entitled "Anthropological Perspectives."

One third of this book consists of a rather good historical and literary approach to social dancing in England from the 13th century to the present, but the relation of this section to the rest of the study presents serious inconsistencies. We might be reminded of an earlier author, Oesterley (1923) who put excellent historical materials, a sophisticated knowledge of Hebrew and the Classics into the service of Frazerian interpretations of dancing and adjusted these to Marett's notions about primitive religion (see *supra*, pp. 51–52).

Rust puts the ninety-odd pages of good socio-historical research on English dancing into the service of a functional explanation and a statistical survey, defining her study as a "small-scale pioneer approach to the sociology of dance" that is concerned with one particular classification of dance and "scaled down to one particular country and to a specific period of history" (1969:xiii). Fair enough, but if that is the case, then it is impossible to understand the comparison of "primitive" dance and modern English forms of dancing contained in the following passage:

> Although this style of dancing is new, so far as England is concerned, it is of course anything but new in the history of dance. [She refers to "beat," "disco" and other open-partnered styles of social dancing.] All primitive dancing is of this nature, the partnered up style being the product of the ballroom of civilization, and, in comparison, artificial and inhibiting. It may be that today's young people want to dissociate themselves completely from the traditional ballroom style of dancing and much prefer a link with primitive man. Indeed, in view of the theory that dancing precedes speech, one might go further and claim that contemporary social dancing has returned to the very beginning of the cycle—to the jungle! Certainly beat music played in the modern idiom is so loud that conversation is both unnecessary and impossible during the dance, and thus 'the language of words is replaced by the language of the body' [Rust, 1969:199].

On a basis of Rust's study, we must now add another group of people to the already over-loaded and meaningless category of "primitive dance," i.e., English teen-agers and "beat dancing." Rust shares these ethnocentric and hopelessly provincial attitudes with many people. However, if "good theory" is tested only by the *numbers* of people who espouse it, her assessments of the situation would seem to be accurate and her theory sound.

By the middle of the 1950's in the United States, "primitive dance" had come to refer to

> ...a kind of pseudo Afro-Caribbean type of dance. This so-called primitive dance has been stylized ... until it has become a kind of contrived tradition in itself. But are Afro-Caribbeans primitive? The answer is that these groups whether or not we can designate them as 'primitive' have their own dance traditions which are totally unlike each other. There is no such thing as 'primitive dance.' The term is meaningless [Keali'inohomoku, 1970:90].

Rust's careless and injudicious usage of the term not only does pseudo-Afro-Caribbean/dancing a disservice (it is a highly regarded form of commercial dancing); it adds nothing to her account of English dancing. What is interesting is that the author herself does not seem fully convinced:

> This 'function' (i.e., pure pleasure in motor activity and expressive body movement) may not be in any way comparable to the function that dancing has in primitive society, but it is nevertheless an important factor in explaining the universality and the persistence of dancing as a pastime, especially if allied with the view, expressed in Chapter II, that this method of expression is part of man's innate biological make-up [Rust, 1969:132].

It is difficult to be patient and tactful with this kind of talk, because if function "X" *is not comparable* to the function of dance in "primitive society" *then why compare them*? If it is the case that this "incomparable function" is "an important factor in explaining the universality and the persistence of dancing as a pastime," one would appreciate knowing more about why one is meant to think so and how this kind of dancing is "part of man's innate biological make-up." To assume that because ballroom dancing is a "pastime" in one's own society and therefore, the activity must constitute a pastime in others, is to make a serious conceptual mistake, in the eyes of many social anthropologists, at any rate.

Furthermore, are we to expect, then, the same biological triggering mechanisms in the neurological systems of English teenagers that exists in the neurological system of language-less creatures, such that we might expect seasonal or cyclic expression of "beat" dancing? How are we to understand the hypothesis that the present-day changed style of teen-aged dancing can be interrelated with certain concomitant changes in society when no explanation is provided except the author's judgement that "beat" dancing is a "return to the jungle"? Nor does the author provide any solid evidence regarding her hypothesis that there is a basic similarity between modern "beat" dancing and the dancing of primitive societies, except for the absence of "partnered up" styles of dancing.

We may well ask, *what* "similarity" is being referred to in *what* "primitive society"? If the reference is to the dancing of "African Society," then we can repeat what has by now been said many times: it is a gross error to think of "African dance" (or "Asian dance" or "Polynesian dance") as a monolithic whole. If it is to the Anuak people that the author refers, then from Lienhardt's research

(1957/58:3) we learn that the Agwaga dance consists of *a dramatic representation* of the relation between a headman and his villagers, so there could be no similarity. If multi-racial Zambia and the Kalela dance is referred to, then there is no similarity because this dance, as described by Mitchell, is supposed to reveal tribalism and tradition (1957). If we think of other so-called "primitive societies," say, in Oceania, or of the dancing of the "under-developed" countries of the middle East and Asia, then Rust's assertions simply make less and less sense as we go along. Reading Rust's entire book forces one to the conclusion that the dancing of English teen-agers, contemporaneous with the author's study, was a result of features internal to English society, just as the dance called "The Twist," which originated at the Peppermint Lounge in New York City, was a result of features of American society. Many West Africans whom I met thought that this was a vulgar, "lewd" dance; others liked it very much. None of them judged it to be a "return to the jungle" (whatever that is). One can only submit that Rust's hypotheses remain unsubstantiated.

It is not surprising that early dance ethnologists saw in functionalist anthropology a way of writing about the dance which was thought to be "scientific" and "respectable," nor is it surprising that they saw in the dances of the world a potential field of enquiry that had, up to Kurath's time, remained largely untapped. What *is* puzzling is that so little time seems to have been devoted to inquiries into the question of whether or not a functionalist paradigm of explanation (based on a mechanical model of society and human beings) was *appropriate to* explanations of an activity that in many of its manifestations throughout the world runs directly *counter to* the nature of the activity. On the whole, to explain any form of dancing or ritual ceremonies of human beings as "adaptations" or "adjustments" to an "environment," whether physical or geographical, is simply to ignore what the people themselves say about it—and I include here the writers who tell us that mountain peoples tend to include jumping into their dances, where "plains" peoples or coastal peoples tend to avoid the vertical dimension in their dances. One is perplexed when field researchers do not seem to perceive the fundamental incompatibilities between their data and the explanatory paradigms which are available to them.

Status-holders in the American dance world in the 'forties and 'fifties seemed eager to tie the little rowboat of dance ethnology to the big tugboat of functional anthropology, seen as one of the vessels that guided the bigger ship of social and cultural anthropology, not realizing, perhaps, that as time passed, the tugboat was beached through the rejection, in anthropology, of a functionalist type of integration, thus rendering the continued uncritical usage of the paradigm for explanation of the dance somewhat anachronistic. Allegiance to a single theory of explanation seems to have rendered dance ethnologists unprepared to deal with the many challenges and refutations that were brought against their parent theory and methodology with the result, perhaps, that rescue operations are in order in 1988, but that cannot really occur unless and until dance ethnologists are willing to distinguish among their many potential rescuers.

They would be well-advised, too, I believe, to recognize contemporary developments in social and cultural anthropology (to continue the metaphor, they might take some interest in what is going on aboard the ship). A short list of these developments might help them to understand why status-holders in the discipline seem preoccupied with other things than the fate of dance studies in anthropology: the shift in the discipline from its sole concern with "primitive" societies, for a start; the many objections that have been brought against being objects of study by anthropologists that have come from members of third-world countries; the problematic nature of field-work itself (viz., the criticism of "collection" rather than "systematization"); the typology problem, plus the rejection of functionalist integration and the fear that structuralist challenges to functionalism might "de-humanize" the discipline; the welcome appearance of many non-western anthropologists; the ever-present "language barriers"; a tradition of specialization over the past fifty years and the current dilemmas of many modern anthropologists, who seem to be faced with a choice between anthropology seen as a moral mission vs. the "disinterested scientist" position,[7] and the current depressing world economic situation insofar as it pertains to higher education and research.

Specialization within the discipline has created something like an epistemological fragmentation all too visible in the bewildering variety of "anthropologies" that presently exist. Dance ethnologists will have to present a much stronger, unified case than they have up to now in order to be convincing. While it is true that anthropology is the logical discipline to provide an umbrella for dance ethnology (or, an anthropology of human movement), one doubts that such cases as Kurath presented or that Hanna (1976) presents, and the general disarray of the theoretical foundations are very convincing.

Then, too, few dance ethnologists seem to be aware of current issues in social and cultural anthropology, to the extent that one wonders if they are really concerned over the fact that it is the very preoccupation with humanistic values in these kinds of anthropology (in contrast to the more behaviorally-based, functional, cybernetic or ethological approaches to human movement and dancing) that makes it such a desirable haven? Anthropologists are, on the whole, concerned over just what it is that ensures that the findings of an empirically-based science conforms to benign human values (for example, see Berreman, 1982). With reference to movement, whether it is "danced" or not, to make "the organism" different from the spirit of humanity; to take refuge in dualisms is no more an answer for anthropology than it is for human movement studies (see Best, 1974 and 1978 for thorough discussion).

More recent anthropological studies of human movement— those carried out from a semasiological standpoint for instance,[8] affirm incarnation. That is to say that they stress the unity of body and spirit, thus there is a sense in which they affirm a kind of anthropological monism (*not* the doctrine that there is only one kind of substance of ultimate reality and *not* an ontological monism, as in Materialism, which denies the spirit, or its reverse, Spiritualism, which denies the body), but a kind of epistemological monism, referred to, but not explained in Williams (1976) that is concerned with *knowledge* rather than being.

At the end of the decade that was marked (for dance studies) by Kurath's article in *Current Anthropology*, another functionalist synthesis of dance materials appeared that is probably more well-known than any other: choreometrics. Persons concerned with studies of the dance seemed to ask, "If we do not have general statements to make about dancing except those which pertain to its role in society, which are as diverse as the societies to which they belong, then how can we go beyond innumerable studies?" The need for a different approach was answered by the creation of a "new" type of functionalism that would accommodate cross-cultural comparisons of dances. In the late 'sixties, a pioneering study, a socio-statistical survey of dances, rooted in Murdockian functionalism was carried out. This project, housed at Columbia University and funded by the A.A.A.S. could achieve, it was thought, what individual ethnographers working alone could never achieve, thus "choreometrics" was born; a coined word that is defined as "...the measure of dance, or dance as the measure of culture" (Lomax, 1968:22). Instead of a "Panorama of Dance Ethnology," we are now confronted with the "Panorama of Human Dance(s)."

The choreometrics project formed a relatively small part of a larger project, Cantometrics, and responsibility for the dance project is distributed by its director. It is said, for example, that the burden of accuracy for the ethnographic data and its relevance to research, together with many of the hypotheses put forward, is placed on Conrad Arensberg, to whom the project "...owes its principal intellectual debt" (Lomax, xiv). The standardized ethnographic ratings for the *song*-style "cross-cultural match" in cantometrics (after which the ratings for the dance were devised) were made with data from Murdock's ethnographic atlas (1962–67) and he also contributed unpublished materials to the project. In the words of the Project Director:

Choreometrics arose out of the Cantometrics Project—or the study of song style as the measure of society—which began in the summer of 1961. Then, in 1968, two seminar courses with Ray Birdwhistell of the Eastern Pennsylvania Psychiatric Institute ... exposed me to the study of body communication. Inspired by his work and seeing the study of body rhythms as a logical extension of, and necessary ingredient in, my work with song style structure as an image of human communication, I asked Irmgard Bartenieff and Forrestine Paulay to work with me. Up until then these two had been analyzing dance movement in terms of a background primarily Western European and American dance traditions. When they suddenly confronted the whole panorama of human dance from every continent and felt for the first time how many patterns of beautiful and appropriate movements had been created, their vision of the dance was sharply altered. In their enthusiasm, they then began to teach me, a non-dancer, their new-found perceptions of the dance. I in turn was able to interest them in the study of song, a system based on the theories of Conrad Arensberg and Ray Birdwhistell [Lomax, 1971:23].

The "panorama of human dance from every continent" was a series of approximately two hundred films. Lomax wrote extensively explaining the use of film as ethnographic data and its biased nature, noting that cameramen have to be oriented and trained to grasp the "sizes and shapes" of the postural habits of a people and their "dynamic patterns." He points out several reasons why films are culture-bound; how they tend to emphasize the main conventions of western art and how they are oriented to the tastes of western audiences who have "ingrained preferences for swiftly paced narrative and plots concerning the fates of individuals" which are not "the central concerns of other cultures." "Furthermore," he tells us, the "theme of romantic love seems to be a peculiarly western hang-up" (1971:30). Despite these problems, he advocates the use of film because filmed behavior rather than the real thing can "split behavior into a series of small segments which can be inspected one by one and studied at leisure." Moreover, "the filmed incident can be something which would be impossible in real life."

Despite the many grave objections to this kind of thing that have been pointed out in painful detail by the many critics of the choreometrics project (see Keali'inohomoku, 1976; Hanna, 1979; Williams, 1972a; and others,[9] Lomax attempts to persuade the anthropological community and laypersons alike of the validity of the data-base because "Non-western cultures are being destroyed so rapidly that this film may one day be the only witness to a way of life which has vanished" (1971:28). He is centrally preoccupied with recording the "culture styles" of the peoples of the world, and one wishes he had simply developed his films of "life" and "dances" from all parts of the world, without any further attempts to uncover their significance because this project has contributed (perhaps more than anyone is aware) to the stultification of further subsidized research on the dance and other structured systems of human actions. Having failed to produce a viable "measure of dance," *or* a reliable "theory of dance as the measure of culture," policy-makers and those who exercise control over research monies now seem to believe, owing to these failures, that there are simply "too many variables" connected, especially with the dance, and that it cannot be studied in a "scientific manner" or in any manner that would make a further contribution to knowledge. The main reason for this seems to turn around units of comparison.

Rust's statistical survey rested on *units of dances*. Lomax's study is based on units (not even of movement, it turns out) which go below—perhaps "above" or "to the side of"—the level of *a* dance, a group of dances or parts of dances. They are not units of movement comparable to those sought after (and found) by the East European school of folk dance research, viz., Lange (1970), or Martin and Pesovar (1961). The latter theoretical approach is summarized in Kürti (1980) and is based on the structural-functional methods of descriptive linguistics exemplified by the Prague School of linguistics. Choreometric units are not the units of movement used by Kurath (1964), which are units devised from the system of Labanalysis. These types of unitary descriptions *are* empirically-based. Choreometric units do not seem to be—both because they are taken from films and because

> Since our intent is not to translate or evoke the entire content of any movement series, we take these dance phrases, with their strongly punctuated and highly crystallized sequences, as our primary data. When we find analogous bits occurring with notable frequency in life activity outside the dance, we assume that the bit in the dance and the bit in life stand for each other [Lomax, 1968:228].

The basis for unjustifiable assumptions like these is never explained, nor is the naïve notion of causality upon which the project is based justified: "…the dance style varies in a regular way in terms of the level of complexity and the type of subsistence activity of the culture which supports it" (1968:xv). Lomax suggests correlations, presumably between the level of complexity to be found in a dance and the level of agricultural or technological complexity in the society as a whole. We are led to believe that we can expect to find "simple" dances among hunting and gathering peoples; "more complex" dances among agricultural peoples. Dancing of peoples who till their fields with the aid of a buffalo (or other animals) and a plough or a tractor: "It seems both obvious and logical that transition in movement should grow more elaborate in structure as a more complex productive technology makes further demands on the body for control" (Lomax, 1968:241).

It is astonishing that none of the negative evidence which could have been brought forward is even mentioned, C.F. McPhee's work on Bali (1970), Wirz's studies in Ceylon (1954), or from other areas of the world where authors have stressed the *complexity* of the dances of peoples who are not technologically advanced. Apart from that, is it true that "more productive complex technology" (the contrast between using a hand-plough and a tractor, for instance) "makes further demands on the body for control"? I think not. And, one would have thought that one of the main reasons for technology of any sort is to make *less*, not *more* demands on the human body, both in terms of energy expenditure and control, than is required of the body lacking the aid of complex equipment.

For example, if a stretch of movement required to wield a hoe, a hand-plough or a kayak and harpoon is mentally compared with a stretch of movement required to operate a tractor in motion, then it is obvious that the amount of movement and the number of joints involved in the first three instances are demonstrably more complex. They involve far more energy expenditure and control than do the movements required in the fourth case. If Lomax had proposed to show an *inverse* relationship between the *complexity* of danced movements and the *simplicity* of farming techniques; between the simplicity of danced movements and the complexity of farming techniques, then his project might have been interesting from this point of view.

He could have shown, for instance, that the masked Bedu dance of the Nafana of east central Ivory Coast (Williams, 1968) is highly elaborate and complex, although they are subsistence farmers who till the soil with hoes. In contrast, he could have shown that the square-dances and conventional social dances of the rural peoples of my native state of Oregon (specifically, Baker county) in the northwest United States are simple to the point of being "primitive" compared with the Bedu dance, although rural Oregonians are industrialized farmers who till the soil with tractors.

Motor complexity in one set of activities connected with agricultural technology is *assumed to be a constant factor* in danced movement activities. A *causal* relation is thus implied between *danced* "motor activities" and those pertaining to the securing of food. The two independent activities of dancing and working, connected *only* by virtue of the fact that they are both "group organizational activities" are further connected by a statistical relation between them which is established by finding constantly recurring motion patterns, "shapes" or "dynamic somethings" in both. But, lest it is believed that I simply grind axes, placing unsympathetic interpretations on the choreometric project's research, I will let the project director speak for himself:

> The expansion of the African agricultural system depended upon the involvement of women in agriculture, on the synchronized activity of large labor gangs, on the polygynous family, and on the increasing and budding lineage systems that the fertility of women supported. Without the high birthrate, without the ardent participation of both men and women in swift-paced communal labor in the blazing heat, the Negro people could never have conquered the African continent. The overtly sexual content of their songs and dances and the constant pelvic play in everyday movement supported the main institutions of the society (polygyny, expanding lineage villages) and gave a pleasant and stimulating tone to the whole of life. More work gets done, a high birthrate is maintained in polygynous families, and the electric current of sexuality touches everyone [Lomax, 1969:238–239].

Quantitative occurrences of pelvic articulation are noted in danced movements from filmed data, and in virtue of the fact that pelvic movement also occurs in sexual intercourse, these two activities are further connected by statistical relations such that the Dogon people (who are, incidentally, called "Bantu") and "Afro-American" end up in choreometric classifications of "distribution style clusters" as "erotic" (1968:231–234). I shall restrain myself from making further comment on the project for the moment and will continue to let the author speak for himself. A summation of the criteria for the movement units in choreometrics reads as follows:

> a) body parts most frequently articulated, b) body attitude or active stance, c) shape of the movement path and of transitions. d) patterns that link body and limb, e) dynamic qualities. The relative prominence of each characterizer is rated on a seven-point scale. For example, a parameter concerned with forcefulness contrasts the most lax movements we have found to the most vigorous we have seen in film and includes as well the degrees that lie between these two extremes. The position that a particular dance occupies on a number of such rating scales forms a unique profile which can be logically compared to any other such profile [Lomax, 1971:25].

Although it is repeatedly pointed out in research reports to the A.A.A.S., and elsewhere, that dance phrases and dances are *not* what is being measured, we are told that

> In every culture we found some one document of movement style. This model seems to serve two main functions for all individuals: (1) Identification: It identifies the individual as a member of his culture who understands and is in tune with its communication systems. (2) Synchrony: It forms and molds together the dynamic qualities which make it possible for the members of a culture to act together in dance, work, movement, love-making, speech—in fact, in all their interactions [1971:25].

On the other hand,

> The choreometric approach does not include step by step analyses from which dances may be reproduced in detail. The pattern and succession of patterns of step and movement *were omitted from our choreometric descriptions*, just as in cantometrics detail of rhythm and melody were merely summarized because it was felt that they referred to cultural but not cross-cultural pattern [1968:224—italics supplied].

In other words, there are no units in choreometrics that are straightforward movement units. There are only

> dynamic qualities that animate the activities of a culture. Thus a very outlandish passage of movement in a dance may present, in a stylized way, a movement quality that runs through all the humdrum activity of everyday [1968:224].

We might well ask what is an "outlandish passage of movement" and what determines its "outlandishness"? What we have in fact discovered is this:

> Each dance type somehow expresses the needs and the nature of a people and one has the impression that the distribution of dance styles on the planet corresponds in some way to the distribution of the families of mankind [1968:273].

In this masterful statement of the obvious, Lomax tells us that we may expect to find "Africans" doing "African dances," "Indians" doing "Indian" dances, Swedes doing Swedish dances ... and so on.

It is necessary to draw attention to two paragraphs that describe the sampling context of choreometrics, since the project has been heavily criticized for this:

> The sample will, for some time, be too small for the final establishment of stable areas and regions. Even so, the similarity wave program has found regional clusters that compare in a remarkable way with the distributions picked out for song-style. The 43 cultures from which we have extracted dance profiles fall into eight regional sets: (1) Amerindia; (2) Australia; (3) New Guinea; (4) Maritime Pacific; (5) Africa; (6) Europe; (7) India and (8) Old High Culture, east and west, whose similarity scores above the quartile (Table 59) form two super-regional sets.
>
> The world of the primitive Pacific splits away from the more complex cultures of Africa and Eurasia, with Australia and New Guinea clustering in a special sub-group. This circum-Pacific tribal area, which includes the Amerindian cultures of North and South America, has turned up again and again in Cantometric research. Its pervasive stylistic homogeneity may trace one of the ancient distribution patterns of human culture.

The second cluster is Afro-Eurasian. Within it the super-region, Old High Culture, emerges again with a linked similarity between the dance styles, east and west, of the Indian subcontinent. Africa's dance style affiliations with the nearby Orient and India correspond to only one aspect of Cantometric findings, owing to the nature of the sample in which two out of the five African cultures are typically agricultural Bantu (Dogon and Afro-American) [Lomax, 1968:281].

Since when, we wonder, has "Afro-America" become a "typically agricultural Bantu culture"? And what justification could there be for classifying the two together in these ways, besides some "quartile" on some statistical table? Lomax could not have chosen more unfortunately: there is documented evidence regarding the taxonomy of the body among the Dogon (see Ellen, 1977, for more complete discussion and references and see Williams, 1980, for a discussion of taxonomies of the body and the semantics of biological classifications of the body). Because of this, we can totally reject Lomax's claims for "similarity," because the Dogon taxonomy of the body bears no similarity whatever to that of Afro-Americans, for a start. Apart from his appalling naïveté about language and his total disregard for ethnography by qualified writers in the field, we need to know of what specific choreometric "samples" consist:

Africa. The African sample which includes several of the cultural extremes of the continent, is very different in its composition from the cantometric sample; it consists of one African Hunter culture (Kung) [sic]; one imperial cattle culture with Cushite affiliations (Bahima); Fulani cattle culture (Garuna); and two complex West African, or West African derived, cultures (Dogon and Afro-American). These dances bear provocative similarity to one another. The Kung [sic] and Bahima are more similar to Africa than to any other region, but have an almost equal attachment to Europe and the Maritime Pacific. Thus, just as in song, these cultures exemplify two distinct peripheries of African style, the first pre-Bantu, the second, Cushitic. The style of the Garuna, a pastoral group near Lake Chad (belonging to the cluster) is centrally African with decisive affiliations to Oceania. The wildly energetic hip-swinging dances of Dogon and Afro-America form a tight sub-cluster at the level of 82%; moreover, the high (100 and 80 percent) attachment of these two profiles to Africa and their relatively weaker ties to other regions put them at the center of the African cluster [Lomax, 1968:234].

Readers are left to make their own assessments of this stupefying example of jargon and to ponder, perhaps, over just how it is that Africa, a geographical land-mass that is 11,708,000 sq.m. (km. 30,323,000) in area, having a population of 490,300,000 people, with a population density of 42 people per sq.m (16 per km.), is adequately represented in terms of its linguistic groupings, its dances or much of anything else of the same genre by *five* groups of people, one of whom is American.

Compared to a choreometric treatment of dances, the methods of classifying artifacts after the manner biological and zoological taxonomic constructions, used by an earlier writer, Haddon (1895) are infinitely preferable, although they do no more justice, ultimately, to the phenomena than does choreometrics. In Haddon's theoretical context, we are presented with a straightforward classification of human cultural artifacts treated as if they were comparable to any of the flora and fauna of the physical environment with no pretenses made about "observations of behavior" and no attempt to discuss or compare the semantic significances of them.

Earlier writers, like Haddon, adhered to scientific paradigms of explanation which did not pretend to deal with people, or with the problems of culture in contrast to nature. If they included the dances of a people into their classificatory schemes, they did so under the same rules that they used for taxonomic features of any element of the physical environment. The methods of functionalist social and cultural anthropology could be said to be a real improvement over some of the older styles of historical reconstruction against which Malinowski and his followers rebelled. Unfortunately, the same cannot be said of the use of functionalism with regard to the dance; in particular, with regard to the choreometrics project.

Not only is choreometrics based on filmed and not actual behavior, it purports to be a "cultural" and not a "natural" scientific investigation. Its data are both inaccurate and incomplete. It is internally inconsistent owing to the ambiguities surrounding the movement units upon which it is based. In addition, it represents an abuse of statistical models, with particular reference to correlation variables. It is impossible to tell upon what population parameters choreometric samples are based: are they geographical or political boundaries, linguistic similarities, agricultural distributions, skin-pigmentation or continental units? The distinctive feature of the whole expensive enterprise and its ultimate contribution seems to lie in the fact that whatever may be seen to be the problems and difficulties of functionalist method and approach on a small scale, can now be seen on a global scale. The significance of the choreometrics project may well consist in its attempts to push functional theory and a statistical, quantitative model of events to their limits. Seeing both in such larger than human life perspectives is perhaps the only way of seeing that an entirely different approach to the study of movement and dance is necessary. In fact, there are other approaches available, and we will examine these in the two subsequent lectures.

For now, it will suffice to say that one of the major claims to freedom from values, hence to scientific objectivity in a functional *qua* behavioral paradigm of explanation, rests on the strict emphasis that is placed on external causes and on the system-maintaining character of the activity under investigation. In a positivistic universe of discourse, these features are emphasized in order to avoid "subjectivity," of course, but the baby gets thrown out with the bathwater. In their attempts to avoid any attribution of subjective, emotional, or self-reflexive understanding, either to the investigator or to the subjects of the investigation, heavy emphasis is placed on the body predicates of dancers alone. There have been so many misconceptions surrounding the concepts "subjective" and "objective" that one hardly knows where to begin to try to unravel the Gordian knots which prevent, sometimes, even rational discussion between subjectivists and objectivists regarding the interpretation and explanation of dances. However, I can do no better than to suggest a cogent treatment of the problem, i.e., Best (1985), and a review of current discussion in the *Journal for the Anthropological Study of Human Movement* (JASHM), volumes 3 and 4, and leave the matter there, for it is too muddled a topic to deal with in these lectures.

In choreometric explanations, the dancers pictured on the films are assigned only biological or physical identities, and the dances, whatever they were—they are not even named—are lost in the investigator's preoccupations with raw movements bereft of any semantic content or significance whatever. This is not unusual in the contexts of the kinds of explanatory strategies used by Lomax and his team: it simply means that these investigators were living up to a view of objectivity which continues to come under heavier and heavier attack (see Pocock, 1977; Grene, 1971; Gouldner, 1973; Polanyi, 1962; Harré and Secord, 1972; and Gould, 1971).

To conclude this lecture, one would want to caution students who are new to the field against misconstruing the intent of the foregoing criticism of functionalism: it is not my aim to characterize functionalists as the "bad guys" and non-functionalists as the "good guys" of human movement studies or any other field. Used out of context, and without honesty and sensibility, *any* paradigm of explanation can be inappropriate. And in any case, the world is not readily comprehended through rigid, mutually exclusive distinctions of any kind.

Notes

1. It would seem, in retrospect, that this collection of essays might have been a brave attempt on Boas's part to elicit response to the application of this paradigm to non-western dances, but what seems to have happened was that the articles were used as "authority" and not to generate discussions or further inquiry into the implications and consequences of using this paradigm for research into dances.

2. Beattie (1964), in the first section of his book, has the best overview and explanation of "armchair anthropologists" that I know of.

3. An anthropologically untrained observer does not know how to separate his or her cultural values and judgments from those of the people who are being investigated, with the result that the published research is a curious mixture of opinions, projections, and identifications which render the work useless in the ongoing life of the discipline. The differences between the two viewpoints is spelled out in Williams (1976)—see Appendix, *infra*. pp. 289–302—where my own pre-anthropological writing is used as an

example of the kinds of objectivism, objectification, and sheer nonsense that can arise, quite unintentionally.

4. Some of the predecessors to whom I refer are Frazer (1911 & 1912), Tylor (1895), Harrison (1913/1948), and Grove (1896).

5. All of these terms derive from functional explanation in general, which is explanation of phenomena in terms of describing the inter-related activities ("functions" or "actions") that elements of a thing undergo during its existence. For example, a functional explanation of "Why does the heart beat?" would be connected with the further activities that depend upon the heart's activities, such as the circulation of the blood, and/or the physical, chemical, and possibly artificial processes (functions) of those parts of the heart and body upon which the beating of the heart depend. Used in a strictly biological context, this kind of explanation is useful. It is questionable how useful it is when it is transferred *carte blanche* to a whole society seen as an "organism." In general, this type of explanation is contrasted with explanations in terms of purposes, intentionality, goals, or drives to fulfill an end.

6. In the Fleshman *Anthology*, Chapter 9 (1986), this basically historicist problem is discussed more fully under the sub-heading, "who are anthropologists of human movement?"

7. See Weaver (1973) for cogent discussion of the social issues involved, and Berreman (1982) for more recent political commentary.

8. The semasiological standpoint is set out in part in Williams (1979 & 1982).

9. So far as I am aware, this project and the writing which has resulted from it has not received *any* positive reviews—even the films that were used for it and the films which have resulted from it have come under considerable attack (See Keali'inohomoku, 1979, for further discussion).

VII. BIBLIOGRAPHIC CONTROLS

THE MAIN PURPOSE OF THIS LECTURE is to examine the kind of literature presently included in the category "dance ethnology" or "dance anthropology," since by now, I trust that my audience is aware (in broad outline, at least) of the intellectual context in British social and American cultural anthropology in conjunction with which this literature developed, especially in the United States.

Before getting on with an analysis of two bibliographies offered to the field by Kurath (1960), a well-known pioneer dance ethnologist, and Hanna (1976), an equally well-known contemporary dance anthropologist, one would want to say two things: (1) I have actual people in mind with regard to this subject, namely, students and librarians primarily, whom I think of as the *users* and the *points of access to* these materials, and (2) usually, it is the case that

> Before developing a research proposal, the scholar will be interested
> in determining the already existing body of research related to the
> subject. Which sources will provide that information: Do manuals
> or guides exist, prepared for the master's or doctoral student, which
> cover the topic? Do separate publications exist which list theses and
> dissertations on the topic (and) how can these be located? [Lair,
> 1984].

The answers to the questions in the quoted passage above, asked by a professor of library science, is "no." There is virtually no bibliographic control over this field of study at present, such as librarians might understand or be able to use, and graduate students are faced with bibliographies that are little more than book lists, or lists of items most of which are unavailable (or at best, extremely difficult to acquire). This is not to say that libraries cannot make any needed item available. They can and do. The point I wish to make will be clarified as we go along. Suffice to say here that a bibliography is often prepared, not with its potential *users* in mind, but with a view mainly toward the preparation of a list which is impressive by virtue of length alone.

Twenty six years ago (and for many years prior to the publication of the 1960 bibliography), Kurath suggested that dance ethnology be included in general ethnology, a major sub-field of American cultural anthropology. There is an updated version of this bibliography that was prepared by Joann Keali'inohomoku and Frank Gillis (1970), and it should be said at the outset that there are certain allowances that must be made for Kurath's work as it is represented in the *Current Anthropology* article: she had little or no formal anthropological training, and when she went into the field to do work with Fenton on the Iroquois, she was an apprentice. Historically, she was in a position to see what might develop from an ethnological study of dances, but she lacked sufficient training and the theoretical sophistication necessary to develop her vision. She was, however, an inspiration to many who were to come after her, including Kaeppler and Keali'inohomoku, and her legacy and her name command respect for that which she attempted.

The work I have done with regard to Kurath's and Hanna's bibliographies reflects a fundamental anthropological purpose, seeking to understand how and in what ways the claim that Kurath makes, i.e., that the "...literature as a whole is comprehensive enough so that the time is ripe for a coordination of the many different approaches" (Kurath, 1960:223) is credible, and the claim that Hanna makes, i.e., that her bibliography consists of materials that dance researchers should be familiar with, is reasonable.

Even if the literature can be seen to be "comprehensive" enough, it sadly lacks in bibliographic controls and those attempts to establish control, e.g., by Davis (1972 and 1982) and Hanna (1976) are basically unsatisfactory because they do not clearly delineate specific fundamental distinctions that are made by anthropologists.[1] Davis's reference works are, like Kurath's bibliography and, to a somewhat lesser extent, Hanna's, simply a list of books. This statement suggests a negative and deliberately so. Neither states a satisfactory *user's purpose* of their lists, and neither comments upon why it is that students should read these works—or read them in juxtaposition. There is nothing *inherently negative* about a list of books, but there is nothing *inherently positive* about a list of books either, just as there is nothing "positive" or "negative" about a list of ingredients for a beef stew. The positive or negative character of a grocery list or a recipe for beef stew, however, might be discerned if the list is used to construct clam chowder or chocolate mousse. Of course, this kind of thing would only rarely, if ever, happen with regard to a recipe for beef stew or cookery in general, but it frequently happens with reference to descriptive concoctions of materials about dancing.

Very little of what follows will be new to librarians, because bibliographic problems are well known in that field, however, the problems are not any less important because they are well known. The first of these pertains to the questions of whether or not the references cited at the end of Kurath's paper, entitled "A Panorama of Dance Ethnology" (1960:233–254) is a bibliography or not. When, we might ask, does a book list become a bibliography and what causes it to remain simply a random list of books?

Presumably, the organizing principle of Kurath's and Hanna's bibliographies is "the dance" (or is it "dancing" or some group of dances?). The difficulty here is that *dancing* is too broad a subject category; the term possesses too many definitions and interpretations if considered on a worldwide basis, and "dancing" is an activity, not an intellectual enterprise, in any case. "The dance" is a phrase that, as we have seen, is equally ill-defined, and in my opinion, undefinable, except in the context of an ethnicity's, a nation's or a specific group's conception (as in "ballet-dancing," "flamenco dancing," high-life or Kpanlogo dancing, and such).

In other words, we shall see—from yet another perspective—how this deceptively simple distinction, even limited to "dancing" and "the" dance crops up over and over again, and there are other problems which are equally perplexing: much of the writing about dancing is not of an analytical nature; it is wholly descriptive, and if any theoretical content does exist, it is generally implicit, not explicit. Moreover, other subjects tend to creep in and become subsumed under the same heading: sign languages, for example, and ceremonies, rituals, etiquette, and the like, and items pertaining to movement writing, dance notation, and the like.

In one way of looking at it, a bibliography is simply a list of items that an individual scholar has read or *knows about*, but may not really *know*. Hanna precedes her selected bibliography for "dance anthropology" with the statement:

> This bibliography is not meant to be comprehensive or to include items of uniform quality. The material presented reflects my view of what dance researchers should be familiar with and what the field of dance anthropology should encompass. It emerged through training in dance and the social sciences. Since this bibliography will be periodically updated, users are requested to send me their suggestions [Hanna, 1976: contents page].

From time to time during the examination of Kurath's work, I shall refer to Hanna's list for comparative purposes, and will discuss it more thoroughly later on. It is necessary to say at this stage of the discussion, however, that students and librarians should take the statements quoted above quite seriously. Hanna's list of books is not representative a) of any anthropological approach to the study of dancing, the dance or "dances," nor is it b) representative of any school of thought or any broadly held point of view with regard to the subject of the dance and human movement. Her list does precisely what it says it does. Maybe the problem lies in the fact that users do not read contents pages or prefaces—I do not know. What does become very clear in a teaching situation is the fact that this book list has been cited (naïvely) as a reflection of the views of anthropologists, or a period of anthropology, or something of the kind.

I have been asked many times why such problems exist at all, and apart from the explanation of "sloppy scholarship" the only answer I can give forces me to turn, momentarily, to a review of the information sources listed in Sheehy (1976:408-410), which is a standard reference work used by many librarians when asked questions concerning the dance. Under the heading, "The Dance, Bibliography," six items are listed. All of these refer either to ballet dancing (BG79, 80, 82, 84) or to collections (BG81) or to "lists of books and articles on the dance and related subjects" (BG82) that are largely, if not wholly, confined to western dancing (i.e., ballet, jazz, tap, folk and square-dancing, social dancing, and such). There is nothing in any of these references that would contribute to an anthropological study of the dance unless the researcher was attempting the study of ballet as an ethnic form, or ballroom-dancing, perhaps.[2]

The Indexes listed in Sheehy (1976), i.e., BG85 and BG86, are mainly concerned with trade newspapers, focussing heavily on what is happening on the current professional dance scene—mainly in the United States—or, they point to descriptive materials that are of interest, perhaps, to someone doing research from a less analytical view-point than is required in anthropology. The problem here is a disciplinary one, really: an anthropologist is required to "describe" what he or she is talking about, but there are two other required steps as well; interpretation and explanation. It is these two steps that more than any others, make anthropological writing different from that of novel writing or other general scholarly approaches.

The point is that *every description is not an anthropological description*: like any other academic discipline, anthropology is in part a "craft," and the craft of writing good anthropological descriptive accounts is an essential feature of training—or should be. Since my purpose here is to focus on content, not literary merit, I would want to say that anthropological literature itself is extremely uneven with regard to style and form. Even so, it has to meet certain criteria of its particular style of investigation, because otherwise, it is not considered to be anthropology at all. Content always takes precedence over form and ethnographic accuracy is more important than such things as "plot development" and the like. Also, it must be said that a novelist can make his or her characters do anything he or she likes. An anthropologist cannot do this and stay an anthropologist for very long. If there is such a thing as "dance anthropology" or "dance ethnology," then, by definition, the writings are pre-supposed to conform to some of the rules of anthropological writing.

The Annuals listed in Sheehy (1976:409) are those which concern ballet and the New York Theatre world. I do not really understand why periodicals like the *Dance Research Journal* or *Ethnomusicology* are not cited in a volume like this, although librarians would understand that Sheehy lists few or no "content" journals or monographs. Also, they are aware of the differences between, say, an *index* as a reference work, a *bibliography* and such. But, how many *users* are aware of these differences? How many users consult the listings in Sheehy precisely *for* "content"? This is not to say that a work like Sheehy's should necessarily list Journals, Annuals and the like that stem from groups who are interested in content, but it is to say that Sheehy is a major reference work for the dance, used nationally in the United States and that as such, it is too often the case that the "research" stops there. "Not Sheehy's fault," I have had critics of my position on these matters say. My reply? It does not matter whose "fault" it is: the fact is that the area of research suffers greatly because of it, and that is my sole concern.

In spite of many defects the *Dance Research Journal* and the Annuals produced by CORD (The Committee on Research in Dance), do provide some references specific to the combined studies of the dance, anthropology, ethnology, folklore, and ethnomusicology, and the editors over the years have published articles by qualified professional anthropologists that are works of serious theoretical understanding and scholarly worth. Perhaps the problem is that Sheehy does not cite works like the *Humanities* or *Social Sciences Indexes* under the heading of "The Dance," or any of the *further* sources that need to be consulted. This lack means that the librarian is required to have some intellectual access to the subject and the larger topics which pertain to the dance so that he or she can lead the user towards these. Some of the sources are discussed in Williams (1986:184–185), so that no more need be said here, except to point out that often, the librarian is the *only* link that a student may have with regard to "content" materials. This is because all too often, students are merely *exposed to* writings on the subject of the dance and anthropology in courses in folklore, ethnomusicology, anthropology, and dance and dance education: they are not given any guidance and/or training in how to deal with any of it. I am not suggesting that librarians attempt to replace "professors," but I do suggest that the keen students of the subject, if given half a chance at what is available, will begin to see on their own, some of what is needed for the research area to progress towards something other than a literature that is both tedious and mediocre.

All but five of the Encyclopedias and Handbooks listed in Sheehy are primarily about the ballet (i.e. BG87, BG88, BG89, BG90, BG92, BG97). One handbook is devoted to the subject of American cowboy dances (BG100). The five non-balletically oriented reference sources are instructive because here, we discover attempts to deal with the dances of the entire world. It is this *kind* of reference that presents the major problems for teachers and students of anthropology, for the reasons outlined in previous lectures. The non-balletically oriented sources are these: Bowers's *Survey of Asian Dance and Drama* (BG93); The Chujoy and Manchester *Dance Encyclopedia* (BG94); Sachs's *World History of the Dance* (BG99); DeMille's *Book of the Dance* (BG95) and Martin's *Book of the Dance* (BG98). This kind of book has been critically discussed in Keali'inohomoku (1980a) and in previous lectures; in particular, Sachs's work, i.e., Kaeppler (1978), Youngerman (1974) and Williams (1976c), but apparently with no real effects. Of interest to reference librarians may be the fact that these five works are all very much outdated, and it is necessary to explain why.[3]

Reference works are often outdated in one way of looking at them because of the vicissitudes of publishing, book production, and all the rest, but that is not what is meant. That sense of outdatedness probably cannot be helped, and in any case, it really does not matter from the standpoint of serious research, because (1) anthropological research at the doctoral level usually always involves fieldwork and there is very little dependence on published sources at that level, because the anthropologist already knows them and (2) research at a doctoral level in anthropology does not consist of a re-interpretation of what is already there. Finally, it is at the master's level in social anthropology that the investigator goes through a rigorous examination of sources that are specifically tied to his or her area of research, which is probably tied to a geographical area. At this level, it *is* important for the student to know everything which has been written by any other anthropologist who has done work in the area, and by the time the student has completed work at a master's level, he or she is also familiar enough with the history, theory, and relations to other disciplines in general anthropology that he or she does not require instruction regarding the mode of analysis, the methodological strategies that are available that are to be used.

These features of standard social anthropological training and practice are what make reference works like those immediately cited above so problematical to anthropologists. They are, without exception, totally outdated from a *theoretical* standpoint. For example, when Sachs first published his "World History," the schools of thought now known as "semiotics" or "cognitive anthropology" or "ethnoscience" did not yet exist. Now, they do. Anthropology itself has changed. Methods have improved and have grown far more sophisticated, especially linguistically, than they were in 1936. On the one hand, one does not want to stigmatize Sachs for something that he could not possibly have known, but on the other hand, one does wonder why this volume keeps reappearing—and worse, continues to be cited—with the regularity of the seasons.

It is the content of these works that is simply inaccurate, owing to changes which have taken place internally in the discipline. At this time, they can be considered valuable historical documents, but they are useless as guides for current research. Then too, they are on the whole, ethnocentric in the extreme. They are shot through with unsubstantiated arguments, as we have seen, regarding other peoples of the world. Their authors unblushingly use explanatory paradigms taken from anthropology that modern anthropologists have long since abandoned, yet, because none of the writers are anthropologists, they lay the scholarly, ethical, and moral responsibility for their explanations at anthropology's door (for a recent example, see Lange, 1975). Some of this kind of thing is dealt with specifically later on in this lecture, so no more will be said here.

Of the five remaining reference works in Sheehy, which are dictionaries, one can be included with the works mentioned above; Raffee's *Dictionary of the Dance* (BG104), which, unlike its companions (i.e. BG101, BG102, BG103 and BG105) is not a dictionary of the ballet, but purports to "define numerous terms relating to dances and dancing in all countries and periods." A more arrogant, inflated, and impossible task could hardly be imagined for a single book of this size. The reference works given on the ballet are in general, very good.

For a start, the ballet is tied to a specific language, French, which has become a *lingua franca* for the ballet wherever it may be found in the world, but the same thing could not be said of the languages of other danced forms. Raffee's *Dictionary* is wholly without merit from an anthropological and linguistic point of view, because it represents a kind of linguistic and cultural imperialism that is, in this decade of greater global awareness, to be deplored. (For further "positive" discussion of the subject of the language of the ballet and some of its anthropological significances, see Williams, 1980 and 1980a.)

In sum, the six reference works which include anthropological (more accurately, quasi-anthropological) materials are totally useless from a graduate student's point of view, unless they are used negatively: that is, used as examples of how *not* to "define" the dances or the dancing of other cultures, and how *not* to comprehend an anthropological approach to the activity. Having reviewed some of the extant reference works on the dance, we will now turn to Kurath's bibliography, "The Panorama of Dance Ethnology."

The list of materials at the end of Kurath's article consists of 251 items, 209 of which are books, journal articles, theses, or unpublished manuscripts. Thirteen of the items are "Projects" and 29 of the items are films.[4] The interest here will focus on the printed items, which are not annotated, beyond an occasional parenthetical comment that the article alluded to has a "huge bibliography" or that the piece duplicates in English something written in another language, or that the piece consists of Labanotation.[5] The list seems intended to support the main thesis of the paper, which is to offer evidence of widespread interest in the subject of dance ethnology. It is also meant somehow to indicate the basis for a coherent field of research and to point to sources for finding materials, especially about movement writing that might not be well-known to scholars in ethnology, folklore, or anthropology (see Kurath, 1960:251, section on Selected Source Materials). *Neither the article nor the list itself offers students any critical or evaluative means of dealing with it.*

This difficulty was alluded to in the "Comments" section of Kurath's paper (p. 250) by Erna Gunther, who would prefer

> ...a separation between the true ethnological field and the folk dance of the American and European cultures. I can see the relationship theoretically, but the students in these two fields have such totally different background and orientation that it is difficult to include all their needs and attitudes in a single study.... (Kurath, 1960:250).

The kinds of study that I would prefer to see were set out in the last lecture (Chapter VI). Suffice it to say at the moment that only some of the materials listed by Kurath are available, either because their only existence was in manuscript form to be presented at a seminar, but never published, or, some were published but are now out of print. It would represent a major task for a reference-bibliographer to track down all of the items cited for any purpose. It is an impossible task for an average, or even above average graduate student.

Kurath is clear regarding the purpose of her essay: to define "dance ethnology" and failing that, to initiate such an enterprise. She intends to outline the scope of the proposed discipline that is meant to use a data-base consisting of the dances of the entire world, and to raise some issues which pertain to dance ethnology as she conceived of it. My purpose is to try to evaluate these references in context—in an anthropological context, which is understood by Kurath to mean "ethnological research."

Of the 209 items listed which are printed materials, 57 pertain to the subject of North American Indian dance. Not unexpectedly, this is where the concentration of trained anthropological writing lies, although its representation is not very large: Boas, Speck and Broom, Beals, and a few others. The following is a list, by author, of those items:

Barbeau. 1957. Record of Canadian Indian Lore.
Barbeau, *et al.* (in French). 1958. Dansons a la ronde.

Beals. 1945. Article in Bureau of Ethnology Bulletin. *Cahita.*

Boas. 1944. Article in Boas' (Fka.) published seminar. *Kwakiutl.*

Brown. 1959. MA Thesis, Harvard. *Taos Pueblo.*

Cavello-Bosso. 1956. BA Thesis, Wesleyan. *Zuni.*

Dempsey. 1956. Article in Journal of American Folklore. *Blood Indians,* (Alberta, Canada).

Dozier. 1956. (ms.) *Rio Grande Pueblos.*

Dutton. 1955. Article for New Mexico Association on Indian Affairs, *"New Mexico Indians."*

Evans. 1931. Book published by A.S. Barnes on *"American Indian"* dance steps.

Fenton. 1941. Article in Bureau of American Indian Ethnology publication. *Tonawanda.*

————. 1941a. Smithsonian Report for 1940. *Iroquois.*

————.1941b. Unclear whether book or article; University of State of N.Y., *Iroquois.*

Fenton and Kurath. 1953. Article in Ethnography Bulletin. *Iroquois.*

Gamble. 1952. Article in book edited by Sol Tax. *Kiowa.*

Gillespie. (no date). *Shawnee.*

————. (n.d.) *Eastern Cherokee.*

Gunther (ms., n.d.) *Kwakiutl.*

Howard. 1955. Article in Scientific Monthly; *Pan-Indian culture* of Oklahoma.

————. (ms., n.d.) Turtle Mountain Plains *Ojibway.*

Howard and Kurath. 1959. Article in Ethnomusicology Magazine. *Ponca.*

Kurath. 1949. Article in Journal of American Folklore. *Mexico.*

————. 1949–50. Entries in Dictionary of Folklore, Mythology and Legend, Funk and Wagnall.

————. 1951. Article in Bureau of Amer. Ethnology Bulletin. *Iroqois.*

————. 1952. Article in book edited by Sol Tax. *"Dance Acculturation."*

————. 1953. Article in American Anthropologist. "*Native Choreographic Areas.*"

————. 1954. Article in Scientific Monthly. *Tutelo.*

————. 1956. Article in Journal of Amer. Folklore. "*Dance Relatives of mid-Europe and middle America.*"

————. 1956a. Article in Musical Quarterly on songs. *East Woodland Indians.*

————. 1957. Article, i.e. "Reprint 22," Indian Institute of Culture, Bangalore, India. *Algonquin.*

————. 1957a. Article in Dance Notation Record. "*American Indian.*"

————. 1957b. Article in Dance Notation Record. *Pueblo Indian.*

————. 1958. Article in El Palacio, 65. *Tewa.*

————. 1958a. Article in Southwest Journal of Anthropology. *Rio Grande.*

————. 1959. Article in Midwest Folklore. *Menomini.*

————. Notation. "Manuscript a": *Seneca* (Amer. Philosophical Society Library).

————. Notation. "Manuscript b": *Onondaga* (N.Y. State Museum Education Library).

————. Notation. "Manuscript c": *Tutelo.* No location.

————. Notation. "Manuscript d": *Eastern Woodland.* No location.

————. Notation, Film and Tape. "Manuscript e": *Tewa.* No location.

————. and Ettawageshik. 1955. (Manuscript and Notation). *Modern Algonquin.* Amer. Philosophical Society Library.

Lambert. (n.d.) '*Danses Canadiennes.*'

Lange. 1953. Article in American Anthropologist. *Cochiti.*

————. (ms., n.d.) in preparation for publication at University of Texas Press, Austin.

Mason. 1944. Book published by A.S. Barnes. *American Indian.*

McAllister. 1941. (ms.) Paper given at Columbia University on Ethnomusicology; *Commanche Sign Language.*

Pollenz. 1946. MA Thesis, Columbia University. *Seneca* (mainly notation).

Schusky. 1957. Article in Anthropology Today. *Pan-Indianism* in East United States.

Slotkin. 1955. Article in Amer. Journal of Folklore. *"Intertribal."*

———. 1957. Article in Milwaukee Public Museum Publications in Anthropology. *Menomini.*

Speck. 1949. Book, University of Pennsylvania Press. *Cayuga.*

——— and Broom. 1951. Book, University of California Press, Los Angeles, *Cherokee.*

Sturtevant. 1954. Article in Florida Anthropologist. *Seminole.*

Tomkins. 1929. Book, published by author on 'universal' *Indian Sign Language.*

Turley. 1959. (ms., n.d.) Present day *Oklahoma* war dancing.

Wilder. 1940. MA Thesis, University of Arizona. *Yaqui.*

Of the 57 items listed above, one is record (disk) with minimal written explanation (Barbeau, 1957); 2 are on sign languages, 1 is not available except through the author and the other, (Tomkins, 1929) is a handbook used by Boy Scouts, and a work which has virtually no credibility in anthropology, having for some time been subject to stringent anthropological criticism (see Farnell, 1984, for full discussion). This leaves 54 items.

Of these, one is out of print (Boas, 1944, discussed later on), one item consists of dictionary entries (Kurath, 1949–50), two are manuscripts that are unavailable except through the authors,[6] and 6 of the items have no dates. This reduces the list to 44. I do not know whether the dictionary published by Funk and Wagnall is still in print or not. The theses of Brown, Cavello-Bosso, Pollenz, and Wilder *may* still be in existence and might be available, although if all universities have maintained the present policies of New York University, master's theses are not required to be kept on record. In any case, one of these concerns notation and the problems of notation, which presents as much of a language barrier as if the item were written in an unknown spoken language.

Of the 40 remaining items, 8 (all by Kurath; one with an informant) are specifically notation scores. This limits their intellectual accessibility severely, except to those who can read the script. Apart from these, there are four items that I have judged to be "miscellaneous"; those of Dutton (1955), Fenton (1955), Kurath (1957), and Kurath (1958). The reasons are these: the Dutton item was written for an association which may or may not have kept records. The Fenton item may or may not be a book published by SUNY; the Kurath item from Bangalore would constitute an expensive search, and the citation of "El Palacia" may or may not be valid—given that one could track down what it means.

There are 21 items on the list that are available through professional journals, but at least two of these emphasize songs, the dance receiving only incidental treatment, leaving 19. There are 4 books represented; those of Evans, Mason, Speck, and Speck and Broom. Two more books are represented, both edited by Sol Tax (1952 and 1952a) that we are aware of only through the references to articles by Gamble and Kurath (both 1952). This book list is, perforce, not even minimally cross-referenced.

The upshot is this: there are 6 books, 19 articles and 3 theses which would be available to a majority of graduate students throughout the country from an original list of 57 items that concern North American Indians and some aspect of dancing (or rituals, ceremonies, pow-wows, and such). Twenty of the original 57 items were written by Kurath herself and one was done with an informant. Out of the 57 items, there are 28 which pertain more or less directly to North American Indian Dancing, but these are stretched over such widely differing peoples as the Cahita, the Blood Indians of Alberta, Canada, the Tonawanda, Iroquois, Ponca, Tutelo, Rio Grande Pueblos, Taos Pueblos, Zuni, Menomini, Seminole, Kiowa, Cayuga and Cherokee ethnicities. Seven of the items are about "American Indians" or "Pan-Indian" matters; inter-tribal affairs, choreography, composition and "acculturation". These different peoples represent a mind-boggling potpourri of languages, customs, beliefs, political organization, ecological conditions for living—the list is nearly endless. As represented, it is an anthropological hotchpotch.

Skill 2.0 OK [Functionalism] pp 119

2002 On the Web OR

SEPTEMBER

2 MONDAY No matter whether for political, economic, or vehicle to accomplish psychological advantages for Samoan + other teenages, overall theoretical framework is to provide a change, drive Elan throughout dance

pp 180 dance as education/entertainment + video

3 TUESDAY "They have successfully removed Indians, encouraged ingredients form the term dance"

4

FRIDAY **30**

SATURDAY **31**

1

SUNDAY

NOTES:

5 THURSDAY

ASSIGNMENTS:

DEADLINE: Parochial

Before we continue with the analysis of Kurath's list, one would want to draw attention to the initial questions asked at the beginning of this lecture: what is the difference between a book list and a bibliography? There are some who would say that there is no difference; any list of books is a bibliography, which means that a list of holdings from any bookshop constitutes a bibliography. That kind of lowest common denominator definition may suffice for some, but it is not the interpretation given to the term in any academic discipline of which I am aware. First, a bibliography would most probably be over 25 items long, but it should consist of items which have a structure. That is to say that it should possess a coherent organizing principle such that an investigator could discern a clear pattern of relations among the items. Perhaps the purpose of the bibliography is to introduce the reader to a universe of discourse; perhaps the purpose is to uncover an important theoretical or methodological concept; perhaps the readings simply reflect the many voices which have engaged in a debate over an important issue. Sometimes, items in a bibliography are there because they support an author's arguments, as in a paper, thesis, essay or dissertation, but the total structure should serve some other purpose besides that of supporting references and testimony to the fact that the author is demonstrating his or her knowledge.

A good bibliography is cross-indexed. That is, if there is a citation for Williams, D. 1975. "The Brides of Christ," in *Perceiving Women* (ed. S. Ardener), Malaby Press, London, then one should expect to find under the "A's," a reference to Ardener, S. (ed.). 1975. *Perceiving Women*. Malaby, London; Halsted, New York. In a working, scholarly bibliography such as the ones provided for students in certain teaching contexts, the bibliography is indexed according to subject, and annotated with regard to emphasis.

In a good bibliography, one can cite items which are still in manuscript form, but it is a better plan to group them together at the end of the other published and available materials than it is to document them, as Kurath did, along with everything else. If they are included in the general list, then they should have addresses where librarians and students may write to secure the work, i.e., a

University department, perhaps, or something of the kind. It is also a good plan for the author to contact the sources of such manuscripts, seeking permission to publish an address where a reader might write to secure the work, or at least write to the source author to find out if the piece is available from an institution or some other site of information access. If an item is known to be out-of-print, this information should be given to readers along with the citation. Materials should be grouped according to format, especially concerning a subject like the dance. In other words, there are strong relationships that a really good bibliography has with the notion of a *syllabus*.

One of the best bibliographic works with which I am acquainted is that of Paden and Soja (1970),[7] which has (among many admirable features) a separation of contents that provides some key to levels of intellectual access to the items as well. In Volume III of *The African Experience*, the editors-compilers make all of the points necessary with reference to features of a *selected* bibliography; the criteria for selection, style of annotation and such. They then point out that

> The Bibliography, like the Syllabus, is essentially experimental. Our experience in the selection of bibliographic references, therefore, is probably less a model then a pilot effort from which lessons may be learned. There have been six distinct stages in the generation of this bibliography [Paden and Soja, 1970:xiii].

What is needed is to have a comparable reference work for the anthropology of dance and human movement, perhaps entitled, "The Human Danced and Moved Experience," which would then arrange reference works, books, materials from different countries and the like in a similar way. Paden and Soja's volume is the only one I have seen in my experience with reference works that could serve as a model for a subject so broad as that suggested by Kurath, but her subject—specifically dance ethnology or "dance anthropology" would need be one category in the work that I envision.

The digression above into the characteristics of a good bibliography and the suggestion of a model for a reference work which might be able to handle such a vast data base as the dance traditions of the entire world was necessary, however, in order to put the critical evaluation of Kurath's work into perspective. What is sorely needed is a reference work that includes introductory materials, further references for teachers, librarians, and students who have specialized interests in the topic, general theoretical references which may not pertain specifically to the dance, but which provide insights into the problems and issues of the subject. Moreover, theories of notation should be included, and the contributions of disciplines so widely different in their handling of the subject of dance and human movement as are anthropology, psychology, kinesiology, philosophy, aesthetics, and linguistics, for a start.

One could, as the compilers of the splendid work on Africa have done, include a section on less accessible sources (such as journals with limited circulation, materials in other languages than English, government documents, etc.). It would be possible to include case study references, and, according to country, bibliographic materials with locally established controls that are appropriate to the study of the dance in other cultures. The examination of the remainder of Kurath's book list will illustrate well why an entirely different kind of bibliographic vehicle is needed to handle the subject of dance and human movement on a global basis—or even on a national basis, if one *only* thinks of the dance forms which are represented in the United States. This means that we will now look at the "Panorama" minus 57 items.

Excluding the items concerning North American Indians, the notion of these kinds of dances, and such, roughly 152 items remain. Of these, 23 are in German, and of these, at least three (read in translation) do not concern dancing, but Kinetography (Laban), Effort (Laban), and a naïve evolutionary theory of the dance that we know by now has been abandoned by anthropologists—that of Curt Sachs. I cannot comment on the remaining 20 items because I do not read German, but I suspect that those of Wolfram, for example, are heavily orientated towards notation. It would require a German reader or translations to make assessments of the contents of these items.

In the best scholarly sense, one would want to have the bibliography represent German views, theories, bibliographic controls, and such. In fact, one would want this for each ethnicity that was included in the work. Of the remaining 129 items, 8 are written in Russian; 12 are written in East European languages; 10 are in Spanish; and 4 in Scandinavian languages. There is nothing wrong with that, but Kurath does not mention the basis for selection of these articles and no others. I doubt that she was fluent (or even conversant) in all of these languages. All in all, there are 95 items remaining, of which one is written in French and one in Turkish, leaving 93.[8] The anthropological point one would wish to make is this: the 59 items written in different languages represent such diverse cultures as Ukraine, Turkey, Chile and other Latin American countries, Mexico, Yugoslavia. All of this represents (like the 57 American Indian items) a hotchpotch of languages, cultures, customs, beliefs and what-have-you which are not rightly lumped into an homogeneous mass.

Into this mixture are included items identifying something called "primitive" dance. We have learned from Kaeppler that anthropologists do not, on the whole, ascribe to the notion that modern non-western peoples represent earlier stages of "cultural evolution" in the west, nor do they hold that the dance or "art" in general can be understood cross-culturally without understanding the individual tradition in terms of the cultural tradition of which it is a part. Yet, the very structure of Kurath's bibliography would indicate either a lack of knowledge of the anthropological position or deliberate neglect of it.

Given that 57 of the items listed concern alleged "primitive" peoples (North American Indians) and 59 of the items concern European and/or European-derived dance forms, one would want to ask, "how and in what ways does the author conceive of the relations between them?" Before examining the more "theoretical" contents of the references cited, however, it is necessary to complete the list of items which pertain to still *more* linguistic and ethnic groups, although these items are all written in English.

There are 5 items representing India—Agakar, Bouwers, Hein, Kaplan, Singer, and Spreen; 3 representing Japan, i.e., Akimoto, Kawano and Matida; 2 represent "Asia" (Holt and Bateson and Moerdowo); 2 are Caribbean (Courlander and Lekis);

2 are from Israel (Kadmon and Lapson); 6 are on South American materials (Almeida, Dmitri, Garcia, and Lekis); 3 are on Mexico (Mansfield, Mooney, and Sedilla); and finally, 1 on Samoa (Mead). These total 24 items, leaving roughly 69 items more or less.[9]

The 60 remaining clearly identifiable items fall easily into the following classifications: "theoretical" (21—including one encyclopedia); "dance notation" (13 items); "psychology" (2 items); "other European dances, including English" (10 items); "U.S.A. folk, jazz, and Hawaiian" (12 items); "theatre dance" (2 items).

It would be merely tedious to subject the 21 items of a vaguely theoretical nature to closer examination. Suffice it to say that this list includes 5 unpublished manuscripts, 6 articles, 8 books, 1 seminar and 1 encyclopedia. The cited works cover a 44-year span of time, from 1916 through 1960, and there is no indication, either in Kurath's article or in the structure of the bibliography which provides readers with any intellectual connections between them. "Why," students ask, "should we read Boas's book on primitive art?" It is a good question and one which could be asked about any one of these items. I do not mean to infer that students should *not* read Boas's book, nor do I hold with a philosophy of pragmatism regarding the reading of books in general, however, students have a legitimate cause for mutiny, it seems to me, if they do not know *why* they are reading things, especially in these days, when they are often handed an enormous book list which, even for a fast reader would take more time than is given in a usual course length to read.

The picture that one is left with of the field of study from this survey is that dancing, choreography, and studies of dancing can *produce* anthropology or ethnology. This belief is fairly widespread among the uninitiated, and unfortunately it is a misconception, but more of that later. The picture that one gets from examining Hanna's bibliography is somewhat different, but it resembles that of Kurath, because it, too, is a list of books that are basically unconnected except by a few subject headings, some of which are misleading. At the end of his review of *To Dance Is Human* (Hanna, 1979), Powers remarks:

...this book should have been called *To Dance Is Scientific*: all
humanism has disappeared.... Finally in Chapter 9 we are given
future directions and a recapitulation of just about everything that
just about everybody has theorized about the universe—as it potentially pertains to dance research and communications.... In general,
much of what is arrogantly passed off as semiotics is an uncritical
assortment of theories in physical anthropology, archeology, socio-
linguistics, cultural anthropology, communications theory, structuralism, symbolic analysis, etc. *ad infinitum*. Dance is simply stuck
onto these existing interdisciplinary theories as if it were a self-con-
scious appendage. Furthermore, there is a rather naïve assumption
that all these "theories"—if they are that—are somehow accepted
by their respective disciplines as absolute, and that there is an
agreement on just what "semiotics" is [Powers, 1983:51].

A quick glance at the citations under the first heading of Hanna's
book list for dance anthropology students, i.e., *I. General Theory
Relevant to the Study of Dance: A. Communication and Semiotics*
amply illustrates her critic's point. Because there are no annotations
and because the compiler does not explain *why* these books and no
others should be read by students, the list simply appears to be a
polyglot assembly of authors, one of whom (Barthes, 1967) is a
semiotician. One is not sure that the other writers listed would claim
the title—or if Barthes still does. In particular, is Birdwhistell's
"kinesics" strangely placed, both because he is not a semiotician
and because his approach (as originally conceived) was not really
meant to be applied to dancing. However, there is a sense in which
he is concerned with "communication"—but then, so are the writers
at the Bell Telephone Laboratory; why were they not included?

Kinesics was designed primarily to suit a diagnostic model of
events, and much of the published analysis available is attuned to
dyadic (two-person) interactional interchanges. Where more than
two people are involved, the context is usually that of conversations
in clinical or ordinary situations. Theatrical performances, religious
rituals, dramas and opera, are of "collateral interest only" to the
kinesicist (Birdwhistell, 1970:181). One wonders if Hanna really
read Birdwhistell's book, and if she did, then to what purpose? But
then, as far as I can see, this book list has no recognizable boundaries: it is as if each authority figure cited can somehow be

understood in isolation—and usually, from one or two examples of their writings.

Under category *1. D. Cognition, Perception and Emotion— Mind and Body*, the one author who has devoted an entire book to the mind-body problem specifically in regard to the dance is left out (see Best, 1974). Although the philosopher, Merlou-Ponty, finds his way into this list, the only philosopher who has written a volume on phenomenology and dance does not (see Sheets, 1966).

Hanna has told us that this "bibliography" represents material that she thinks that dance researchers should be familiar with and that the field of dance anthropology should encompass. If this is the case, then why does she think that a dance researcher should be familiar with one or two of Kaeppler's writings, but not be familiar with "ethnoscientific" approaches to ethnography in American anthropology, or with Pikean linguistics and discourse analysis? How can dance researchers understand Kaeppler if they do not understand whence the terms "emic" and "etic" arose and what they mean? Similarly, Williams's "Deep Structures" paper is cited, but without accompanying references to (1) Chomsky, (2) Saussure or (3) any reference to aid the user to understand what the usage of formal models of analysis entails. "Deep Structures" (1976a and b) was not written with dance researchers in mind. It is a complex, difficult paper which is highly condensed and which was written for one purpose only: to avoid the possibility of the theoretical structure of semasiology being pre-empted before more extensive discussion and explanation could be published. Williams (1972) would have been more useful to Hanna's intended audience.

Hanna's subject-categories are so general as to be virtually meaningless and together, they present a decidedly over-inflated picture of what is actually available in the literature on the dance. For example, "Symbolism and Ritual," "Aesthetics: Arts and Performance," "Creativity," "Structural Analysis of the Dance," "Politics and Dance," "Transcendence and Dance." Perhaps the compiler used these categories because she *wishes* that there were solid pieces of scholarly work on, e.g., "Transcendence and Dance"? Or, perhaps she wants to set students thinking about the possibility of a combined subject like "Politics and Dance"? One simply does not know. The point is that these subject-categories conflate disciplines, explanatory strategies, theories, and just about everything else. They rest, apparently, on the naïve assumption that "dance researchers" as a group are going to possess the necessary academic and scholarly preparation which might be able to handle works in philosophy, structuralism, socio-linguistics, anthropology, history, and all the rest that the list of citations implies. The fact is that the majority of dance researchers do not have that kind of background. At the risk of making myself even more unpopular in certain circles, I would have to say that a curriculum for a standard dance education, art education or dance "performance" degree—even at a master's level in the United States—does *not* provide the necessary preparation; nor does a "dance ethnology" degree. We have neither the time nor the space to enter into discussions of curricula for graduate degrees in the combined studies of the dance and anthropology in these lectures, but it is a subject that wants examination in the near future, lest we continue to produce bibliographies and other written work that ultimately amount to little more than fantasies.

Apart from all that, most of the subject-categories in Hanna's book list are relatively meaningless, e.g., "Music and Dance." *What* music, *whose* dance, from *which* part of the world? There is no theory about "music and dance" that covers everything in the field of music *or* the dance, but subject-categories like these tend to lead the untutored or the unwary to believe that there *might* be—or that a survey, say, of materials in that combined field might exist. It doesn't, although someone in future might do us the favor of providing such a thing.

Some advances had been made with regard to explanations of the dance and more or less viable methodologies for its systematic study by the year 1976; many of these were not available to Kurath when she wrote in 1960. Sixteen years is a long time in the life of a new field of enquiry, and Hanna cannot claim the excuses that are legitimately to be made for Kurath and her work. Hanna's omission of all but one of Kaeppler's impressive list of contributions, which started in 1967 if her unpublished doctoral dissertation is included, and her omission of Keali'inohomoku's work except for two items, is simply shocking. Blacking (1971) is omitted and Royce (1977) and Williams are not cited.

No bibliography can be "comprehensive" in the fullest sense of that term—or in the librarian's understanding of the term, for in that field it means quite simply that the bibliography (or the holdings of a library) is an attempt to include *all* references, or *everything* which has been written on a given subject. No one blames Hanna because her list is *incomplete*. Many blame her because she excludes the writings of colleagues who not only preceded her in the study of the subject, but who far outstrip her in scholarly ability and contributions. Hanna's book list reminds me in a strange way of a student essay (fortunately the only one of its kind which has so far surfaced), written for an assignment in an introductory course in the anthropology of human movement at New York University in 1981. The paper's title was "Myself and My Society" and it was restricted to five pages in length, with concise instructions regarding an approach to the subject-title. The student's paper began with the sentence, "I am Atman." It proceeded from there through 5 pages of totally disconnected, unrelated statements about the nature of society, god, the world, social science, art, and just about everything else, including the author's cat.

It was necessary to inform this student that I was unqualified to criticize an essay which emanated from Deity, and there is a peculiar sense in which I feel similarly unqualified to criticize Hanna's bibliography—or her books—because they all include a not inconsiderable slice of the scholarly universe, several academic disciplines, and such mighty subject areas as "Communication," "Perception," "Transcendence," "Cognition," "Structure," "Semiotics," and "Politics." In the face of this kind of thing, my world seems very humdrum and mundane indeed. "How," I have asked myself time and again before entering a classroom to lecture, "can I more effectively prepare these students for what they are up against, given the sprawling, intractable nature of the literature on the subject?" "How can I get University librarians to cooperate with me in providing intellectual access to a subject which is virtually 'wide-open'?" "How can the students' expectations be brought into alignment with the realities of the extant literature?"

The role that the librarian plays (or might play) in the development of the subject of combined studies of the dance and anthropology—or any of the other disciplines which have been mentioned—is crucial. Often, the librarian is the only person who controls bibliographic and/or physical access to the items which are needed for study, and if they have taken the trouble to prepare themselves adequately, they are also valuable resources for intellectual access as well. The addition to the reference literature of Fleshman's *Anthology* (1986) should be of enormous assistance to librarians, who may well ask, "what are we to make of all this?" The *Anthology* highlights the *enormity* of the subject, for a start, and each author for this volume was asked to write a bibliographic essay that did something more than provide an unstructured list of books: writers were encouraged to exercise critical judgments—to assess and to evaluate the literature—and while readers may disagree with any given writer, the attempt was made to provide a standpoint from which users might depart if they so wished—or build upon.

Faced with questions from master's and doctoral level students which pertain to research in this area (other than "ready-reference" types of questions), university librarians can simply be honest: that is, let the student know that the present state of reference works for the study of dance and anthropology is virtually nonexistent, and that in many cases, the student is not going to "find answers" to some of the questions that he or she might assume to have been "answered" by someone. They might also attempt to encourage students to recognize the disciplinary boundaries which are involved, and try to discourage them from "random reading" that will, in the end, produce nothing more than a disconnected, ill-begotten hotchpotch of materials that will do them no good whatsoever. I take it that colleagues in library science will understand that by "random reading" I do not mean to deprive the student of the time-honored practice of "browsing," upon which our cataloging systems are largely based.

Sometimes the librarian is the only person who is in a position to inform students about the differences, say, in Humanities and Social Science reference works, and they are important guides, too, into the *further* citations which will help the student go beyond a superficial examination of one available reference work.

In conclusion, I would want to say that I am still basically unprepared to handle comments on the part of students, librarians, or anyone else which might be summarized in the statement: "I can't believe that some of this has actually been written." My response to that has been in the past, "If you don't believe it, then go read these materials for yourself." Or, "If you don't believe that I have given an accurate account of, for example, choreometrics, then read the book and write a review of it yourself." In other words, I would want to say that in general, students of this field could well do *without* a certain innocence and naivete: an "innocence" which assumes that it is unnecessary to exercise critical judgments regarding the bibliographies, book lists, monographs, and such that are available, including my own, and a "naïveté" which dictates that they withhold critical judgment for a time in the nebulous future when they, too, are going to be "experts," and therefore qualified to criticize. I do not know how this attitude develops—I only know that it is there. It is a pity, because through such misguided beliefs, if they have them, students are setting themselves up, as Pocock says, for a posture of "alienation," with the result that the field of dance studies itself becomes alienated from the disciplines on which it must depend and with which it must interact, and this is more than a pity. If continued unchecked, it represents the death of the subject and/or its continued isolation.

Our problem does not consist in having *enough* literature to get on with; our problems lie in the kind of literature that it is, but now, we shall turn our attention to "body languages" and the kinds of language that are typically used about human bodies when they dance, sign, "gesture," or otherwise attempt to communicate through the medium of movement instead of speech.

Notes

1. Specifically I refer to curricular and/or area study distinctions, or to theoretical or methodological distinctions. For example, some works on dances are archaeologically biased; that is, their

methodologies are rooted in archaeological or historical method, and they are, so to speak, reconstructions from documents or artifacts, rather than the results of fieldwork participation and observation using social/cultural anthropological method and explanatory strategies. Both kinds of work are valuable and, in a loose sense, they are both "anthropological," but they are not the same. One wonders, therefore, why they are cited together. What does the undifferentiated listing mean? Over the span of her lifetime, Kurath attempted both kinds of analysis. Two examples are the dances of the Ana'huac (1964) and the dances studied whilst she was an apprentice with Fenton in the field. From a standpoint of research, they are entirely different kinds of work, yet they are listed without comment or annotation.

2. Keali'inohomoku's article, treating ballet as an ethnic form of dancing, continues to be controversial, not among anthropologists of human movement, who would, as she points out, tend to view any form of dancing whatever as "ethnic." But to non-anthropologists (and even some anthropologists) who seem to have vested interests in keeping the ballet separate from the category "ethnic," the idea is resisted, although I have yet to discover the grounds for the resistance. It is as if they believe that we are not "ethnics" too. One of the biggest problems with studies of the dance turns around classificatory and categorical distinctions like this. In a section of her article entitled "Objectives of Dance Ethnology" (Kurath, 1960:234), the author discusses the problem indicated by the notion of treating ballet as an ethnic form of dancing, but she reaches no conclusions.

3. I do not advocate the view that simply because a book is "old" that it is out of date. There are seminal works in every field which continue to be up to date from a theoretical, a methodological or an epistemological viewpoint, even if they were written many years ago. Unfortunately, Sachs's book is not one of these.

4. I am aware that other types of materials, i.e., films, audio and visual recordings and the like are valuable documents, but they are not, in this context, really relevant to the discussion. Moreover, the notion of the use of film in anthropology is a matter of some debate and is outside the scope of these lectures. An excellent

reference, however, is that of Worth and Adair (1972) which includes a structured bibliography of references pertaining to the usage of filmed data.

5. Again, the subject is beyond the scope of these lectures. Suffice it to say that there is considerable interest in the subject (see Farnell, 1984b, for a report on a recent International Conference held in Israel).

6. David McAllister, now retired, is still at Wesleyan and could be reached, but one doubts that he would want to hand this manuscript over for general consumption without considerable revision. It was not really an important paper of his and one wonders why this and the other item on sign language were included in the first instance? One also wonders how students are meant to make the connections between sign languages and dances, apart from the rather obvious fact that they both use movement as a fundamental mode of communication? (see Hart-Johnson, 1984, for full discussion).

7. In spite of the fact that the authors of this work consider it to be a pilot project and not a model, one could certainly use it as a model for a similar work on human danced experience.

8. One is aware of the arguments for representation of multi-language works in a bibliography: to assure the user that significant works are represented. What one protests against is not the argument itself, but its use in dance ethnology literature. How can a user be assured that these works *are* the significant works if the author cannot assess their value either in terms of the different anthropological viewpoints from which they originate or in terms of the thesis of the author's paper? The only message that seems to emerge is that someone has written about dances in another language—an altogether trivial point, surely.

9. There are "69 items more or less" for reasons which should by now be obvious. For example, if Boas's second seminar was ever published, I have not been able to find a record of it anywhere. That means that many of the items listed are lost, and some items, like those of Gillespie are the kinds of items which create the numerical discrepancy.

VIII. BODY LANGUAGE(S)[1]

IN PREVIOUS LECTURES SO FAR, I have given an account of some theories and explanations of the dance, with numerous illustrations, of many influential ways in which dancing has been viewed in English-speaking countries for approximately one hundred years. On the whole, most of the explanations that we have discussed are, for anthropologists of human movement at least, as dead as doornails. Today, these explanations are chiefly of interest only as specimens of the thought of their times, and they are evidence of the rich opportunities that exist to develop alternative explanations, descriptions, and interpretations of the dance.

Only the functionalist writers, of those we have reviewed, recognized the importance of cultural context, and for that, they are owed gratitude. However, the outcome of their efforts in the form of "dance ethnology," "dance anthropology" and the choreometric synthesis that was produced during the late sixties and early seventies in the United States reflected the same kinds of over-arching notions of functionalist integration of societies that single ethnographical accounts had also adhered to, indicating in a small way, a need for a paradigm shift from function to structure (in a Lévi-Straussian sense) perhaps, or a shift from function to semantics; from function to more viable modes of explanation of some kind which would permit new and different syntheses of date, interpretive and explanatory strategies, models, and descriptive language.

The shift in explanatory paradigm in British social anthropology which in a very real sense permitted a small-scale shift in the field of movement studies to occur in the form of semasiology was the shift in the parent discipline from function to meaning. This newer style of anthropology was not a development of older, functional styles of anthropology and it does not point to a theoretical and procedural foundation which emphasizes "meaning" *more* and "function" *less*: it is an anthropology that is rooted in a different conception of people; simply put, a conception of humanity as meaning-makers.

> It was Evans-Pritchard who so crucially stimulated this trend (Pocock, 1971:72), but it is the misfortune of our discipline that his manner of expressing it prevented his offering a more vigourous statement of the fact that what was involved in his dissent was a fundamental disagreement over the nature of anthropology.... Evans-Pritchard's basic contention was that anthropology was not a natural science studying physical systems, but one of the humanities investigating moral systems. Our experiences in British social anthropology since the early 1960's have now provided us with better conceptual resources for stating the contrasts at which Evans-Pritchard hinted, and we are now also far more adequately equipped to see what the opposition involves [Crick, 1976:2].

Because Crick has so ably defined the map of the territory of a semantic anthropology and its relations to historical and theoretical developments in Britain, France, and the United States, I need not reiterate any of it here. It is enough to say that for students of anthropology and human movement, some consideration must be taken of recent paradigms of explanation in social anthropology itself, otherwise the standpoint from which theories and explanations of the dance have been (and will be) presented in these lectures will remain unclear. With specific reference to semasiology, no understanding of it is really possible at any level without some comprehension of the context out of which it arose. Crick's book was published a few months after I had completed a doctoral thesis (Williams, 1975), and as I have insisted that students attempt to understand the intellectual contexts of writers in the past, so I shall also insist that they understand those of contemporary writers in the field of human movement studies.

Most of the books and articles which have been reviewed in past lectures, for example, those of Sachs, Hambly, Lady Frazer, Frobenius, Tylor, Frazer, Harrison, and Darwin, will continue to be read—and they should be—because like early functionalist writings on the dance, they enable students to comprehend the historical and intellectual backgrounds for their more contemporary interests, but they are of little or no value used as guides for current research. That these explanations no longer possess much interest for anthropologists of human movement is due to a number of factors, a few of which I will mention.

First, the disciplines of social and cultural anthropology themselves continue to grow and change, and modern researchers have grown and changed along with them. In the next lecture, I shall review the extant linguistic approaches to human movement, including the East European school of folklore analysis, which stems from the Prague school of structural functionalism; some features of the American "ethnoscientific" approaches, heavily influenced by Pikean linguistics, that has contributed much to Kaeppler's "emic" style of movement analysis; and others, including kinesics (Birdwhistell) and proxemics (Hall), but more of that later.

The single most powerful instrument of change in social anthropology has been the differing views of language that have emerged and the effects which these views have had, both on base-line definitions of humanity and (internal to the discipline) the notions of what "doing anthropology" amounts to. Because of the changing nature of their preoccupations with language (see Ardener, 1971, and Henson, 1974, for more thorough discussion), not all modern social anthropologists now go into the field guided by the notion that they are simply "observing behavior" in the same or similar ways that one might "observe behavior" among language-less creatures, say, chimpanzees.

Ethnography is now regarded by a significant number of social and cultural anthropologists, more as a cooperative enterprise between informants and anthropologist that produces a theory of culture of any given ethnicity. It is no longer the case that an ethnography is a product of a relation between an alleged "objective" observer and the "observed." I do not mean to imply that ethnographies of the latter kind are non-existent, or that all anthropologists agree with me in my interpretations of what a good ethnography is; I merely wish to point out that contemporary and future generations of aspiring anthropologists have the advantages of *choice* in these matters in rather different ways from their predecessors. For an example of the newer kind of ethnography to which I refer which pertains specifically to a form of dancing, read Schieffelin (1976). To students, one would want to say that a reading of this work will be doubly profitable if it is read with a sensitivity a) to the usage of descriptive language and b) to the underlying conceptions of humanity that inform the work throughout.

Older definitions of humanity as "tool-makers," "the imperial animal," the "social," "political," or "economic animal," the "weapon-maker," and such are noticeably absent in Schieffelin's work, and it is gratifying to note that in general, such definitions are gradually giving way to others like "the language-user," "the meaning-maker," "the role-creator and rule-follower." Simplistic though these phrases may seem, stated by themselves in this way, the changes to which they point are profound. The latter set tends towards viewing humanity, not so much as products of their environments, but as a self-defining, self-regulating species who create the cultures in which they exist. Think about it. And think about the differences in explanations of dances, dancing and "the dance" that could arise from such different kinds of conceptualizations.

Second, coupled with changes internal to the discipline of social anthropology itself, there have been the beginnings of a general gradual breakdown of what I think of as hard-core provincialism and ethnocentrism regarding other cultures which may have been aided by the current state of mass-media access to the customs, conventions, habits, and bodily and spoken languages of other peoples. Ethnocentrism, although it still exists and probably always will, becomes ever more difficult to defend. Then too, the appearance of television has drawn attention to purely *visual* modes of communication and to the semantic nature of the human body itself as a symbol in all forms of cultural semiotic in ways that may have been apparent to experts in human movement studies in the past, but which were only dimly perceived, if at all, by the majority of people.

Perhaps the same interest in bodily forms of communication has been stimulated by television as was stimulated in aural forms of communication through radio, such that visual modes of information, knowledge, and expression can now come into their own, so to speak. The concept of "body languages," although greatly hampered by naïve, dictionary-definitional interpretations of popularizers like Fast (1970), is not fully (nor even partially) understood, but the phrase *is* commonly used these days, thus providing both an alternative to the ubiquitous natural science phrase "non-verbal behavior," and a loophole, perhaps, through which a few new ideas about human non-vocalised communication might slip. The notion, for example, that body languages comprise systems of *the same degree of logical and semantic complexity* as spoken languages—although different from them in important ways—is not a new idea to some social anthropologists, but it is not an idea that is widespread enough to be popularly held. Still, the notion, even on that level, is not rejected out-of-hand, either.

For the moment, I should like to illustrate the problem to which I allude through the use of an example of the kind of descriptive language that is used for human movement that is rarely, if ever, examined. In the past, we have limited ourselves, through the influence of "scientific" literature, to the descriptive languages of physiological, anatomical, or kinesiological accounts of human movement and the technical, descriptive terms which are appropriate in those contexts. However, as Harré and Secord so rightly point out, if human *actions* are reduced to gross physical *movements* set in a physiological or biological context, *the significance of the action as part of human social life is lost* (1972:39).

For example: we all know what a hitch-hiker thumbing a ride might look like. Nearly everyone has seen them and experienced them in a variety of ways; perhaps we have hitch-hiked ourselves. Whatever else might be said, we can conceive of a hitch-hiker as a *person* "thumbing" a ride. The action (thumbing a ride) is thus described as a socially and semantically-laden action that is part of a prescribed social set of actions that are rule-governed and language-based. In Fig. 1 is a written version *of that action* in its completeness. In the technical terminology of semasiology, we refer to this as a "kineseme." That term is purely for our own analytical use; the person(s) whose actions are recorded in Fig. 1 probably has never heard of a "kineseme"; probably does not care to, and certainly does not imagine herself or himself performing a "kineseme." No. He or she is "thumbing a ride." Full stop. From the written, recorded Figure, if one can read the script, we can see that in this case, there are two persons involved: two males, who are standing astride their duffelbags on a highway, where a motorcar is approaching them at 70 m.p.h. We can read that their left thumbs are hooked into their belt loops, and that their right arms are performing the action of "thumbing". From the amount of text available to us in Fig. 1, we do not know *why* they are standing there, or where they are going, or if the motorcar stopped and picked them up, or *who* they are: we only know that two fellows are standing at the side of a highway thumbing a ride.

Now, I would ask that readers examine *this* kind of text (and script): "TWO MEN STOOD ASTRIDE THEIR DUFFEL BAGS, THUMBING A RIDE ON HIGHWAY 66." This text represents the situation in linguistic signs. The text in Fig. 1 represents the situation in action signs. The text in Fig. 1 does not *reduce* the actions of the two men to the status of a sign, as Jackson (1983:329) would have us believe, nor does it make the body into an "object of purely mental operations, a 'thing' onto which social patterns are

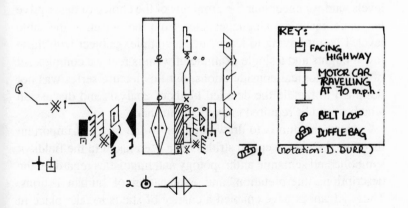

FIG 1.

projected" (1983:329), any more than the conventional language text does. Both forms of text simply describe a state of affairs.

However, when we are told by Birdwhistell that a "macro-kinesic" *explanation* of this state of affairs is something like this: "two members of the species, *homo sapiens*, standing with an intra-femoral index of approximately 45°, right humeral append-ages raised to an 80° angle to their torsos, in an antero-posterior sweep, using a double pivot at the scapular-clavicular joint, accomplish a communicative signal," we are justified in saying, "no." That is not what we see. We see *persons* thumbing a ride.

Descriptive language that is appropriate and necessary to a functional anatomical explanation of the hitch-hikers' movements and posture is both necessary and useful in certain contexts and for certain purposes, but the same kinds of description and explanation are inappropriate and unnecessary in other contexts.[2] Moreover, that stretch of the technical terminology of functional anatomy does not "explain" anything: in particular, it explains nothing about the socio-linguistic or semantic properties of the *action* involved. We do not see each other, respond to one another, nor do we conceive of ourselves and others in human social life in these ways. Thus, we encounter the problem of *people* and descriptions of people (in contrast to organisms or animals or machines) even at the simplest levels, and we encounter the problems of the choice of descriptive language, technical languages, etc., from the outset, at the same level. I regret having to leave such a complex subject with these few thoughts and a single example of what is really a complex set of methodological considerations, but this lecture series was not designed to handle the detailed kinds of analysis and discussion which would be required to explicate further.

Here, the aim is to draw attention to the fact that important theoretical and conceptual strides *have* been taken in the fields of symbolic and semantic anthropology and linguistics regarding the description, interpretation, and explanation of human actions. These advances have enabled a change of status to take place in scholarly thinking with reference, e.g., to the sign languages of deaf culture (see Stokoe, 1960, 1980 and Frishberg, 1983 and their bibliographies). Signing is no longer thought of among those familiar with the literature in the field to be essentially "mimicry" or some kind of intellectual poor relation to conventional spoken languages.

The emerging interest in, and research into, the problems of body languages has also provoked a renewed and continuing interest in the nature of the language-using creatures—human beings—who produce such systems. This renewed interest can be discerned by noticing a shift of emphasis in many contemporary works to an "agentive point of view"; that is, to a point of view which stresses the role of the "agent," (or "actor" or "dancer," or "performer"—the person who creates) as well as the spectator's or observer's points of view. The creator is now thought to be at least a partial determinant of meaning, no less than the spectator or "watcher" in visual modes of communication (see Williams, 1980c for more thorough discussion).

Many older studies of the dance and the explanations that were put forward to rationalize the activities of signing, dancing, and the like, are now seen to be seriously flawed both because they make too strong a contrast between dancing and ordinary movement, and because some authors, in their attempts to define, especially dancing, were prey to a number of definitional fallacies, a more thorough examination of which is to be found in Best (1978:88–90ff). Any single definition of "the dance" or a succinct definition of "dancing" is going to make a number of presuppositions and beg a number of questions. Anthropologically speaking, I would want to say that there are exactly as many succinct definitions of "dancing" or "the dance" as there are cultures or ethnicities, and groups of people within them, that support them.

It is this cultural diversity, richness, and variety that anthropologists of human movement would seek to preserve, along with the theories of what dancing *is* and *is not* to each ethnicity which constitutes the "folk anthropology" of the activity. However, each of these local definitions and the unique cultural practices that go along with them are to be understood, in semasiology at least, as single modes of bodily communication among all of the structured systems of human actions that an ethnicity may possess.

A number of considerations enter into a sophisticated understanding of "body languages" as a subject to practicing professionals, of which the following ten are perhaps the most significant.

It is important to keep in mind that "dances"—when and where the term is appropriate—are merely sub-sets of the larger synthesizing concept of "body languages":

1. Every physiologically and mentally "normal" person (also defined and definable only by the ethnicity under investigation) in any linguistically recognizable group, acquires from childhood the ability to make use of, both as a "mover" and a "watcher," the system(s) of bodily communication that comprises a circumscribed set of movements, called "actions," resulting from the habits, customs, conventions and such that are established in his or her ethnicity for the semantic (the meaningful) usage of the body, the person, or of groups of people. By means of these, together with the spoken language(s) available, the individual is able to impart information, to express feelings and emotions and to influence—and be influenced by—the actions of others. In particular, he or she is able to comport himself or herself with varying degrees of intimacy, friendliness, hostility, indifference, enthusiasm, or withdrawal (or comparable values, as "expressed" or "held" within the culture towards persons who use the same body language or set of structured human actions.

2. Different systems of bodily communication constitute different "idioms," "dialects" or systems of meaningful actions, be they connected with the political, economic, religious, legal, military, domestic, mythological, artistic, private or public aspects of the ethnicity. These are what anthropologists of human movement understand as the different "sets" of body language(s) within a given ethnicity.

   The degree of difference that is required to establish a totally different idiom of body language cannot, perhaps, ever be stated precisely, yet we can recognize both different usages of the same body language (based upon criteria established by samenesses in the rule-structure) by two or more individuals and we can also recognize two or more systems that use similar counters or units of body language in entirely different ways (see Williams, 1981 and Puri, 1981a, for more complete discussion).

No two people move or behave in exactly the same ways, thus it is possible through a sophisticated conception of "body language" to (1) recognize the actions of friends and family, for instance, but we can also (2) keep distinct the stylistic differences of strangers separate, recognizing idiosyncratic usages, even though they are using the same idiom. In these cases, we are dealing with dialectical or idiolectical differences within the same body language.

3. In general, different systems of movement communication are recognized as different "idioms" of body language, or different body languages entirely *if they cannot be understood without specific learning by both mover(s) and watcher(s)*, although again, precise limits of mutual intelligibility are hard to draw and belong on a scale rather than on either side of a clearly drawn dividing line.

Substantially different systems of bodily communication which may impede, but do not prevent mutual comprehension are referred to as "dialects" of an idiom, as e.g., in the idiom of American modern dance, several dialects exist in the form of "techniques" (the folk term used by modern dancers to describe what it is that they learn). These are known currently as Graham technique, Limon, Humphrey-Weidman, Hawkins, Cunningham, Tharp "technique," and others. In order to describe substantially different movement patterns of a body language, say, Bharatanatyam, with reference to dances, or the different movement patterns of a signing system, e.g., Plains' Indian sign language (hereafter referred to as PSL) American Sign Language (ASL), the Indian *hasta mudra* system of gestures, an Anglo-Saxon system of manual counting, the idiom of ballet, or American ballroom dancing, the term "idiolect" is sometimes used to describe the different movement patterns of a single actor or agent within an idiom.

4. Normally, people acquire the components of their native body language from their parents or guardians and the extended family groupings on out into peer groups, and other groups, from infancy. Subsequent "second" body languages are learned to varying degrees of competency under various conditions, through change of location to another ethnicity, perhaps, or through contact with members of another ethnicity and such.

   Through learning and mastering of an idiom of dancing, signing, certain rituals, and the like, an individual not only learns to "perform" his or her own culture, but can learn to "perform" elements of other cultures as well, whether these elements consist of military arts, dancing, ceremonies, or what-you-will. But, just as a significant majority of people on this planet remain monolingual in a conventional language sense, the majority of people in the world remain "mono-somatic"[3] with reference to body languages as well.

5. Body language, as conceived of by semasiologists, is "species-specific" to human beings. Indeed, that is why the term "semasiology" is used to distinguish this approach from more general semiotic approaches[4]—because of the irrevocable ties that are believed to hold between body languages and the neurological capacities, including all of the language-using and meaning-making faculties, of the human mind. Other creatures have the capacity to move, certainly, and they can monitor their movements on a restricted level, but humans possess the capacity to *act*, to monitor their movements according to preconceived notions of behaving and what it is and *means to "behave."* Humans have *conceptions of acting*, thus it is a serious error to reduce the notion of body language in the human social context to meaningless physical movement and leave it at that (see Williams, 1982:173 for reasons why this often happens).

6. The most important single feature characterizing human body languages (which includes every individual human body language) as against the organized movement be-

haviors of other sensate animal or marine life (i.e., every known mode of animal communication) is its infinite productivity and creativity. Human beings are unrestricted in what they can act upon and what they can move, act, or dance about, although there are certain intransitive structures of local Euclidean space, movement of the body, and locally-experienced time which impose constraints on a structural level.

7. No area of human experience is accepted as generally incommunicable through some system of human body language, although there exists great cultural variety in the systems available in each ethnicity for the communication of experience through body languages and some ethnicities may be richer in these forms of communication than others. Human body languages also provide the opportunities for change and adaptation to new fashions, new concepts, or new modes of thought. The pre-existing set of moves; the existing conceptual structures which cause any given body language to hang together, as it were, are capable of including innovation and change, which is another feature that likens them to conventional spoken languages. Colloquial and formal usages are evident in body languages, and it is possible to recognize "grammatical" and "ungrammatical" elements (see Myers, 1981, for discussion of phrase structural aspects).

8. Body language interacts with every other aspect of cultural life in human societies. As Best puts it: "Human movement does not symbolize reality, it is reality" (1978:87), although human action signs can be devised which "symbolize reality", many action signs *are* themselves the reality.

9. Like the concept of human "culture," human movement is not itself a material phenomenon. Human movement is a cognitive and semantic organization of a material phenomenon; the human body (or bodies) in a four-dimensional space/time. Just as there is a sense in which "culture" can be seen as a cognitive, and ultimately mean-

ingful, organization of material phenomena and the external environment, so human actions in any of their manifestations are cognitive, and ultimately meaningful, organizations of bodies and the structured spaces in which they move.

10. Act*ing*, like danc*ing*, or mov*ing* or perform*ing* in the human realm is essentially the termination, through actions, dances, movement systems, and/or performances, of a certain kind of symbolic transformation of experience (see Williams, 1972, for further discussion). Where the more familiar terminal symbols of speech are expressed in words, sentences, and paragraphs, the less familiar terminal symbols of movement are expressed in action signs, action utterances, and an impressive array of structured systems of meaning that include deaf-signing, dances, martial arts, liturgies, games, ceremonies of all kinds, manual counting systems, systems of greeting, and many others. We merely reiterate an anthropological truism when we say that from the outset, we are considering a global array of human body languages, an astonishing variety of systems.

Some reflections, however brief, on the ten descriptive paragraphs above seem necessary: for a start, there is intra-cultural variation as well as inter-cultural variation in meaningful systems of movement such that some comprehension of the socio-linguistic facts of these constitutes an important first step towards a semasiological understanding of human movement. Simply put, if the *code* of the body language is not understood, then the empirically perceived messages will be misunderstood (see Pouwer, 1973:1–13, for further comment). To facilitate understanding of what human movement *is*, we must recognize the non-material conceptual boundaries that are placed on it, and this is why rather elaborate theoretical and methodological means are required whereby we can assure ourselves and others that our analytical redescriptions are both accurate and truthful (see Williams, 1976a and 1976b for fuller discussion).

Human movement study is not "simple." It may turn out that

in the end, it is more complex than spoken language. Each individual user of a body language may have a unique, personalized model of what his or her movement experiences and manifestations consist. Each user may or may not be cognizant, even of other models of actions held by other members of other cultures, far less those of his or her own segment of the ethnicity. But, it is just here that neo-Durkheimian preoccupations with the relation between individual and society become important.

They are important to trained investigators insofar as they are couched in the Saussurian notion that in separating body languages from individual manifestations of "moving," "acting," "dancing," we are at the same time separating (1) what is social from what is individual and (2) what is essential from what is more or less accessory or accidental. "Body language" is not a function of the individual mover, actor, or dancer. While it is true that many movers, like most speakers, behave *as if* only a limited number of ways of acting exist, this does not alter the fact that it is a trained investigator who, as a result of discipline and extended study, thought and reflection, plus a far greater than average visual and spatial awareness, is able to transcend these particular models and who is able, in a clear and elegant manner, to describe, interpret, and explain to others of what these systems consist. It is necessary, in other words, to acquire the means whereby one can study the codes of body languages *minus the acting*,[5] otherwise human movement studies will remain condemned to the prison of the level of *la parole*, or to a slavish allegiance to "commonsense" interpretations which, like earlier commonsense interpretations of the shape of the planet (as flat instead of spherical) and much else, are decidedly lacking.

It is probably clear by now that the theoretical standpoint from which I speak is not a "theory of the dance" *per se*. Rather, it is a theory of culturally and semantically-laden *actions*: a theory of "body language" if you will. It is not a "theory of movement" comparable to, say, kinesiological theories about measurements of latent kinetic energy and muscular movements that are susceptible to quantitative, metric mathematical models of interpretation and explanation, because these proceed, both from a different definition of humanity and from a philosophical doctrine regarding "objec-

tivity" that begs the question of human, self-reflexive understanding.

Movements, in particular action sign systems, are so complex
that they require non-metric mathematical modes of explanation—
a requirement that was perceived by many anthropologists, notable
among them Leach (1961) and Lévi-Strauss (1966), but which
status-holders in the discipline did not flesh-out with reference to
human movement studies. Instead, they suggested a rich untapped
field of investigation which has resulted in semasiological theory,
a theory that postulates a set of organizing principles that consists
of certain invariant features of (1) the human body, (2) the space in
which it moves, and (3) certain transitive and intransitive features
of hierarchy of human choice, such that we can say that there are
elements of body languages that are in complementary distribution
throughout the world, and so do not, at one level, conflict with one
another, but from a level of empirically perceivable data, may seem
to conflict with one another.

A developed conception of body languages encourages the
view that "unity" or "universality" of any kind in human movement
does exist on a structural, but not on a semantic level of manifestations, and that a different conception of "unity" will manifest itself
after we comprehend the variations in ordered relations between
individual systems of movements and their contexts. There is a
significant body of research in hand that can be offered to support
these contentions, but much more is needed before comprehensive,
sweeping generalizations are made to the anthropological community or to the public at large. The point is that this kind of research
is possible only if one sees variety, including the sometimes incompatible ideologies and beliefs perceived in the systems "on the
ground," not as deviations from an assumed "norm," or as positive,
latent, or dysfunctional functions of some kind, but as manifestations of intricate sets of rules that, at base, can be seen to reiterate
a linguistic truism: the medium, in this case, movement, *is* the
message.[6]

At the simplest level of enquiry, one might start by asking,
"how would the people of some other culture (or of some segment
of my own culture), or the users of some other body language,
expect me to behave if I were a member of that culture or wanted

to use their body language?" This is a good question with which to begin an anthropological investigation into a system of meaningful actions because to learn and then to explicate the rules of the body language of "X" is to provide a few beginning answers to that question and at the same time lay the groundwork for a low-level theory of that body language which is based upon how the folk themselves conceive of it.

The whole of the anthropological process does not stop there, of course, and because modern styles of doing anthropology are self-critical and self-reflexive and point towards a different consensual notion of what "objectivity" amounts to,[7] the emerging rule-structure which is being learned by the anthropologist is constantly compared with the known rules of his or her idioms of body language, thus the "knowledge" that eventually emerges from the investigation is basically of a self-reflexive nature.

It is thus that the description of the rules of "X" body language (dance, signing system, or whatever) itself constitutes a "theory" of that culture or of some part of a culture, because it represents *the conceptual model of organization* used for the body language(s) of that culture. We validate such theories by an increased ability to communicate, and to anticipate successfully how "X" people would expect us to behave if we were members of that culture, plus other modes of theoretical and procedural validation offered by the discipline of anthropology that, owing to the general nature of these lectures, will not detain us here.

The complexity of the subject of body languages is difficult to comprehend, mainly because they are taken for granted by their users in many of the same ways that spoken languages are taken for granted. That is, a body language, like a spoken language can be used to live out a people's lives, to communicate and all the rest, permitting individuals to operate in the world with more or less success without any awareness whatever of the rule-structures that govern the usages of the body language or its connection with the culture as a whole, far less the metaphysics of self that is involved.

Where spoken languages are known to require translation across cultures, the popularly held belief among many peoples of the world is that their body languages do *not* require translation. Chapman states the matter succinctly and well:

It will be clear that the possibility for misjudgment and misinterpretation of the kind that I have described is very great in "non-verbal" matters. Character, emotional states, and changes of mood, are judged and expressed according to a great diversity of non-verbal "semantic" phenomena, including bodily posture, gesture, stress or rapidity of pitch in speech, frequency or rapidity of movement of the body, avoidance or seeking of bodily contact, and so on. All these things are semantically loaded, rule governed, and category based, and vary greatly from culture to culture. There is not however, any serious popular conception that such things require "translation" from one culture to another. Most people, when faced with an unintelligible foreign language, will recognize the need for "translation"; non-verbal "language" gestures, and generally semantic use of the body, of the person, or of groups of people, are not usually granted the same status as language in this respect. Translation will not be thought necessary. In general, an "English-speaker" will interpret the gestures of, say, a "Breton-speaker," a "French-speaker," or a "Gaelic-speaker" according to an entirely "English" set of rules of interpretation, without feeling any need to go to the bother of "translating" [Chapman, 1982:133-134].

Not only does the rule-structure of spoken English differ significantly from the rule-structures of other spoken languages, the role/rule structures of British body language differs significantly, even from American forms of body languages, Canadian or Australian body languages—and these co-exist, presumably, within the same domain of the same linguistic group. Yet, we treat the differences in body languages as insignificant, as somehow "unimportant," perhaps manifesting a steadfast refusal to give up or change commonsensical, received notions about the nature and complexities of human behavior, as if its humble, everyday character were so well-known and understood that it requires no explanation beyond those already assigned to it.

Unfortunately, in the immediate present, there are those among anthropologists and other investigators into the subject of human movement to whom it would seem that "the body" is the last stronghold of a kind of cultic searching out of some "experience" which is behind or beyond appearances; a kind of "real reality" which, as far as I can determine, is a-historical, a-linguistic, a-cultural, a-conceptual, but which is nevertheless, "there," which is based on "embodied experience" and "bodily praxis"—both extremely problematical, trendy terms which, under scrutiny, do not hold up very well. Some authors (the example which springs to mind is Jackson, 1983), are convinced that the recent emphasis on semiotic, linguistic approaches to the study of movement are merely over-intellectualized and that such approaches either subjugate or ignore the somatic and the biological.[8]

This kind of argument nearly always plays heavily on the term "praxis," which at this writing is an "in" word that originated, I believe, with Marxist writers. As far as I can make out, it has been used for some time as a marker for attempts to put all the strands of phenomenology, Marxism, Wittgensteinian philosophy, and much else into a new synthesis. The "praxis" element is tied to an old Marxian concept concerning a "real" world of the work of laborers and the lower classes in economic systems. "Bodily praxis" partakes of this flavor, for in one of its definitions, at least, it designates common, everyday movement—movement that can be "shared" and "sensed" in a different way from e.g., "ritual movements" or "danced movements" and such.

I mention this kind of thing in passing, because it seems that we are asked to view the body as if there were some kind of "bodily logos" present, which is a kind of bodily "mind" with which we are supposed to become acquainted at the expense of our other notion of mind (see Sheets-Johnstone, 1983, for a fully developed argument for this kind of notion and Varela [1983] for a criticism of the position), or else we are to conceive of the body as some sort of mystical event which is capable of providing us with an equally mystical communion or "shared experience" which partakes of the "real reality" that is meant to be the culmination of this kind of search. Jackson says

> While words and concepts distinguish and divide, bodiliness unites and forms the grounds of an empathic, even a universal, understanding. This may be why the body so often takes the place of speech and eclipses thought in rituals ... whose point is the creation of community.... And, because one's body is "the nearest approach to the universe" which lies beyond cognition and words, it is the body which in so many esoteric traditions forms the bridge to universality, the means of yolking [*sic*] self and cosmos [Jackson, 1983:341].

But, enough of that kind of thing.

Humor often provides interesting insights: leafing through the kinds of magazines provided for airline passengers' light reading and entertainment, one begins to find articles about the disparities that exist between our received notions of the universality of body languages and actual cases, like that of an American English teacher and her experiences in Japan:

> I thought I could always rely on hand gestures and signs when the going got rough.... But I quickly learned that they never worked as well as I had hoped. None of my hosts knew my sign language. One time when I pointed to my chest with my forefinger to indicate 'me,' I was shown to the bathroom because to the Japanese that same gesture means 'I want a bath.' The Japanese point their fingers to their noses to mean 'me' (Simmons, 1983:107).

One wonders if this teacher, or her many counterparts throughout the world, would have believed a semasiologist who could have told her that this would be the case; that she probably does not understand the body languages of her own culture very well, far less those of another. The same teacher *expected not to understand Japanese spoken language*, but she expected to understand and to be understood with reference to body languages. She is not alone.

The same article suggests Morris *et al.* (1979) as a guide to further comprehension; a questionable suggestion because of the naïveté with which this author approaches the complexities of the subject (see Puri, 1981, for review). Old ideas and fixed mental sets regarding any subject are difficult to change, however, and because body languages, like spoken languages are intricately tied to notions of self-identity, political identity and cultural identity, it is as if we thought that to really learn something about them is going to destroy us in some peculiar way. No matter how hard people continue to resist the notion that body languages require translation, the fact remains that they do. Body languages are not "universal," nor are the dance forms that arise from them. It is quite another thing to say that body languages (or dances) are to be found universally throughout the world.

Many dancers know this (although they might not know that

they know it), especially those who have tried to become proficient in more than one idiom of dancing. Just one item of interest regarding this theme is the phenomenon of "naming" that goes on in many professional companies: nearly everyone is familiar these days with the necessity faced by Alice Marks (Alicia Markova), Patrick Kay (Anton Dolin) and Edris Stannus (Ninette de Valois) and others, to change their names to Russian and/or French names, during a time when it was believed that native-born English men and women could not dance as well as their European or Russian colleagues. No studies have been done on this, but it is an interesting potential area of research, for reasons which will soon become clear which have to do with proficiency, status, and identity.

Lay audiences are frequently surprised to discover, along the same lines, that Spanish names "authenticate" or "legitimize" American performers of Flamenco dancing and body language or Indian dancing and body language. Many other examples could be given. The point is this: it is entirely possible for a non-native "speaker" (i.e., performer) of a body language to become so proficient in a particular idiom that he or she is acceptable to native performers as "one of us"—even to the extent of representing the ethnic group in an "ethnic performance" setting. As dancers are well aware, this level of accomplishment involves more than simply learning the movements involved: a non-Gypsy Flamenco dancer could not perform in that context if he or she did not also *speak* Spanish, enabling him or her to converse, sing the songs connected with the body language and such.

What is interesting is that in a *body* language context (in contrast to strictly spoken language applications) non-native performers of a body language will often be looked upon as frauds or cheats (or, if that is too strong, then as questionable or suspect), where a non-dancer who is a fluent speaker of the conventional language, or a musician, will be applauded for the ability and skill that he or she displays. The only explanation that I can offer for this lies in the history of theories of the dance and human movement, where, sadly, we do not find thorough-going examinations of the myths that enthrall the field of study, such as can be found in the field of linguistics regarding the same kinds of myths that once surrounded sign languages, but I will discuss these in more detail later on.

All of these considerations raise interesting and pertinent issues concerning the notions of "blood" and "birth" as against "adoption" and the capacity to learn, and they point to the central place that studies of body languages might play in the "innateness arguments" that preoccupy philosophical anthropology today. Further to the point: there was a time in the history of western spoken language studies (generally known as the period of philology) when the majority of linguists thought that if, for example, the sound [e] (the "phone") occurred in three or four different languages, that at some level, there *must* be a similarity of meaning. Early semasiologists (*circa* 1877) argued that this was not the case, that where two words may seem to be phonetically linked, semasiologically, their connection is likely to be improbable. Words, or "phones" may indeed *sound* the same across two or more languages, but it cannot be assumed that therefore, they *mean* the same things. Exactly the same thing is true of elements of body languages.

In an illuminating and pioneering book for its time, Wundt (1973) pointed such things out, but his work has been virtually ignored by modern movement and gesture theorists. It is the case that human movement studies have lagged far behind conventional language studies, not only because of the problem of literacy, but because of the putative 'universality' of the semantics of human actions. The current renewed interest among linguists in gesture can probably be attributed to Stokoe (1960), whose work was the original impetus behind changing the status of sign languages from a complex classification of "non-verbal" behavior to the status of a language (or languages) proper.

Despite such progress over the last three decades in the field of linguistics, the majority of human movement theorists still believe that an "eme" of movement, for example, the hand position used for thumbing a ride ( ), if seen to occur in two or more systems of body language (i.e. as the mudra "sikara" in Bharatanatyam; as a substitute for the verbal expression "right on" in the body language of the streets of New York; as "thumbs up" or "thumbs down," possibly surviving from the body language of the Roman Circus—and other usages) *must* point to a similarity of *meaning*—of semantic content. Modern semasiologists argue that this is not the case, that where two gestures or two utterances of body language may seem kinesiologically linked, semasiologically, their connection is improbable (or simply false) given the results of specific research where actual comparisons have been made (see Hart-Johnson, 1983; Farnell, 1985; and Puri, 1983)

Since these lectures are meant primarily to concern the dance, we may well ask at this stage of the discussion "what are we seeing when we see a dance, if it is the case that we are not seeing a great many things that we thought we saw?" Are we, when we see a dance, seeing a set repertoire of genetically programmed movements that are comparable to the courting or mating displays of birds, perhaps, or chimpanzees? Are we seeing *symptoms* of the dancer(s)' internal states, or are the empirically perceivable moves to be understood as *signs* that represent something else: Are the actions that we see *symbols* in a logical (and not wholly psychological) sense that express the choreographer's and the dancer(s)' knowledge of human thought, feeling and experience? These are interesting questions, and questions which might lead to more reasonable theories of the dance out of the maze of unexamined mythology that surrounds the subject.

It is worth quoting Langer's succinct formulation of an answer to the "symbol" question because her distinctions between the logical and psychological properties of non-discursive symbols with reference to the dance provides considerable aid in clearing one's mind of so many received ideas about it:

> As soon as an expressive act is performed without inner momentary compulsion it is no longer *self*-expressive; it is expressive in a logical sense. It is not a sign of the emotion it conveys, but a symbol of it; instead of completing the natural history of a feeling, it denotes the feeling, and may merely bring it to mind, even for the actor. When an action acquires such a meaning, it becomes a gesture....[Langer, 1942:134—italics supplied].

What this means is that when we see a dance, what we are seeing is not a *symptom* of the dancer's feelings (see Langer, 1957:7), but a symbolic exposition of the composer's and participants' *knowledge of* human feelings and experience, manifested through their culture-specific forms of body language.

Philosophers tell us that we can say at least two things about symbols: we can say that a symbol, "x" means an object (concept or idea) TO a person or persons, or, that someone means an object (concept or idea) BY the symbol. In the first instance, meaning is created in a *logical* sense. In the second instance, meaning is created in a *psychological* sense. Many dances in western culture and elsewhere in the world use symbolic action and gesture *only* in the first, and not in the second, sense (see Hart-Johnson, 1983, for fuller discussion). The importance of Langer's distinction cannot be overstressed.

Both mediums of human expression, movement and spoken language, share the function of meaning, for that is what any symbolic system is about, and in the human realm, meaning is based on conditions that are logical, although it is also true to say that "meaning" has both logical and psychological aspects. In semasiology, the logical aspects are stressed, if for no other reason than to redress a balance of discourse that has for a long time (in English-speaking civilizations, at least) only enjoyed interpretations that have stressed the psychological aspects of meaning. Semasiologically, utterances in either medium, sound or motion, must in the first place *be employed as* signals or symbols, then they must be signals or symbols *to* someone or to a group of people in order to qualify as signals or symbols—both of which subsumed under the general designation, for analytical purposes, in this kind of approach, as "action signs."

In other words, until a movement is employed as a sign or symbol, we believe that it is "natural." When movements are employed as signs and symbols, and when they are not specifically symptomatic of internal states or disease, they are cultural. That is to say that the movement has undergone the initial transformation which makes it "body language," thus we may say that dancing is essentially the termination, through actions, of human, symbolic transformations of experience. The terminal symbols of speech (that which we hear, or see on a page) are expressed in words, sentences, and paragraphs. The terminal symbols of a dance (that which we apperceive visually), either in performance or on a printed page, as in a Labanotation score, are expressed in gestures, poses, movements phrases.

Let me be very clear about this; the movements manifested by an individual having an hysterical fit, an epileptic fit, or convulsions of some kind are *not*, by this definition, *danced* movements. They are neither signal nor symbolic. They are symptomatic of internal states or conditions. In general, they are conceived to be movements that are made where human agency and the faculties of intention are either temporarily or permanently absent. To determine whether movements are either signal or symbolic requires knowledge, first, of the system of body language(s) of the ethnicity concerned. To talk of "movement" with no accompanying distinctions being made as to the system of movement involved, whether it is signal or symbolic—and how and in what ways it is signal or symbolic—is simply a nonsense, or, more charitably, such talk is simply composed of commonsensical, unexamined observations that "something" has (or is) moved, or does move, and we have every right to persist in asking, "so what"?

The "same" movement or movement shape may be symptomatic, signal, or symbolic and a great deal hangs on the differences among these distinctions, whether they are used, methodologically, at the level of the investigator's "home-made models" of the ethnicity under investigation, or whether they are used later in the analytical redescription. For example, a thumb in a baby's mouth may be symptomatic of an inner condition of hunger or a sign of some physiological or psycho-biological condition for which sucking is a necessary accompaniment. A thumb in an adult's mouth may be a symptom of regressive behavior, but a thumb-nail flicked against the teeth in Italy (or a thumb pulled quickly out of a sucking position in the mouth in Milwaukee, Wisconsin, USA) is a socio-cultural sign of abuse and may lead to a fight. The baby's thumb-sucking is a natural sign which is perhaps symptomatic; an adult's thumb-sucking in our culture is clearly symptomatic and the

Italian's thumb gesture is a socio-cultural sign of impending violence.

A dancer who employs the Italian gesture of abuse in a dance is not completing the natural history of his or her feelings, making the gesture under the stress of momentary compulsion. The dancer makes the gesture because it has been employed *as a symbol* in the dance to convey a *conception about* violence, perhaps, or a concept of an abusive person or group of people or something of the kind. Peter Janiero's masterful handling of movements and gesture for the Puerto Ricans in the well-known American musical comedy, *West Side Story* is an excellent instantiation of what is meant. In that context, the gestures became vehicles for the *conceptions of* people, objects, attitudes, or situations. Exactly the same things could be said of the rude, abusive gestures incorporated into the Ga dance, *Kpanlogo*. These gestures, which out of context might invite immediate and perhaps violent responses, do not do so in the context of the dance because they are no longer "signal," but "symbolic" in a hard sense, and everyone knows it.

The interesting thing is that everyone "knows" these kinds of things at some level, just as everyone knows when spoken language is used in a symptomatic, a signal, or a symbolic way, yet knowing of this kind is of very little use to the investigator who attempts to decode the system and find out how it is put together. Although he or she may rely on informants' accounts of a given system of body language, it will not be at the level of the folk model of the body language that the paradigmatic or panchronic rules and laws governing its usage will be found. It is not my purpose in these lectures to enter into the intricacies of analytical and methodological practices connected with semasiology, however, so we will return to the main themes of the general examination.

In preceding lectures, we have examined many theories of the dance in which the notions of "origins" and "expression" were emphasized. Methods consisted mainly of reconstruction, especially by adherents of the German *Kulturkreislehre*; attempts to manufacture chronologies of the dances of the world through circumstantial evidence. Behind these chronologies (the most developed recent examples with reference to the dance being those of Curt Sachs [1937] and Roderyk Lange [1975]) lies the notion that there exist peoples who are ethnologically older than all others: any people who lack the arts of agriculture and who are "sedentary," as e.g., the Eskimos, some Australian Aborigines, some North American Indian tribes, the pygmies and pygmoids of Africa and Asia, and the peoples of Tierra Del Fuego.

These peoples are thought to belong to a "primitive culture" which then developed along three independent, but parallel lines: matrilineal and agricultural, patrilineal and totemic, patriarchal and nomadic, each with their own habits, customs, dances, rituals, and general outlook on the world. We can still see shadows of these ideas in Lomax's synthesis of the world's dances, where instead of *real* comparison we are offered a synthesis of "dance culture" that is based on observations of filmed data and inferences from the data regarding the relative "primitiveness" of human be-ing throughout the world. As always, the real complexities of the rule-structures, composition, and organization of the dances were ignored and the conclusions that we are offered are, to my mind, not only tendentious, but based on unsound premises.

I believe that, in spite of their many differences, most anthropologists today would agree that it is useless to seek for a *primordium* for the dance because it would appear that all evolutionary schemas for the dance—all attempts to determine a locus of "origin" and to postulate alleged serial stages of development—proceed along purely idiosyncratic and fairly ethnocentric lines, apart from the fact that social and cultural anthropology have moved away from such origins arguments and the rather simplistic cause-effect relations that were implicit in these unsupported theorizings. Modern social anthropologists seek rather to understand and to reveal constant relations of time, space and motion that are comprehensible through the study of dance cycles and ritual processes and their rule-structures.

In nearly all of the theories we have examined, excepting those of functionalism, it was assumed that "we" were at one end of the scale of human "progress" and that "they," the so-called "primitives" were at the other end. "We" are logical, rational beings. "They" are pre-logical and pre-rational and living in a world of dreams and make-believe about which they dance and perform ceremonies. It is not my intention here to unravel the rationality debates (cf. Wilson, *et al.*, 1970), for that would require several lectures as a subject on its own. I merely point to the fact that thinking along these lines has changed drastically, largely owing to the efforts of cognitive anthropologists (see Tyler, 1969), symbolic anthropologists (see Dolgin, Kemnitzer and Schneider, 1977), ethnoscientists (see especially Kaeppler, 1985, 1986, and 1972 with regard to the dance), plus the work of semioticians and semantic anthropologists (see Williams, 1986, for an overview regarding human movement studies).

Interestingly, some of the older, ethnocentric kinds of thinking still exist in the dance world itself in the form of a taxonomic distinction that is widely used among dancers, teachers, choreographers, critics, and dance historians, i.e., that of "ethnic" dancing, which simply distinguishes "their" dancing from "ours" (see Durr, 1986, for a recent evaluation of Keali'inohomoku [1980a], and the value of seeing the ballet, too, as an "ethnic" form of dancing). In erecting a category "ethnic dance" which does not include western forms of dancing, we have simply slavishly repeated an unexamined process of treating history, not as a dynamic process from which we can learn, but as a repository of "dogma" which we tediously repeat.

"Primitive dance" can include many kinds of things, of course, but it is usually conceived of to be "simple," "crude," "earthy," "powerful," "fundamental," "primal" (whatever that means), and last but by no means least, "animalistic." This dancing is thought to be comparable to primitive dancing *in situ*—but it is not, of course. Would that I could suggest cogent books or articles comparing, for example, a form of pseudo-Caribbean dancing with that of one of the peoples of West Africa, the Caribbean, or Polynesia, but I cannot. These books have yet to be written.

Such hard-headed, down-to-earth comparisons are nowhere to be found in the literature on dancing, probably because they would have to be by definition too iconoclastic with reference to the many myths that surround, not only the origins of dancing, but the universality of dancing, the "primitiveness" of dancing, the monolithic nature of dancing and all the rest. The "ethnic dance" category is particularly damaging, because while the ballet and American modern dancing may be thought to be on the superior end of a continuum of "progress," these forms of body language in turn become "primitive" as modes of expression contrasted with other human social activities that are thought to be "rational" by comparison, say, to speaking.

The past few years of research have shown that such denigrations of dancing were, and are, simply ill-formed misconceptions, but such categories tend to serve certain educational, political, and ideological purposes, the discussion of which would be peripheral to the mainstream of this lecture. Let me simply say that to my mind, no one, American, English, European, Canadian, or Australian, is exempt from the discredit that accompanies these kinds of thinking (for cogent discussion, see Barish, 1981). Marett was not alone in his beliefs that "savage religion" was not *thought* out, but *danced* out, nor was he alone in his belief that actions and movements precede thought.

Harrison (1913) was not alone in thinking that the dance was "inchoate" and without form, nor was Havemeyer (1916) alone in thinking that Plains' Indian dancing preceded Greek drama. Lowie (1925) shared his beliefs that Freudian psychology could account for forms of social life other than those of upper middle-class Viennese people. The myths that prevail, both about dancing and signing, are legion: some of them have been made explicit by Hart-Johnson, who enumerates five that are widely believed by thousands of people:

1. Sign language is universal...

2. Reality must be word-based....

3. Signs are glorified gestures....

4. Sign language is "concrete"....

5. ASL is ungrammatical....

As this author points out, both ASL and Martha Graham technique (hereafter referred to as MGT) and American Modern

Dance in general "...have suffered because of these myths. With regard to ASL, they have been explicitly stated and explained *as myths* by linguists; with regard to MGT and American Modern Dance, they are found explicitly and implicitly in much dance literature, *not stated as myths but as truths*" (Hart-Johnson, 1983:198). She suggests that instead of reading "Sign language is universal....," we read "MGT is universal...."; instead of "ASL is ungrammatical....," we read that MGT (or any other dance technique) is ungrammatical, and so on.

The message is clear: these myths must be explicitly stated and *explained as myths* by anthropologists of human movement, otherwise the field of study, specifically with reference to the dance, is doomed to remain in the quiescent state in which it has existed for the past century. But, just as the discredit is only fairly distributed among many disciplines and shared for the disproportionate amount of nonsense which has been written about the dance and theories of the dance, the "credits," so to speak, for advances in our thinking about the dance and ritual practices must also be distributed and shared, for there have been theoretical, methodological, and other kinds of advances made, although these are undoubtedly less well known generally than are the approaches to the study of the dance that we have previously examined. Therefore, it is to more contemporary theories of the dance (and study of the dance) that we will now turn, beginning with the Prague school of linguistics and the East European school of Folkloristics, bearing in mind that we now enter a different world of conceptualization and understanding than we have encountered up to now.

Notes

1. Harrison (1986) points out that Fast's book has sold more than two-and-a-half million copies. That means that two-and-a-half million people have bought oversimplified, basically misguided ideas of what "body language" comprises. One is in complete agreement with scholars who "...consider Fast's book superficial—and even misleading..." and who "...feel uncomfortable with that label" (Harrison, 1986:79), although I have been forced

to continue to use it because I cannot think of a better alternative, and the term "body language" in semasiology was taken up originally as an alternative for "nonverbal communication" (see *supra*, p. 67, note 1).

2. See Williams, *et al.* (1981) for a more developed discussion of this and other elements belonging to the analysis of action signs.

3. This is an awkward term, but is meant to convey the notion that only one body language is learned by the majority of people.

4. An explanation of this is given in Williams (1986b) with particular reference to Sebeok (1979).

5. It cannot be overstressed that by saying this, I do not suggest *reducing* all human movement study to the study of "codes." I mean to imply that a study of acting *alone* will not suffice.

6. Long experience has taught me that the notion of "rule(s)" as it is understood by philosophers of science, linguists, and semantic anthropologists is fairly difficult to grasp for students who have nothing to go on save the commonly understood application of the term as in lists of prohibitions for conduct in dormitories and the like or merely as "orders" or "commands"). The meaning of "rule" with reference to body language is far more complex than that and deserving of an entire lecture on its own.

7. See Best (1985) for cogent discussions of "subjectivism" and "objectivism" and the fallacies and misconceptions pertaining thereto.

8. Rorty (1979) would deny all of this, saying that the tradition of this kind of search is sterile. It is also necessary to say that in a private communication, Jackson said that he did not mean to imply that his statement meant "anti-intellectualism" or that intellectual approaches to movement study were "bad".

IX. MODERN THEORIES OF HUMAN MOVEMENT

IN THIS NEXT TO LAST LECTURE, I am aware that I have a difficult task confronting me: that of suggesting what lines of thought might be followed by those who are interested in pursuing investigations into some dance form, sign language, martial art, or "ritual." Are there existing works that might form the basis for cumulative study? What is available for students who want to proceed, not from private interpretations of what anthropology or the dance are, but from some standpoint which might interest, especially social anthropologists or scholars of high calibre from other disciplines? How might one proceed to provide systematic analyses, interpretations and explanations of dancing that avoid some of the more obvious errors of reasoning, judgment, and scholarship which form part of the common heritage of inherited literature on the subject? Before getting on with an examination of more modern theories of human movement, including the dance, the following comments seem relevant.

I do not deny that *the* dance, *a* dance, or the act of danc*ing* can be studied in many ways, nor do I deny the fact that dancing is an activity that can be interpreted differently according to disciplinary interests. I do not deny that people who dance do so for many reasons. The important point is that they *have* reasons for the beliefs and intentions which produce their forms of dancing, thus I do deny that dancing is usefully seen as an undifferentiated 'behavior' that is separate from the language-using faculties of the total person. I do not deny that dances may be accompanied by emotional and/or spiritual experiences or that such "feelings" may constitute an important feature of the performance of dances, and I certainly do not deny that danced ideas and practices are directly associated with ritual actions and with practical actions. I simply affirm that whatever else they may be, dances are human sociolinguistic phenomena.

What I *do* emphatically deny is that "the" dance is explained by any collection of observed facts about one, two, or more dance forms, or that "the dance" is explainable from procedures which begin with simple dictionary definitions. I also deny that the traditional Darwinian-universalist position, which treats movement and behavior (including the dance) as something that is prior to and independent of human intentions, beliefs, or socio-linguistic contexts, provides an adequate theoretical framework from which we may proceed towards comprehension of that which *people* (not chimps, bower-birds, dung-beetles, dolphins, or scorpions) are doing when they dance, but as I will revert to this subject in detail in the last lecture, I will say no more about it at the moment.

I hold that it is not sound social anthropological method to seek for the origins of dancing or its essences because those lines of thinking not only do *not* deal with the many cross-cultural problems and semantic predicaments (foremost among them the notion of "translation") that continuously arise, they do not enable us adequately to deal with several important ontological and epistemological questions that, as I have attempted to point out in the first seven lectures of this series, conspire to bedevil us at every turn. Just one of the issues to which I refer turns around the question of whether it is possible to maintain a positivistic *qua* behavioral notion of *passive observation* with regard to the study of dances, rituals, ceremonies, and such.[1]

Unless we wish to limit ourselves to that period in general scientific history preceding ours which can be characterized as the period of belief in the non-disruptive observer who existed in a mechanical universe of empty spaces filled with particles of matter, we cannot ignore the paradigm changes in science itself, nor can we afford to ignore the language revolution that has so deeply affected every sphere of thinking in all walks of life in western cultures. Modern social anthropology, together with post-Newtonian physical science, deals with relations—not with "origins" and "essences" in any case. Insofar as they can be explained at all by social/cultural anthropologists, these facts must be interpreted and explained not only in relation to the many other facts which are external to the given dance itself (in connection with which it forms a system of ideas and practices that are associated with it) but the facts internal to the dance: its composition and organization. The idiom of body language that the dance represents must also be interpreted and explained.

In the relation of an individual case of "a" dance to the totality of any given ethnicity's experience, a characteristic recurs which can always be established where the problem is to define a "whole" that is not merely the sum of its parts, but is *a systematic totality arising from the relations of the parts*. As Cassirer pointed out:

> Logic traditionally distinguished between "discrete" and "continuous" wholes. In the first, the parts precede the whole, and independently of the connection into which they subsequently enter, are possible, and distinguishable as independent pieces. The "element" of the continuum, on the contrary, is opposed to any such separation; it gains its content only from relations to the totality of the system to which it belongs, and apart from it loses all meaning [1953:248].

An investigator is thus required—if he or she is to attempt to speak to scientists at all—to seek out a comprehensive and fairly sophisticated set of procedures whereby such complex socio-linguistic phenomena as dances can be approached.[2]

As examples of the kind of thing we are involved with here, I would instance (1) any *single* dance from any stable tradition in the world, or (2) any attempt to distinguish, for analytical purposes, the dance (derived from the infinitive "to dance," i.e., the act, not a party) from ordinary or practical actions. To try to understand "dance" (used with no preceding article or without an "ing" ending in English) as an idea in itself; *what* it is, or the *essence* of it, is a hopeless task. Dancing, "a" dance or "some" dances become more intelligible when they are viewed, not only in relation to other rituals, ceremonies, exercise techniques, games, and the like, but also in relation to other systems of manifest cultural belief—as parts of a system of thought—for it is the case, first, that dancing, as it is understood by the investigator's own culture may not exist in the given ethnicity under consideration, or, if it does, it may be the result of entirely different historical and sociolinguistic developments. Bear in mind, here, that I believe these assertions to be as true of an English, American, Canadian, or Australian investigator working in "other cultures," as they are of, say, a Japanese, African, Samoan, or Indian (either variety) anthropologist working in England, America, Canada, or Australia. Second, the study of any single dance in isolation from the rest of the ethnicity to which it belongs makes about as much sense as does the study of one isolated example of the oral or written poetry of an ethnicity in isolation from the rest of the language.

A non-specialist [3] seeing a new dance, rite, or exercise technique for the first time is often at a loss as to how the empirically observable successions of movements or the relationships of the agents should be understood. Considered by themselves, a sequence of danced actions is comparable to a sequence of utterances in an unknown conventional language—the actions, like the sound images, only become intelligible when the sequences are divided by meanings. If the danced sequence is unknown, there are few, if any, clear-cut divisions in the sequences, just as there are few clear-cut divisions in the acoustically perceivable utterances of an unfamiliar spoken language or sign language to someone who does not understand it.

Understanding is impossible if only the substantive aspects of the action signs that are represented are considered, but when the meanings and the sign functions of the sequences are known, the significant elements of the system begin to detach themselves one from the other. The apparently shapeless, chaotic successions and simultaneities begin to break themselves into units, thus *coherent units* begin to emerge within the context of the larger whole. Notice that I have not said that the successions of movements in all cases will conform to a pre-conceived notion of "units of movement" that the investigator may have learned somewhere from a teacher, a textbook, or from the ethnography of another danced form. The interesting thing about dancing, sign languages, and all structured systems of human movement is that *any* conscious spatial differential connected with any bodily part (or combination of parts) or *any*

spatial dimension (or combination of them) *may form a unit,* but
the same differential or dimensional usage may constitute an entirely different unit within the context of two different rites or
dances.

> ...just as the game of chess is entirely in the combination of the
> different chess pieces, language is characterized as a system based
> entirely on the opposition of its concrete units. We can neither
> dispense with becoming acquainted with them, nor take a single step
> without coming back to them; and still, delimiting them is such a
> delicate problem that we may wonder at first if they really exist
> [Saussure, 1966:107].

Similarly, the body language game of, say, the ballet dancers
in the ballet Checkmate[4] lies entirely in the combination of the
different role/rule relations of the characters and, coincidentally, in
what those characters do while they are dancing. An idiom of body
language is based entirely on the oppositions of *its* concrete units.
Exactly the same things could be said of any dance, rite, ceremony,
or exercise technique and such anywhere in the world, but nothing
at all is to be gained by viewing these language-like phenomena as
"overt behaviors" in the same analytical and explanatory modes
that are used by investigators who undertake studies of the overt
behaviors of, say, Makak monkeys or chimpanzees.

Unlike human body languages, systems of animal behavior
and their accompanying limited ranges of communicational signals
exist within tightly circumscribed biological and genetic constraints,[5] both with reference to what may be communicated and to
which individual specie-members. Speechless creatures' communicational systems do not incorporate displaced references, the
ability to communicate about things and persons outside of spatial
and temporal contiguity, nor do they include metaphor, metonymy,
linguistic reflexivity, and all the paraphernalia of the human mind
that is tied to the uniqueness of specifically human concepts of
person and to the usage of person-categories. In other words, we
cannot say of our furred and feathered friends that spatial points of
reference are points of application for linguistic predicates (see
Hampshire, 1959).

I will only draw passing attention again to the extraordinary confusions, especially apparent in the literature of dancing, that arise because of the lack of any real reflection regarding the nature of investigative contacts between human investigators and other sensate species of life (ethology and physical anthropology) and human investigators and other human beings (social and cultural anthropology). The problem, simply stated, is that of a science in which the human observer studies a human subject, rather than a non-human subject, and we identify such considerations in modern anthropological discourse under the general rubrics of "reflexivity." With regard to primates, Ardener (1977) has provided us with substantial evidence that primate vocalic utterances (called, by some, "primate phonetics") are *not* human phonetics. It can be asserted with equal assurance, that *primate kinetics are not human kinetics* (see Williams, 1986b). Human dancers have conceptions of what they do. Moreover, human dancers, unlike bees or chimpanzees, can talk back. All of this amounts to saying that we have to account for the facts of dances and all other structured systems of human actions in terms of the totality of the ethnicity and of the wider societies or national entities and linguistic groupings to which they belong insofar as that is humanly possible in each single instance.

None of this will be new to trained social and cultural anthropologists. Perhaps, to them, it simply amounts to tedious repetition to say that we must attempt to understand systems of human movement in terms of what Marcel Mauss called *le fait total*. Yet, I also believe that they, perhaps more than anyone, will be struck by the paucity of cogent writings on the subject. Of the several hundred publications produced in any given year in social and cultural anthropology, only a handful, if that, take the dance as their subject. I am delighted to be able to say, however, since it was only through the study of social anthropology that I was finally able to realize the many significances of a lifetime's preoccupation with five idioms of dancing, that there are signs of a renewed interest in the subject not only on the part of practicing anthropologists, but linguists as well—especially those who are concerned with deaf culture.

For anyone interested in modern modes of anthropological analysis to fail to respond to the challenge of language automatically deprives them of entrance into the current field of relevant discourse.[6] Nearly all of the works of modern researchers, whether in anthropology, ethnology, or folklore, are closely connected with developments in modern linguistics. For example, thoroughly to comprehend Kaeppler's *emic* analysis of Tongan dance, students must be acquainted with certain basic notions concerning Pikean linguistics and the historical and methodological connections between these and modern ethnoscientific approaches in American anthropology. Knowledge of Birdwhistell's *kinesics* requires correlative understanding of some of the technical developments and advances made in the field of linguistics since the 1930's, because kinesics can superficially seem to be so similar, especially to semasiology, that students are sometimes puzzled about why the two theories developed as separate entities. The surface similarities in these two approaches tend to mask deeper, more fundamental epistemological and ontological differences. In fact, of the three approaches mentioned above, Kaeppler's and Williams's approaches are more compatible with each other than either of them is to kinesics or to the work of anthropologists, like Bateson, who advocated a "culture-personality" approach to the study of social phenomena. Faced with such complexities, students tend to wonder, "where do I start?"

The Prague School of linguistics is relevant to the three approaches mentioned above—and to any other linguistically-based approach —as a general background for two main reasons: first, for its importance in the period immediately following publication of Saussure's *Cours*, owing to the fact that many of its characteristic ideas, like those of Saussurian linguistics, have been taken up by other schools of linguistics and because, with specific reference to the dance, the Hungarian school of dance studies (but one segment of the East European School of Folkloristics) has developed highly sophisticated research models, methods, and an analytical style that is based on structural-functional types of explanation and description taken directly from the Prague School.

Second, the Prague School's notion of "distinctive features" in phonology and the later development of an approach to the functional analysis of syntax has greatly influenced theories of human movement in some theoretical contexts. With reference to the Hungarian school, these have been summarized by Kürti (1980), thus what follows here will simply take note of some of the highlights of this approach. Restrictions of time and space prevent detailed examination, not only of structural-functional styles of linguistic analyses of the dance and movement, but of other major theoretical orientations as well. In any case, detailed exegeses on my part are inappropriate in general lectures such as these because intelligible discussion of any of them would require students' knowledge of the sources.

Since this course of lectures assumes no prior knowledge (or very little) of that kind of in-depth knowledge, I can only point out that dance researchers who, for example, cannot explain the differences between using a linguistic *analogy* for human movement and a linguistic *model* with reference to the same data, will be "sent back to the drawing-board," so to speak. Similarly (using examples now from many years of teaching experience), if students attempt to convince me that they know of what Kaeppler's considerable contributions to the field really amount to, but they are unable to explain her usage of the term "emic" with reference to the opposition "emic/etic" in which it is included, then one is justified in saying that their assessments of Kaeppler's work—whether "positive" or "negative"—are immaterial and irrelevant. Researchers, like dances, can also be torn out of context, subjected to superficial criticisms and misunderstood generally, thus I would want to say that young investigators who want to use Kaeppler's work as a model should first emulate the care and responsible attitudes that she brought to such study herself, and they should tell themselves that they do not understand Kaeppler at all if they try to understand her in isolation; out of the context of American ethno-science, and out of the context of her contemporary colleagues and so on.

Similarly, Williams's concept of the "action sign" and the general semasiological point of view, based upon an application of Saussurian ideas to movement instead of speech, cannot be comprehended without coincident knowledge and understanding of Saussurian linguistics, because the approach presupposes some understanding of fundamental Saussurian notions: *la langue* and *la parole,* the principles of "arbitrariness," "synchrony," and "diachrony," "panchrony," the concept of the linguistic sign, i.e., the relations between *signifiant* and *signifié,* "valeur," and the original Saussurian definition of semiology.

Curiously, I have met even advanced students who did not seem to see (or know) how and in what ways this theoretical approach differs from (and to what extent is incompatible or compatible with) the school of folklore studies that is presently headed by Dell Hymes at the University of Pennsylvania.[7] Birdwhistell (also at University of Pennsylvania, but now retired from the Annenberg School of Communications) establishes his relations to the field of linguistics in several ways, but makes it clear that he relies " ... on the observations of Smith and Trager, modified by discussion with Hockett and McQuown, and strained through [his] conceptions which are, at least in part, the result of kinesic observation" (1970:7).

In an earlier lecture (see *supra,* pp. 16–17), I alluded to the problematic character of bibliographies prevalent in the dance field, that include disparate items of writings, all of which require additional readings for their understanding. There is a sense in which I emphasize the same point here: that is, there is no "one" methodological formula that over-arches, even the four linguistically-based approaches listed above, far less one that includes these and other, non-linguistically based methodologies and theories. It is worth saying, therefore, that Kaeppler's and Williams's approaches are based on linguistic *analogies,* and Birdwhistell's is based on an application of linguistic *models.*[8] I know of no published piece of writing that clarifies this point with reference to the dance and the application of Hymes's socio-linguistic approach. Even among three comparatively compatible views there exist important, underlying differences, and make no mistake about it—the differences in these cases are, perhaps, more important than the similarities.

Because kinesics is primarily concerned with an application of a model, Birdwhistell can postulate a 'macrokinesic' level of explanation that, in the end, views human "behavior" as a "kinesic stream" that is somehow independent of, and prior to, human contexts, beliefs, and intentions. He can thus lapse into functional anatomical descriptions of phenomena like "thumbing a ride" with no apologies (see *supra*, pp. 182–183). The *emic* theorist, or the semasiologist, or the researcher who, like Sherzer (1982 and 1983), subjects movement materials to discourse analysis cannot, because they see a strong analogy between the properties of conventional languages and body languages. Writers who are concerned, as is Bastien (1985), primarily with the *semantics* of physiology and biology in terms of folk-models of body concepts, also cannot resort to functional-anatomical explanations of data.

Time and again, students go wrong because they are unaware of matters like these with reference to superficially compatible approaches, or, I have known a few who took the line that such matters were better left to "experts" and that at some level, all these researchers were "really talking about the same things" anyway. They go even farther wrong when they are faced with less compatible approaches, for instance, that which is outlined in " ... the summary of the Darwinian-universalist tradition in Hinde's *Non-Verbal Communication* (1972), [or] a focus of the psychological literature dealing with the human body in Fishers and Cleveland's *Body Image and Personality* (1958), [or] a résumé of the phenomenological-philosophical literature on the subject in Zaner's *The Problem of Embodiment* (1971)" (Polhemus, 1978:10). I will revert to the themes of differences among these identifiable schools of thought regarding human movement later on when I discuss anthropological and non-anthropological studies of the subject. For now, we will turn to the Hungarian school of movement analysis, one of the East-European group that is centrally informed by a Prague School approach to phonological analysis in linguistics.

In Hungary, the scientific study of dance forms is referred to as "dance folkloristics" and the field of study developed during the decade of the 'fifties, when serious study of the dances was undertaken on any kind of large scale for the first time. The International Folk Music Council (IFMC), an organization that is strongly supported by third-world and East-European countries, has been largely responsible for publishing ongoing research and for keeping alive a sustained interest in the work of dance scholars. For those who are specifically interested in Polish, East German, Czechoslovak, Rumanian, Yugoslavian, Bulgarian, and Hungarian dances, the publications of this organization are useful, starting with a syllabus of "foundations" for the type of research that these scholars do (see IFMC syallabus, 1975). There is also available now the work of an American anthropologist, Diane Freedman recently graduated from Temple University, on Rumanian materials. Although more work has probably been done by researchers and scholars on the dance by East Europeans using a linguistic approach than has been done elsewhere, both the language and the political barriers between these countries and the west are formidable. A few things have broken through: probably the best known publication to English-speaking students is that of Martin and Pesovar (1961), which clearly sets out their style of "motif-morphology" and its connection with phonological analysis reminiscent of traditional descriptive linguistics.

> Based on this linguistic model, motivization (the process itself is referred to as 'motif-morphology' in the Hungarian School) became a working premise for dance folklorists not only in Hungary, but among other Eastern European scholars as well ... . The initial studies in Hungary only analyzed dance to the smallest compositional unit, the 'motif' which is similar to a 'morpheme' in linguistic analysis. Later studies stressed the importance of existing smaller movement units that would be akin to 'phonemes'. By the beginning of the nineteen-seventies the whole system of morphological methodology was worked out and an internationally accepted terminology was invented [Kürti, 1980:46].

For those who are interested in this style of analysis, and the applications of a descriptive linguistic model to dance materials, Kürti's article is invaluable because it is thorough in relation to one dance, the *Pontozo,* and it gives a clear indication of how Labanotation is used by these scholars.

It is appropriate here to mention a group of six essays in a volume entitled *The Performing Arts,* edited by John Blacking (1979), written by Petrosian, Mladenovic, Zhornikskaia, Sikharulidze, Anjelic, and Comiçel, that were reviewed by Kürti (1980). Since we possess so few articles that have been written in, or translated into English by scholars from East European countries and Russia, the essays are significant as examples of the thinking about the dance that comes from a relatively unified approach different from that of most western-trained scholars, some of which have been created by a desire on the part of these peoples to organize cultural materials that are closely tied to their ethnic identities and to their unique cultural expressions.

> Movement and dance are very complex, highly symbolic phenomena that vary from individual to individual, as [the preceding] analysis of the five versions of the *pontozo* would clearly indicate. Just like 'primitive dances' were described in the nineteenth century as 'frenzied', 'wild' and 'trance-like', Hungarian dances suffered similar treatment in the sixteenth and seventeeth centuries and earlier. Only in our time have some of us come to understand that the dance, together with art, social structure, religion, oral literature and ritual, exists as a truly cognitive product of the human mind, and presumably projects humanity's capability for symbolic communication.
>
> It is simplistic to assert that this type of research is the only method capable of dealing with dance. Nevertheless, the Hungarian School has gone much further toward sophisticated understanding than seems to exist in other parts of the world. With this in mind, I hope that by advancing the linguistic model outlined here I have presented an accepted structure of analysis that others might find useful in cross-cultural investigations in the anthropology of human movement [Kürti, 1980:55].

Any attempt to treat modern theories of human movement, including the dance, from the standpoint I have so far adopted—that of semantic anthropology—presents a problem that cannot be solved easily, if it can be "solved" like an arithmetic sum at all. On the other hand, I risk oversimplification because the modern/approaches that I have so far mentioned are anthropological, in that their protagonists and the architects of the theories (Martin and Pesovar, Kaeppler, Birdwhistell, Hymes, Williams, plus Hall, the originator of Proxemics, and Kendon, who emphasizes a concept of "gesture") are all anthropologists. The theories and methods that they have generated or that they use, i.e., "folkloristics," the "emic" approach to the dance, "kinesics," "semasiology," "proxemics" and

Kendon's gestural approach, respectively represent, not merely
theories or methodological formulae whereby movement might be
analyzed, but whole bundles of presuppositions, procedures, ethnographic materials, and analyses that are as complex as any
"school" of anthropology say, functionalism or structuralism. Regarded in this way, this lecture is about current, rival, social and
cultural anthropological theories of human movement, including
those of Gell (1985), Sherzer (1983), Blacking (1977), and the
writers in Benthall and Polhemus (1975).

On the other hand, these approaches (with the possible exception of folkloristics) represent a kind of disciplinary commitment,
established from the beginnings of social and cultural anthropology, to deal with gesture and movement that had its roots in
Tylorian preoccupations with sign languages and all aspects of
human culture. Seen in this way, we cannot regard the theorists who
generated or implemented these differing anthropological approaches as a random aggregate of individuals who happen to be
interested in "dance," "ritual," "cermony," "gesture," or "spatial
relations" for each of these individuals had intellectual predecessors, and while many of them may have discarded, amended or
modified much of what their predecessors thought and said on the
subject, the theories are a result of their interactions with received
authorities, plus their different social origins, roles, and circumstances.

It is because of this that I regard the above-mentioned approaches to be very different from the non-social/cultural anthropological tradition exemplified by Hinde (1972), who, in an edited
collection, has gathered together writers who carry on a tradition
established by Darwin, arguing that bodily expression is a cross-
cultural universal and that it is transmitted from generation to
generation through biological inheritance. Although Hinde has
included some more sociologically-minded authors in this collection (from social anthropology, Leach), their contributions seem
oddly placed, because it is highly unlikely that Leach, anyway,
would defend the biological argument with reference to human
communication, unless he has recanted at some point from the
earlier position he took in published writings on ritual and human

communication (see Leach, 1966). Polhemus's collection (1978) although a required text for students of the anthropology of human movement, is prefaced by remarks that strike a decidedly strange note to some of us, because he says that

> Except in the writings of anthropologists such as Mary Douglas, this Durkheimian-based approach (stemming from Hertz, Mauss and the Annee Sociologique tradition) to the study of the human body has been largely ignored [1978:9].

Unless one interprets these remarks to pertain strictly to the human *body,* and not to the movements it makes, one wonders to whom Polhemus refers? Other works that refer to the human body *and* to its movements were excluded (see Williams, 1986:176–177 for further comments and review).

In fact, what was ignored in *The Body Reader* was the entire ethnoscientific approach and Kaeppler's work, East European folkloristics, and semasiology, all of which are based on a social level of experience, presupposing the notion of the Durkheimian "social fact," with particular emphasis on that most primary of all human social facts: language-using. All three approaches mentioned above are centrally concerned with the relationships between spoken languages and body languages, as is that of Kendon (1983), and they are all rooted, one way or another, in similar apperceptions about movement as their French predecessors, namely, that a purely physical or biological understanding of the human body and of its movement is insufficient to explain the majority of aspects of human life and forms of life.

Fisher and Cleveland (1958) offer students more understanding of the psychological *qua* phenomenological approach in outline form, and Zaner's work (1971) addresses some of the philosophical problems that have arisen over the notions of "embodiment" and "incarnation." Polhemus's volume, apart from its significant omissions, which also include Best (1974 and 1978) seems to provide students with a range of articles from widely differing sources, some of them anthropological, others that are not. It is difficult to comprehend just how it is that the novice student in the field is meant to deal with them, or how they are to organize them into a coherent, systematic structure that might support the research that they may wish to undertake. I unashamedly take the part of actual or potential students here, because they are the "consumers." They represent a significant portion of the other half of the academic publication exchange, and they are frequently both the unwitting and unwilling victims of the "publish or perish" syndrome.

Very few collections of essays or bibliographies have been written with them and their needs in mind, thus I would want to stress the fact that the importance of such collections as Polhemus's, Blacking's, or Hinde's, in the end, lies in the fact that they represent compendiums of *different modes of thought* regarding the subject of human movement studies. The question that students might address themselves to at first is this: "Are all of these theories simply rival accounts of the same things, or are they theories about different things entirely?" Thus, I refer back to a point made in the opening lecture: it really *is* necessary to conceive of the field of human movement studies as an intellectual territory which has many accounts of what human movement consists and how it should be studied.

Modern students are faced with a wide variety of theories of human movement (including the dance) and because of this they discover very quickly that *they have some significant choices* to make as they leave the world of alleged "common knowledge" regarding the subject and enter into the world of educated discourse and research. The clearest measure, to my way of thinking, of the quality of a student's training in this field, regardless of the parent discipline to which it is tied, is whether or not the student is aware of these choices and of the alternatives that are available. One of the interesting things about students' present plight (whether they start out in ethnomusicology, anthropology, folklore, museum studies, dance and dance education, or 'performing arts' departments) is that, were they to undertake studies in any other subject, they would know beforehand that rival theories, outmoded theories, blatant popularization and all the rest exist. They would expect to have to sort it all out, but they could also expect some of the more traditional aids in this project than are available to them with regard to the subjects of movement and the dance. It seems to come as a shock to many students to discover that a) there are so many theories of the dance and movement generally, and b) like "African dance," the notion of "the" theory of dance, or "a" theory of human movement is illusory. Comparatively little has actually been figured out about this field of study, and expectations of a pluralistic intellectual universe of discourse are certainly more realistic, if less appealing, than other kinds of initial expectations which are geared towards the hope, at least, that there is a unified body of work available.

Some of the published accounts of human dancing and the explanatory frameworks which support them are compatible, and some are not. Metaphorically speaking, some lead to Budapest, some to Turkestan, and to other places on the map. Nearly all theories of the dance, sport, art, ritual, ceremony, or what-you-will either explicitly or implicitly include some narrative ordering of human life and theories of the nature of human be-ing, plus direct or indirect implications and inferences regarding "human nature" *writ large*. The latter-day status of such theorizing, or of the traditions and academic disciplines that support them is not something that can be predicted, but they are all modifications and re-interpretations of previous theories. My purpose here is to try to deal mainly with those which have been developed by social and/or cultural anthropologists, thus it is to Birdwhistell and "kinesics" that we will now turn.

"Kinesics" is a term that refers to a body of knowledge that, given its stage of development in 1970,[9] is prior to a field of study that the author would have liked to refer to as "kinesiology." Kinesics is based upon "psychiatrically oriented interview material" and this kind of data is offered as the most appropriate for the practical application of kinesic investigations because psychiatrists and psychologists have a tradition of awareness that body motion and gesture are "…important sources of information regarding personality and symptomatology." Kinesics draws heavily on Deutsch's posturology (1947, 1949, 1952). An impressive array of the works of investigators in psychology is invoked and used, including early work on communications models (see

Deutsch, C. W., 1952). The reasons for this interdisciplinary connection is plain: "[F. W. Deutsch's] is one of the clearest statements
concerning the diagnostic value of body motion and posture"
(Birdwhistell, 1970:180). Birdwhistell was aware that body motion
and gesture can be seen to have symptomatic, signal and/or symbolic values, and he was primarily interested in the symptomatic or
diagnostic interpretive mode of investigation. In fact, he stresses
that kinesics has only minimal interest in formalized systems of
gestures:

> Theatrical performances, whether centering around dancing,
> drama, opera, or the mime have long emphasized the role of gesture,
> particularly in its stereotyped or conventional form. Integral to
> every religious ritual, the gesture is stressed in all novitiational
> training...which evidences the international character of the interest
> in gestures, and their *proper* performance. *Most of these writings
> are of collateral interest to the kinesicist* [1970:181—italics sup-
> plied].

In other words, kinesics was designed primarily to suit a diagnostic
model of events, and much of the published analysis available is
attuned to dyadic interactions.[10] Where more than two people are
involved, the social context is usually that of conversations in
clinical or "ordinary" situations.

     Given the kinds of strictures and constraints that the architect
of kinesic theory himself placed on kinesics, it comes as a surprise
to find kinesic theory underpinning a modern theory of theatre
semiotics (see Elam, 1980, and see *infra*, pp. 265-267 for further
discussion), because kinesics was not developed for use in that
context and it is ill-suited indeed for the purpose. It may be that
kinesic theory has been amended during the past fourteen years, but
if it has, it is not available for us to examine in publication, thus we
are forced to rely on what has been published in the past. Birdwhistell developed a theoretical and methodological departure from
studies that had preceded his work, stressing personal activities and
individual performances, hoping that kinesic research (in the larger
context of communicational research) would provide a methodology, an annotational system and a set of "norms" against which
prior, basically intuitional systems that had been offered could be

checked. He seemed convinced that significant statements concerning the behavior of particular individuals had to be based on an understanding of the patterns of intercommunication of more than one actor, postulating that the significance of *individual* variations in behavior could only be assessed when the range of permissible *group* variation had been established, and with these assertions, plus the many that he made about *learned* patterns of behavior, he seems to remain most clearly the cultural anthropologist. He concludes that bodily motion and facial expression are strongly conditioned, if not largely determined, by the "socialization process" in particular cultural milieux, and while he affirms an "ultimate biological basis for all human behavior," he is convinced that, given the vast range of possible combinations of muscular adjustments, each society *selects* certain ones for recognition and utilization in the "interaction process."

A careful scholar, and certainly the outstanding pioneer in anthropological research on bodily communication, Birdwhistell considered his work with kinesics to be a natural follow-up of Sapir's intuitive insights:

> Gestures are hard to classify and it is difficult to make a conscious separation between that in gesture which is of merely individual origin and that which is referable to the habits of a group as a whole...we respond to gestures with an extreme alertness and, one might almost say, in accordance with an elaborate and secret code that is written nowhere, known by none and understood by all [Sapir, 1949:556],[11]

Birdwhistell is never unclear in his published work about what he means:

> While Efron's experimental approach (1942) has not been pursued by other investigators, Labarre (1947) and Hewes (1955, 1957) with quite different emphases have directed the attention of field workers to the importance of recording and analyzing the gestural behavior of human groups. However, the most important anthropological contributions to the development of the study of body motion as a communication system have come from the work of Mead and Bateson (1942). Their concern with the relationship between socialization and communication, assisted by considerable skill

with and appreciation for the camera as a research instrument, set the stage for the development of kinesics as a behavioral science. Not only has their field work provided a body of materials for cross-cultural study, but their insights into the systemic quality of the communicational process have prevailed upon the writer to take up his profitable association with the linguists [Birdwhistell, 1970:183].

The underlying assumptions which guided Birdwhistell's work in the study of movement are set out on p. 159 of his book and repeated on pp. 183–184, so that it is not necessary to draw them out here. Similarly, it should not be necessary to set out the terms of Birdwhistell's meta-theoretical premises for extended analytical interpretation and explanation, because he does that so well himself, i.e., "The initial descriptive statement is totally inadequate for purposes of extended analysis" (1970:177). He goes on to say that *any* event, like his example of thumbing a ride, constitutes a "communicational transaction" that takes place in the contexts of social groups and social rituals that affect the lives of the persons involved. "Thumbing a ride" together with all such actions are "pieces of microculture whose natural history we may attempt to relate" (1970:177). Much of the explanatory control at the highest meta-levels of explanation of kinesics is given over to biology and to natural history. The same could not be said either of the meta-levels of explanation either of "emic/etic" theory or semasiology. While neither of these approaches *deny* certain facts of biology, they tend not to give these facts a privileged position in the general scheme of things, thus causing Jackson (1983) to conclude somewhat misguidedly that they are, perhaps, anthropological approaches, "which play up the intellectual and linguistic characteristics of human social existence to the exclusion of somatic and biological processes" (1983:328). Students are well-advised to see epistemological differences in explanatory strategies concerning the dance *not* as liabilities, but as assets, which can provide the basis for productive thinking and dialog.

Before leaving the above bare outline of some of the basic features of kinesics, it is appropriate to update the remarks made regarding the camera as a research instrument with reference to the study of human movement. A most significant and important contribution to this kind of research was made by Worth and Adair in the late 'sixties in the United States. Their book, subtitled "An Exploration in Film Communication and Anthropology" (1972) is an invaluable reference, not only because of their discussions about how people structure reality through the use of film, but because these authors offer a student interested in such modes of investigation a complete overview, not only of researchers who have used film, but of the problems and issues that surround filmed data—and there are many.

Worth and Adair set out in 1966 to determine whether or not they could teach people with a different cultural and linguistic background from theirs to make motion pictures depicting their culture and themselves as *they* saw fit. They assumed that

> ...if such people would use motion pictures in their own way, they would use them in a patterned rather than a random fashion, and that the particular patterns they used would reflect their culture and their particular cognitive style [Worth and Adair, 1972:11].

They report on three areas of what in my opinion are the major issues surrounding the use of film and anthropological research. *Through Navajo Eyes* is a required text (or should be) for any beginning student in the subject of human movement studies, and more, regrettably, cannot be said about such matters here.

Instead, we will move on to a brief discussion of proxemics and the "emic/etic" approaches to the study of human movement, hoping thereby to introduce students to theories and methods that are in many ways different from kinesics, but whose advocates share with Birdwhistell and with Worth and Adair a major anthropological concern, namely that the "folk model" of events and the classifications and categories of the people to whom the body language belongs be understood.

> If a folk classification is ever to be fully understood, an ethnoscientific analysis must ultimately reduce to a description in terms approximating culture-free characteristics...full understanding of a culture or an aspect of a culture and particularly its full description in a foreign language require the ultimate reduction of the significant attributes of the local classifications into culture-free

terms.... Culture-free features of the real world may be called 'etics'
(Pike, 1954). The label may also be applied to features that are not
truly culture-free, but which at least have been derived from the
examination of more than one culture, or to the sum of all the
significant attributes in the folk classifications of all cultures [Stur-
tevant, 1964, reprinted in Manners and Kaplan, 1968:477].

Just what the "etics" of ethnoscientific analysis consist of is
not always clear, but it is safe to say, for the purposes of these
lectures, that the search indicated by the term is for universal,
culture-free elements of the world which transcend or in some way
over-arch the diversity of local usages and references. On the "etic"
side of the "emic/etic" opposition lie all those concerns with universals and invariants that preoccupy investigators in all of the
physical sciences and linguistics.[12] The "emic" side of this
ethnoscientific, basically linguistic theoretical equation is usually
easier for the novice student to understand, both because if deals
with the collection of local, non-culture-free elements of the investigation, and because it concerns methods whereby the anthropologist discovers of what the "significant elements" of any given
system of folk classifications and categories consist.

No one has done a better job than Adrienne Kaeppler of setting
out for us the "emic" elements of Tongan dance and she also offers
us a clear picture of what the investigatory techniques and methods
that are used in ethnoscience consist, insofar as they can be applied
to the study of dances. Her article, published in 1972, on the
structures of Tongan dance is, therefore, basic to the understanding
of the ethnoscientific approach as it might be used to further studies
of the dance anywhere in the world from (as she calls it) "an
anthropological perspective." Although I cannot enter into a discussion of "etics" here, I nevertheless want to include a passage
which might provide an opening gambit into anthropological discourse from this point of view. At the same time, it is with overtones
of apology that I present just these few snippets from Sturtevant's
cogent discussion of emic and etic analysis. I take comfort in the
fact that in a series of lectures like this, one cannot hope to do more
than to "introduce" subjects.

Pike contrasts an etic approach with one which he calls emic, which amounts to an ethnoscientific one: an attempt "to discover and describe the behavioral system (of a given culture) in its own terms, identifying not only the structural units but also the Structural classes to which they belong" (French, 1963:398). An emic description should ultimately indicate which etic characters are locally significant. The more we know of the etics of culture, the easier is the task of ethnoscientific analysis.... Furthermore, in material culture the objects classified are concrete and easily examined and usually readily observable in many examples during the time available for normal field work.... The nature of learning and of communication implies that a culture consists of shared classification of phenomena, that not every etic difference is emic. But it should be emphasized that an emic analysis refers to one society, to a set of interacting individuals. Cross-cultural comparison, if we take culture in Goodenough's sense, is another level of analysis which involves the comparison of different emic systems. There is no reason why one should expect to find emic regularities shared by cultures differing in space or time [Sturtevant, 1968:477–478].

However inadequate the presentation of this one passage may be, it nevertheless points to some of the relevant issues and problems that preoccupy ethnoscientific investigators, and, having said that, we will now turn to Proxemics, and to the work of E.T. Hall.

Proxemics may be the best known of extant anthropological theories and methods pertaining to the field of anthropology and human movement in the United States. Started as a result of Hall's extended applied anthropological studies carried out for the American Foreign Service, the approach from proxemics deals with a theory of *spatial interaction* between two or more persons. The *proximity* of persons whilst communicating is of chief interest, for it is postulated that there are measurable zones, socially or culturally established, surrounding individuals that are generally out-of-awareness, but that influence (and may determine) daily interactions greatly.

In my opinion, it is unfortunate that so much interesting and valuable work as Hall has done has had to be tied to the notion of "critical distances" in animals because human beings possess in unparalleled abundance the characteristic of flexibility in their so-called "behavioral responses." All of the cultural data which

Hall uses to support his thesis about culturally defined spaces can be brought forward to support the claim that human beings are *not* confined to rigidly programmed responses including those of "critical distance." Perhaps it is because we are a unique, unspecialized group of creatures who are not rigidly programmed that Hall was able to point to the richness and variety of the culturally defined spaces that are to be found in the world. But, it is possible to read (and greatly to benefit) from Hall's many astute insights into the spatial relations of human beings, and to share his many excellent ethnographic observations about spatial usages as well as his interesting and lively exegesis of some of the wide variety of cultural observations about concepts of time without concerning onself over whether or not the implied link between animal and human neural capacities is an implicit or an explicit theoretical point. One can effectively disregard the rather loose, basically commonsensical comments he makes regarding the similarity between the biologically-based mechanism of critical distance in animals and the culturally defined zones of expressive space which play such a large role in human interactions (see Hall, 1966, 1966a and 1977). [13]

This writer's work is also valuable in that he is a movement theorist who assigns more time and attention to space and spatial relations than he does to "gesture" or "movements" of the body *per se*. For this, he is owed thanks, surely, although proxemics concerns itself primarily with only *one* of the spatial oppositions which, structurally, define human interactions, i.e., "inside/outside"; specifically, the "near/far" dimension.[14] This is not a negative assessment of Hall's work: his convictions regarding the zones of space which surround a human individual (i.e., the personal zone closest to the body— which many dancers would call the "kinesphere"; the informal zone—a concentric sphere of space that, as it were, encloses the personal space, and a formal zone—another larger concentric sphere of space that encloses the informal and the personal zones, somewhat like a series of three nested boxes), are, upon reflection and examination, unexceptionable.

The beauty of Hall's concept of personal spaces and their relations is that these are a) culturally defined spaces that b) could also define the relations of the "self" to an "other," whether the "other" consists of objects (as in a room, house, garden, office, or whatever) or "other people" and specific features of social interactions. In contrast to another modern theorist, Kendon, Hall does not enter into a close, finely tuned analysis of what "gesture" consists. This, too, is not a "criticism" in the commonly understood use of that term. I introduce Kendon's work at this stage of the discussion simply to point out to students that, on the whole, scholars like Hall, Kendon, Kaeppler, Birdwhistell, Williams, Martin and Pesovar, Sherzer, and others of the same calibre do not, like Hanna (1979) propose to embrace *all* theories at *all* times or to use *all* methodologies in an undiscriminating fashion.

It seems that so prevalent is the misconception regarding the universality of movement, we often fail to realize that, empirically, "An exact definition is not possible" (Kendon, 1983:13). That Kendon is skeptical of pat definitions is clear, and he defines "gesture" as "...any visible bodily action by which meaning is given to bodily expression" (1983:13), a delimitation of the field of interest, surely but not a "definition" of it. Further limitations are imposed by this writer: 1) gesture is to be considered separate from emotional expression, and 2) gesture (in Kendon's usage) does not include "nervous movements," i.e., tics, unconscious mannerisms, and such, thus we can understand "gestures" to mean voluntary (and presumably intentional) actions. "Practical actions" are ruled out, and by these we assume that he means, e.g., all the moves required to cook a meal or to repair a motorcar, wash hands, shave faces, and the like; however, a mimed re-creation of a practical action for communicative purposes *is* to be considered "gesture."

Kendon seems mainly interested in gesture as it appears in social interactions and because of this we can safely assume, from his published work and the bibliographies that are included in them, that he would be interested in the gestures of dancers participating in everyday communicative interactions, but that he has not concerned himself with what they are doing while they are in classes, rehearsals, or on stage. An overview of his writings suggests that students approaching Kendon's work as a guide to understanding the complexities of human actions would find in him a reliable, conscientious scholar, whose view would not conflict, say, with an emic/etic, a proxemic, or a semasiological viewpoint regarding the ground rules, so to speak, of human gesture and actions. However, if those students were specifically interested in the dance or rituals, one would be hard put to say how Kendon would handle such materials—or if he would.

His interest in "gesticulation," "autonomous gesture," and sign languages suggests that he might classify idioms of dancing as stable, standardized forms of gesture which are autonomous, but one is not sure, because he seems to have avoided references to dancing and/or ritual, or to those theorists who have come to the subject from that field of interest, who have dealt with it and with sign languages as well. Despite this limitation, it is gratifying to read of his basic commitment to the fact that "...the gestural modality is as fundamental as the verbal modality as an instrument for the representation of meaning" (Kendon, 1983:38). He also maintains that "...the employment of gesture is not dependent upon the employment of verbal language" (1983:39) and that gesture is in principle equal to, but not separate from, speech, even though they are used simultaneously in many cases.

These are good words and phrases to hear from a scholar of Kendon's stature, maturity, and development. Indeed, it is Kendon's development, apparently from one paradigm of explanation (basically Behaviorist) to another, towards the notion of human movement (or some forms of it) as "language," that makes his work especially interesting. He seems to have shifted in his intellectual lifetime, from a view of human movement as a quantifiable universal which can be treated as if it were prior to and/or independent of human intentions, beliefs, and socio-linguistic contexts, to a view of human actions that he realizes cannot be effectively understood independently of language-use, rule-following, role-creating, and meaning-making. One is struck with reference to this shift, by the fact that such a shift is necessary if the study of human actions in anthropology is ever to grow beyond objectivism and relativism (see Bernstein, 1983), or beyond that to which I have already referred as a "cultic search" for a "real reality" such as Jackson seems to suggest (see Rorty, 1979, for counter-arguments). However tentative, any move in this direction by anyone interested in this field of study is all to the good. For future generations of students, Kendon can (among other things) be an exemplar: even if one starts out committed to one set of theories and methods, one does not have to remain "stuck" to them, especially if one discovers (as Wittgenstein clearly did in philosophy) that the original theories and paradigms are, in the end, unsupportable.

By now, the heterogeneity of this field of study should be clear. It should also be clear that the subject of dancing, although recognized in anthropology, is *not* a prominent feature of the discipline on either side of the Atlantic—or the Pacific, for that matter. I say this to warn students against their own naïve assumptions. Many anthropologists are interested in the subject of "the dance" and they are sympathetic towards it and some are not. By far the greater majority of British social and American cultural anthropologists (and I believe that the same applies to Canadian, Australian, and South African anthropologists as well as a great many semioticians, ethnomusicologists, folklorists, and their European, Asian, and African counterparts) *have received no training,* nor have they had any background in the subject of movement *per se.*

In fact, the subject has probably received more attention in the past two or three decades than it had in the entire history of the discipline before that time. Unspecified, unqualified "attention" is a mixed blessing, of course, and can have both positive and negative effects. Apart from making the trite observation that nothing is easy, students may expect to find, even among those anthropologists who *do* take movement or the dance to be their specialization in the discipline, little agreement regarding theory, practice or hermeneutics. As I have remarked elsewhere (Williams, 1986), the fragility of the field of interest is really its outstanding characteristic at this time. For those students who see this as a creative challenge rather than a disadvantage, however, I would want to say that adequate preparation is imperative. By that I mean a careful examination of the extant, ongoing work that is being done at this time, plus some real awareness of that which we have inherited from the past with reference to the subject of dancing.

With that, we will now turn to another genre of thinking about the dance which I have not so far mentioned in any of these lectures: I think of this as "common-sense" theorizing and approaches to the study of dances. Having collected a fairly large number of these over the past ten years, I want to share one or two which seem to be outstanding, mainly because, even in the work of academically qualified scholars like Gell (1985), it is often the case that common-sense theorizing is at the base of the thinking that was done with reference to the analysis, interpretation, and explanation of dances.[15] I would want it understood at the outset that what is to follow does not consist of "theories" comparable to those discussed at the beginning of this lecture; commonsense thinking about dancing is mainly composed of an individualized aggregate of received ideas, assumptions, personal experiences, casual observation, prejudices, which, taken together do not amount to very much, yet, the influence of this kind of thinking should not be underestimated. Because there is little or no formal preparation in social and cultural anthropology for the study of movement, actions, or the dance, the investigator is often forced to fabricate *some* kind of thinking. Our purpose is to discover some of the elements of it, not to stigmatize an investigator who has had to resort to this kind of thing in the absence of adequate preparation.

It seems reasonable, for example, to imagine that since most of us are aware that danced movements and ordinary movements are (in our cultural context) very different from one another, that it would be "natural" to begin a systematic investigation by attempting to define "dance," or at least define the *difference* in the observed material. It then follows that we must separate the dance from all other modes of human activity. Oesterley (see *supra*, pp.95–97) had this in mind, and it is clear that this dilemma (from which he concluded that definition of this kind was impossible) is not very different from that of many other investigators and keen students, past and present. The literature on dancing is cluttered with hundreds of such definitions,[16] all of which are either inadequate, fallacious or, if not, then applicable only to one, maybe two idioms of dancing. On the whole, they are definitions which conflict with folk categories and classifications of the activity and are, therefore, anthropologically unsound. They assume an *a priori,* universal conception of the activity—as if "dancing" were itself an "etic" category, to use the ethnoscientific term. I discovered to my cost (see Appendix, p.311) that writing about the dances of other cultures starting from such definitions and assumptions can prove to be an embarrassment.

Another type of commonsense theorizing begins by dividing all human behavior into symbolic and instrumental categories, seeing the vast field of meaningful human actions as a divided field of study from the standpoint of "practical" and "non-practical"—or "symbolic"—actions. It is this, more than anything, that for me flaws Jackson's work on Kuranko ritual (1983) and Gell's work on Umeda dance (1985: 183–202). From this initial dichotomy, one may be led in a number of different directions, of course, but one of the more common is that of distinctions between "art" and "non-art," or between people who dance and those who do not (leading, obviously, to problems of further definition and the criteria by which it will be decided, for example, whether "dance" will include only, say, the ballet and modern contemporary dancing, *and* social dancing, and whether the criteria will include or exclude the notions of formal or informal training and such), which may be very different in the culture under examination than it is in our own society.

Years of experience grappling with this kind of thing have taught me that those who hold to these kinds of initial dichotomization either consider *danced* movements to be "interesting" and everyday movements to be "mundane" and comparatively uninteresting, or the reverse. The problems are multi-levelled, but seem to rest on *a firmly held conviction that there must be some way of getting at the danced movement directly,* as it were, and this leads in turn to the notion of a generalized, universally present "behavior" which can be broken down into modular units—into little sequences, perhaps, like "walking" or "sitting" or "standing" "aiming" or something of the kind so that it will be possible to 1) see how smaller units fit into larger sets of "behavioral routines" and thereby define movement that possesses some definable instrumentality, and 2) from this basis, state that "X" is what makes some other kind of behavior "dance."[17]

These approaches, although they may seem reasonable on the face of it, are based on important conceptual errors to begin with, and they will inevitably lead to the division of sequences of movement in distorted and unnatural ways.[18] For a start, the people performing the actions may not themselves think of the world in terms of a division between "symbolic" and "instrumental" features, as we tend to do, and second, one is rendered impotent using these lines of thought when sequences of movement or whole sets of idioms of body language are used in rituals like the Latin post-Tridentine Mass.[19] Here, the entire ritual is composed of so-called "mundane" movements or "practical" actions, such as washing of hands, offering of gifts, pouring of wine and the like. In contrast to this, we may ask how, even in our own culture, are we to classify the movements made by olympic gymnasts? Are these sets of actions "symbolic" or "instrumental"; "impractical" or "practical"? Commonsense theorists usually classify *dancing* as "symbolic" and not "instrumental," but, what makes the actions of a gymnast or a footballer, an ice-skater or a tennis player, taken as a whole, any more instrumental or any less symbolic than the dancer's actions, say, in a performance of *Checkmate* or at a Harvest Moon Ball?

An argument that is repeatedly brought up by those who identify themselves with such "theories" (even if they concede that there are "difficult areas") is an argument for a vaguely conceived notion of "style." That is, the difference between danced movements and ordinary movements is to be discovered, first, by isolating "X," which shall equal some element of "stylization." Having hit upon that (and never mind that we do not understand what it means—we are meant to discover *that* by doing the research), we are then meant to accept stylization as a *system* with reference to *all* human movement. Not only that, if the protagonist of these views is also a hard core empiricist and a materialist, we must accept *stylization as a system that is susceptible to physical description.* What this seems to mean is that we will land up, either during the process of the research or afterwards, with charts or graphs of *measurable muscular activity.*

Not only are we meant to be able to pin down all the complexities of (even) the simplest human action sign, we are then meant to "prove scientifically" that "X" (whatever it is) *physically* exists. The same kind of approach, applied, say, to operatic singing, would attempt to persuade us that in order to understand or explain an aria, its meaning or its context, we must engage in an examination of the muscular changes in the singer's throat. There are those who might be persuaded by this argument, but to those having more theoretical and philosophical sophistication, such arguments are less than convincing. Moreover, it has been my experience that, when challenged, the lack of conceptual clarity which pervades these kinds of ideas is defended by an appeal to *techniques*; that is, we are told that conceptual clarity "will come" when we have subjected the data to computational analysis, perhaps, so that, in the end, our research and our conclusions will depend on the sophistication of the instruments and equipment that we may or may not have to hand. Conceptual clarity will only "come," like Godot, through following these notions and practices.

In his attempts to define the linguistic object, Saussure drew attention to the fact that in the production of sounds necessary for speaking, the vocal organs were external to the notion of "language" in the same way that the material and electrical devices used in transmitting the Morse code are external to the code itself. "Phonation," by which he meant the *execution* of the sound images, in no way affected the system itself. Poorly spoken English, to put matters simply, does not affect the systemic character of the English *language* itself. Similarly, in the production of *movements* necessary for the execution of action sign images, the physical members or organs of the body are external to the notion of *body languages*, as semasiologists conceive of them. The "organism" is external to the code itself, and performance in no way affects the idiomatic system itself. Thinking like this, which encourages thought about the non-material codes of any given body language is a kind of thinking which, although by no means commonsensical, leads one in totally different directions—to a totally different "place" on a notional map of the territory of human movement studies.

No amount of measurements of the material bodies of dancers is ever going to lead to an understanding of the semantic and communicational features of any danced form of human expression and representation—or any other form of expression which uses movement as its primary medium of communication. Just as one cannot usefully study, or explain, the spoken languages of the peoples of the world through analyses of the physical and chemical composition of the body parts that are relevant to the production of the sound images of human languages, so we cannot explain body languages in these ways. Perhaps I should say, not that we "cannot," because people attempt to do this sort of thing all the time, but that we cannot "succesfully," or "rightly" do that kind of thing if what we aim to do is to comprehend systems of bodily or movement communication.

> The principles of semasiology do not preclude a chemical exami-
> nation of a dancer's body, a kinesiological examination of a 'grande
> battement' or any other move in any dancer's body language game.
> Nor does it preclude a biological comparison, say, of circular
> formations of body parts, or circular spatial patterns which appear
> in human dances and rituals and in those, say, of primates, but we
> think it both misguided and foolish to invoke chemistry, kinesiology
> or biology—even evolutionary biology—as explanatory paradigms
> for, say, a performance of *Seraphic Dialogue,* Bharatanatyam, a
> Haitian *vudu* ritual, the Catholic Mass, or any other manifestations
> of human dancing, ritual, ceremony, martial art or sign language in
> the world [Williams, 1986b:76].

I hold that if we insist on retaining such commonsense beliefs as I have described above (as we once insisted on retaining the commonsense notion that the earth is flat), then we will never generate any ideas that will advance our thinking about the dance, or any other structured system of meaningful human actions. Although it could be argued that science itself has its roots in commonsense thinking about nature and the world, and that one's entry into any field of study is accompanied by such thinking, there have been changes in the 20th century in concept formation, from substance to function, that shifted scientific thinking itself from the analysis of materiality to the analysis of relationships, thus providing the strongest arguments for more sophisticated modes of analysis in every discipline. This kind of thinking is relational, symbolic, and formal, simply because these are known to be better ways of thinking than those which are not (see Cassirer, 1953).

In the first lecture, I emphasized three main themes to which I have held throughout the series of lectures thus far: (1) there are alternative and competing conceptions, explanations and theories of (and about) the dance; (2) the growth of knowledge in the field and the noticeable lack of sophisticated theorizing exists because we possess no comprehensive map of the territory with which to begin, and (3) the kinds of questions that are asked about the activity of dancing and the kinds of questions that guide each investigative process are crucial, not only to the knowledge we may or may not possess about the subject, but to the outcome or results of any research that is undertaken.

It will perhaps come as no surprise, therefore, that the last lecture will address this question:

> Is human "behavior" something that can be treated as if it were prior to and/or independent of, human intentions, beliefs and socio-linguistic contexts, or is human "behavior" better thought of as "action signs" that are embedded in ethnographically intelligible narratives of human lives which cannot be effectively understood independently of language-use, rule-following, role-creating, meaning-making and person categories?

As I survey the map of my own making of the territory that I have discussed in the past eight lectures, I would want to say two things: other cartographers, so to speak, might concern themselves with different features of the landscape. Indeed, they might not see human movement studies (or dance studies) as a "landscape" at all. If this is the case, then they will probably not see the metaphorical "valleys", the epistemological gaps that I see as a dominant feature of the landscape between older and more current modes of thinking. "Behavior-land" in its older natural science definition is occupied by a large number of people, including many social scientists of different persuasions. The territory on the other side of the valley is more sparsely populated, although emigration has picked up recently. For those who occupy Behavior-land, it may seem that my excursions into their territory present them and their ideas, not as they would themselves, but from a biased, antagonistic standpoint. If so, I invite them, with friendly interest, to produce maps of the whole terrain which seem to them to be more accurate, for in the next lecture, I shall argue from a semantic anthropological/semasiological point of view with no apologies whatsoever. I would hope, however, to be understood by all concerned, both as a worthy adversary and as a fellow traveller.

Notes

1. See Wolf (1981) for more complete discussion. Suffice it to say here that social anthropologists have for some time known that they were "disturbing observers" and there is a sense in which their perceptions have been vindicated by the emergence of new paradigms of explanation in the "hard" sciences. Also see Harré (1970) with specific reference to the chapter on models.

2. To students, I would want to say that a choice is involved here—a *significant* choice: either an approach from the standpoint that *a whole dance is the product of the sum of its parts* (an aggregative approach), or an approach from the standpoint of "structure," i.e., *that the parts of an entire dance are elements of a wholeness that is the defining characteristic of its structure.* The first approach is "aggregative" in that the whole dance is conceived of merely as a composite formed of elements that are independent of the whole complex into which they enter (that is, the whole is

the sum of its parts). The second approach is "structural," in that the whole dance is conceived of as a composite formed of elements which are *subordinate to* laws and rules, in terms of which the whole dance is defined. These "laws" and "rules" that govern a danced structure's composition are not reducible to a cumulative one-by-one association of elements.

3. By "non-specialist" in this context, I mean someone who has not addressed the problems and conceptual issues inherent in the investigation of dances or any structured system of human movement; this could be anyone, regardless of disciplinary orientation, including many anthropologists.

4. See Williams (1975, Volume II) for an ethnography of the ballet *Checkmate,* for the analogy, using *Checkmate,* to body language, and the relation to the game of chess.

5. See Williams (1986b) for further discussion.

6. This in spite of the fact that writers like Jackson (1983) talk as if language-based approaches are a dead issue and no longer interesting because they are "over-intellectualized."

7. A graduate of this school, Dr. Barbara Kirschonblatt-Gimblett, Jr., now heads the department of performance studies in the Drama department, Faculty of the Arts, New York University.

8. See Kaeppler (1986) for full discussion.

9. From Lee Ellen Friedland, a student at University of Pennsylvania, comes the information that kinesics has been changed, and that she will use the newer approach in a major study on New York "break" dancing, but at this writing, nothing is publicly available.

10. Furthermore, much of Birdwhistell's work concerned the gesturing which accompanied two-party spoken conversations.

11. At the time Sapir wrote, this "code" was perhaps both "secret" and "unknown." Today, parts of it at least have been written, and I find it difficult to believe that it was "understood by all," then or now.

12. It has never been clear to me what Pike meant by "culture-free features of the real world," especially when he says that the term "etics" can also be "applied to features that are not truly

culture-free...." (Sturtevant, 1968:477). To semasiologists, there is a conflation of levels in Pikean linguistics that is difficult to assent to, which is why applications of Saussurian ideas to movement were used to form the basis of semasiology, because they include the notion of levels.

13. Hall's recent contribution (1983), entitled *The Dance of Life,* is disappointing for reasons outlined in Williams (1986a).

14. Structurally speaking, there are four primary spatial dimensions which pertain to all human movement: up/down, right/left, front/back, inside/outside. The "near/far" relationship is a permutation of the latter, i.e., inside/outside.

15. I refer to the theoretical underpinnings of a recently published article of Gell's entitled "Style and Meaning in Umeda Dance," in the collection edited by Spencer (1985:183–202).

16. It is commonsense, for example, which tells us that if we are going to treat systems of movement like conventional spoken languages, then we will find similar units, similar semantic structures, etc., and it also tells us that we should be able to construct "dictionaries," "grammar" books and all the rest.

17. These are not verbatim quotations, but paraphrases of statements made by Gell at a seminar held by the Society for the Anthropological Study of Human Movement (SASHM) at New York University in the spring of 1984.

18. How is one to deal, for example, with the movements of, say a yam farmer in the Cameroon? Yam planting is pre-eminently "practical" and "instrumental," but what are we to do with the bits of sacred potash or herbs dropped into the mound and/or the ritual which may precede or follow the planting? (see Ardener, 1973). To the farmer, all of these actions may form a structural whole. The actions may not constitute a distinction between "instrumental" and "symbolic" actions at all. Yet, how many times are they described in this way, as if the western categorical distinctions were also part of the folk model of the actions? And yet another example: what is one to do with the movements in the Roman Catholic Mass, all of which can be performed by anyone, and all of which (excepting one) are "instrumental" actions, i.e., taking, distributing, breaking,

and pouring. "Blessing" is the problematical action to the investigator who starts with a dichotomy between instrumental and symbolic or practical and artistic actions, or something of the kind. And how does one explain so-called "everyday" movements when they are incorporated into a ritual or a dance?

19. See Williams (1978) for further clarification and explanation, and see, e.g., Barakat (1975) for one type of monastic (Cistercian) sign language.

X. HUMAN BEHAVIOR

THE TERM "BEHAVIOR" HAS HAD A PECULIAR and interesting set of usages in western societies over the centuries. No one draws out the socio-historical implications of these usages more succinctly than Ardener (1973) in a short term paper presented to tutors of the Human Science degree at Oxford. Despite its brevity, it introduces an issue central to the field of human movement studies that none, regardless of differing disciplinary persuasions, can usefully afford to ignore.

"Behavior," we are told, is a term that is used as a cross-disciplinary concept all the time, but its *usefulness* with regard to its diverse applications can be doubted. I would want to add, particularly in those instances where—in the manner of B. F. Skinner and his followers—it becomes something that can be identified prior to and independently of, human intentions, beliefs and socio-linguistic contexts. I choose to let Ardener speak at length, however, because I can neither paraphrase nor improve upon his exegesis:

> It is a strange term to use, for it is a genuine product of social life, with a characteristic socio-linguistic history.... Like its verb 'be-have,' it seems to be a fifteenth century coinage. This verb was always reflexive and consciously derived from 'have,' (so that a person 'behad' himself), and the force of the *be*-preverb was to denote the imposition of a constraint on the person involved. The substantive was formed upon *havour,* or *haviour,* 'possession,' which came straight from the French *avoir* of the same period. Although *haviour* and behaviour were thus of independent origin, the new substantive was, by its French ornamentation, quite appropriate to express a certain conception of deportment, or socially

This chapter was originally given as a paper at a weekend conference, convened by Michael Herzfeld of ISISSS '85, Indiana University, Bloomington, in July.

prescribed and sanctioned conduct. It became a semantic doublet of *demeanour,* but differently marked. *Demeanour* had a more lower class application: *behaviour* thus emerges in a period when an expectation of restraint in upper class behaviour could be regarded as desirable. The positive marking of concepts that referred to courtly life in the late middle-ages is well documented by Trier and his successors. *Behaviour* without modifier, was marked as 'good': the 'behaviour' being watched for was 'good deportment.' Bad behaviour was failed behaviour. *Demeanour* without modifier was marked as 'bad': the 'demeanour' being watched for was 'bad deportment.' 'Good' demeanour was corrected demeanour. After-wards the semantic field of behaviour invaded not only that of *demeanour,* but of *conduct, comportment* and the rest.

It is important then to stress that *behaviour* is a term from a set of terms, and a set of terms from a particular historical period. It is strange to social anthropologists, steeped as we are in language, to be shown the term as something quasi-objective: as an 'idea' or 'concept' to be exemplified, even 'defined' in various supposed manifestations in disparate kinds of data. *Behaviour* when we meet it first is, we note, a coining and a slightly grandiose one. It thus labels a new kind of component. In that world, there could be no such thing as 'random' behaviour.

The extension of 'behave' and 'behaviour' into scientific discourse is Victorian. The first applications are in Chemistry in the 1850's and '60's ('It combines violently with water, behaving like the bichloride of tin,' 1854); ('In Chemistry the behaviour of different substances towards each other, in respect of combination and affinity,' 1866—Oxford English Dictionary). These early ex-amples have still some of the direct living metaphor about them. The very model or orderly discrimination of the conditions under which things acted as they did, was derived from social behaviour. *Behaviour* was marked therefore for its knowability in advance: an image or aspiration for the natural order. When in 1878 T. H. Huxley is talking of the "behaviour of water," he is reducing to orderly terms the activities of a supremely unpredictable element. No doubt it was the continual use of 'behaviour' in contexts in which the activity was far from understood, that led to its association with 'activity in general,' and even 'behaviour problems' towards relatively violent activity. The generalization of 'behaviour' to the inanimate world has since then gone so far that the use of the term 'animal behaviour' probably owes more to its natural science uses than it does to its original social use. Paradoxically, then, we are offered 'behaviour' as a quantifiable universal, a mere century after its metaphorical use in natural science began. Of course, there has been retained throughout the essential component of 'constraint in action.' At all times, 'behaviour' has been conceived of as *rule-governed:* the natural science shift *has moved the locus of the rules* (these italics supplied). At one time behaviour is expressly the subject of rules, at another it is the subject of an aspiration that it will turn out to be governed by rules [Ardener, 1973:152–153].

I cited Ardener at length for several reasons: (1) because I wish to explain in detail why it is axiomatic in semasiology that there is no such thing in the human domain as "behavior" to be identified prior to and independently of human intentions, beliefs and socio-linguistic contexts; (2) because it seems necessary to emphasize, yet again, the concept of an "action sign" as against the unqualified usage of the single word "behavior" (or "action," or "movement" —even "gesture ") and "person category" as against "person" and other such unmarked terms. Finally, I wish to record the many perplexities that arise over the formulations of those who advocate a "human movement science" (as, e.g., Whiting, *et al,* in the Journal of the same name published in The Netherlands), or a "science" of "behavior" that is based on uninterpreted physical movements, *sans* language, *sans* social context, *sans* semantics, in a theoretical setting, either of an old or a neo-positivistic, Behavioralist, or "practical" kind. Advocates of a natural science usage of "behavior" seem to propound sciences into which semasiology and its related social and semantic anthropological concepts cannot be made to fit.

It is not my purpose here to enter into a discussion of Skinnerian (or a generally Behaviorist) approach to movement studies, nor is it my purpose to discuss the problematic nature of the works of those researchers who, like Peng (1978) and Argyle (1975) advocate experimental research in human movement studies. I merely wish to point out that I am puzzled by their work as I am by Jackson's and Gell's (see *supra,* pp. 234ff and 235ff, respectively), and that it is not clear just what such experiments, or notions of "bodily praxis" and commonsense theorizing amount to, although for many years I have made serious efforts to try to understand these points of view.

This genre of work seems to point to a trend towards the inclusion of human movement studies into a kind of "human ethology" (with regard to the dance, see Sebeok, 1979, and Williams' criticisms, 1986b). It would seem that we are meant to be persuaded of the neutral, value-free and "objective" nature of "behavior," defined as a universal phenomenon that can be attached equally to animals, molecules, human beings, machines, the tides, or what-you-will. On the other hand, we seem to be asked to suspend our knowledge that such experiments are themselves based on a human conception of scientific experiments and whole stretches of behavior that are closely connected with human intentions, values, and belief-formed behaviors that take place in specific socio-historical circumstances and contexts.

One therefore has to begin with a confession of bafflement: what does the phrase "human movement science" mean? Is it a science of uninterpreted, non-linguified physical movements which seeks only to explain the physical *mechanics* of movement, in which case, the emerging human movement science is simply a verbal gloss for kinesiology, functional anatomy, and body mechanics? But that, I am told, is *not* what it means because human movement science or a natural science of behavior means much more than that. The root definitions, stated in many ways, seem to boil down to this: the science is defined as dealing with actions (i.e., "behaviors" or "movements") that include "subjective behaviors," such as attitudes, beliefs, motivations, expectations, and aspirations, as well as "overt acts."

What this wording in any of its permutations seems to imply is that there are *two* distinct sets of items available for independent study by all of us who are concerned with the nature of human actions :"the movements," i.e., the "overt acts" and "all the rest," i.e., the attitudes, beliefs, intentions, and such. The problem that haunts those of us who advocate a semasiological point of view concerns the underlying dualisms. If the underlying assumptions and axioms of semasiology are correct (see Williams, 1982:173), then there can be only *one* set of items available for study in the human domain, *not two*. There can be no division between behavior (as raw movement) and social settings, intentions, beliefs, and value systems.

The importance of the initial standpoint from which one proceeds with reference to the subsequent description, analysis, interpretation, and explanation of human systems of action *cannot be overstressed,* whether the actions occur at the level of one gesture of one single body part, or whether they are longer stretches, or episodes, or whole genres of actions, e.g., "dances," "ceremonies," "exercise techniques," or something else.

It is a conceptual commonplace for anthropologists, philosophers, linguists, and many social scientists, that one and the same stretch of human actions may be correctly characterized in different ways, but that is not the point at issue here. It is not the case that kinesics, proxemics, behavioralist approaches, an emic/etic style of analyses, and semasiology simply characterize actions in different ways. The issues lie at a much deeper level than that and they are more significant, when considered at the level to which I draw attention; i.e., that level where statements are made regarding what human behavior or human movement *is.* The issues begin at the level of ontological considerations. Because of this, movement theorists (as we shall see) are not simply characterizing the same things in different ways. In many cases, we are talking of different things entirely.

"An action" is, as we all know, an analytically useful abstraction, but left only to that, it is a dangerous and misleading abstraction because it is so easy in human cases to begin to see it only as "a movement," thereby seeing it out of context. This is why the concept of an *action sign* is useful because the "sign" part of the phrase tends to help locate it as part of a relational sequence or as part of a situational bundle of relations that are part of, or potentially part of, some ethnographical narrative. I will revert to this notion of ethnography later on, as it is central to my thesis about "behavior."

For now, I should like to consider momentarily, the irony of Sartre, who insisted that human actions had no sense, no sequence, no "narrative," no beginnings, middles, or ends. The irony lies in the fact that in order to convey his ideas, he had to write books and plays that *had* beginnings, middles, and ends in order to make his characters (and his thesis that human life is random, basically unintelligible, and sense-less) and his bitterness about the human estate as he saw it, intelligible. It is no wonder that Lévi-Strauss argued with Sartre, who may have claimed to have found an "anthropology" of sorts during his long and distinguished career, but if he did, it was one that separated French society from others, and ultimately separated Sartre himself from others. Lévi-Strauss says of him, "A Cogito—which strives to be ingenuous and raw—retreats into individualism and empiricism and is lost in the blind alleys of social psychology" (1966a:250), by which he meant that the Sartrean style of "anthropology" focussed on secondary incidentals of social life, never coming to grips with its foundations.

It is no wonder, either, that there is a problem regarding the analysis of events in the minds of those moderns who, along with Sartre, would like to remove the *intelligibility* from human actions, human presence, and human experience. It is not surprising that in a Sartrean intellectual space, events are only "output," a "stream," as it were, of emitted behaviors for which there is no metaphorical program. There is no "program" in this context (with the possible exception of a genetic program) because this would imply some higher-order, cultural meta-logic of patterning or sequences of events—together with some notion that empirically perceivable events are potentially "true," or "false," "intelligible," or "unintelligible," "orderly" or "disorderly," and the like. If Sartrean actors or agents can be conceived to be the authors of their scenarios, episodes, and their actions at all (and not merely passive-receptive information processing machines), then they would have to be convinced, one would have thought, that they must conceive of themselves as meaningless ciphers in a sense-less universe. I do not need to be reminded that there are people who do believe that, but that is, quite simply, their problem, not ours or mine.

While I have great admiration for Sartre's scholarship, and sympathy with his metaphysical discomforts about many features of a post-World War I world, and with his dissatisfactions with the prevailing philosophies of science and features of the society of his times, I cannot consent to his conclusions, for, to Sartre, it would appear that the "subjecthood" of other people and the freedoms of others—thus the very nature of humanity—was practically and otherwise forever inaccessible. It seems that for him, love, carrying with it its congruent potentialities for understanding and accessibility, is always doomed to frustration. Indeed, as is well known, other people constitute the Sartrean hell, because although they seem to *need* each other, they can never really be *known,* nor can they ever be anything but "other." One wonders what the Sartrean heaven would have been like? His extreme pessimism about humankind and his commitment to a thesis of absurdity, even when converted to a quasi-religious view, for example, by Marcel, still does not solve the anthropoligical problem.

If Lévi-Strauss is right, i.e., that "The pre-eminent value of anthropology is that it represents the first step in a procedure which involves others" (1966a:247), then social anthropologists and semasiologists cannot adopt the position that other people are ultimately unknowable or untranslatable, although all of us are aware of the dangers, difficulties, and potential pitfalls that surround the enterprise of offering ethnographical reports that are "true" and which have universal intent. It is unnecessary to discuss those here, in addition to which, I would like to stick closely to the original point, which consists of the question of whether or not movement, actions, or behavior can be treated, in the human domain, as if it were somehow independent of everything else. Another way of putting this is to ask, can we really study people as if they were ants, dung-beetles, bower-birds, or chimps? Can these creatures enter into our debates? If they have intentions, language-use, role-playing, and rule-following capacities in the same ways and in the same senses as human beings, then semasiology is, at a very fundamental level, wrong.

Having said all that, I would want to return to the Sartrean theme, saying that one cannot really practice anthropology or semasiology successfully if one is convinced of the Sartrean premises that (a) "the other" is ultimately inaccessible and (b) that "playing a role" is not coincident with being an authentic human being. Role-playing seems to be defined narrowly in the Existentialist context as a kind of cogship in one or the other kind of social, class, or political machine. With all due respect, one simply cannot

consent to Existentialist or Phenomenological views of the world—
or of the dance—even if one takes into consideration the debts of
gratitude which are owed scholars of these persuasions for picking
up the cudgels with reference to the notion of "person" against older
styles of entrenched establishment positivism, and their evidently
sincere efforts to humanize western science.

Consent is withheld because social and cultural anthropology
as I conceive of them are human(e) sciences that devote themselves
to the study of "others," whether outside or inside of one's own
ethnicity, and because one recognizes a post-structuralist point of
view (see Ardener, 1980) in British social anthropology as an
attempt, in one way of looking at it, to free oneself and one's
students from the intellectual imperialisms of the "objectivities" of
Logical Positivism and the "subjectivities" of Existentialism and
Phenomenology. To us, they are merely opposite sides of the same
coin.

An interesting way of viewing some of these problems, in
particular, the dualism implied by the separation of the active and
the verbal (as in Jackson's "verbal praxis-bodily praxis" dichotomy) is to split the human world into the domains of the "lived
story" and the "told story." One is tempted to say of those who place
the *told* story over the *lived* story (or the reverse) that they offer an
extremely impoverished view of human culture and human nature
and its significances, but one has to admit that if the proponents of
this kind of view are correct, then anthropology is itself a fairly
ridiculous enterprise because the anthropologist is no more than a
creator of fiction. Two authors—i.e., Hardy (1968) and Mink
(1970)—address the underlying issues behind the problems with
which I have tried to grapple regarding the concept of the "action
sign" as against the unmarked usage of "action" or "movement" as
quantifiable universals. Their pre-occupations seem directly relevant to the issue of whether or not the dance and other non-vocalized forms of human communication are in fact body languages, or
whether they are merely overt acts which can be understood apart
from human intentions, beliefs, and contexts.

Hardy takes the position that "narrative" is not solely the work
of novelists, poets, and dramatists *reflecting upon* events which had
no narrative order before one was imposed upon them, whether by

those involved in the literary arts or, one imagines, by historians, anthropologists, sociologists, psychologists, and others. Narrative *form,* in Hardy's view, neither disguises nor decorates. Although Hardy is not an anthropologist, she takes what semasiologists would identify with as an anthropological point of view, especially when she writes that we dream in narrative, daydream in narrative, remember, interpret, anticipate, hope, despair, believe, doubt, plan, revise, criticise, construct, gossip, learn, hate, and love by narrative. If I understand her, she argues for human actions as *enacted narratives* (see Hardy, 1968, especially p. 5). Her opponent, Mink, tells us that

> Stories are not *lived* but *told* [italics supplied]. Life has no begin-nings, middles or ends; there are meetings, but the start of an affair belongs to the story that we tell ourselves *later* and there are partings, but final partings only in the story. There are hopes, plans, battles and ideas, but only in retrospective stories are hopes fulfilled, plans miscarried, battles decisive and ideas seminal. Only in the story is it America which Columbus discovers and only in the story is the kingdom lost for want of a nail [Mink, 1970:557–558].

This literary debate is important because we who say that the concept of an "action sign" or "signs" does not consist solely of movement that can be understood prior to or independently of human intentions, beliefs, and contexts will stand solidly with Hardy and her thesis of lived narratives. We would be obliged to agree *in part* with Mink that retrospectively, hopes, and all the rest, are characterized in a variety of ways, but we would have to add that to us, they are so characterized in life and thus, they are lived as well. One does not need an historian, for example, or a poet or an anthropologist to tell one that one has committed a *gaffe* at a dinner party, or that one has been successful in achieving an agreement that results in the signing of a contract. I do not have to be *told* later on, by myself or anyone else, whether I won or lost a battle, or that I have become an aunt, a mother, or a grandmother, nor do I have to be told whether I have achieved a good perfor-mance—on or off-stage.

I have spent a lot of time wondering, along with all of my anthropological colleagues, just what it means when we talk of social facts; their obligatoriness, their general traditional character, their modes of transmission, and their "stacked deck" characteristics. I have concluded that it means that, as human beings, we begin by being born into an ongoing "story." What happens to human children following birth usually includes some ceremony or rite that marks the child's inclusion into the story of the ethnicity: the public recognition among the Orakaiva, for instance, that the child is no longer to be classified with nature and the pigs, but with culture and the human society (see Iteanu, 1984). The many "bringing forth" and naming ceremonies in Africa that (although very different in ethnographic details) nevertheless perform the function of including the child into the social contexts and the ongoing *lived narrative* of the ethnicity. In Christian tradition, the baptism, i.e., the plunging of the child into (or the sprinkling of) the symbolic water(s) is the act which effectively plunges the child into the *story* of that tradition. I need not continue to offer examples of what every novice anthropology student should know, and what may seem overly obvious to colleagues who are seasoned scholars.

My point is this: we enter into an ongoing ethnographic narrative of events which is, so to speak, "told" in a particular time, a particular language, and this narrative defines the import, even of the event of our births in certain definite ways. And if we are born into a situation that is defined by the attitude that we are *not* born into a "story," that such things as baptisms or any other ceremonies celebrating our arrival into the world are essentially meaningless, then *this* kind of event still takes place within the confines of the social facts that everyone knows and inherits, thus, whether the unmarked birth event constitutes a "rebellion" on the part of the parents, a pathetic happenstance, perhaps, a circumstantial necessity, or what-you-will, it nevertheless takes place in the human domain with reference to *an already established set of customs and practices the absence of which is itself significant.*

A striking feature of human life seems to be the fact that we do not begin where we please, and only a few of us seem to go on entirely as we please—or as we think we please. As symbols in the semiotics of our ethnicity, we are constrained by others, and we, in turn, constrain others. We are constrained by the ethnographic contexts in which we find ourselves, and by that stock of stories and narratives that our ethnicity and our language represent. We spend most of our lives, as Pocock has pointed out, not finding out the truth about ourselves and the world, but simply trying to make sense out of the semiotic, even if we believe that the semiotic is a nonsense, as Sartre did. We can see that there are intelligible aspects of this almost unbelievably intricate and complex semiotic. We can also perceive that we individually occupy a certain place in it that changes as we go along. It is at all times "marked" or "bracketed" by inescapable facts: we begin (birth) and we end (death) both as individuals and as members of groups—peer groups, professional groups, age-groups, political, economic, literary, historical, or religious groups. Embedded in the total story are other stories of like kind, and our individual stories intersect with many others of a like nature on ever-ascending (sometimes descending) levels.

A Sartrean view, or any view that starts by separating our movements or our actions from this semiotic, seems to deny certain ethnographic realities of human life. It seems to deny that human beings are, or ever were, symbols in the semiotics of their own and others' authorship and co-authorship. It is true, I believe, that with reference to our lived stories and our lived personal ethnographies that when we begin in them, we enter a story that is not of our own making and which for some time, we are relatively unaware, but the story of our growth and maturation as human beings can be seen to be parallel with the growth of our knowledge(s) concerning the ethnographical narrative of our ethnicity and its relation to others.[1]

For many years, the authors of our personal ethnographic realities and the (usually) unwritten records of our personal anthropologies (see Pocock, 1973) are those to whom we refer as "mother," "father," and other kindred, and surrogate kin: teachers, spiritual and intellectual "brothers" and "sisters," and the like. They, together with "me" create the lived story that, as it unfolds, can be seen to be marked by two main characteristics: (1) the story is unpredictable and (2) the story is teleological. We live our lives from the start by coming into a shared story, the beginnings of which are already made for us by what and who has gone before.

We go through the middle of our lives between birth and death both individually and as a member of various groups, in the light of shared language(s) and possible shared futures, some of which repel, others that entice, others that seem inevitable; some are "open" and some are "closed "—the list is long and multi-levelled, for a start, because we are at once the central figure or "character" in our own personal ethnographies and at the same time, we are supporting characters in the personal ethnographies of those around us.

It seems constantly to be overlooked, possibly because it is so obvious, that "I" am simultaneously "female," "daughter," "sister," "grand-daughter," "niece," "student," "friend," "mentor," "tax-payer," "professor," "thin" or "fat," tall or short, old or young, and all the rest. Some of these classifications and social roles and their accompanying modifiers have been constant since the beginning, some have been acquired (or only can be acquired) through various means as "I" grow older. These lists of person-categories and their modifiers are not the same for everyone, although in any given ethnicity, there are overlaps, just as there are also "empty slots," anomalies, and such. Person categories such as "wife," "aunt," "mother," "teacher" are role/rule categories which tend to indicate greater maturity, and they are not really relevant when "I" begin, although "I" am a *potential* wife or mother. As a human child, "I" am potentially many things, in whatever ethnicity "I" may be born, but this potential is constrained in many ways. At the same time, that cluster of person-categories, whatever they may turn out to be, also offers many freedoms. Perhaps my personal ethnographic narrative will not include the person-categories of wife and mother; perhaps I will be a nun—and so it goes. The permutations are virtually endless, and I say "virtually" because they are not infinite in our own or any other ethnicity, although they may seem to be so when "I" am young.

The point of view that I have elaborated very briefly is a familiar one to anthropologists: it is basically van Gennepian, as I understand him, and it is a point of view that makes a case for the *intelligibility* of human life and its features of *accountability*. It is a point of view that is entirely incompatible, not only with a Sartrean view, but to any view that would make of human behavior something that is identifiable prior to or independently of person-categories, social contexts, language-use, role-playing, and rule-following. Neither view can usefully be grafted onto the other. One can only arrive at conceptual confusion if one attempts to synthesize them.

But now, I should like to examine more closely the unmarked term "action," thinking of it first as a human action and returning to the theme of the action sign, because I am convinced that many readers will still believe that the subject of our discussion in this lecture, i.e., "behavior," has remained on a theoretical rather than a practical level. Instead of seeing the discussion as an attempt to clarify the "praxis" connected with the theories so far outlined, they will secretly hold to the idea that what I am *really* doing is dressing up old concepts in a new verbal disguise. At best, skeptics and critics will prefer to think that all of this talk is relevant only to the fringe-areas of mainstream anthropology, as if their own preoccupations with political behavior, economic behavior, and such did not include an examination of actions. Thus, it is necessary to assume an ethnographical mode for the moment and examine some thought exercises that will attempt to make sense out of a short stretch of observable actions on the ground.

To the question, "what is she doing?", the answers might be (A) she is exercising, (B) she is preparing for a dance class, (C) she is pleasing her teacher, or (D) she is dancing. Some of these answers characterize the agent's intentions, and others point to unintended consequences of her actions, and of these, the agent may or may not be aware. What is important to notice is that *any* answer to the questions of how we are to understand or explain this, or any stretch of actions, will presuppose some *prior* answer to the question of how these different correct answers to the question "what is she doing?" are related to each other.

If someone's primary intention is to exercise [answer (A) above], then it is only incidentally the case that she is pleasing a teacher of dancing, and it is to some extent irrelevant whether or not preparation for a dance class is involved. We need only explain, in this context, what it is "to exercise." But, if the agent's primary intention is to "please the teacher" [answer (C) above], we have another *kind* of action that requires explanation. In the first case (A), the actions will be explainable in terms of a cycle of personal behaviors that have differing values in the context. Moreover, the intention of "exercising" embodies an intention that presupposes certain attitudes towards the aims, purposes and ends of personal exercise within a certain context, and, probably, a certain system of designated movement.

In other words, there is a kind of narrative, ethnographical setting that is involved in order for us to understand what is meant by "exercise" with reference to the agent's actions. Is the exercise a "warm-up" performed by an Olympic athlete, or by a housewife preliminary to a half-hour's morning jog, or by a dancer before a performance? The notion of "exercise" will not be the same in all three cases. Neither will the form, length, duration, tempo, or quantity of actions be the same. The ethnographic description of the action should not be the same because (a) the movements will not be performed in the same way in all three cases and (b) each case should be seen as a short episode in a different ethnographic narrative. Here, we are considering the movements themselves, but it is clear that even at this fundamental level, in order for the actions to be intelligible, we have to deal with intentions, beliefs, and contexts.

In contrast to sorting out answer (A), "she is exercising," answer (C) has placed the set of actions (i.e., the tiny movement episode) in any hypothetical ethnographical narrative of teacher-student relations, and probably a dance class, although the person-categories and the relations involved could be those of "coach-athlete," which moves the *locus* of the episode into a different *model* of actions; an agonistic (for the athlete) rather than a dramaturgical modular context (for the dancer). With reference to a general notion of "exercise," the episode can be seen to be very different, depending as it does, on whether the ethnographical narrative setting is a gonistic, dramaturgical, or domestic, i.e., the housewife at the moment of daily jogging. The point is that whether the example of movements is short or long, whether it is trivial or non-trivial in the investigator's eyes, we cannot rightly characterize human actions independently of intentions, and the intentions themselves cannot be characterized independently of the socio-linguistic contexts which make the intentions intelligible, both to the agents and to the observers.[2]

The word "context," like the word "ethnography" is a familiar one in anthropology. Both terms are used in a number of ways, but I mean for them to be understood fairly inclusively with reference to this discussion. A "social context" in the context of this argument, can be taken to be an institution, or a system of formal practices, or a danced idiom, a linguistic exchange, a geographical location or any combination of these. Central to the notion of context, however, is the notion of ethnography as I conceive of it: in its broadest sense taken to mean some narrative "story," if you will, in which context the set or sets of actions take place. Thus "context" in this definition generally has a history and a projected future. Because the context can be deemed valuable or useless, significant or insignificant, and the like, it is seen to be connected with a belief system—with an ideology, perhaps, and in accordance with our own cultural categories, it can be seen to be political, religious, economic, artistic, or any combination of these—or none of these, but a social category that is designated by some other comparable classification. One and the same stretch of actions may belong to more than one context.

In the first illustration given [answer (A) above], the agent's activity may be part of a purely personal regime of selected activities that are included in her daily cycle of living and generally domestic events. Here, the ethnographic character of the agent's history of participation in exercise activities and the ethnography of domestic structures in the ethnicity intersect. However, if the domestic life to which the agent belongs is a family of acrobats or a circus family, the family itself may possess a history and a narrative of participation in "exercise activities" that extends far past the individual agent's lifetime, such that the particular family may have a reputation and a life of its own in a particular town, village, or nation. In this case, the agent's exercising would possess a relationship to the sequences of actions in the observed episode in such a way that it can be presupposed that the sequence has a certain life of *its* own in a set of "routines" or "techniques" which itself has been handed down for generations, such as certain systems of exercise which are handed down with reference to dance idioms or circus routines, the military arts, and such (see Bouissac, 1976, for some discussion of this in circuses). If an investigator is to relate some particular segment of "behavior" in any precise way to an agent(s) intentions and thus to the contexts in the extended sense that I have outlined then he or she will have to understand in a precise way how the variety of correct characterizations of the agent(s) actions relate to each other, first, by identifying which characteristics refer the reader to an intention and which do not, and then by classifying further the items in both categories.

Where intentions are concerned (as I have pointed out at length in Williams, 1978, in the work on the Catholic Mass), it is necessary to know which intention or intentions are primary. That is to say, of which it is the case that, had the agent intended otherwise, "it," i.e., the particular episode, *would not have been that action.* If we know that an agent is acting with the self-avowed purpose of exercising and of pleasing a (dance) teacher, we do not yet know how to understand what she is doing until we know the answers to such questions of whether she continues to believe that dancing and the contingent warming-up exercises are effective *and* whether she would continue dancing if she ceased to believe that dancing was a valued exercise, but continued to believe that the actions "pleased teachers" and whether she would continue dancing if her beliefs were changed on both points. That is to say that we *must know* what the agent's beliefs are. Not only that, we must know which of those beliefs are *causally effective* such that they produce the actions that we are able to observe. To know that, we also have to know whether certain contrary to fact hypothetical statements are "true" or "false." Until we know these things, semasiologists do not think that they know how to characterize correctly *what* an agent is doing.

Consider momentarily this set of contextually compatible and correct answers to the question "what is she doing?": (P) "Putting on makeup"; (Q) "Finishing a phrase of movements from the end of Seraphic Dialogue"; (R) "Choreographing a dance"; or (S) "Auditioning for Martha Graham's company." Here the intentions of the agent can be ordered in terms of the stretch of time to which the reference is made. Each shorter-term intention is (and can only be) made intelligible by reference to some of the longer-term intentions. The characterization of the actions in terms of the longer-term intentions are, however, also correct. Suppose for a moment we have Labanotated stretches of the episodes to which I have referred above. We have, written down, stretches P,Q,R,S.

The first question is, could we have written those stretches and designated them by the linguistic utterances used above, if we had not known the agent's intentions? The answer is "no," we could not. For a start, putting makeup on for a performance of Seraphic Dialogue is a rather different process from applying street makeup for the purpose of auditioning for a company and "finishing a phrase of movements from the end of Seraphic Dialogue" for a dancer in that already prescribed piece is quite different from "choreographing a dance." Although the four action sign stretches bear contextual relations to one another, we are obliged to know more of the story before we can know what to write down in Laban script. The second question is, can we isolate the movements or the "observed behaviors" from the agent's capacities for language-use, hence for making intelligible actions for which she is *accountable* and for which she can give *reasons,* and still usefully call it by the unmarked term "behavior," whose definitions include some unmarked, equivalent "things" that are quantifiable universals?

In our theoretical context, we cannot (see Durr, 1981, for further discussion with reference to writing movement as against writing action signs). The point is that the actions that we write are only adequately characterized as action *signs* when we know what the longer, shorter, and longest term intentions are that are invoked and how these are related to one another. "Aha," a critic might say, "what an elaborate and basically unnecessary exegesis of how to do an ethnography. You insult us by assuming that we do not know," to which I can only reply that this extended explanation of some important elements of writing ethnography was not meant to tell anthropologists what ethnography is but to explain why it is that semasiologists cannot treat episodes of human actions as if they were raw "movement" which can be treated as if they were prior to or independent of human intentions, language-use, human beliefs, and socio-linguistic contexts. I have simply attempted to point to some of the ethnographic realities behind this statement: "...an intentional action is not the same as a physical movement since the latter can be described in various ways according to one's point of view and one's beliefs about the person performing it. One cannot specify an action as opposed to a purely physical movement without taking into account what the agent intended" (Best, 1974:193).

Human intentions, as they are manifested in dances, signing systems, the martial arts, greeting systems, ceremonies, rituals, and all of that to which we refer as "body languages" have to be ordered both causally and temporally, and both orderings will make reference to settings—to "context," writ large. This, in our view, is something that does not only happen in *told* stories, but also happens in *lived* stories as well. As we live our lives, whatever they may consist of, we make reference obliquely to such orderings as I refer to through our usages of elementary terms such as "exercising," "teacher," "dancing," "makeup," "auditioning" (as in the examples I have used) or any other set of related terms which can be culled from the ordinary, everyday usages of the agent.

What this means is that the correct identification of the agent(s) beliefs *will be a constituent part of the investigative task.* Failure with this means failure with the whole enterprise. Investigative tasks which are conceived of *without* identifying the agents' intentions and beliefs are, we believe, studying something other than human movements. We do not, by the way, imagine that we expound something wholly new: it is an axiom of semantic anthropology that the investigation itself is a symbolic interchange (see Crick, 1975, for extended discussion). In the anthropology of human movement, we identify an action only by invoking at least three kinds of context: (1) we place the action signs in a causal or temporal order with reference to their role in agents' personal narratives or "stories", (2) we place them in their social contextual settings, and (3) we place them with reference to the idiom or system of body language that is being used.

We are, I would say, even over-familiar with this kind of thing with regard to danced idioms and systems of sign languages. "When," we ask, "is a plié not a plié?" The answer? When the same apparent "shape" or "move" appears in an idiom other than the ballet. In Bharatanatyam, for instance, where *mandi* (sitting on the heels) and *aramandi* ("half-sitting") are entirely different actions from *grande* or *demi-plié*. In determining what causal efficacy the agent's intentions have in one or more directions, and how these intentions succeed or fail to be constitutive of long-term intentions, the investigator writes, as it were, a further part of the socio-historical narrative or ethnography of the actions.

The ideal (or is it the illusion?) that human actions can be free of their narratives, that their social values, beliefs, intentions, and features of intelligibility and accountability is a dangerous myth, for it denies the very substance and meaning of the action(s) from the start. Like any social or cultural anthropologist, an anthropologist of human movement is concerned, not with the *mechanics* of movement or "motor actions" *per se,* but with intelligible acts, actions, and sequences of events or patterns of events. Unintelligible actions are failed candidates for intelligible actions: there is no way that we can lump together a Balinese trance dance, for example, with an epileptic fit, trying to discern what they both have in common, because in doing so, we have ignored the concept of intelligibility and have failed to make the distinction, fundamental to semasiology, between *actions* and movements.

The concept of intelligibility, like that of story-telling is thus important because of a basic distinction between human beings and other kinds of sensate beings, because human beings can be held accountable for their actions—at least those of which they are the authors. To identify a movement occurrence as an "action sign" and therefore as some part of an intelligible event is to identify it under a type of description that enables us to see the event as a sequence flowing intelligibly from a human agent(s) intentions, motives, purposes and passions. It therefore means that we understand human actions, and the concept of the action sign, as something for which someone (or some group) is "accountable," about which it is not only appropriate but necessary, to ask for an intelligible account. We are not obliged to pass judgment on the actions as anthropologists—another obvious point, perhaps, but one that is worth making, considering the fact that we describe sets of human actions all the time that, like the cattle raids among the Nuer, horse-raiding among the American Indians, or the sheep raids among certain Greek herders, are not *judged* by the anthropologist to be "stealing," but *described* in terms of the values of the ethnicity among whom the practise might represent something entirely other.

When we are faced with sequences or clusters of actions that are apparently intended, but that we cannot identify, we are both practically and intellectually puzzled. We are perplexed—baffled.[3] How are we meant to respond? How do we explain? In some cases, the distinction between the human and cultural and the natural seems to break down. What are we to do with the movement manifestations of an epileptic, for instance? First, it is the movement manifestations themselves which are a product of this and similar types of affliction that lead to those having such diseases being treated as "patients," and it is such manifestations of movements that places them, in our culture, in the ongoing ethnography or narrative of medicine. In another culture, the same manifestations might lead them into another category or classification of persons. In our own context, however, when we are confronted in these cases with actions which are not only unintelligible to observers, but to the agents who manifest them, we understand this type of unintelligibility as a kind of suffering.

Sometimes, our bafflement with sequences of actions does not indicate that kind of breakdown between the human and the natural; sometimes the perplexity arises simply because we do not know or understand the rationale that organizes the actions or that causes the "behavior." Encounters with alien cultures and alien social structures within our own social context, all that to which we refer when we use the term "culture shock," turns around this kind of perplexity. Although we experience the perplexities and bafflements of unintelligibility in many ways, we seem to overlook the importance of a concept of intelligibility, especially when speaking of movement partly because it is so all pervasive in all social interactions that we take it entirely for granted.[4]

Suppose, for example, that one is standing in a subway train headed for home and a young lady standing close-by says, "This is a plié," "rond-de-jambe," and after a few seconds lapse of time, she says, "*Swan Lake*." Suppose that she articulates these vocal utterances with action signs and looks at me, as if awaiting a response. Such utterances, in either linguistic signs or action signs, addressed to me at random, could constitute a possible form of madness. Is it possible to imagine some context that would render this young woman's actions intelligible?

It is. Suppose that she has just come from her psychotherapist, who, in the interests of getting her to overcome her extreme shyness has suggested to her that she must address some person with whatever comes into her head. Suppose that she and I have attended the same ballet performance of *Swan Lake* and she has seen me musing over the experience and perhaps "talking with my hands" over what I have just seen. Suppose that she is a spy and that these terms are code-words that are really addressed to the person sitting next to me, but the danger of the situation for her and her companion spy demands that she not overtly address her partner in espionage.

With these thought exercises, I hope to open a door to understanding an important premise in semasiology: the understanding of any human movement as an action sign requires an understanding of intentions and context at the very least, because the simple identification of a movement (i.e., she did "this," or "that") is not enough. There are those who would say that to supply the context, such as I have tried to do in the above examples, or to supply a bit of notional ethnography of the situation is wholly unnecessary—just frills. There are those who would argue that all that is required of us is that the young woman's utterances, in either medium of expression, spoken or acted, be *identifiable*. In other words, all that "I" need to know or to do in the situation is to identify the speech acts ("This is a plié" and "rond-de-jambe") as belonging to the technical language of the ballet and the actions she performed as examples of the ballet dancer's body language game. But, there is a problem here.

With reference to speech acts and action signs, the *purpose* of either can be intelligible or unintelligible. Suppose, for example, that the young woman explains what she said and did by saying, "My words and actions were in response to a question you asked me about the ballet." My reply: "But I didn't ask you any question to which those utterances, either spoken or acted, could have been a possible reply." She says; "Oh, I know *that*," and once again, her actions become unintelligible. There are many examples that can be constructed to illustrate the point that the mere fact that an action sign serves some purpose of a recognized type—that is, an action sign may be identified as "plié," "thumbing a ride," "praying," or whatever, but the mere identification is not sufficient to render the action *intelligible*. The conclusion: both linguistic signs and actions signs *and their purposes* require contexts.

All too often, movement theorists of whatever disciplinary persuasion, seem to want to be able to excise the action signs away from the linguistic signs and vice-versa. It is thus that they seem to try to persuade us that human actions can be treated apart from intentions, beliefs, purposes and contexts, as, indeed the organized movement "behavior" of language-less creatures *can* be treated, but the presupposition in the human realm seems to include a level of "non-verbal behavior" that can be identified independently of the human capacity for language-use, and semasiology says "no" to that, because we do not consent to the notion that in the human realm there are two independent sets of items which can be studied: the "overt acts" (movements) and "all the rest," i.e., attitudes, beliefs, intentions, and the entire apparatus that accompanies the human faculty for language-use.

It is the treatment of action signs separately from linguistic signs that renders Elam's position regarding movement in the theater highly questionable from a semasiological standpoint, for we simply cannot understand what is meant by "the kinesic components of performance," supported by the ideas of those who, like Artaud, "dreamed of a 'pure theatrical language' freed from the tyranny of verbal discourse—a language of signs, gestures and attitudes having an ideographic value as they exist in certain unperverted pantomimes (Artaud, 1958:39)" (Elam, 1980:69). Elam's arguments seem to support our contentions that there is a basic incomprehensibility built into notions of a "plastic stage language" that is separate from the language-using faculties and capacities of the human mind.

Positivism, as we all know, was suffused with a dream of a conventional, scientific *spoken* language that would be perfect; a language that would in some sense permit us to speak and write "objectively"; free, as it were, of all the warts, blemishes, and other imperfections of human emotion and action. The counterpart of the positivistic dream seems to exist in theater and religion, where many authors seem to long for some kind of universal esperanto of gestures and bodily motions that would be "unperverted" by language.

We are offered a choice that is ultimately based on the Cartesian mind-body split: a spoken language shorn of actions, passions, and such, or a body language split off from conventional languages. Such dreams are not to be taken seriously, and because he uncritically offers us a non-choice, we cannot take Elam seriously either, especially in view of the fact that he asks that we consider one of the most powerful systems of combined linguistic and actions sign systems in the world in support of his contentions about "kinesic paradigms": the Indian dance theatre. He offers this material under the misguided belief that there are no such "powerful subcodes" in Western dance theater, which is patently false, apart from the fact that to separate the Indian *hasta* system from the spoken and written languages to which it is irrevocably tied is a gross error (see Puri, 1981a, for full discussion).

One thus finds Elam's exegesis of kinesics and the properties of "body motion as a communicative medium" virtually unintelligible, especially with regard to what he calls a "gestural fallacy" common to "…popular handbooks on 'body talk' and most writing on theatrical movement" (Elam, 1980:71), keeping in mind, of course, that we would agree with him if his meaning is restricted to notions of a universal "dictionary" of gesture, such as Fast describes. However,

> It is tempting to conceive of the 'gesture' as a discrete and well-marked item, especially in the case of a highly expressive actor or, say, a demonstrative Neapolitan fruit-vendor, since we may note characteristic movements which appear distinct from their behavioural context. In reality, the gesture does not exist as an isolated entity and cannot, unlike the word or morpheme, be separated from the general continuum [Elam, 1980:71].

Attempts to unpack his arguments result in the following questions: (1) if gestures do not exist as isolable entities, like words or morphemes, then how are we to account for the gestures in the Indian *hasta* system, or for the isolable gestures like "thumbing a ride" and many others with which we are all familiar; (2) what is meant by Elam's usage of the phrase "behavioural context"? Does this phrase imply, as we suspect, *two* sets of items available for study, and (3) are we meant to understand that because a "highly expressive actor" moves when he or she is *not* "acting," and also moves while "acting," that it is impossible to identify these sets of actions and to discover their purposes, contexts, and intelligibility? And, are we to understand that the actor is never *still*—that he or she is *constantly* in motion? What kind of "reality" is this? Examination of another passage answers these questions:

> One cannot tabulate a gestural 'lexicon' in which kinesic paradigms may be conveniently set out: movement, in effect, is continuous, and is open to analysis only through the overall syntactic patterns of a (preferably filmed) stretch of kinesic behaviour [1980:71].

But this hypothesis simply cannot survive the avalanche of negative evidence that any novice anthropology student of human movement could produce: I refer to Bharatanatyam, for a start; to Martha Graham technique, to the ballet or to any other danced form, and to the lexicon of Tongan gestures that can be culled from Kaeppler's work (1985). American Sign Language, British Sign Language, or Plains' Indian Sign Language are all based on lexicons of gestures, as is the body language of Orthodox and Roman Catholic Masses. Are we to disregard the long and short forms of T'ai Chi Ch'uan or any other military art, or the greeting ceremonies and "routines" that are characteristic of hundreds of

peoples throughout the world? Are we to ignore gestures of ridicule
and abuse? But, one could go on and on with this. The significant
feature of all the ethnographic evidence in this case is that, taken
singly or together, all of these systems represent negative evidence
with reference to an hypothesis postulating a "behavioral continuum" that supposedly consists of *non*-discrete unmarked items.

We can now understand Elam's phrase "behavioral context"
to mean "continuous movement" that is open to analysis *only*
through overall *syntactic* (not semantic) patterns of "behavior" that
are independent of and prior to intentions, beliefs, and contexts,
hence any semantic content at all. And we would be forced to agree,
if this is what one is looking for, that such "behavior" is better
studied through filmed stretches because there, the agent's intentions can well and truly be disregarded. Finally, we are to understand, or so it would seem, that we need not concern ourselves with
stillness, or with the semantics involved in the human act of *not*
moving. We are told that movement is, "in effect" continuous
(whatever that means) so that we must repress our certain knowledges that a "highly expressive actor" or a "Neapolitan fruit-ven-
dor" like anyone else we have ever known or imagined, surely does
not *move all the time*. Nor do we need to be reminded that hearts
beat and breathing continues, because to that kind of observation,
one is tempted to say, "so what?" with reference to considerations
of movement as a communicative medium.

Perhaps we would be better advised to recall Wittgenstein's
remarks on movement from *Philosophical Investigations*: "I don't
need to wait for my arm to go up—I can raise it" (1958:159e, no.
612), because there, human agency and human intentions are not
disregarded. Or, perhaps we should reexamine the work of
Hampshire (1959), whose investigations on thought and action
yielded the conclusion that *human spatial points of reference are*
points of application for linguistic predicates, thus reminding us of
the indissoluble connection between human actions, time/space,
and thought. Such reminders, however, will not lead us in the
direction of a conception of "behavior" as a non-linguified, quantifiable universal, but towards the concept of an "action sign" and
a different point of view entirely, for not only is a significant portion

of human behavior marked, such that it can be talked about as "discrete items" somewhat like "words" and "morphemes," human actions can be classified into genres of act/action structures using the medium of human movement as a basic form of communication.

Semasiologists allocate stretches of action signs as they are manifested on the ground to genres, using the classifications and categories assigned to them by the ethnicities to which they belong. Thus, signing (as in ASL, PSL, BSL or other sign language) is a genre of act/action structures using the medium of movement, much in the same way that it could be said that conversation is a genre of speech acts. Signing is a kind of performance, just as a conversation in the spoken domain can be understood as a kind of performance, using a dramaturgical model of events. It is necessary, however, to exercise extreme care when using terms like "performance" in these ways because signing is a "performance-with-a-difference" with reference to comparative work. A conversation in ASL, for example, tends to be an on-the-spot improvisation of an idiom of body language, where the agents are both the joint actors and authors of the resulting "story," unlike a "drama" where there are (barring improvisational forms, like the *Commedia*) prescribed scripts and blocking of the actions and body language. I am fully aware that there are, besides the *Commedia,* certain dramatic art forms that on an hypothetical continuum, would tend more towards on-the-spot improvisation. In a discussion as unspecific as this, one's examples tend to be over-generalized and somewhat rough and ready, but such risks must be taken, otherwise one bogs the reader down in too much analytical detail.

My point is this: to juxtapose drama as it is conventionally understood with signing as it is conventionally understood, is to focus on two forms of the communicative usage of action signs and two "spaces" wherein beliefs, ideas, and information are exchanged. The genre of dramatic performances in western theater incorporates both speech and movement in situations where the actors can be, but usually are not, the authors, either of the sets of linguistic signs or action signs. To contrast this kind of sign-space with the signing space of, say, ASL, is to compare and contrast the dramatic forms with a genre of actions signs that do not include a speech component. Or, if signing can be said to include a speech component, then we enter a world of verbal glosses onto action signs, made primarily for hearing persons and not for the people who use signing as a primary form of communication.

To enter the spaces of western theatrical dancing is to enter another genre of idioms of body languages that are devoid of speech in their observable manifestations, but one that is not devoid of speech acts in the same way as the signing space of ASL. One would not want to characterize the danced action sign spaces either as "dramatic spaces" that merely repress the speech acts or as "non-verbal behavior." In other words, dancing does *not* consist of the same kinds of act/action structures as the blocking of a drama, and neither is the danced space a "movement conversation" in the same sense as the signing space of ASL. The relations of actions to language can be seen to be very different in all three spaces. Regardless of their differences, all these genres of actions can be treated as "lived events" or "lived stories," and this leads me to the final problem that the separation of language from human actions represents.

When semasiologists say that human beings are language-users, role-creators, rule-followers, and meaning-makers (a declamatory proposition that quickly becomes tedious), what we mean to say, in encapsulated form, is that we proceed from the assumption that human beings are story-makers and story-tellers. Recognition of these features of the nature of human beings is not, we insist, merely a reiteration of a self-evident statement of that which everyone knows, but a base-line definition of the constitutive elements of human nature and human be-ing. We mean for it to be understood, moreover, that humans, besides telling stories in a conventional sense, also *live* stories in a less conventionally understood sense. Human stories include animals, plants—everything that can be perceived in their universes. Semasiologists tend to see these lived stories, individual or collective, as action signs. What we mean by that is that any one action sign or any combination of them always constitutes some episode or part of an episode in a possible, a past, or a potential ethnographically describable narrative.

The implications of this are fairly broad and I cannot discuss all of them here, but in the interests of wrapping-up all of the unmarked terms with which I began this lecture, one of the consequences of our point of view is that we say "no" to the psychologists' idea that human continuity consists solely of a personal identity seen as a continuum of psychological states and conditions. It also means that we say "no" to certain forms of hard-core empiricism, and "no" to cultic searches for some experience which is behind appearances to a "reality" which is a-historical, a-cultural, a-conceptual, and a-linguistic.

In the extended sense in which I have used the word, "ethnography" is not a simple diachronic or synchronic account of sequence of events or actions conceived of as movements bereft of meanings, but a conception of sequences and patterns of actions abstracted from the lived stories or ethnographies of a person, a people, or a group of people. An action sign (or any stretch of them, written or unwritten) is not a "raw movement" or "piece of emitted behavior" which can usefully be thought of independently from socio-linguistic contexts, but an element, usually of larger stretches or patterns, of lived ethnographic narratives which have significance and semantic content *only* in relation to the other signs that accompany it, and with reference to the ethnicity and the language context from which it was derived.

The notion of a "personal anthropology," then (see Pocock, 1973, and the Appendix, *infra,* pp. 288–289), means that "x" is the subject of a personal, narratable ethnography and history. "X" is seen as living out his or her personal ethnography. As this *kind* of subject, "x" is the subject of an ethnography that is peculiarly "x's" own and no one else's; the individual story has its own peculiar meanings, but that feature of "x's" personal ethnography does not alter the facts of that ethnography intersecting with that of other individuals, nor with general features of the ethnicity in which "x's" personal ethnography began, or with others which may have been adopted. Chief among these shared characteristics is the spoken language(s) and body language(s) that are shared social facts, plus the languages that may be learned in addition to the native languages.

At any given time, one's personal identity is pre-supposed to "be" or to possess a certain unity of character that the unities of the kinds of social narratives to which one belongs (and those which one attempts to write about) require. Without such unities that are indissoluble "welds" of the individual and social—especially with reference to the stock of person categories that are available—there could be no stories and no notion of a personal anthropology, a personal "ethnography" and no ethnographical reports, whatever or whomever they might concern.

The notion of the lived story or the lived narrative is one that is, I think, particularly well-understood by some anthropologists who, like myself, have been engaged for part of their lives in professional theatre. A significant feature of the discipline of professional western theatre in any of its forms involves intense and acute awarenesses of an array of notions about personal identity, of the complexities of role-playing and *being a symbol* in a semiotic of one's own or another's creation.[5] I do not wish to imply that no one else is cognizant of these things, and I have not omitted discussion of the works of Goffman (1959 and 1961), Harré and Secord (1972) and others because I am unaware of their concerns for a dramaturgical model of events, but because, interesting though it all is, it would have distracted us from the main theme of this lecture: how are we to understand the term, "behavior"?

As I move towards the conclusion of this lecture—and of the entire series of lectures—it is appropriate to ask, "what are we to make of it all?" First, I hope that we can agree that all of the terms with which this lecture started, especially "behavior," are important terms that, however obvious their meanings and definitions may seem to be, nevertheless want constant reevaluation and study. It has not been my purpose to persuade my audiences towards judgments of the greater or lesser value of any of the features of ethnographic investigation to which I have alluded, but I *would* ask for a judgment concerning the contrasting proposition with which this lecture began:

Is "behavior" something that can usefully be treated as if it were prior to, or independent of, intentions, beliefs and social contexts, or does "behavior" consist of actions signs embedded in ethnographic narratives of human lives that cannot rightly be treated independently of language-use, rule-following, role-creating, meaning-making, and story-telling?

I ask for this judgment because by now, it should be clear that all of the theories and explanations of the dance which have been discussed in the previous eight lectures do not, in one way of looking at them, stand by themselves, nor have most of the authors we have discussed in the first six lectures addressed the above question. Only a few of the modern theories of the dance and human movement concern themselves with these issues. As for the rest, they all depend upon implicit theories of human "behavior" and human "being." I have attempted to survey these theories from a social anthropological standpoint which is informed by years of experience as a dancer, choreographer, and teacher of dancing. I have examined the claims that it seems to me that the authors of various theories have made, asking whether or not the explanations given are plausible or implausible, with a view towards pointing out the implications and consequences of holding such views.

My years of teaching the anthropology of human movement have convinced me beyond all doubt that on the whole, students come to the study of this subject relatively ill-prepared because they do not know, for a start, what explanations-cum-theories have been offered them from the past, or what views are available to them in the present. Because they are unaware of the problems and issues that surround the literature, especially on dancing, its lack of bibliographic controls, and its general state of disarray, they are often—and all too easily, led astray, either by teachers who know very little more than they do, or by their own incredulity and naïveté. Let no one say, if they have been patient and kind enough to accompany me through the exercises of these lectures, that he or she now "does not know"—and that, yes, all of that which has preceded this lecture has been said, believed, and acted upon with reference to the dance.

Perhaps, to the relatively small part of my audience which consists of professional anthropologists, linguists, sociologists, and philosophers, all that I have accomplished specifically in this last lecture, is to drive yet another nail into the coffin of Cartesianism—or into the coffin of Positivism, with all of its attendant notions about a passive, objective observer, in which case, this lecture might end with the lyrics of the Moody Blues: "I think, I think that I am. Therefore, I am, I think?" But, I prefer not to retreat into in-jokes of this kind, because they may not be meaningful to readers who are interested in a more general approach to human movement studies.

With them in mind, I will conclude this discussion with an anecdote about a committee of the French Academy employed in the preparation of the Academy dictionary, who defined the word "crab" as follows: "Crab: a small red fish which walks backwards." Commenting on this definition, the celebrated naturalist Cuvier said: "Your definition, gentlemen, would be perfect, only for three exceptions. The crab is not a fish, it is not red and it does not walk backwards."

The current natural definition of "human behavior" would be perfect, too, only for three exceptions: human behavior is not universal, we do not understand it, nor does it come to us *sans* language, and it is not caused by something apart from human intentions, beliefs, passions, and contexts.

Notes

1. I am aware that there are people who do not grow, but this is not the point. The capacity and potential for growth is there: whether it is realized or not does not alter the fact of the existence of the capacity.

2. The expectation on the part of young field investigators that intentions will be made conveniently explicit by informants is somewhat sophomoric, to say the least. There is no more reason why an informant in Africa, Melanesia, or Siberia should give an unequivocal account of *their* intentions for their actions, any more than an informant in the United States, Great Britain, Australia, or Canada can be explicit about intentions at this level. Try asking a secretary or an "average person" why they drink coffee or tea at an

appointed time of day, or why certain foods are considered "breakfast food" and others are not, and then ask them if they "intend" coffee breaks or "elevenses," and such. Their answers will be similar to answers with which anthropologists are familiar elsewhere: "everyone does it," or, "this is what we always do." I will not belabor the point further, except to say that I am convinced, because of this, that part of graduate study (or upperlevel graduate study) of this subject should include a "junk ethnography"; that is to say, a study of some form of movement system carried out in the student's own culture that is of value simply because it gives the novice fieldworker some notion of the complexities of the fieldwork process, and the importance of questions and answers with regard to the study of human actions.

3. For example, Jackson (1983) was puzzled by the ritual actions of Karanko women in Sierra Leone—and he evidently remained puzzled, according to his own accounts. He apparently did not ask them what they were doing, or, perhaps he could not, or did not want to believe what they seemed to mean by their actions, reminiscent, at least on the face of it, of the sort of thing described by Shirley Ardener in her fine article on female militancy and Kom and Bekwari women (1977).

4. There is an additional problem with practical experiences of unintelligibility: in many cases, we do not (cannot, or will not) take responsibility for our side of the communicative process. That is, an act, a thing, an utterance, or a concept may be poorly or unintelligibly expressed or presented, and in cases like these, the agent (actor, speaker, creator) bears the burden of clarification. On the other hand, unintelligibility may occur because the "receiver" (listener, observer, audience) may not have intellectual, cultural, or linguistic access to that which is being expressed. In these cases, the burden of clarification is not on the agent or originator of the communication, but on the recipient.

5. The awareness of being a symbol in a semiotic is neither a "commonsense" perception nor is it an experience common to a majority of people on a conscious level. The fact that it is not common experience does not alter its reality or the perceptions which arise therefrom. It does not alter the fact that human natures,

powers, and capacities provide the possibility for this kind of experience. I am convinced that every individual who has experienced "culture shock" knows, on some level, what it is like to be a symbol *out of the context of* their own "group semiotic" or group sign-system, whatever it may be, but these perceptions are frequently unarticulated or classified as something else, thus admitting the possibility of "knowing" something, but "not knowing" that one "knows."

CONCLUSION

THIRTY-ODD YEARS AGO, WHEN I WAS beginning to be aware of the differences in modes of explanation for the dance, their variety, incompatibilities, and contradictions, I was particularly interested in theories of the dance and theatre which viewed both as "illusion."[1] At the time, I was deeply shocked, and often hurt by the fact that others (including several members of my family) evidently considered the life that I had chosen as an artist and dancer as an elaborate deception of some kind. "When are you going to get a *real* job?" they would ask. " When are you going to face up to the realities of life?" It was as if my real life as an artist and dancer was less of a real life than the lives of lumberjacks, secretaries, college professors or waitresses, lawyers or truck drivers, insurance salesmen, priests, nurses, or any other profession.

During the intervening years, I have occupied other social roles than that of artist/dancer. I have done many kinds of work and have had many experiences of life all of which taught me that there is a common misconception about artists and "artistic experience" which is thought to be isolated from other kinds of experience in important ways. The misconception is based on the notion that imagination and creativity *are* required of artists, but *not required* of, say, sociologists, lumberjacks, college professors, priests, anthropologists, lawyers, or secretaries.

The reason for the misconception lies in the nature of theatrical, especially danced theatrical events. The confusions that surround this kind of event arise mainly because the majority of persons seem not to understand very clearly either the event of a dance as it is understood by its participants or their own responses to it. Here, I would ask that readers recall comments made in the second lecture, i.e, " ...we might expect that a ballerina who dances

Giselle will go mad and actually kill herself at the end of the ballet"
(see *supra*, p. 21).

The audience in this case, does not *imagine* that Giselle kills
herself: Giselle actually *does* go mad and kill herself, but Alicia
Markova (or any other ballerina who ever danced the part) does *not*
kill herself. The question here is not one of "illusion" or "deception"
on the part of the artist: the question turns around how we respond
to the facts of unrequited love and despair which leads to suicide
in "real life." Had we no experience of despair or suicide in real
life, we would have no basis for comprehending the artistic intention of Giselle. If we cannot be moved by the madness and suicide
in Giselle, then we probably have not developed the capacity to
respond emotionally to despair and suicide in life, either.[2]

The fact is that the response to the situation in Giselle is an
analogue to many situations in real life, just as the power of illusion
(a central theme of the ballet *Swan Lake*) is an analogue to many
life situations. There are many who wonder why this "old" ballet,
so well-known—and so out-dated in the minds of many—remains
so popular that it cannot be dropped from a company's repertoire
without immediate complaints from audiences. I believe that the
continued fascination for this work lies in the preoccupations that
we all have with the notion of choices: *Swan Lake* is about a man
who makes a wrong choice because of a magician's powers of
illusion, which created Odile, the "other" and evil Swan Queen. The
prince is dazzled and fooled and he makes the wrong choice. He is
deluded and cannot see through the fakery. In the original version
of the ballet, he and Odette (the " right" choice) do not sail off into
never-never land in a swan-boat.

The point is that we respond to *real* characters in a dance, that
are portrayed by *real* people with *real* knowledge of human emotions. It is thoughts like these which prompt me to say that a
theatrical or dramaturgical *model of* events looks very different
from an agent's (actor's or dancer's) point of view than it does from
an audience's point of view. Erving Goffman (1959) uses a theatrical type of model of events with power and authority, but it is one
which is taken entirely from aspects of a *physical* theater, not from
the standpoint of the actors who use it.

It is no real criticism of Goffman's pioneering and valuable use of the model in the field of sociology to say that from a semasiological viewpoint, his overall conception of the theater seems somewhat impoverished. He seems to have conceived of the theater mainly as a piece of architecture, and he applies fairly superficial aspects of it to human social events in western society, using some of the technical terminology, connected with the stage, i.e., "backstage," "frontstage," etc., but in the end, he is prepared to discard the structure; for once having served its purpose, it is expendable, like the painted sets it contains, and we are left to get on with "real life."

Keen students of anthropology and human movement cannot afford this kind of facile oversimplification. If they use Goffman's work, they must be prepared to go beyond it, and much more deeply into the notion of a dramaturgical model of events than Goffman did, although he is owed gratitude because he introduced the model once more into social science. It had laid dormant in the history of science at least since the time of Erasmus. While it may be argued that Goffman, because of this, is the Newton of the social sciences, as a teacher, I am obliged to point out that we are now in need of an Einstein, perhaps, or a Faraday or Planck—someone who has ventured beyond the boundaries of Newtonian social science, as someone had to reach beyond Newton in the physical sciences. We need studies of the semantic values of some of the people to whom the theater *is* "real life" in our own culture, and studies which draw attention to aspects of the theater which seem to be consistently overlooked: the people in it.

It is true that a theater can be seen as a stable image of the cultural environment in most western societies, and it is equally true that usage of the model is familiar in common language terms. Nearly every English-speaker has at some time referred to, e.g., "theaters of war," or "operating theaters" in hospitals, or the "scenes of the crime," "the international scene," and so on. These phrases encapsulate that which can be thought of as the beginnings of "implicit theory" regarding the events they describe. It is implicit theorizing in common usage cases, because the person(s) using the terms and phrases have never stopped to consider in how far they *really* believe that a war is like a theatrical event. It is interesting, and semantically significant, that while men play " war *games*," the real war is assigned to a theater model of events, consciously or unconsciously. And when people refer to " the political scene," they usually characterize real political "battles" as happening in an "arena," as in a circus or stadium. Thus, I do not speak of anything with which we are not all familiar; the unfamiliarity begins when students of anthropology and human movement are asked to bring these familiar things into their consciousness and examine them. This process is a part of the process of familiarizing oneself with "theorizing" in semasiology.

Viewed as examples of architecture—as physical spaces alone—theaters, circuses, gymnasia, stadia, and churches present stable images of the non-biological, spatio-linguistic environments of people, but their semantic spaces[3] are far more difficult to comprehend. They are also very different indeed, both in degree and kind. We all know, for instance, that the movement events which occur in a Catholic church are very different from those which occur, say, in a football stadium, but what makes the space different? Is it merely the physical building? It is not, and the "proof" of this, if you will, lies in the fact that the space *internal to* a rite of a Mass can be shown to be different from the space *internal to* a football game. If the physical spaces of churches, stadiums, and such were the determinants of the actions which take place within them then we should be unable to recognize an event of a Mass or an event of a football game in any other context. No. The physical properties of the buildings are secondary to the semantic spaces which they stand for, just as the physical structure of the larynx and throat muscles are secondary and external to the notion of "language."[4]

What is meant by this? Consider, momentarily, Gell's analysis of an Umeda dance. Ask these questions of the data we are offered: how is the space internal to the dance organized? Is it around the notion of cardinal directions, is it around the conventional use of the body in ordinary, daily life? Is it around a concept of social roles and rules that are peculiar to the Umeda concept of be-ing? What are these people doing when they dance? What are the stable images of Umeda cultural environments which are the "facts" which determine what their dance(s) and ceremonies look like. We shall never know, partly because the anthropologist chooses an "observer's model, using behavioural data" (Gell, 1985:185) to convince us that if we measure Umeda muscle actions using the same kinds of charts and graphs which are used to measure the movements of the legs in kinesiological studies of walking and running, that we can understand what the *ida* ceremony is all about. The spatial organization of the dance is not, apparently, a matter worthy of consideration.

As a "non-dance expert" (1985:187) this writer admits his lack of skill as a notator, but complains of the "incomprehensibility" of movement writing scripts and expresses his own (and he assumes, the rest of the anthropological profession's) unwillingness to learn. Instead, he offers, with no apologies, a reductionist view of Umeda dance movements "simply to movements of the leg, seen sideways on." From this model, which is also a reduction from an original which was "too sensitive and too abstract" for Gell's purposes, we are treated to several paragraphs of totally unilluminating technical jargon which the author admits is problematical, as there is a difficulty of translating the graphs into concrete movements—precisely his problem with the notational "hieroglyphs" he derides in movement scripts (1985:188).

His banal conclusion consists of the declaration that "Dance is finally interpretable as a stylised deformation of nondance mobility, just as poetry is a deformation or modulation of language, a deviation from the norm of expression that enhances expressiveness" (1985:204). This anthropologist also learnedly informs us, by way of *explanation* that " ... the way Umedas walk is related to their environment...and their technology (lack of shoes of any kind)" (1985:193). We shall hear more about environmental explanations in a moment. For now, I would want to say that in this conclusion, as in all of the preceding lectures, I have attempted to point out that different *levels* of understanding, different *levels* of comprehension are required before we can even begin to discuss human actions in an honest and sensible way. I have also stressed to the point of tedium the importance of the informants' views of what they are doing.

"But how," students have asked, "can I begin to understand

all that?" My reply? The process begins with the quality of reading and thinking that one does from the outset regarding the literature on dancing, and with the skill one develops over a period of years with reference to the articulation of one's ideas. Individual success in this kind of study, as well as the future success of the field of study itself, depends upon people who can read and write clearly, articulately, and cogently about the dance, dances, and the act of dancing. It is essential that students recognize theories and theorizing from the beginning, and that they develop their capacities to think in these ways.

It is with some regret that I am forced to say that the prevailing intellectual climate of these times is not very hospitable, and not conducive to the kinds of thinking that are required, because it is not the kind of thinking that is useful in passing multiple choice and true-false examinations. The knowledge of language required in these cases amounts to little more than the ability to write check-marks that are the equivalents of verbal grunts, for a start. One hopes that this is merely a passing fashion in the educational world, of course, but it is well for aspiring students to recognize what they are up against.

If anything, these kinds of testing, the course structures which accompany them and the educational philosophies which inform them are little more than an encouragement to adopt an a-theoretical, even anti-intellectual attitude towards studies of human actions. On the whole, thinking of the kind to which I have consistently alluded is not much appreciated. One is forced to this conclusion because of the astonishment and incredulity that is often expressed with regard to higher levels of thinking in relation to any form of dancing. Astonishment, is, of course, a dead give-away because it reveals the extent to which a-theoretical and anti-intellectual attitudes prevail. The condition exists partly because students are merely *exposed to* different theoretical and explanatory modes of thinking about the dance. They are rarely, if ever, actually *taught* anything about them, which is the main justification for writing a book of this kind. [5]

I have been asked, by status-holders in the educational dance field, for example, to "have patience"; to understand that functionalist kinds of thinking and generally sloppy scholarship are a "stage" that has to be got through in the life of the field of dance ethnology (somewhat like teen-aged thinking is conceived to be a stage in the developmental progress of an individual towards maturity). "In thirty or forty years," they tell me, "we may catch up with you and your students. But we have to progress towards that kind of sophisticated thinking. Not everyone thinks the way you do." I am aware that many people do not think the way I do, and I am not flattered, but saddened, by this kind of response, apart from the fact that the mere passage of time has nothing to do with the case. *More* functionalist thinking, or the same kinds of thinking for thirty or forty more years will not lead to semantic, semiotic, or any other more sophisticated modes of thought about the dance. Forty years ago, I might have believed that kind of argument. Now, forty years later, I do not, and I attempt, wherever possible, to encourage students in the disbelief, although I know that for them to resist the kinds of entrenched thinking that the above-mentioned attitudes imply can be both costly and discouraging. It requires extraordinary stamina to maintain one's original aims and purpose in this field, however, I am convinced that there are a significant number of people who are prepared to undertake the task, and it is primarily for them that these lectures have been written.

The practical advice that I would want to leave with these students of anthropology and the dance is this: from the beginnings (whatever those may be in specific, individual cases), LEARN TO READ DIFFERENTLY. Follow Dutton's advice (1979) regarding ethnographies and their levels of explanation when he says (in criticism of Titiev's explanation of Hopi ceremony),

> So all of Hopi sacred drama—those moving texts and elaborate ceremonies, those magnificent dances—can be seen merely as an apparatus to cope with the threat of hostile desert environment. Here is yet another example: In her discussion of Hopi socialization, Goldfrank tells us that "large scale cooperation" seen among members of the Pueblo tribes is "no spontaneous expression of good will or sociability," but results from a "long process of conditioning" required by trying to engage in irrigation agriculture in a desert environment. To achieve the cooperation necessary for a functioning irrigated agriculture, the Zunis and Hopis strive from infancy

for "a yielding disposition. From early childhood, quarrelling, even in play is discouraged ... " (1945:527) ... And so it goes. Why are the Navaho so concerned with witchcraft? asks an anthropologist, who learnedly informs us that it is because of the strain of living in a hostile desert environment. Why this vast and rich spectacle of Hopi sacred life? asks another, who wisely tells us that it is all just a device intended to counteract the hostile desert environment ... . [Dutton, 1979:204].

Dutton has focussed his criticism on one type of meta-explanation—an environmental explanation, although there are several others. The reason that his short paper is so good is that he elucidates very clearly the fact that anthropological writing requires more than one level of description: Crick's discussion of fieldwork problems and techniques (1982) is apposite.

Novice anthropologists of human movement tend not to understand what is required of them at first, thus, when they are asked, for example, to give a précis of some anthroplogist's argument, say, regarding Hopi dance or ceremony, they mistakenly offer a discussion of what the anthropologist has described about features of the dance or ceremony itself, usually with negative results. That is, the answer will rate "B–" or "C," perhaps, on an essay examination, and usually the student does not understand why, especially if the "ethnographic facts" that were presented by the student about what the anthropologist described are accurate. The simple explantion is this: a précis of a writer's argument (anthropologist or not) concerning any set of facts is not the same as an account of the writer's *exegesis of those facts.* Students should learn to read asking at least three questions: 1) What is being talked about here? 2) How is this material interpreted? and 3) What is the disciplinary or private explanation for that which is being talked about? If the student is encouraged to interact honestly and sensibly with received authorities and if he or she is encouraged to examine his or her privately held convictions, beliefs and such as part of the process, the results are usually extremely satisfying, both to teacher and student.

It is quite possible, in anthropology, to "...go far astray if we try to impute to a primitive people *our* notion of their natural habitat.

For it is not their physical environment *as we experience and understand it* which influences them, but that environment *as they experience and understand it"* (Dutton, 1979:205) which is important. This is why one wishes that Gell (1985) had simply written an article about his problems with describing, understanding, or writing about Umeda dance instead of leading us to believe that we might learn something of the dances themselves. Instead of "Style and Meaning in Umeda Dance," his article should have been entitled, "A graphic representation of one leg in Umeda dance; with special attention to an observer's model."

Human actions always stand in some relationship (a) to the spoken language(s) and to the body language(s) which are relevant to the people themselves, (b) to the context(s) in which they are found, and (c) to the individual's "self" and the social "selves" of the investigator's ethnicity. This is a rather lengthy way of saying that it is necessary in semasiology, at least, to recognize the human basis of human knowledge. That there are limitations on this is, one would have thought, self-evident. There is a great deal which is mysterious, infinitely beautiful and inexpressible about dances, rituals, and such. One would hope that this kind of mystery and beauty will always exist, otherwise, the destiny of the human race may consist of becoming a rather complicated bipedal anthill—not a desirable prospect, surely.

But, whatever the future may hold, students of anthropology and the dance should keep in mind the fact that dances, if they are "products" of anything, are the products of the mind/bodies of language-using creatures who work with their circumstances in order that those circumstances may become intelligible to themselves and others, on a spectrum of danced activities which ranges from the trivial and banal to the profound—and the mysterious, the poignant and the beautiful.

Notes

1. For those who are interested in a discussion of the intellectual life of the notion of the theater as a model of life in western society, see Barish (1981), for the "anti-theatrical bias" which,

according to this author's excellent analysis, appears to have been with us for a very long time.

2. For further discussion of the relation of emotional responses, art and life, see Best (1985) and Barish (1981).

3. The notion of semantic spaces is exemplified in the concept of the liturgical space (in contrast to the physical or geographical) spaces of the Dominican post-Tridentine Mass. Liturgical east, west, north, and south and their various meanings provide the key, in that context, to understanding important elements, both of the ways in which the celebrants move and of the distributions of objects in the space (see Williams 1975:Volume II, for complete discussion).

4. And, we might add, as the physical body is secondary to the notion of body languages.

5. It seems necessary to say that there is a current fashion for no "teaching" of the kind that I suggest, because, I am told, this kind of teaching is really hidden persuasion and influence. According to the "exposure method" of instruction, the intellectual self of the instructor is to be kept as far out of the matter as possible, on the belief that the student will somehow find his or her own way, and that the possibility of "objectivity" in teaching will be thereby increased. This is not the place to enter into a discussion of pedagogy, but I must assert that I find this method and the beliefs on which it is based both pointless and silly because in the end, it is a method of teaching which offers the student no real *choice,* thereby destroying the foundation for the development of any real individuality as a scholar. My views on teaching in any subject admittedly stem from the teaching of dancing, and from an ideal of many artists which, simply stated, is the notion of freedom through discipline, in contrast to the notion that freedom consists either of formlessness or the absence of discipline and techniques (see Best, 1982, for apposite discussion).

Appendix I.
AN EXERCISE IN APPLIED
PERSONAL ANTHROPOLOGY

Introduction

This paper represents an attempt to raise three points with regard to the study of dance and social anthropology. First, I have stressed the importance of an anthropological perspective in contrast to other perspectives in connection with ethnographies of the dance. Second, I have briefly outlined a few ontological and epistemological implications of treating social anthropology itself as a language-based, rather than as a Behavioral[1] science. Third, I have only barely indicated the epistemological consequences involved in accepting the idea of a personal anthropology.

In fact, it is the latter point which suffers most from the following brief treatment, for while the subject matter for a deeper analysis is present in this essay (i.e., the parts of texts of articles written before I read anthropology), it has mainly been subjected to a fairly standard anthropological critique. There are those who might say that this could have been done without the benefit of the idea of a personal anthropology. It seems appropriate, therefore, to justify the approach I have taken, since I would not agree that a public criticism of one's own writing could be legitimately undertaken unless it was connected with the idea of a personal anthropology and the related notion of a different kind of objectivity. Thus, as an initial foray into the idea, I have chosen what I conceive to be a pragmatic approach, which explains the choice of title and why,

This article is reprinted by kind permission of the *Dance Research Journal*, (CORD) and *The Journal for the Anthropological Study of Human Movement* (JASHM).

out of many possibilities, I stress the notion of "an exercise" and of the *application* of these ideas.[2]

If one applies Pocock's idea to one's own writing retrospectively, as I have done, one of the consequences of doing so is that one subjects one's earlier writing to stringent anthropological criticism, assuming, of course, that the newly acquired criteria apply to one's own work as they do the works of other authors. In other words, I have taken Pocock's "counsel of perfection" to include a continuous process of destruction of cherished axioms and a perpetual coping with apparent paradox and contradiction. This has meant facing up to the vagueness of all that I previously took for granted. It further involved, on a more general level, the often painful collapse of long established, firmly believed-in parameters of social interaction, models of reality and the world, moral and behavior "laws," etc.

But, it is not unusual to discover, as I have done through gaining an anthropological perspective, that what were once thought to be "laws" (or more accurately, fixed ideas) about life and the world are merely rules for living in a state of mild neurosis—mostly contained in that complex of bigotry, fears, prejudices, polarizations, and dichotomies which anthropologists generally refer to as ethnocentrism—which tends to remain unnoticed simply because it is shared by many of the people who happen to be around.

It seems to me that the idea of a personal anthropology requires seeing the world in itself and of itself in rather profound ways, rather than seeing it as a playground or a circus put there for egocentric purposes—whatever those purposes may be. And this is why I develop the philosophers' metaphor of "mental spectacles." It has occurred to me that perceiving the world—our own or that of others—merely as something to be used or to be afraid of, defended, protected, or otherwise reacted to, merely amounts to fitting it into pre-formed categories; to classifying ourselves and others in fallacious ways, hence the struggle mentioned below with received notions about "primitive/civilized," "developed/underdeveloped," and all the rest. In my view, perception is illusory if it tends to make everything look the same and if it leads to naïve universalism, boredom, cynicism, and familiarization based on the belief that our own needs, fears, etc., are the *determinants* of perception. This is a supremely egocentric and ethnocentric point of view which leaves out of account the human capacity to transcend both ego and societal values. The objectivity which the idea of a personal anthropology points to is, in my interpretation of it, connected with the general human capacity to be conscious of being conscious, of being conscious...and so on.

My interpretations of Pocock's ideas are surely not the only ones, nor does this essay draw out all of the consequences of adopting such a point of view. One could have written a paper on the relevance of the idea of a personal anthropology or written an extended essay on the implications of a new kind of consensual objectivity. Numerous subjects come to mind, which merely serve to indicate the richness and power of the idea. However, in this essay, I proceed from the assumption that the ideas are relevant and have tried to show some of the practical consequences involved, as e.g., a far superior approach to the ethnography of dance and human actions that I was capable of producing without the anthropological perspective and without the kinds of disciplined approach to dance ethnography I would now advocate. The paper is mainly addressed to those who would venture into the field as I did, to do "research" on their own: an interesting and instructive thing to do, but which in the end has little to offer a wider readership than one's friends and acquaintances.

Thus, in my writings since the year 1967 two distinct categories seem to appear, as follows:[3]

I. *Pre-anthropology*
   1. The Ghanaian Dancer's Environment (1967)
   2. The Dance of the Bedu Moon (1968)
   3. Primordial Time and the Abafoc Dance (1969)
   4. Towards Understanding African and Western Dance Art Forms (1969)
   5. Sokodae: Come and Dance (1970)
   6. Dance and Krachi Tradition (1970)

Ia. *Transition*
   1. Sokodae: A West African Dance (1971)

II. *Post-anthropology*
   1. Social Anthropology and Dance: B.Litt. Thesis (1972)
   2. Signs, Symptoms and Symbols (1972)
   3. The Relevance of Anthropological Studies in Dance (1973)
   4. The Human Action Sign and Semasiology (1974)
   5. Reviews: (1974)
       Women in Between (JASO)
       Choreometrics (CORD)
       Dance in Society (CORD)
   6. The Brides of Christ (1975)
   7. A Note on Human Action and the Language Machine (CORD, DRJ 1974–75)
   8. Reviews: (1975)
       Method and Theory in Analyzing Dance Structure with an Analysis of Tongan Dance *(Ethnomusicology)*
       Expression in Movement and the Arts: A Philosophical Enquiry *(Ethnomusicology)*
   9. The Role of Movement in Selected Symbolic Systems: D.Phil. Thesis (1975)
   10. Deep Structures of the Dance (1976).

A few facts connected with the above categorical division seem relevant: I first came to anthropology six years ago (August, 1970). I was teaching western dance history and choreography at the University of Ghana and in 1969, I sent some articles to the late Professor Sir E.E. Evans-Pritchard. It was thanks to his encouragement that I came to Oxford and it was initially owing to his good will and guidance (and subsequently to that of many others) that a gradual transformation from amateur to professional anthropologist has taken place.

The desire to study social anthropology crystallized because, while in Ghana, I realized that what I did was amateur anthropology; that is, the study of dances on their own, conceived of as isolated social phenomena, or conceived of as special activities having a privileged place in the total scheme of things. Three-and-a-half years in Ghana taught me much. I came from there an altered person, but one significant impression stands out as a result of the fieldwork done there. It consists of "...the daily experience of not knowing" (Ardener).[4]

While in Ghana my main concern was with learning some Ghanaian dances and attempting to absorb, insofar as I was then capable, elements of societies quite different from my own. The interest in West African dance had been awakened some years before, through intensive study with Pearl Primus and Percival Borde in New York City between 1956 and 1961. I arrived in Ghana having had extensive study and performing experience in four idioms of dance, three years of undergraduate philosophy and aesthetics, many years of teaching experience—and boundless energy and enthusiasm.

It would be difficult to assess, now, which was the greater: the enthusiasm or my naïveté. Both fortunately, were exceeded by the patience, generosity, and hospitality of my many teachers of dancing in several parts of Ghana and the Ivory Coast. If truth in communication had depended entirely on their good will, there would be no need to write this essay. If the accuracy of verbal reports of dance events and experience depended solely on the desire to learn or the willingness to teach, there would be few, if any problems of communication. But as I tried to learn from them and tried to record the dance events in which I had participated, I slowly realized that I did not know how to translate any of the experiences—my own or theirs—into any other terms or any other system or mode of expression.

This dissatisfaction was expressed obliquely in the article entitled "Towards Understanding African and Western Dance Art Forms." The chief value to be gained from that article, in my view, lies in the above insight and in the crude attempts made at that time to conceive of dances as systems; as body languages, which I tried to formalize in a kind of block diagram of the situational elements involved. This later provided the basis for a chapter in a B. Litt. thesis on the nature of communication through structured systems of meaningful actions.

On the whole, the writings produced between 1967–70 seem to reflect a genuine recognition of some of the important issues involved in the complex relations between dances and ordinary body languages of a people; between the body languages and their spoken languages; between the microcosmic world of "a dance" and the macrocosm of the wider society in which it is embedded, but at that time, I did not possess a sufficiently sophisticated meta-language[5] through which I could make, or express accurate connections among all the above-mentioned elements of a society. At that time, I possessed no systematic knowledge of a necessary kind which would have enabled me to write economically and concisely about the relations I saw and understood through my teachers' modes of specification of what they were doing. Looked at in one way, it may be that such experience as I had, grappling with fieldwork problems prior to the study of anthropology, was valuable. It has encouraged a view of anthropological theory and method as something other than tiresome academic abstractions and it has developed an awareness of the inevitability of a personal anthropology.

From "Objectification" Towards Objectivity

The writing done after the year 1971 reflects the above insights and the many I continue to gain from formal anthropological study, which I have consistently combined with a study of philosophy of science. Because of this, the writings listed under the heading "post-anthropology" (see *supra*, p. 290) will not provide objects of discussion. The elements of personal anthropology in them have undergone many profound changes, mainly owing to the gradual development of a meta-language. This in turn stems from touching, through formal study, higher levels of conceptualization and aware-ness. In Vygotskian terms, this would be described as reaching higher orders of structuring capacity. In common parlance, we might say, "an increase of understanding"; new and significantly different views of people and of the world.

For the remainder of this essay, I propose to comment on those articles of mine which are

...untrammeled by anthropological theory, or, for the most part, any experience of alternative ways of looking at the world...[Pocock, 1973:2.2].

The "pre-anthropology" articles I wrote bear strong resemblances to the student writings Pocock examines in his essay, but with one major difference: the student essays are entitled "Myself and My Society," where mine could all be effectively sub-titled, "Myself and Another Society" or "Myself Between Societies." It is slightly more difficult to tease out the elements of personal anthropology in these articles than in those Pocock comments upon, mainly because the relationship of the writer to the material is so different. In fact, I think of the relation as being disguised by the overt aim of writing about "them"; about "the other."

On one level, there is evidence of an *a priori* assumption of a type of objectification which Pocock rightly considers dangerous; that is, where the self of the enquirer is presumably excluded from the investigation and/or where the selves of the people are being investigated are somehow isolated, "cut-off," as it were, from the investigator and the rest of the world. The phrase "presumably excluded" is used for a specific reason, for as we shall see, the self of the investigator was not by any means excluded. The self of the writer is almost painfully evident in the form of

...a whole set of judgments about human nature, authority, sex, money, family, nation, etc. [Pocock, 1973:1.3]

As an initial example, we will look at the following paragraphs from "The Ghanaian Dancer's Environment":

Next we must consider certain factors pertaining to the dance itself which create radical differences in the Ghanaian dancer's milieu if compared to that of a Western dancer.

There are no Ghanaians who do *not* dance.

In the U.S., the dance belongs to informal aspects of the total culture, as recreation or entertainment; or to highly technical aspects, as in theatrical or educational dance. In these specialized areas, a high level of professional expertise, an academic degree or teacher training is the goal of long years of study. In Ghana the dance belongs first to the formal, traditional, ceremonial aspects of the total culture. Ghanaian dance has no highly organized technical structure. Ghana's dances are just now in the process of becoming theatrical phenomena and academic disciplines [Williams, 1967:34].

Here, the writer states what Pocock would call "conscious pressures" explicitly, drawing attention to western classifications of dance and dancers. We are led to think of some of the social facts of western dancers, i.e., they can be commercial entertainers, concert artists, or they can become professional dance educators— all fairly low status, not to say marginal professions in the United States.

Following these comments in the passage above, we find a somewhat appalling generalization, i.e., "there are no Ghanaians who do not dance," for which the author could have produced no evidence whatsoever, and which also participated (*N.B.*: past tense) in the "Africans-have-such-a-wonderful-sense-of-rhythm" syndrome. But we may safely assume that such statements only disguise the real message in the above paragraphs. The writer's implicit judgment is quite clear: in her view, the United States compared unfavorably with Ghana because, in the latter country, people dance. The dance is part of everyday life; it has a role in the overall pattern of life. It is not something "special," different, or inherently demeaning or degrading socially or intellectually. Of course, the statements also assume that dancing represents a kind of universal "good thing," which is, after all, a debatable point, too.

In the paragraph below, the author elaborates on the theme of general western categories of art, including the dance, noting with approval that the broad classifications of "fine" vs. "applied" art do not seem to hold in Ghana, yet, she perceives a problem here: her own awareness of this arbitrary, culture-specific distinction conflicts with the evident trend towards appropriation of these distinctions in urban areas of Ghana:

Much of what I have seen that is called 'art' in Ghana is a curious mixture indeed! It is some kind of adapted or adopted 'synthesis' of African form, concept or rhythms with an overseas overlay from a supposedly 'higher' civilization [Williams, 1967:34]

The author's struggle with and animosity towards received notions about such spurious, over-simplified oppositions as "primitive/civilized," "less complex/more complex," "literate/illiterate" are not very well disguised, and it is also questionable as to whether the struggle did not amount to a rather romantic understatement of them i.e., the pure untouched indigenous romanticism of early functionalism. The confusion becomes complete in, for example, the statement that "Ghanaian dance has no highly organized technical structure," which must be taken by a reader to mean theaters and academies of dance, for the words "technical" and "structure" can be interpreted in at least a dozen different ways. Even if one makes charitable excuses for the author based on her obvious naïveté with reference to language-use, the ambiguities remain. They exist because there is no real comparison made between features that Ghanaian dance has or has not and features that forms of dancing in the U.S. have or have not.

Perhaps it is to the writer's credit that in later publications she stresses the internal complexity of structures in several Ghanaian dances, and that in later articles she writes in such a way that readers might perceive her dawning awareness that words have more than one meaning. However, the intense conflict the writer experiences regarding the confusion over a categorical "fit" between western and Ghanaian classifications of dance is fully revealed in the following paragraph:

A significant feature of the Ghanaian dancer's psychological and intellectual environment is a confusion which often manifests itself in intense personal conflict. The pressures to which they are (and have been) subjected which have produced this 'pseudo-art' are largely subliminal: the result of cant, colonization and economic underdevelopment.They find it difficult to advance the values and ideas which their dances represent. It is an understandable reticence: the fear is that they (and the dances) will be labelled 'primitive', 'uncivilized', 'simple' etc. *ad nauseam* [Ibid: 1967:34]

But, we may well ask, whose "intense personal conflict" are we called upon to witnesss here? Whose reticence? Whose fears? And this is just the point.

The reader has lost the Ghanaians completely by the eleventh paragraph in an article consisting of nineteen-odd paragraphs. The author did not intend this to happen, nor at the time was she aware that such a thing *could* happen. And this, too, is just the point: lacking adequate training in and awareness of language and the complex process involved in making verbal accounts of others, the author simply managed to absorb the Ghanaian dancer's environment into her own set of received notions in ways which not only did disservice to the Ghanaian's uniqueness and humanity, but to her own as well. The comments below are truly apposite here:

> The recognition of unconscious operations in our communications is no alibi or excuse for irresponsibility. On the contrary it heightens the demand for responsibility; one aims simply to be as conscious as one possibly can recognizing the limitations built into the enterprise [Pocock, 1973:13.3].

Thus, one's unconsciousness gives rise to a mixture of reductionism, ethnocentrism and naïveté; not an "error" in one sense, simply because one is unaware of any alternative structures, theories, models and what have you. *Ignorance only becomes an error if one persists in maintaining it.* But one of the most important points made by Pocock can appropriately be stated here:

> This outside other becomes an object for my knowledge and understanding when I enter into relationship with it, and what I call my understanding is a report on that relationship <u>not on the essential being of that other</u> [underline is mine]. I personally enter into this relationship and make my report upon it. It is this making of a report, the offering of my understanding of the relationship as *true*, having universal intent, and therefore open to the acceptance, modification or rejection of my colleagues that constitutes the difference between my subjective experience and my personal anthropology [1973:13.4].

Objectivity Re-examined

It has been instructive to try to determine the nature of the pressures to which this writer was subject in 1967. It seems necessary to add that this exercise is very different from indulging in two-penny-halfpenny psychologizing, or an orgy of self-recrimination. Some of the unconscious pressures are summarized by Heisenberg when he questions,

> To what extent, then, have we finally come to an objective description of the world, especially of the atomic world? In classical physics science started from the belief—or should one say from the illusion?—that we could describe the world or at least parts of the world without any reference to ourselves.... Its success (that of "science") has led to the general ideal of an objective description of the world.... This division is arbitrary and historically a direct consequence of our scientific method [1958:54–55].

But, not all the pressures were unconscious. Some of those which were not were the products of many experiences which any western dancer has had (to a degree and with a frequency only vaguely understood by non-dancers, I think) of what it is like to be "the other" in relation to his or her own society. That is to say, in the United States, the dancer is often considered to be "exotic," perhaps "primitive," often "illiterate," and all the rest, hence the explanation for the author's easily constructed identifications with groups who are categorized in similar ways.

Notwithstanding how easily understood these particular elements are which contributed to the formation of an individual personal anthropology, they distract our attention from the issue of "objectivity" in the human(e) sciences. For, if we reject cheap psychologizing or litanies of criticism of our own or others' personal anthropologies, as Pocock advises, and turn to consider modification of our traditional notions of objectivity, where might we begin?

If we express dissatisfaction with the methodological divisions and patterns bequeathed to us by natural science and natural historians, then we may well ask what these notions are to be replaced by, or how they might be usefully modified? As is well known, many current developments in anthropology express acute dissatisfaction with some of the more dominant "pure" social science outlooks, as e.g., a construal of "the social" as an autonomous domain, or a construal of "the social" as epiphenomena, determined by physiological or biological mechanisms of some kind. There seems to be a widespread, increasing emphasis on *semantic* aspects of the social which cannot adequately be accommodated in the traditional social science paradigms and there have been many useful guidelines and productive suggests made; viz., *Explorations in Language and Meaning. Towards a Semantic Anthropology.* M. Crick, 1975, Malaby, London, and Halsted, New York.

What might be said of anthropologists who deny themselves the security of the kinds of objectivity that many of their colleagues have, and nearly all their predecessors had? What would characterize an anthropology which has, as it were, "...cut the painters..." connecting it to natural or Behavioral science paradigms? (see Ardener, 1980a). First, a semantic anthropology would be conceived of as a language-based science, in contrast, for example, to ethology, entomology, or biology, which are not. Second, to a working field anthropologist, a semantic anthropology would be characterized by a different ontological base from older styles of anthropology. That is, the nature of its subject matter would be defined differently, i.e., informants (whether from one's own or another society) would be looked upon as *subjects* in their own languages, spoken or unspoken. They would not be seen as "objects" divided from the rest of the world, or from the anthropologist. They would be conceived of as people, not as "organisms" or "mechanisms"; cf. Harré (1971).

An anthropology of this kind would have a different epistemology: the relations between investigator and data would differ. Winch (1958) discusses these relations at length, emphasizing these points. Harré (1970) discusses the relations between investigator and data at the meta-level of models and conceptual structures. Toulmin (1953) contrasts different kinds of relations between investigator and data with reference to physicists and natural historians, providing some valuable insights into conceptual problems in these sciences. Ardener (1973a and 1975) has effectively discussed such relations with regard to the analysis of events in anthropology. Pocock (1973) provides us with a new and wholly legitimate direction to take with reference to the notion of objectivity.

Theoretically and methodologically, the importance of such enquiries and relations cannot be over-estimated, for in my view, and in that of many of my colleagues in anthropology anyway, of simply "telling it like it is." Immediately that experiences or events are transposed into written language, they have had an order imposed upon them. The same thing is true, of course, of any type of human "languaging" or notation system, whether in the realm of body languages or dances, music, mathematics, films, etc. Thus, following Pocock, we can quite readily see that the more conscious one is of one's own implicit, *a priori* judgments regarding events and experiences, then the more objective in a new and different sense one might hope to become. I am convinced that only thus can we aspire to approach truth in communication or accuracy in any "languaged" formulations of any kind, whether they are about the world, others or ourselves.

An intriguing and wholly satisfying consequence of assuming Pocock's point of view and taking his "counsel of perfection" (1973:8.3 & 8.4) seriously is that it makes of the practice of anthropology a dynamic, living, open-ended process rather than a static, dead block of reified "knowledge" of some kind; a transformation altogether compatible with an Einsteinian universe of genuine "becoming" and the human world of languages and change which we presently inhabit. In fact, I would want to say that Pocock is too modest (or else he is merely a good tactician) in his assessment of the teaching practice of assigning initial essays to students of the kind he suggests. He refers to the exercise as a pedagogic device, which it undoubtedly is, but its value is far deeper than that, and its consequences are profound.

One is irresistibly reminded of Wittgenstein's and, later, Toulmin's and other philosophers' usage of the image of "spectacles." Toulmin remarks:

> There is only one way of seeing one's own spectacles clearly; that is, to take them off. It is impossible to focus both on them and through them at the same time [1961:101].

The main thrust of Pocock's idea of a personal anthropology, if I understand and interpret his arguments rightly, is that it enables one, first, to be aware of and then to remove, one's mental spectacles. In the process of removing and examining them, one is not bound to throw them away, discard them or label them "bad." In fact, one may prefer another image of the matter—one given to me by Pocock in a private communication: we can look at the soles of our feet, but not while walking. In either case, the crucial difference lies in our individual awareness of what we are doing.

There is, of course, a difficulty attached to the notion of mental spectacles which is, I think, a common human problem. Call the spectacles "conditioning," "socialization" or what you will, we all acquire at least one set of mental spectacles in virtue of the fact of being born into a specific language, into a given society and all the complex network of systems of communications which that implies. Then too, other sets of spectacles may be acquired: the professional sets, as e.g., physics, architecture, engineering, literature, anthropology, music, psychology, etc. Here, too, the analogy applies; if we fail to recognize the conceptual elements of the academic discipline to which we are committed, we will fail to recognize the true character of our ideas and our intellectual, or other kinds of problems. This is equally true, of course, if we consider the intellectual problems of our predecessors, many of whom thought, felt and saw "reality" and the world in very different ways. They did not, nor do we, "float free," as Pocock puts it, of their historical selves, or of their personal anthropologies.

The main difficulty is that we are so used to viewing the world, ourselves and its other inhabitants through our particular sets of spectacles that we forget what it would be like to see without them. Our very identification of ourselves with one, or many, sets of mental spectacles tends to prevent us from seeing that other possibilities exist. Perhaps they also prevent us from realizing that having at least one pair of mental spectacles is fundamental to the common human estate. Unfortunately, there is no analogous image for the mental "spectacles" in relation to the other senses, yet, we might imagine that we experience similar impediments in relation to them—in our hearing, for example.

The Status of the Essays

On a basis of the reflections made thus far, it is appropriate to ask what status I would now assign to these pre-anthropology essays. The answer is: differing statuses to each, depending upon where the particular essay stood in relation to the process of discovery mentioned at the beginning of this writing, i.e., that of realizing I was doing amateur anthropology. It must also be remembered that although the articles are listed in their chronological order of publication, they were not necessarily written in that order, thus the list does not reflect the process of realization. *The Dance of the Bedu Moon* was written after the article on time and the Abafɔ dance, although they were published in the reverse of that order. The Bedu article is a much better article, simply because in it, the writing is confined mainly to reportage; to the best descriptive writing of which I was then capable. These remarks, by the way, should not be construed by students to mean that one should not attempt to fit ethnographic material into a larger societal or theoretical context—far from it. Nor is the statement intended to mean that descriptive writing is better than some of the more technical kinds of languages I might use now. I would merely wish to draw attention to the fact that the Bedu article is better than the one on the Abafɔ dance because in it, I did not try to explain why or to give any reason for, the disparities between the Nafana year, the Muslim calendar and our own. I did not mention that the Nafana months appeared to be movable and to depend upon when "the right conditions" *as defined by them* were present for their purposes. I did not attempt to unravel the problems of why lunar months are not equal to or the same as those specified by the Christian calendar, as I had no desire to measure Nafana concepts of time against astronomical "realities" of one sort or another.

I was aware, as nearly any serious dancer is aware, of the *indeterminacy* of time; that is to say, whether time is measured in days, seasons, rhythms, hours, events, dates, micro-seconds, or occasions. Most of us are aware that one of our own dances, lasting approximately half an hour measured in clock time, can be the expansion of a moment in someone's life—as in Antony Tudor's

Jardin aux Lilas—or that a dance lasting one hour might cover several years of "historical time"or that "time" in any case, can as easily be defined as rhythm as anything else, or the regular reoccurrence of accented beats, etc. Yet, time systems are of central anthropological interest, as the search for "real" time and "real" space has preoccupied western peoples for centuries; cf. Ardener (1975). Some of these and similar points will be expanded later. Here, I should like to comment briefly on each of the essays in the order in which they were written.

In the first essay, the "environment" article, the writer depended heavily upon one author, E.T. Hall (1966). Whether that fact is immediately apparent to others is not known, however, at the time, Hall's writing had little impact on the author beyond emphasizing the inadequacies of general American attitudes towards "art," "dance," "space," "non-verbal" communication, etc. And this is not in any way meant to be a criticism of Hall. The writer was prepared, albeit totally unconsciously, to use his work as a justification for the ill-concealed animosities which were noted as "conflicts" earlier. In this observation there is, we might imagine, a cautionary tale: many writers, students, and others, seem to make the common mistake of using another author's work in a cavalier fashion, for they too seem to choose another's work to support a hidden message or to advance an implicit point of view. Doubtless they are also unconscious of the process, but the results are somewhat ludicrous. To an informed and/or careful reader, it is clear that no actual dialogue takes place between two positions or two arguments, just as no dialogue with Hall's thesis was undertaken in the "environment" article. The upshot is simply a naïve and undocumented appeal to vaguely defines "authority" which is not only misguided, but irrelevant.

When the "time and the Abafɔɔ dance" article was written, the author had recognized the need for some other kind of language or some other means of conveying the concepts of time to be found in different ethnicities from her own, but she again resorts to heavy dependence upon other authors for terms which seemed to be adequate. This is probably clear to a sophisticated reader through her adoption of the term "primordial," a word used by many psychologists when discussing the differences they think they perceive between, say, the lived, experiential time of a people and the standard western concept of "real" time.

Of the four earlier articles, the one on *understanding* African and Western dance is, from my present standpoint, the most important (although I would never use the words "Africa" or "art" in this context now). It was severely criticized by those who read it at the time, for it expressed dissatisfaction with many prevailing, and I might add, banal, notions of dance. It pointed to very awkward questions, such as, *what is the basis* for our generalizations about the universality of dance and human movements? By this time, the author had become relatively insecure in the face of different human systems of time, space, motion, and meanings. She had begun to glimpse the patterns on her own mental spectacles and this recognition marked the turning point in her intellectual career, for the disillusionment was painful, but the message was clear. It read, "you are not writing about the dance or the Ghanaians; you are writing about yourself and what you think the dance ought to be like in your own country, or what you wish it were like there." It was a sobering thought, but it provided the energy for work in a new direction, and perhaps, interestingly, the means for pursuing a new career. It was the article on *Dance and Krachi Tradition* which prompted Evans-Pritchard (or so he said) to suggest that social anthropology might provide useful lines of study—and it has. Moreover, this article is sufficiently different from the rest that we might usefully examine it in more detail.

The Dance and Krachi Tradition[6]

The core of this article is to be found in the extended diagram to be found on pages 318–320 at the end of this article. The diagram or "chart" of the role/rule relations between the religious hierarchy of persons and the two figures outside of it reflect the radical changes in thinking mentioned above. The ethnographic material to follow is taken from the chart, as it is a brief explanation of some of the person categories of the Krachi people.

In the article, "Dance and Krachi Tradition," more is said about Krachi tradition than about any particular dance of those people. In fact, four dances were studied in the Krachi-Ntwumuru area: the Sokodae, the Abafɔɔ, the Tigari and Boame, a trance dance. They are all as different from each other as, say, pieces of literature of a people might be different. As individual items, their *variety* is as great as that which a student of English literature might perceive between a Shakespeare play, a comic book, an historical narrative of a war, and an essay on psychology. The previous examples are meant to point up the variety. They are not meant to be analogues for the dances. My point is probably clear: to study any of these dances in isolation is as misguided as isolated studies of the examples of literature, and in the "Tradition" article, the author does not make that fundamental mistake.

The Krachi have many dances, many ceremonies, and many rituals. It is true that some are more important than others; of those listed, the Sokodae is probably the most important of them all simply because it involves more people. It is in its way a com-memoration of important events in the past of the Krachi which they value highly and the dance is strongly tied up with Ntwumuru social identity and with Krachi religious identity. In contrast to this, Tigari is the least important because 1) it is an imported dance, 2) it is connected with the figure of the Odunsini (lit: the root man) and not with the religious hierarchy, and 3) Tigari is a special cult to which only a few Krachi belong. Moreover, its powers or its attributes are man-made in contrast to those associated with Boame, which is connected with a lesser divinity. The Abafɔɔ is not so important as it once was because this dance is a hunter's dance and the men hunt less today than they have done in the past.

The basis for these generalizations lies in the self-definitions of this people and in a constellation of roles, rules and meanings which define the place of men and women in the universe as they see it. Krachi reality is neither "empiricist," "idealist," nor can any other such term be legitimately applied. Krachi reality generates its own space/time and terminology, as does any world-structure, and in the charts on pp. 318-320 this reality is sketched out in terms of seven person categories:

Hierarchy connected with divinities (Ikisi)					Outside Hierarchy	
Dente-okisipo	Other Okisipo	Ojya	Osuamfo	Okurafé	Odunsini	Ɔkpé
1	2	3	4	5	6	7

These words are, except in the cases of 4 and 6, Krachi words; numbers 4 and 6 are Twi, i.e., Akan language terms. If one were to travel to Ketekrachi now, one could ask to "see" or "meet" any of the above-named people, and doubtless be conducted to their presence. That is, with the exception of number 7, the ɔkpe, because this term defines one who possesses "kékpé," i.e., an evil, destructive spirit.

None of the above person categories can be accurately defined without reference to the others. Meanings here are relational (as they are in any society): that is, the terms map a certain conceptual territory, even though they also refer to real human beings who are known by the terms. We might usefully recall the Saussurian observation about the various pieces in a chess set: none have any meaning on their own, isolated from the rest of the set.

We will briefly look at only two of the categories so that we might grasp something of the relational character of the meanings and to further illustrate the changes in thinking experienced by the author which led, ultimately, to a transformation of what is sometimes referred to as a "world-view."

Ojya and Odunsini (numbers 3 and 6 above)

The dances Boame and Tigari are associated with the persons of the Ojya and Odunsini respectively and with their conceptual definitions. The outstanding characteristic of the Ojya, who can be either male or female, is that this role (occupied in the religious hierarchy) can only be acquired through possession by a divinity. In West Africa, someone may say, "we have come to watch the gods dance" if they are asked about their presence at, say, an annual festival of some kind. The basis for such a statement lies in person categories such as that of Ojya. The dances in which trance occurs are called "Njakoe" in Krachi, i.e., "nja" = the person who is in trance, the Ojya; and "akoe" ="dance." The dance to which I refer is thus properly called "Njakoe Boame"; the trance dance of the Ojya of Boame.

Similarly, one could say "Njakoe Yentumi". Notice that on the attached chart (pp.318-320), the Ojya is the only person defined by possession of a divinity. Read vertically, the chart is a brief, but fair definition of the person category as given by the Krachi. Read horizontally, the chart is a concession to the propensity towards comparison characteristic of our own thinking. The *Ojya,* you will see, is the assistant to the *Okisipo* for the divinity and ranks third in the hierarchy. In Krachi, if the *Okisi* (a divinity) is a creation of *Dente* (as in *Yentumi,* known as one of the "sons" of *Dente*), then both *Yentumi*'s *Okisipo* and *Ojya* will be subject to the *Denteokisipo,* because *Dente* possesses no one, has no articles such as drums, bracelets, etc. which represent him, thus he requires no *Ojya* and no one to "carry" (the meaning of *Osuamfo*) the shrine articles which represent him.

Anything which an *Ojya* does, directs, prescribes, or anything else is done while in a trance state. It is through the *Ojya* that the divinity tells the people what is wanted by way of rituals, dances, carvings and all the rest. When an *Ojya* is in trance, according to the elders at Dadekro, it means that it is not the person's ordinary "persona" or "self" which is in ascendence or control. The *Okisi* takes possession of the *Ojya's sunsum,* and for the duration of the time of the trance, it is as if the *Okisi* were using the individual's body in order to manifest himself (or herself, for there are female divinities too) to the people.

Briefly, in order to comprehend the above statement, the Krachi man has three aspects which together make up his total "self." These are the *Ɔkra,* the *Sunsum* and the *Nyenkpasa.* A Krachi woman has four components: the above-named three, which she shares with the man, and a fourth called "Kokoe," which distinguishes her unique power to bear children; to "bring forth," as they say. The ordinary aspect of a person—what we usually see, listen to, etc.—is the *Nyenkpasa,* defined in the following way:

1. Nyenkpasa is the (mental) picture which you may have of another person.
2. It is the Nyenkpasa which you remember about another person and it is Wuruboale's gift to that person (lit: "wuru" = "lord"; "boale" = who made us).
3. It is the general term used for all human beings.

The Nyenkpasa is the sum of the acquired characteristics of a person, including the mannerisims of speech and gesture, the shape of the body and face, etc. It dies at the same time the physical body dies, so I was told, but the ckra returns to Wuruboale and can come to earth again as another person.

Wuruboale has both "good" and "bad" *Akra* (plural of *ɔkra*). The old people used to say that there are certain periods during the day and night when a man and woman should not have sex, because during these times, there are bad *Akra* moving about who wish to come to earth as people. In the traditional belief the *ɔkra* enters the human being at the moment conception takes place. The *ɔkra* was defined as "a little piece of Wuruboale in each person."

The *Sunsum* amounts to "the breath of Wuruboale" in people. There are many diffferent kinds of *sunsums;* all divinities have (or are) one, and so does *Kisimen,* which I shall explain later. *Kekpe* (an evil destructive force) also has (or is) one. Just about anything which moves, or which lives, has a *sunsum. Sunsum* is a major classificatory term for life as distinct from non-life. All persons have a *sunsum* and some are more powerful than others. When the body dies, the *sunsum* leaves the body, but it does not die. It is the *sunsum* of the ancestor which is invoked, when for instance, a libation is poured at an ancestral stool shrine.

During the *Ojya's* state of possession, the *Nyenkpasa* recedes; becomes, as it were, the out-of-focus background of the *sunsum,* for the divinity possesses the *sunsum* of the person. The *ɔkra* is not in any way involved in the possession. A real *Ojya* does not take any drink, for example, because drink can affect the *sunsum,* and one would not want to be an inadequate vehicle for the divinity. Contrary to many opinions which attribute states of possession or trance to hysteria, drunkenness or drugs, the trance states of the

Ojya are heightened states of awareness which are not induced by these kinds of external means. Extraordinary feats of physical prowess, balance, and control are performed by Ojyas whom I have seen in trance, feats which by no means could be accomplished if they did not have perfect neuromuscular control, and no drug addict, hysteric, or drunk has this.

When asked if anyone at all could be possessed, I was told that there are some people who cannot be. I, for example, was one of these. The reason given is that there are some people whose *sunsum* is so strong that possession cannot take place. Also, it is necessary for the *Okisi* to ask the person's *sunsum* before possessing him or her. It is at this point that the *sunsum* can refuse, and there is simply an end to the matter.

In contrast to the *Ojya,* the *Odunsini* is the only person out of the seven listed who maintains his title or who holds his position through personal volition. 'Odunsini' thus defines a profession, an occupation by which a man or woman can make a living. The term is potentially a confusing one for most westerners, for there are three distinct types of *Odunsini* in Krachi, and sometimes the same person will combine features of more than one of the categories designated by the term at the same time. An *Odunsini* can be

1. an herbalist; one who knows the healing properties of herbs, roots, etc., who has learned the native pharmaco-poeia, or
2. a nurse, a midwife, or a physician who administers or practices western medicine (note how foreigners are assimilated into the traditional lexicon), or
3. the creator and/or owner of *Kisimen. Kisimen* is a powerful object, man-made and man-owned, from which power is derived with which to manipulate the world in some way.

Both the terms *Odunsini* and *Kisimen* have great density of meanings. *Odunsini* number 3, as listed above, always has *Kisimen.* This requires three elements: (1) an object, and theoretically, it can be any object, (2) some herbs and (3) the blood of a chicken, goat or sheep—usually a chicken. These elements symbolically represent the "power" or "force" of whatever part of the natural or human world from which they came. For example, if the object used for the *kisimen* is a piece of rock from a certain hillside or cliff, the piece of rock will symbolically carry the strength of that hill or cliff. In other words, the piece of rock represents what the hill represents on the *conceptual* map of the territory. Plants and the vegetable world have a different kind of power, and blood, of course, represents the life force itself.

The major difference between *Ojya* and *Odunsini* is fairly easy to see, even in the abbreviated account given above: the *Ojya* is *acted upon* by a divinity, one of many, all of which can ultimately be traced back to *Wuruboale,* hence the *Ojya* represents people in a universe of powers or forces (or what you will), some of which are of a higher nature, having fewer limitations than human beings. The *Odunsini* on the other hand, uses bits of the world and its forces to create power with which to act upon the world, and thus represents a certain ambivalence in human beings, because sometimes *kisimen* can be protective and constructive to the human community, but in more cases, it is not. In fact, the latter is often expressed spatially in that the owner of *kisimen* will frequently live "in the bush," i.e., nature, separated from the human community, although not too far away.

The distinction was made very clear when the elders said, "If a *Kisimen* is destroyed, then whatever power it contains is also destroyed and another one has to be made. But if, for example, the brass basin which represents Boame is destroyed, or the stool which represents Yentumi is destroyed, then neither Boame nor Yentumi is destroyed, because the power of Yentumi and Boame is not the stool or basin." The distinction between divinities and *kisimen* is also made in these ways: *kisimen* can be bought, sold, transferred, created, or destroyed by people, but the *Ikisi*, i.e., the divinities cannot, nor can anything connected with the ancestors be bought, sold, transferred, created, or destroyed by people. The *kisimen* created by an *Odunsini* has nothing to do with the divinities. Thus, when we see the dance, Njakoe Boame, and then we see the dance Tigari, done by an *Odunsini,* we may well ask, in what ways and in how far can we say we are seeing the *same* things?

The Written Accounts

I have indulged in this rather lengthy exposition of ethnographic detail to underline the kinds of insights to which I drew the reader's attention initially, and perhaps a summary is now in order. I began by stressing the transition made from amateur to professional anthropologist, which included a dawning awareness of the difficulties of making verbal reports of the kind Pocock suggests and an awareness of the general problems of language. The six essays written before 1971 document the process of grappling with fieldwork problems with inadequate, incomplete knowledges of many kinds on the part of their author. By the time *Dance and Krachi Tradition* was written, I had, if nothing else, abandoned the notion that dances could be studied in isolation, or that they could in any way, as it were, "stand on their own." Moreover, I had to make up my own mind about (1) what the "facts" of movement were, and (2) what the relation of these were to myself and to the material I was trying to explain. I did not want to believe that the reports I made about dances or any structured action systems in a society, were of the same genre as letters written home by a tourist.

It is from a basis of these insights that the question "in what ways and in how far can we say we are seeing the same things?" is relevant. It is relevant when we consider two dances from the same geographical area in Ghana. It becomes even more relevant if we consider a cross-cultural comparison of, say, Ghanaian dances with other dance forms from different societies which possess different spoken languages and body languages. For me, the question encodes the changes in thinking which occurred to me between the years 1967 and 1970. The *Dance and Krachi Tradition* article is very different indeed from the ones which preceded it. It even begins with a crude attempt to tackle the language problem in a section entitled "The Problem of Terminology." There are many changes I would make in it were I to rewrite it and it is the only one of the pre-anthroplogy essays I would consider rewriting because in it are the seeds of the approach I would advocate now. I find it necessary to emphasize this because I have been dismayed to find that these articles are quoted by other authors, and I am continually perplexed about what to say when enthusiastic students or colleagues ask me where they might obtain reprints of them.

Perhaps it is needless to say that one *does* try to explain to them (1) that these articles were written at a specific time, under specific circumstances and (2) if they would qualify the statements I made, keeping the historical perspectives in mind—both mine and theirs—or if they would be *critical* of the statements or question them in any way, then their usage of them might be mutually beneficial. However, one discovers that this is usually not the case. Instead, one finds one's works cited in bibliographies (as e.g., in the Dance Perspectives publication of Odette Blum's work on Ghana, which has at the very least all the faults of my own pre-anthropological work) without one being consulted and with no indication in the text to which the essays are attached of *why* the citations are made, so that one does not know why one's writing was cited in the first place. Or, one is asked for a "research model," or told that somebody is going to take a five or ten-week course in "African" dance (whatever that may be) and the articles are needed for "reference material."

Mercifully, most of the essays I have spoken about are nearly impossible to get hold of. I say this, not because they do not contain some valuable information, because they do. The trouble is that this information is, so to speak, wrapped up in packages that are incomplete, untidy, and in some cases, just dead wrong. Extracting the contents from the wrappings would amount to a tedious process and I daresay that few if any students would care to undertake it. A concrete example might be helpful: in the "environment" article, the bits about the forms of the *Kobine* dance are, I think, fairly dependable, but the comments about "wholeness" being a value to this people are not to be taken seriously. Here, I imposed my own personal set of values onto the dance. I have absolutely no idea whether "wholeness" is a value in Lobi society: maybe it is and maybe it is not, but I would regret having unintentionally, through my unconsciousness, misled students who might quote such statements in good faith. In fact, the purpose for doing this exercise in applied personal anthropology has been to prevent, if I can, just such occurrences, which are a potential embarrassment both to students, colleagues, and to me.

I would not have engaged in this critique of my own writing if I believed it to be vulgar self-criticism or that I was peculiar in some way. An exercise of this kind is, to say the least, tedious, but I have publicly criticized the work of several colleagues, notably those who advocate statistical models, functional, or Behavioral explanations of human actions and who insist (or so it seems to me) upon treating dance and human actions as "instinctive behavior" of some kind, rather than treating such material as linguistically orientated subjects. It seemed appropriate therefore to share the insights I have gained, for when I wrote the articles under discussion in the present essay, I had no idea what a "statistical model" amounted to and I see no reason to believe that other dance researchers know any more than I did about these models or what their usage might mean. When I used the word "function," as I used it several times in the essay on the Bedu dance, I had no idea that, to a sophisticated audience, I committed myself to an entire school of thought, which comes complete with definitions of human beings, of what they are about, of the relative importance of their various activities and so on.

What, Then, Do We Mean?

I have in front of me now an essay which I am asked to comment upon for publication. It is a fairly good essay, rather better written than most, by someone who obviously has excellent intentions and who is doing her best to say something about a West African people whose religion and beliefs are living, vibrant and real—as her own probably are not. The author has tried very hard (and her efforts are plain to see) to be as faithful to her research and the people about whom she writes as she can, yet, the essay is sprinkled—as with a pepper-shaker—with terms like "dichotomy," "kinetic," "standard-ized," "dutifully," "deified," "mythical," and many more. One's eyes, and mind, are irritated—as by pepper—with these terms.

How would they translate, if indeed, they would at all, into the spoken language of the people concerned? Are the terms that most faithfully represent the space/time concepts they have? As with my own pre-anthropology essays, I have the curious experience reading this writer's work, that sometimes I get rather large glimpses of "them," but on the whole, I seem to see more of "us," especially "her," and it is this split, this severance, which is so worrying. Yet, I think I understand exactly why it is there and the essential elements of the author's dilemmas, for many of them are exactly the same as my own were in the past.

While I will endorse the publication of her work, I wonder how this author would characterize her relation with the society she writes about or the relation between herself and her own society? I wonder how many of her statements were made with universal intent, "…such that they are believed to be true of all selves in all societies" (Pocock, 1973:13.3). And one wonders, too, how many dance specialists, dance researchers, dance therapists, dance anthropologists, dance ethnologists, and all the rest have committed themselves to the fullest extent possible to the implications for themselves and humanity of the views, theories, and research models they advocate?

I would above all hope that these remarks will be received in the spirit in which they are offered: one which is rooted in deep concern for the future of dance ethnography, but which sees the specific problems of dance as a small part of a much wider contextual field; namely, the field of human actions in general, with all the richness and diversity of human structured systems of meaningful actions. Dancing is only one of the many forms of expression of human structured systems of actions. It is true that it is a potent form, because dances are among the most complex systems of actions, but the field of dance *per se* is limited, as everything else is limited.

While the battle to be *heard* may have been fought over the dance, and while the personal anthropologies of many of us are dominated by our experiences with the dance, we would be foolish if we failed to see the wider applications of our work. Perhaps my major argument is already clear: it is simply that we take so much for granted and we assume too much. These are dangerous attitudes to entertain when a field of research is so new and when so many basic questions remain unanswered chiefly because they remain unexamined, while the field ethnographies seem to proliferate.

We know very little about the relations of human movement to spoken languages, for example, and it is doubtful whether we understand why it is that gestures, no less than spoken words, are arbitrary, to use the Saussurian term (1966:67ff). Different ethnicities have generated different values for the dimensions of right/left, up/down, front/back, inside/outside, to choose obvious instances of the conceptual fields in which dances (or any human actions) take place. These contrary oppositions do not *mean* the same things cross-culturally. No amount of ethnographies based upon naïve assumptions of universality of movement is going to make them *mean* the same things. Of course, if we take the position that ultimately, these dance ethnographies are more properly looked upon as new additions to current ethological research, and that in any case, human dances are simply more complex manifestations of the same kinds of spatial organization displayed by birds and animals, then all the effort will doubtless "prove" the universality of movement—but from what and from whose point of view?

I have protested against the tendency among dance researchers to leave all of "the hard stuff," i.e., the theoretical frameworks in which their material is expressed, to someone else, and I will continue to do so, even if all the protests amount to is a cry in the wilderness, and here, I think, is where one of Pocock's main arguments and my position truly meet. He suggests careful examination of *written texts,* and he says,

> I suppose there is one guiding assumption in the enquiry and that is that nothing is irrelevant to it. The use of this adjective rather than that, or the lack of adjectives is to be taken as significant...approach the text with the rule that every usage, turn of phrase, or cliché must be shown to be irrelevant before it can be discounted. Again, because this sort of analysis is time-consuming and tedious, this is a counsel of perfection [Pocock, 1973:8.4].

His remarks are equally applicable to one's own writing as they are to the writing of others.

Whether we like it or not, those of us who deal with so-called "non-verbal" materials are faced at the outset with major problems of translation, transcription, and transliteration; that of a space/time system, whether it is a dance, a rite, a ceremony, a system of greetings, or what you will, into spoken, and more accurately, into written language. We are all well aware that space/time systems occupy geographical spaces which are at once, (1) physical, (2) social, (3) semantic, and (4) conceptual. We must use written language to communicate to others *about* the system, as we use spoken language to *express* the system, but we also know that spoken or written language introduces other things into the system. As Ardener has pointed out, conventional language intrudes itself into the system (1975), and it is simply a nonsense to imagine that it does not—or worse, attempt to ignore the fact that it does, because "everyone else does" or something equally silly. "But," an uncharitable critic might say, "no one imagines that"; to which I would reply ("non-verbally" or "paralinguistically" or whatever the current term may be) by silently pointing to our extant literature, including my own pre-anthropology essays. Such evidence is as overwhelming as it is undeniable.

If some of my own experiences with these more intractable elements of an anthropology of dance are anything to go on with, I would want to say that I do not think I am unique in having taken "language," and the whole idea of what language is, completely for granted in the past. In fact, until I lived in Ghana, language to me was a rather tasteless, colorless, odorless, medium, much like water must be to a fish. And, like a fish, I only became aware of it when I was either deprived of it or when I found myself enslaved by it, as I was every time I sat down to write.

Conclusion

As I would now be prepared to defend the position that anthropology is a language-based science, I would also be prepared to say that, to me, all human "culture" is a kind of language—or "languaging" process, if you will—and there are two primary systems of human communication: speaking and moving. The latter is a human semiotic system of great logical complexity, no less than the former. Systems of human actions are kinds of languages too: they can be notated, they possess syntax, grammars, and all the rest. They are reflexive, referential, and relational. They structure space. Their "vocabularies" and the degrees of freedom of their executants' bodies may be more or less articulate.

An immobile person is to a semantic space with regard to actions as a vocally impaired person is to a linguistic "space." The problems of translation, therefore are much more complex than we have imagined in the past. If we can adopt the position that language-using is, among other things, a process of ordering our experiences, and of structuring experience so that it is comprehensible to ourselves and to others, then we are in no difficulty at all with such notions as body languages. In fact, human beings express their world-structures through their body languages as much as they do with spoken languages. The two are inseparable, for human actions are indissolubly tied to the human capacity for language-use.

It is very, very difficult to visualize a location or an action in a complex, multi-dimensional space. A human dance is a very complex space indeed. This is what makes dances so important to any enquiry into human actions. Often, however, "common" spoken language or "ordinary" speech is not sufficiently sophisticated to express all the relational elements of that space. Here, we encounter an issue about which some have thought that Pocock and I might disagree: I have used the term "meta-language," which implies that I might regard the study of anthropology as (1) a way of acquiring a "conceptual tool-bag," and (2) as an "emergence out of darkness into light." I readily admit to using some "high-powered" terminologies (as they are commonly called): some of them come from linguistics, and some of my analytical language and notion consists of group and set theory: branches of non-metric mathematics. I also use the Laban system of movement notation as another element of the meta-language to which I referred. I justify the usage of these on the grounds of the complexity of the human semasiological body and the multi-dimensional spaces in which it moves. The nature of action material itself demands additional kinds of notations.

Second, I emphasized the transition from amateur to professional anthropologist at the outset and while I do in some sense conceive of the transition as analogous to an emergence out of darkness into light, I by no means look upon the history of social anthropology as that kind of emergence, thus I would want to say that while I might agree that "...anthropology is its history," as Pocock says, I view that history (as I suppose I view everything else) as a multi-dimensional continuum wherein *one always has a choice,* so to speak, of different conceptual *levels* available to one at any given time.

As a rather trivial example of what I am trying to say, we might imagine a student in the past—one who was genuinely interacting with the anthropologies of received authorities—to have had a choice between, say, Hocart's or Rivers's views on kinship, insofar as they can be represented as two different conceptual frameworks from which to approach that very complicated subject. The notion of *levels* applies in this case, as it does with any aspect of our subject. At any time in the history of a discipline, there seem to be more and less sophisticated notions available about definition, analysis, method, etc. Some of these are advocated by more people, some by fewer. Certain kinds of theory and practice are favored for a while, then replaced by others, which in their turn may be discredited, or shown to be inadequate while an older theory may be revived. In sum, I would wish to draw attention to the *vertical* dimension in history, if such an image can be allowed, and I would describe a passage from "darkness" to "light" more in terms of a "quantum jump" rather than as an "emergence."

In any case, I share Pocock's beliefs in the value of conscious-ness, whether history is viewed in one, two, three, or more dimen-sions, and I certainly agree that our consciousness is predicated on vast areas of knowledge, experience and belief of which we are unaware. As I have tried to indicate in this essay, one's under-standing is undeniably a relationship and it is contingent upon what one does *not* understand. This essay by no means exhausts the subject of the idea of a personal anthropology, indeed, it is hardly more than an initial foray into the subject, but I have so far lived with the idea to my great benefit, and I hope to the benefit of others as well.

Role/Rule Relations in Krachi Traditional Religion.[7]

	Twi: Denteobosomfo Kr: Denteokisipo	Obosomfo Okisipo	Okomfo Ojya
Role:	In religious matters is supreme over everyone in Krachi state. Holds special position in secular matters; is second to Krachiwuru.	Is the local head of the cult of one particular Okisi; is not involved (in office) in political affairs; is the local head of the Okisi's shrine.	Completely subject to Okisi, and is assistant to Okisipo. Is subject to authority of Denteokisipo if his/her Okisi was created by Dente.
Role transmission:	1. Always taken from Dentewiae clan. 2. Most senior male by age. 3. Must be clan member by ancestry, not by slavery. 4. Line can succeed through father or mother.	Both people of cult and Okisi must select or 'elect' him and he must agree; thus 3-party agreement. It could happen that he has to be member of dominant clan, but other would still hold.	Can only become Ojya (either male or female) through direct possession by the divinity.
Rules:	Physical reasons for disqualification: 1. More or less than 5 toes or fingers; 2. Leprosy; 3. Any history of imprisonment; 4. Insanity; 5. Circumcision.	Same as Denteokisipo	Same.
Physical healing:	Does no physical healing of any kind.	Same as Denteokisipo	Does give prescriptions for all manner of ills, but these are by directions of the Okisi and given to the Ojya while in trance.

	Osuamfo No Krachi name	No Twi name Okarufɛ	Odunsini No Krachi name	Obayi Ɔkpɛ
Semantic values:	Dente was created by Wuruboale (the lord who created us), therefore Dente's power is derived from Wuruboale.	Some Okisi were created by Dente, e.g. Yentumi (at request of the people); thus an Okisi's power is ultimately derived from Wuruboale.	Through extension, his power also derives from Wuruboale.	
Economic Gains:	There is no remuneration for the role itself, so living is made otherwise. Traditionally, money gifts were made to the Dente shrine of the smallest possible denomination. If other gifts were brought, these were, together with the money, shared out to needy people.	This role is not an 'occupation' like the previous ones. If the shrine receives gifts, the same thing happens as in previous case.	This role is not an occupation, but the Ojya can receive free gifts. Money gifts are given to poor, along with other shrine offerings.	
Role:	'Osua' means carrier. Office is to carry objects which represent the divinity. Also acts as messenger for Ojya and Okisipo.	Assistant to Denteokisipo; only connected with Dente cult. There are several Akurafɛ; the term means holder of herbs.	Means 'the root-man': there are 3 categories of Odunsini: 1) an herbalist or native doctor; 2) a midwife; 3) a maker of Kisimen.	One who has kɛkpɛ, i.e. an evil destructive spirit.
Role transmission:	Selected through election by community led by Okisipo and the Ojya. After election must be approved by Dente.	Selected through direct inheritance or by father choosing one of the sons. The position is obligatory and cannot be refused.	Becomes Odunsini through personal volition (may be either male or female). Undertaken as a life profession.	1. (Rare) can become through own choice i.e. through seeking for spirit; 2. Can have spirit put into individual without their knowledge; 3. Can be transferred through food or money; 4. A child can have kɛkpɛ put into him/her while still in the womb.

	Osuamfo No Krachi name	No Twi name Okarufé	Odunsini No Krachi name	Obayi Ɔkpé
Rules:	Same.	Same.	No physical restrictions, but leprosy or insanity would be obvious deterrents.	None.
Physical healing:	If Ojya is absent, then this may be taken over by Osuamfo under direction of the Okisipo. Some Osuamfos do private healing, but it is not part of official duty.	He will give medicines for common maladies, for which Dente has prescribed something.	No. 1 is equivalent to a doctor. These prescriptions are given on the basis of knowledge of the native pharmacopoeia. None of it comes from a divinity. No. 3 may be an herbalist.	None whatever.
Semantic values:	Same as Ojya.	Same as previous ones.	Nos. 1 and 2: their power comes from knowledge of herbs etc. No. 3: power derives from object itself; from the amalgamation of elements of blood, object and herbs.	Power created by Wurubo-ale, who created both good and evil. "If there were no evil, then people would not understand what good is."
Economic Gains:	Same as Ojya.	Same as Ojya.	This role represents a full-time occupation and is how the person makes a living.	No economic value.

Notes

1. The reader will notice a distinction, made throughout the essay with regard to the word "behavior" and its derivatives. When a capital "B" is used, the term is meant to refer to a school of thought in the natural and social sciences, i.e., "Behaviorism." Otherwise, the common usage is indicated.

2. When this essay was first completed in July, 1975, it was intended to be read following a reading of David Pocock's paper (see bibliography). It is to be hoped that some day, his paper might be published. In the meantime, there is now a book which develops the idea of a personal anthropology in some detail (see Pocock, 1975).

3. I have chosen to refrain from including this list of articles in the list of references for this article because I wish to avoid possible inferences that an exercise in public criticism of my own pre-anthropological work hides a motive to encourage people to read those articles. No writer can control the use another might make of his or her ideas, but I would regret it if, in this case, Pocock's ideas were misunderstood or trivialized through my attempts to apply them.

4. This quote is from a public communication in lectures, not from a book.

5. For a more complete definition of this term, see paragraph three under the sub-heading "conclusion."

6. This section of the essay, while somewhat tedious, aims in a small way to indicate some of the kinds of information which are needed with reference to the translation of person categories from one cultural context to another.

7. The chart of the person categories of the Krachi religious hierarchy in its original version is greatly extended. Space prevents the inclusion of more detail here yet there are enough points listed to serve the present purpose of the writing, which is to demonstrate the relational character of the manings involved. Notice the derivation of semantic values, for example, from Wuruboale, who creates both "good" and "evil."

Appendix II.
SURVEY OF AUSTRALIAN LITERATURE
ON ABORIGINAL DANCING

But whether one deplores or rejoices in the fact, there are still zones in which savage (that is, untamed) thought, like savage species, is relatively protected. This is the case of art, to which our civilization accords the status of a national park, with all the advantages and inconveniences attending so artificial a formula; and it is particularly the case of so many as yet 'uncleared' sectors of social life, where, through indifference or inability, and most often without our knowing why, primitive thought continues to flourish. [Claude Lévi-Strauss. *La pensée sauvage*, p. 219.]

Introduction

To my mind rightly so, Stanner has said, "Contemporary study (of religion, totemism and symbolism) is weakened by the fact that there is so much bias in the old printed record. One cannot turn very hopefully to it for test or confirmation of new insights. Far too much of the information was the product of minds caught up with special pleadings of one kind or another" (1979:123). Exactly the same things could be said about studies of the dance (or danc*es*, or danc*ing*) in Australia. With regard to the dancing of Aboriginal peoples in particular, the comment above is relevant because a large proportion, although not all, of the dancing referred to in the printed record pertains to religion, totemism or symbolism.

Following Stanner, I would want to ask about studies of dancing, Aboriginal or otherwise, "What are the present limits of our information and what would constitute a reasonable estimate of the present theoretical position(s) concerning the subject of dancing on this continent?" Secondarily, one would want to ask how the answers to these questions would compare with answers which might be given about, say, American dancing, British dancing or any other nation's store of information about the dances and dancers included in its politically defined borders.

Conclusions formed on the basis of intensive study of written resources upon arrival in Australia on 5 August, 1986, are these: a definitive survey of the state of Australian dancing awaits the possibility of more profound assessment (1) after the separation of the real problems of scholarly dance studies become separated from false, mis-stated or imaginary problems, especially with regard to theoretical and methodological questions, and (2) development of a level of thinking and scholarship about the dance that is at present comparatively rare, mainly because of the emphasis at a technical school and college level, on the performance of dancing, i.e., the training of dancers. On the whole, this emphasis exists at that level of education in all English-speaking countries, but in Australia, there are no possibilities at this writing for dancers, teachers, choreographers or directors of companies to pursue further education regarding their subject at University (see Appendix A, page 365, for information from a recent government survey).

Moreover, the notion of "performance" in the tertiary level of education which is available to persons interested in the dance is limited to, indeed dominated by, the study of ballet or various forms of western contemporary dancing (e.g., Martha Graham technique, Cunningham, Horton and others). Writing about dances or thinking about them (and the epistemological and ontological issues that such writing and thinking entail) is rare, as is the comparative study of danced forms, their analysis and/or their relations to other movement-based phenomena, although there are some anthropological works of excellent calibre: Kaeppler on Tonga, Schieffelin on New Guinea, von Sturmer on Cape York dancing, Wild and Clunies-Ross on Walpiri and Arnhem peoples, Goodale on Tiwi dancing—but they are too few.

For some of the reasons why this situation prevails, we can again turn to Stanner, whose critical comments about those who influenced the study of religion in the past can be brought equally to bear upon studies of dancing (see Stanner, 1979:106–143 with reference to Durkheim, Frazer, Lang, Strehlow, Freud and others). One would only want to add some of the names of those who have dealt specifically not with Aboriginal dancing, but with the notion of the dance on a global scale: Lilly Grove (Lady Frazer) who wrote in 1895, Harrison (1913), Havemeyer (1916), Ridgeway (1915), Havelock Ellis (1920) and later on, Hambly (1926), Sachs (1937), Kurath (1960), Lange (1975) and others too numerous to mention here (see Keali'inohomoku, 1980, and Williams, 1986, for further discussion and citations).

The undertaking of a definitive survey of literature about dancing specifically in Australia and with reference to her social context cannot be made manifest in depth until there exists a cadre of Australian scholars of Aboriginal, English, or other ethnic Australian origins with post-graduate university degrees who will be in a position to contribute authoritative theoretical, historical and ethnographic analyses of the subject. These are simply not available at present since the state of the art in 1987–88 does not include such scholars. Specifically, I refer to those who, besides anthropological and/or ethnomusicological and linguistic training, have adequate knowledge and experience in structured systems of human movement, including the dance. These scholars would also have to possess requisite literacy skills with regard to human action sign systems.

Of the studies of dancing that presently exist, there are none of which I am aware that emphasize comparative materials or commentary among the many forms of dancing of Aboriginal peoples or between those forms of dancing, signing or rituals and those of the rest of multicultural Australia. One would wish to stress that there are no overtones of reproach intended here. The same could be said, with a few notable exceptions,[1] of nearly all American and British studies of dancing as well. Australia does not lag very far behind any other English-speaking country in this way, but the lag which does exist is there mainly because her dancers and composers of dancing do not possess the means to develop scholarship in the subject, except by competing for grants in overseas institutions. Owing to the efforts of a few concerned persons[2] this country could be in a position in future to assume leadership in this field, possibly providing adequate models for other countries with regard to the direction that dance and human movement studies might usefully take at university-level educational institutions.

The following survey of specific studies of dances are those which anyone would have to cope with in an attempt to discover the limits, potentialities and substance of research in the subject of dancing up to now in Australia. The studies represented have been chosen from a recent bibliographical overview of writings on Aboriginal dances and dancing (see Appendix B, page 366, which is a reproduction of Wild, 1986).[3] Two writers and one volume of essays have been added to the listing in Appendix B since Wild's article was completed in 1982: Grau (1983),[4] Dail-Jones (1984)[5] and *Songs of Aboriginal Australia* (1987).

Before undertaking the survey, however, it seems important to raise a point which Stanner made in a different context that is highly relevant, especially to the items from the bibliography which are anthropologically uninformed:

> One of the troubles of course is that concepts like 'society' and 'culture' are being used without technical understanding. One often has the strong impression that 'culture' is used to mean only mythology, bark-painting and dancing. I read recently that one politician would reduce it to bark-painting only [1979:313].

Then, too, we must bear in mind the fact that anthropology has not had much to say about western forms of dancing until recently;[6] but then, until recently, it has not had much to say about western forms of anything. It is perhaps understandable that for a long time in the relatively short history of the discipline, anthropology was about "them," not "us," although this has changed drastically over the past thirty years (see Crick, 1975, for the shift in British anthropology from "function" to "meaning"; Burridge, 1973:43–84, for further clarification of the western notion of Aborigines as "other"and as "primitive"; and a recent ASA Monograph, *The Anthropologist At Home* [see Jackson, A., 1987], which treats some of the developments among British-trained anthropologists since the mid-seventies).

Further to the point, a great deal is laid at anthropology's doors by dance scholars who, wishing for something novel and often with a view towards marketable goods in the literary field, have turned to "ethnology" as a source of subject matter and inspiration. The history of thought about dancing in social and cultural anthropology itself, by contrast, bears some striking resemblances to the history of thought about "primitive religion" (see Williams, 1976, for a criticism of my own pre-anthropological writings). In our own culture, the dance has been regularly stigmatized, applauded, derided and elevated over the years in much the same way as drama and dramatic acting (see Barish, 1981, for further discussion).

The point of all this? It is a mistake to imagine that serious study of the subject of dancing is somehow meant only to preserve the "Culture"[7] and/or memories of an "ethnic," a white Australian or an Aboriginal past, or that the study of dancing in any of its manifestations is the kind of feckless enterprise that public opinion often imagines it to be. Dancers as a group (a sub-culture, perhaps?) in English-speaking societies are in some sense a "marginal" group, no matter what form of dancing they practice; they are often classified with "primitives" (see Williams, 1988, for further discussion) and indeed, by the middle of the 1950's in the United States, "primitive dance" had come to refer to

> ... a kind of pseudo Afro-Caribbean type of dance. This so-called primitive dance has been stylized ... until it has become a kind of contrived tradition in itself. But are Afro-Caribbeans primitive? The answer is that these groups whether or not we can designate them as 'primitive' have their own dance traditions which are totally unlike each other. There is no such thing as 'primitive dance'. The term is meaningless [Keali'inohomoku, 1970:90].

Dancers throughout the world are, on the whole, familiar with stereotypes, fantasies and wrong-headed theories about themselves and their activities because they often have to contend with them on a daily basis. If it is the case that Aborigines in Australia are still labeled "primitive," for example, then it is equally true that in much popular thinking, dancers are labeled in the same or similar ways. They seem to be regarded as the "primitives" of the western art world.

There are immense tasks of scholarship awaiting attention in the field of dancing and human movement study. In general, the literature on the subject in the English language is extremely poor.

It is important, therefore, that these introductory remarks are understood in the spirit in which they are intended: as an overall critique which is meant to point to the need for a different *kind* of scholarship with reference to Aboriginal and every other form of dancing in Australia. To comprehend more specifically what is meant, I refer to scholarship that is not based on the kinds of cosmetic treatments of the subject that are all too familiar to those of us who have read it all, from even cursory examination of the titles and subject matters of many of the dance books to be found in performing arts sections of the majority of bookshops. I also refer to a genre of professional writing which is not cosmetic, but is equally disappointing for other reasons, e.g., Spencer (1985) and Richard Moyle's contribution to a recently published Festschrift for Alice Moyle (1984). It is to an article in an edited collection by Berndt and Phillips (1973) that we will now turn.

Australian Aboriginal Dance (Allen, 1973)

Apart from Allen's article, an MFA thesis appeared in this year, *viz.* Quisenberry (1973). Allen's article is better than Quisenberry's thesis, partly because, unlike the thesis, Allen's work is neither sentimental nor patronizing, nor does it depend, as the Texan's work does, for its inspiration dance-wise on the outmoded and basically misguided theories of Curt Sachs about dancing (1973:103–104).[8] The dependence on Sachs is a common flaw of many American Dance Education theses on the subject. Anthropologically, it bespeaks a lack of critical discrimination regarding historical and theoretical sources.

Allen's contribution is not crippled by the same kind of thing as Quisenberry's thesis; however, I use her work as a stalking horse to begin this survey because (1) consideration of the kind of work she did raises several important issues with regard to written accounts of dancing; (2) comparison of this kind of dance study with other possibilities of approach can be instructive, and (3) the author is a trained choreologist and dancer whose work is uninformed by anthropological, linguistic or philosophical insights into the study of dancing.

Allen possesses a finely tuned appreciation of the *movement* aspects of dancing, and she is an experienced notator. She brings considerable intuitive understanding to her study, e.g., of the need for separating the constituent (called "important") features of the movement patterns from the contingent (called "incidental") features of the patterns under investigation, but these insights are spoiled when she remarks that

> Aboriginal dancing is based to a large extent on spontaneity which means that nothing is done exactly the same way a second time [Allen, 1973:276]

The difficulties with her work are four-fold:

(1) Innocent of scholarly discourse on the problems implied in the phrase "nothing is done exactly the same way a second time," the author falls into a well-known philosophical trap. That is, if it is the case that nothing is done the same way a second time, then how does she know it is *the same dance*? Or, given that she means simply that there is a conventionally accepted latitude of performing "steps" and "figures" in the dance (a parallel issue in spoken language would involve, e.g., how we recognize the meaning of *b/a/th* or *b/ae/th* when confronted with trans-Atlantic pronunciations), then the statement regarding "sameness" risks the criticism of falsity.

Although danced spaces are very different in some ways from signing spaces (as in American Sign Language, Plains Indian Sign Languages, etc.), one shared feature of the two kinds of systems exists in the fact that there is a conventionally acceptable latitude of performance of any given action sign or stretch of action signs which is, of course, the real justification of postulating constituent and contingent features of the system in the first instance.

(2) The entire focus of Allen's analysis is on *gestural data alone*. Readers are told nothing about the characteristics of the spaces in which the dancers moved. It is as if any given dance exists solely in the performed actions themselves, bearing no relation to the conceptual features of the spaces in which the patterns of the dance and the dancer(s) exist. For example, there is no information given about referential, directional or locative features of the dan-

ces. We may well ask, Are these dances based on a notion of cardinal directions, or some schema that represents an "embedded" space within the geographical directions, or are the dances talked about spatially organized by the paradigmatic features of Dreaming tracks? Wild's analysis of Walpiri danced spaces (1977) is much more satisfactory from this standpoint.

(3) The writing of *movement,* regardless of the type of script used (that is, whether it is Benesh, Labanotation or Eshkol-Wachmann, the three most viable scripts of movement writing extant today) can be, and with regard to human dances, must be, an entirely different exercise from that of writing human *actions* because

> ... an intentional action is not the same as a physical movement since the latter can be described in various ways according to one's point of view and one's beliefs about the person performing it. One cannot specify an action, as opposed to a purely physical movement, without taking into account what the agent intended [Best, 1974:193].

For a more detailed analysis of this problem connected with the writing of Luo danced actions (Africa), see Durr (1981), where the analysis also includes written samples of both modes of writing and the different results obtainable therefrom.

(4) It has to be said that Allen's article does *not* refer to "Australian Aboriginal Dance" as a whole. Hardly more than mention is made of six dances of four specific peoples in northern Australia: *Wogaidj* (Delissaville) and the "Buffalo," "Crab" and "Birdsong" dances; *Maiali* (Bamyili) and the "Fish" and "Black Crow" dances; *Nunggubuyu* (Rose River) and the "Brolga" dance and *Wanindilyaugwa* (Groote Eylandt), where the author's comments are to the effect that there appears to be the same overall pattern and sequence for all dances. That may indeed have been the case, but if it is, then readers need to know why this is the case with Groote Eylandt dances and not with the others.

Allen's article would have been greatly improved by changing the title to "Six Dances of Four North Australian Peoples" because that is what the main dance content of the piece is about. There is no way that a fifteen-page article, which includes seven pages of photographic plates, can deliver the promise that the title "Australian Aboriginal Dance" implies. For something approaching adequacy in relation to this kind of title, see Wild (forthcoming) in the International Encyclopedia of Dance (Charles Scribner's Sons, New York). Wild's article, in conjunction with others by von Sturmer, Grau, Clunies-Ross and Dail-Jones on specific areas in Australia deliver considerably more of the promise of such a title. In fact, von Sturmer's blunt remark, "The Aboriginal case? There is none–or in fact not one; only many" (1987:65) is surely appropriate here.

I do not deny that popularizations of materials about dances, Aboriginal and otherwise, are necessary, nor do I deny that the casual or occasional reader might want generalized information; but I do deny that such materials have to be written in such a way that they mislead readers and create more stereotypes than they dispel. It is all too easy, for example, to assume that "Aboriginal dancing" is somehow the same. The issue is an old one in anthropology: the relativist's position against various kinds of "universalist" arguments. Specific to Australia is a homogenization (a kind of universalization) which leads people to believe that the *didjeridu,* a musical instrument unique to Arnhem Land and borrowed elsewhere, is (or was) used by *all* Aboriginal peoples. Generally in the past, the relativist rather than the universalist arguments had more force, simply because ethnographies have tended to be based on empirically perceivable elaborations of gestural and spatial patterns of a generic form of dancing found in a specified area.

During the past seventeen years, research in other parts of the world has produced evidence that there is just cause to doubt that a broad classification of dancing—say, "jazz dancing" or "folk dancing" or "Aboriginal dancing"—possesses universal characteristics of need, function, form, meaning, motivation or what-you-will. Forms of body language(s) seem to have developed independently; moreover, they can be shown irrevocably to be tied to the human faculty for language-use. Simply put, Ga, Ewe, Ashanti and Dagomba dancing, and the dances themselves, are very different from one another, although the peoples who generated the dance forms are all "Ghanaians" or "West Africans."[9] Jazz dancing, ballet dancing, tap dancing and square dancing are all performed by Americans, but they are not the same kind of dancing. There is no more reason for lumping Aboriginal dancing into one indistinguishable homogeneous mass either; yet, that seems to be done in the literature, where one would never find comparable usages of the term *American dancing* or *British dancing*. Why?

Universals and "Natural" Dancing

There do exist certain universal features of dancing, whether it is Aboriginal dancing or some other kind of dancing. Furthermore, there is a clearly discernible interface between the spoken (or "natural" language) of any given group of people and their body language(s). These universals are to be found in the locally Euclidean features of the spaces in which any danced action occurs—and for that matter, any human action at all; they are the dimensions of up/down, right/left, front/back and inside/outside. There are structural universals pertaining to the human body as well, which will be mentioned later. These spatial and body-related universals are comparable to the universals of pitch, harmonics and time which cause diverse pieces of music to hang together in important ways, or to the phonological universals which cause all human languages to cohere at a meta-theoretical level, but no one imagines that these universals are to be found in their pristine state in specific languages, specific pieces of music or culture-specific dances. The point is that the notion of universal structures of dancing and human movement is at least as recondite and complex as is the notion of harmonics and pitch in music or phonetics or phonology in human spoken languages (see Williams 1976a and 1976b for further elucidation). The problem for the serious student of danced forms of human movement is that the structures of human actions are not given the same status as are those which pertain to music and language, but this matter cannot detain us further here.

With regard to the "interface" alluded to above, one would want to point to recent work in linguistics, specifically to what Fillmore (1983:317) called the "semantic primitives" (not in the

Wierzbiska sense), i.e., certain fixed, closed class and schematized devices within the syntax and morphology of the spoken language of any given people which characterize space, location, position and direction (see Haviland, 1986, for an excellent discussion of these with regard to Guugu Yimidhirr, a local Paman language spoken at the Hopevale Mission in southeastern Cape York Peninsula).

Clearly, a consideration of universals in dancing (or any structured human system of actions whatsoever) leads to questions of great import. Just one of these is the problem of typologies, for it is with an attempt at a typology of dancing that Allen's article on Aboriginal dancing begins. The author lists what she believes to be all of the ways that dancing is used in an Aboriginal context, although just how she arrived at the list and why we should accept it as authoritative is not given. The four peoples to whom the six dances belong that are talked about in the article are characterized as persons to whom art forms including the dance, comes "naturally."

It is difficult to imagine what the author means by "natural" dancing, and it is unclear whether the dancing is "natural" because it is connected with many life activities—in which case, all danced forms are "natural"—or whether the source of the "naturalness" lies elsewhere, say, in some form of bodily logos, perhaps, that is universal to dancing but not to any other human action or, perhaps what she implies are any number of "origins" arguments and theories about dancing which have been postulated over the years. Statements about the "naturalness" of dancing generally point to unimaginative handling of the dances and to the fact that the investigator did not try to find out how the dances were learned, viewing *a* dance as an isolated artifact of the culture concerned, as if it existed in a conceptual, linguistic, spatial vacuum.

Anthropologists and linguists have produced evidence that there are complex learning processes that accompany the learning of Aboriginal dancing, e.g., Goodale (1971), Kayberry (1939), Elkin (1972 and 1974). Certainly it is the case that often in West Africa (where dancing is also stigmatized as "natural," "unfettered" and "primitive") many years are required for the formation of a dancer, as in the case of the seven years of singing, dancing and drumming needed to produce a *Kple* priestess. It is as if investigators cannot recognize the process of learning if the paraphernalia of learning with which they are familiar is absent. For many years, African peoples were thought to have no law, simply because they had no courts; no government, because they had no rulers of the kind that Europeans were used to. Is it the case that Allen thought that Aboriginal dancing was "natural" because she saw no ballet barres, studios, mirrors and pianos?

In a thoughtful, perceptive article regarding the problems of ethnomusicological fieldwork in general, Ellis may supply part of the answer:

> There is a lack of understanding of the work, a naive belief on the part of some authorities that all that is necessary for successful ethnomusicological work is the mere manipulation of a tape recorder ... [Ellis, 1970:76].

There is a similar lack of understanding of the nature of research into dances; a naive belief on the part of authorities and non-authorities alike that all that is necessary for research into dances is (1) a notator or choreologist who has danced—often in an idiom totally unrelated to that which is being investigated— and (2) a video-camera or a film crew.

One would want to add to this the problem of classification of body parts (see Ardener, 1982 and Williams, 1980a and 1980b). The human body is divided by different criteria in different languages, thus a human action sign in contrast to a raw bodily movement has to be dealt with simultaneously in terms of classification, conceptualization *and* action. Simply put, one would have to know what taxonomies of the body existed among the people Allen talks about and how the body parts are divided. Then the question of how these affect the performed actions in the dances arises, plus the elements of systems of reference and systems of address and their effects on the dances. Through these kinds of co-relations (their presence and/or absence), part of the significance of the danced figures in relation to the rest of the body language of the community begins to emerge. To explain and develop fully the many arguments and issues that are relevant to fieldwork problems and the dance would require another article at least as long as Ellis's, which is 136 pages long. Add to this the problems of the use of film in the field and the comprehension of film and video-taping as yet another "languaging process" in that it involves significant selections, and it is easy to see how much writing about dances, including Allen's, is perhaps best recognized as a kind of simplistic gloss connected with realities which on the whole remain unexamined.

The Notion of Translation

Further to these points, readers would do well to reflect on Chapman's summarization of this kind of problem when he says,

> There is not...any serious popular conception that such things require "translation" from one culture to another. Most people, when faced with an unintelligible foreign language, will recognize the need for "translation"; non-verbal "language" gestures, and generally semantic use of the body, of the person, or of groups of people, are not usually granted the same status as language in this respect. Translation will not be thought necessary. In general, an "English-speaker" will interpret the gestures of, say, a "Breton-speaker," a "French-speaker" or a "Gaelic-speaker," according to an entirely "English" set of rules of interpretation, without feeling any need to go to the bother of "translating" [Chapman, 1982:111].

Field investigators who are going to study the body language of any human group or any sub-set thereof are well-advised, first, to refrain from taking into the field (in their own culture or that of another) the kinds of prejudices, naïvetés, biases and simple igno-rance of the nature of dance research which have consistently been demonstrated by many of their predecessors. If they choose to try to do fieldwork in the 1980's and 1990's carrying this kind of cultural baggage with them, then they will have to expect that savage criticisms will inevitably follow. Again, one turns to Stanner:

> Modern anthropologists criticize their nineteenth-century predeces-sors for many faults, and the force of the criticisms is reflected in

many aboriginal positions. ... But a cardinal fault—the invincible ignorance about Aboriginal religion—has not been criticized sufficiently [1979:111].

I am convinced that there is an "invincible ignorance" about human dancing, dances and "the dance" which has not been sufficiently criticized either. It is simply boring, apart from anything else, to be faced with the same old clichés again with regard to this little known and less understood activity. Since I intend to share some of the more commonly used theories of dancing with readers later on in this essay, I will say no more about the matter here.

Instead, I would want to draw attention to some sentences, chosen at random from von Sturmer (forthcoming) to illustrate the point I am trying to make: He says, " ... all dances, even those now secular, took root in the religious life." There is no awareness of this, hence no mention of it in Allen's article and in many others of the same genre. It cannot be overstressed either, that the very language used to describe a dance either reveals or obscures the investigator's knowledge of the subjects of investigation. For example, talking about Cape York, von Sturmer says,

> ... individuals represent themselves in more or less heightened ways. They are not bonefish, taipan, blue-tongued lizard; they are Bonefish Man, Taipan Man, Blue-tongued Lizard Man. While they may exhibit some of the features of their eponymous animal species, they dance as men—or, perhaps more accurately, as spirits, or as revealing their own spiritual essence. These dances (which are fairly typical) bear little mimetic or even narrative load: they are representational in a highly formalised way, but of human activities and responses, personal identity, social relations, not animal behaviours [forthcoming].

Allen, together with many other writers on Aboriginal dancing, when faced with "Brolga," "Buffalo," "Fish" or other "totemic" dances merely says that the dancers are mimicking the creatures. Someone is wrong. Either what von Sturmer says about the nature of these dances hits the mark, or it is wide of the mark and an imitation theory of human dancing is the more accurate. Thus, we are led to consideration of the nature of the human act of dancing—and a great deal hangs on these considerations, not only for Aborigines, but for ourselves. Yet, many dance researchers will say, Australia and abroad, "All I want to do is to *describe* the dances, I am not interested in all the theoretical stuff."[10] They seem to imagine that one can produce an ethnographic description that is void of theory—an impossibility, as we have seen. The fact is that the pitfalls inherent in alleged "simple description" are legion!

In any case, it simply does not do to talk of any form of Aboriginal dancing, whether it seems to the investigator to be a "fun" dance or a "ceremony," solely in terms of metaphors drawn from the western stage. Allen refers to bushes and trees in the physical spaces of the dances she saw as "set pieces," as if the dances were taking place on a stage in Sydney or Melbourne, and of objects used in the dance by the dancers as "props"; a blatant case of an overlay of the conceptual spaces of Allen's familiar forms of dancing onto the conceptual spaces of dancers and dances to whom these notions are completely alien.

In spite of the fact that movement notators, especially, are aware of the rules of the game in their own idioms of dancing and in the exercise of writing movement itself, they seem able to develop acute myopia when they are faced with idioms of dancing with which they are not familiar. It is as if they see no need for translation; no need for working out the rules of the body language games of the dances under investigation. Clearly, there is no point in working out the rules of the game if the dances under investigation are thought to be "spontaneous" and "natural" (whatever that may mean). It is the case that *dancing is learned,* and there are far better theoretical and methodological frameworks for the study of it than a kind of wooly unilinear evolutionism or the pure, untouched romanticism of early functionalism, i.e., "they have such a marvelous sense of rhythm" syndrome.

Universals Again

At this point, I shall briefly sketch some of the universal features of dances, and, indeed, of all human actions, anywhere in the world, so that readers might more readily comprehend the theoretical underpinnings of a different anthroplogical approach to the study of dances.

It seemed reasonable to assume that it would be useful (1) to know what is in fact universal regarding the phenomenon of human movement and dancing in order that (2) we might possess an objective, scientifically valid foundation for cross-cultural generalization and comparison, and (3) a useful set of *open structures* which are not initially data-laden, on a basis of which we might better understand how and in what ways the enormous variety of semantic elaborations of these structures has developed and been utilized by different peoples of the world.

In other words, in order to talk about "Z" (specific dances of any culture(s) in any historical period anywhere in the world), one has to know something about "X" and "Y"; that is, the structural characteristics of the expressive human body (X) and the space(s) in which it moves (Y). These structures are not the dances themselves, but consist of axiomatic statements about the human body and the space/time in which it moves, e.g., "the elbow only has one degree of freedom," or "the human semasiological[11] body [semasiological = expressive or semantically-laden] is a ninety-dimensional, self-activating, mobile object which operates in a locally Euclidean four-dimensional space/time" (see Williams, 1975 for full discussion).

These structures constitute, as it were, the *rules of the rules* of dancing and human actions. They are necessary for investigators to *know,* but do not necessarily enter explicitly into the ethnographic description of any given danced form encountered in the field. They are encountered, however, at the "interface" between the spoken language of a people and in the notion of the semantic primitives of up/down, right/left, front/back and inside/outside. For example, about Guugu Yimidhirr, Haviland says that this language

> seems to concern itself deeply with location, not only in the frequent
> practise of *describing* where things are, or in the universal need to
> locate referents ... [1986:1],

but with regard to features of motion, position, spatial relations and direction as well. He also points to other significant semasiological features of this spoken language when he says

> There are some specific locational words as well. Hopevale people
> use a familiar contrast in two deictic roots (*yi-* 'here', 'this', and

nha- 'there', 'that') along with the roots *bada* 'down', 'below', and *wangaar* 'up', 'above', to locate and identify things. There are two further complex deictic words, <u>both typically requiring a gesture to specify their meanings</u> (underline suplied): *yarrba* 'thus', 'in this way,' a kind of demonstrative word, and *yarra* 'there', 'that', whose use implies: 'Have a look at that', or 'There it is' … [Haviland, 1986:2].

Later, we are told that Guugu Yimidhirr's "repertoire of distinct locational or deictic *roots* is actually somewhat meagre and underspecified: a simple proximate/distal deictic contrast, supplemented by a basic, if hardworking, vertical opposition, and two further demonstratives which, as I say, typically require gestural supplementation" (Haviland, 1986:2).

To a semasiologist, the locational, directional, demonstrative and deictic features of a spoken language are some of the indices which, combined with ostensive evidentials (that scheme of deictics which places distances relative to an actor) plus all the empirically observable actions which accompany them, are the "stuff" so to speak, of which dances, rituals, rites, signing systems or what-you-will are made. The point of this sketchy overview of some of the relations between empirically perceivable (transitive) structures and intransitive structures (non-empirically perceivable "givens") is simply this: dances do not exist within a conceptual, a spatio-linguistic or a cultural vacuum. It is, in our view, impossible to carry out effective, confirmable, cross-cultural comparison and to avoid a total relativist's position with reference to the study of Aboriginal or any other kind of dancing, without a sufficiently sophisticated theoretical structure with which to begin (see Williams, 1980b for further discussion).

Moreover, without such knowledge, plus certain other features of each individual culture (as I have tried to indicate above)— which includes taxonomies of the body, deictic contrasts and coordinates which are culture-specific, including systems of address, pronominal systems of reference and such—we are ill-placed to comprehend specifically *human* movement as it manifests itself in semantically laden actions, in contrast, say, to the movements of animals and birds or the sign functions of machines (see Williams,

1986b). Because of this, one proceeds from the axiom that *human spatial points of reference are points of application for linguistic predicates,* a summation of perceptions gained through reading Hampshire (1959). Boiled down further, the statement is meant to imply one of the significant differences between the human use of space as against the use of space by other sensate creatures: in the human instance, there is an irrevocable connection between spatial points of reference and the use of language. Simple examples are those explicated by Haviland (1986), the cardinal directions and any permutations of them, spatial metaphors—which abound in any human language—and the canonical coordinate system in which all human actions take place. As in physics, certain relationships between human bodies and the spaces in which they move must be known in advance.

Such universals as I have pointed to are the "gear," so to speak, that (1) all moving human beings possess, and (2) any investigator needs to know in order to elaborate in any way—or to describe the elaborations which exist—with regard to any dance, sign system or other structural system of meanings of an alleged "non-verbal" nature. The reason why these are structural, not semantic, universals is that, for example, there are no grounds for saying that dancing is done for the same reasons everywhere in the world—or anywhere. One is not saying that movements have been found that people use for various purposes everywhere in the world (*pace* Fast, 1970, Morris *et al.,* 1979, and others).

One can legitimately postulate certain structural and semantic primitives[12] which are universal to every manifestation of body language anywhere in the world; indeed, Haviland implies (1986:fn. 16, p.26) that McNeill (1979), and McNeill and Levy (1982), "... seem to suggest that the conceptual structure that underlies gestural production is in some ways *also* the deepest structure that underlies spoken language as well." If that is the case, then the conceptual structures of human actions postulated by semasiology are those to which McNeill and Levy could be seen to refer. It is gratifying to know that colleagues in a sister discipline may have arrived, through independent types of investigation, at one or two of the same conclusions reached in Williams's doctoral work (1975) pertaining to dances and human actions, although I would not want this statement to be misconstrued as a dogmatic assertion that the conclusions *are* the same.

There are certain similarities of approach to the notion of universals referred to as "etic" features of body languages (with specific cultural manifestations being the "emic" characteristics), and this is roughly the theoretical approach taken by Kaeppler (1972), following the intellectual developments of American ethnoscientists and the linguistic researches of Kenneth Pike. In my own frame of reference, we talk of "intransitive" and "transitive" aspects of human action sign systems. Dances, in this context, are seen as extremely powerful, generally very dense encapsulations of the semantic primitives mentioned above, simply because they *are* conventionalized forms of body language(s) which depend for their existence on implicit knowledges of these universals. It is thus *not* the case, as Grau would lead us to believe, that

> The distinction between dance and non-dance must be equivocal, because it depends upon culturally shaped as well as universally objective components. At this stage, *we do not know what these universally objective components are,* but it is possible to find out the culturally relative answers by isolating the appropriate ethno-domains [1983:32, italics added].

While one would agree with Grau that dances "depend upon culturally shaped as well as universally objective components," her assertion that we do not know what these universal components are is based on a narrow and incomplete reading of currently used theories of human actions and the dance.[13]

Grau's positive contribution to the study of Tiwi dancing lies in the excellence of her data, in the meticulous manner in which it was handled, and in the insights she achieved which led her towards the study of the taxonomy of Tiwi bodies and their relation to the danced actions they perform. It is unfortunate that this author's doctoral dissertation lacks in theoretical underpinnings and orientation because the data is extraordinary—but it seems to lack organization *into* anything. We have yet to hear from Grau about the real *design* of Tiwi dancing and signing systems and it is to be hoped that we are not kept too long in suspense, for she is in an admirably placed position, having freed herself from the strictures of a too-limiting supervision, to extend and further discipline her work into major post-doctoral contributions.

In contrast, Dail-Jones's M.A. thesis *has* a theoretical framework; she advances an argument and follows it through, but her choice of theory leaves much to be desired, as it stems from hard-core functionalism and behaviorism (perhaps reflecting what her supervisors deemed to be "scientific"), leading to statements like this:

> For Walpiri women, dance as a whole consists predominantly of adaptors and illustrators interspersed with regulators; it often results in affect displays ... [1984:369].

One can be sure that "for Walpiri women" dancing does not consist of anything of the kind.[14] There is a disastrous confusion here among the investigator's home-made models of events (which generally get totally amended or completely discarded over the period of fieldwork), her analytical models and the folk-models of the events being described. Inevitably, this kind of confusion results in nonsensical statements of the kind quoted above. Fortunately, Dail-Jones has an opportunity to redeem herself through work at a doctoral level where she could acquaint herself with more modern, certainly more rigorous, self-reflexive theorizing and with more anthropologically orientated approaches to the study of movement rather than Behavioristic ones. She was hampered by supervision which came from outside the discipline, and this would not be important except for the fact that the scientistic theorizing she does use tends to obscure and obfuscate her data. This is unfortunate, because Dail-Jones tried to see relationships of other types of Walpiri patterned movement and the danced movements, and no one but Dail-Jones has, up to now, tried to grasp the organization, specifically of women's dances.

Having said that, it is necessary to digress a moment in order to recognize the admirable work of Diane Bell, whose ethnography *Daughters of the Dreaming* points to important features of the dances and ceremonies of women, although not in a specific sense.

That work is reserved for another dimension of this anthropologist's applied approach to the study of central desert women. Unfortunately, much of Bell's work that is specific to the dance is restricted material and is contained in evidence which she helped women to present—in the form of dances and ceremonies—pertaining to land claims and rights. I can therefore cite only two pieces of unrestricted material in this essay and suggest that for further information, the author herself be contacted for anything else which may be available (see Bell, 1982 and 1983–4).

With regard to the two theses mentioned above, it can be said that Grau's and Dail-Jones's work represent the first attempts in Australia scientifically to study human movement and the dance—with the exception of Kendon's work on sign languages (see Kendon, 1983, for a good discussion of the kind of work it is, and see also Haviland, 1986, for his comments on Kendon's theoretical stance). Grau's and Dail-Jones's theses represent a giant step forward from that which one can only call "pre-scientific" writers, e.g., Allen (1973), Quisenberry (1973), Morse (1968), Dean (1955 and 1955a) and Jones (1980). Dean is quoted by Morse as saying, " … research dancers using an accredited dance notation … are also needed" (Morse, 1968:3), and while it is true that people who have danced who use an accredited notation system *are* needed, it is equally true that dance experience alone is not enough, nor is the fact that dancers can usually learn the movements of other danced forms enough.

The reasons for this are two-fold: (1) idioms of dancing are analogous to spoken languages in important ways. The matter of learning a language other than one's own is a complex affair with regard to spoken language(s) and body language(s) alike. A fluent grasp of the phonological characteristics of one's native spoken language does not provide a sufficient basis for the understanding of a different language. Similarly, a fluent grasp of the kinological characteristics of, say, ballet dancing, does not provide a sufficient basis for the understanding and performance of a different danced idiom of body language.

(2) Whether we like it or not, those of us who deal with so-called "non-verbal" materials are faced at the outset with major problems of translation, transliteration and transcription; those of a

space/time system, whether it is a dance, a rite, a ceremony, a system of greetings or what-you-will, into spoken, and more accurately, into written language. These space/time systems occupy geographical spaces which are at once physical, social, semantic and conceptual. We must use written language to communicate to others *about* the system, as we use spoken language to *express* the system, but we also know that spoken or written language introduces other things into the system. As Ardener has pointed out, conventional language intrudes itself into the system (1975) and it is simply a nonsense to imagine that it does not—or worse, attempt to ignore the fact that it *does,* perhaps underlining Wittgenstein's observation that it is easier to bury a problem than to solve it.

The description of the danced actions of another people, whether in our own or another culture, is such a delicate affair, requiring such developed sensibilities of numerous kinds, that it is difficult to know where to begin to explain just what *is* needed for adequate preparation for the task. Suffice it to say here that one can, at least, now point to the works of better educated and trained professionals for guidelines (see Note 1) for list of references.

Process and/or Preservation

Morse's article documents an interesting and important period in the thinking about dancing (dances and "the" dance) in Australia: She was one of three people who carried out a project in the Northern Territory in the second half of the 1960's which was meant to test the efficacy of notating Aboriginal dances in the field. The project was endorsed by several distinguished scholars in the ethnomusicological and anthropological fields, among them Alice Moyle (1977, 1977a and 1978) and McCarthy (1957, 1964 and 1978), who was principal of the A.I.A.S. at the time. Morse says,

> Our aim can be described simply: to obtain a precise record of Aboriginal dances in the form of a written score of both the dance movements and the music to which the dances are performed [1968:3–4].

This kind of aim is heavily "preservation" oriented and there are many parallels in the Australian case with attempts which have been made over the past thirty years in China to preserve minority dances in that country. Space prevents teasing out the issues involved, but we possess an excellent account of the issues and the consequences of the approach in the Chinese context by Fairbank (1985 and 1986). With all due respect to the project in which Morse participated, it must be said that "totemic" dances show themselves to the modern investigator not as simple-minded mimed images of the physical environments of the peoples who generate them. If what von Sturmer says about Cape York dances is true (see *supra,* p. 335), then we can assume that the following statement is simply dead wrong:

> ... the dances we saw were mainly concerned with mimed description of everyday events, such as buffalo hunt, the catching of crabs and of fish. Some dances simply mimicked the activities of creatures such as birds, without human characters at all ... [Morse, 1968:6].

Stanner put the matter in more generalized terms about as succinctly as possible:

> ... a 'totemic' system shows itself as a link between cosmogony, cosmology, and ontology; between Aboriginal intuitions of the beginnings of things and resulting relevances for men's individual and social being, and a continuously meaningful life ... Aboriginal totemic groups were thus sacred corporations in perpetuity. The yearly round of rites let the Aborigines renew both the sources and the bonds of life constituted in that way [1979:143].

Surely, "totemic dances," wherever they may take place in Australia, partake of all this, and dances that use an imagery that is based on vital and significant features of the environment (whether sacred or not) should command enough respect, one would have thought, for us to attempt to look beyond the signifier to the signified. Preservation of our own, or Aboriginal, culture may be a desirable aim, but it is neither the most important (taken in its "museum" sense) with regard to dances nor is it the most fruitful, seen from the standpoint of a semantic anthropology (see Williams, 1982).

Dances provide us with encapsulations of ontological facts. Recognition of this is difficult if too much stress is laid on historicist or functionalist approaches. This is why it is so important to see human action sign systems, including dances, as kinds of languages: they can be notated, they possess syntax, grammars and all the rest. They are reflexive, referential and relational. They structure space. Their vocabularies and the degrees of freedom of their executants' bodies may be more or less articulate. Perhaps it is necessary to make the effort to see human action sign systems as "language processes" which occur not in the medium of sound, but in the medium of movement.

The danger in an unenlightened "preservationist" approach is of course that it focuses almost entirely on the "vehicles"—on the "products," as it were—thus tending to disregard the content. It is possible to focus only on the movements and the ritual *form* in the event so that the meanings and substance of the ritual or dance are entirely forgotten. There is an unconscious separation of the signifier/signified unity, with a resulting distortion of the whole. This is why it is so important to stress the distinction between notating "movement" as against "actions." It is why it is so important to know *why* one is undertaking any given investigation in the first instance.

Early Studies of Dancing

The first publication about dance that had any real relevance to anthropology was Curt Sachs's *Eine Weltgeschichte des Tanzes,* published in 1933 and translated into English in 1937 as World History of the Dance. This book has been widely used, and indeed is still used today, as a definitive anthropological study of dance. Although this book certainly has a place today in the study of anthropological theory, *it has no place in the study of dance in anthropological perspective* [italics added]. Its theoretical stance is derived from the German *Kulturkreis* school of Schmidt and Graebner in which worldwide diffusion resulted in a form of unilineal evolution. But just as modern non-Western peoples do not represent earlier stages of Western cultural evolution, there is no reason to believe that non-Western dance represents earlier stages of Western dance. Yet some anthropologists find it possible to accept the latter without accepting the former (see Youngerman, 1974, for more detailed discussion, and Williams 1976c for a review of Lange [1975] which is a modern version of Sachs's theories).

Much more important for the study of dance in anthropological perspective, although he did not really address himself to the subject, was Franz Boas, whose orientation offers scope for analyzing dance as culture rather than using dance data to fit theories and generalizations. Boas felt that man had a basic need for order and rhythm—a need which Boas used to help explain the universal existence of art. By refusing to accept sweeping generalizations that did not account for cultural variability, he laid a foundation for the possibility of examining dance and responses to it in terms of one's own culture rather than as a universal language. In spite of Boas and others, however, the idea that dance (or art) can be understood cross-culturally without understanding an individual dance tradition in terms of the cultural background of which it is a part, is not yet dead, especially among artists and dancers [Kaeppler, 1978:33].

Just as Boas did not really address himself to the subject, neither did E.B. Tylor or Sir James Frazer address themselves directly to the subject. Students today are sometimes offended when they discover that Tylor referred to dancing as "frivolous and meaningless" and they find it difficult to understand why he was pessimistic about the future of dancing in modern civilization; why he thought that what remnants there were in England of folk dancing were dying out, that sportive dancing was falling off, and that although sacred music was flourishing, civilization had mostly cast off sacred dance. "At low levels in civilization," he said, "dancing and play-acting are one" (1878:15).

Tylor's real interest in symbolic movement did not lie in its manifestations in dancing, rather in the language of gestures used in deaf-signing. Tylor's work on gesture language is a rich and original source of linguistically based movement theory in anthropology (see Henson, 1974, for fuller discussion and see Farnell, 1984a, for recent work on Plains Indian Sign Language and American Sign Language). It requires much more than superficial handling, then, to accommodate his theories of gesture and movement to the dance as we understand it today without risking distortion, either of Tylor's thought or of the dance. But Tylor's name carries with it a cautionary tale: His thinking was in many ways a true reflection of the general evolutionary bias of nineteenth-century anthropology. Most of the writings about dancing during the period 1850–1900, whether contained in works on other subjects or whether they are solely about dancing, begin with sections or whole chapters on early Greek, Roman, or Egyptian dancing, or in the case of Lilly Grove (Sir James Frazer's wife), the emphasis is on "primitive" dancing.

For Frazer, dancing fit into a scheme of stages of an assumed human intellectual development: At the lowest end of the evolutionary continuum, the dance was placed as an exemplar of magic. Frazer thought that "primitives" called on magic when their capacity to deal with situations realistically was exhausted. Magic thus provided a substitute reality: If a tribe could not really make war on a neighboring village, then it could at least do a dance about it. In the Frazerian scheme of things dancing was classified as sympathetic magic, and magic of course was wrong-headed science. The point here is that in the intellectual battles that Frazer was really interested in fighting, he opposed both magic and science to religion. Although social anthropologists no longer accept Frazer's theory of stages of evolution or his assessments of dancing today, many artists, dancers, dance critics and others still use these ideas. It is difficult to understand why. Keali'inohomoku states the problem succinctly:

> Despite all [modern] anthropological evidence to the contrary, however, Western dance scholars set themselves up as authorities on the characteristics of primitive dance. Sorell (1967) combines most of these so-called characteristics of the primitive stereotype. He tells us that primitive dancers have no technique and no artistry, but that they are "unfailing masters of their bodies"! He states that their dances are disorganized and frenzied, but that they are able to translate all their feelings and emotions into movement. Primitive dances, he tells us, are serious but social. He claims that they have "complete freedom" but that men and women can't dance together [a 'fact' of sorts which Sorell may have gleaned from reading about central desert peoples in Australia]. He qualifies this statement by saying that men and women dance together after the dance degenerates into an orgy! Sorell also asserts that primitives cannot

distinguish between the concrete and symbolic, that they dance for every occasion, and that they stamp around a lot! Further, Sorell asserts that dance in primitive societies is a special prerogative of males, especially chieftains, shamans and witch doctors. Kirstein also characterizes the dances of "natural unfettered societies" (whatever that means) [Keali'inohomoku, 1980a:84].

Similar criticism could be leveled at most of the genre of "dance books" that are commonly read and used throughout the English-speaking and European dance worlds: cf. Haskell (1960 and 1969), Kirstein (1924), DeMille (1963), Terry (1956 and 1967), Martin (1939 and 1963), and the many entries in dance encyclopedias under the headings *ethnic dance, primitive dance,* and *ethnologic dance.* There are doubtless parallels in Australian literature on dancing; I have not yet read everything which has been written here, but I have seen the above-mentioned books on the shelves of bookstores, so one can fairly assume that they are there because people read them and swallow them, as it were, book, line and thinker.

Fortunately, anthropology has come a long way since the end of the nineteenth century:

> Descriptions, brief as they are, of the dances are given from time to time to show that choreography is a real art with the Aborigines. Music, rhythm, actions and steps of both men and women dancers are worked out by the composer and master. It is not random or free activity. Directions are given by a leader, if details are not known. Behind each action is meaning. The pattern, however, does allow the virtuoso some latitude for improvising [Elkin, 1972:275—originally written 1949].

Although the kinds of description which could be carried out today are far more rigorous than those used by Elkin, he nevertheless recognized the importance of the dances and music of the peoples he visited and the central place they hold as significant repositories of knowledge and mediators of meanings. The problem is that the writings of anthropologists like Elkin are rarely read by dance scholars or the general public, and it is to another such writer that we will now turn.

Goodale's section of the book *Tiwi Wives* headed "Songs and Dances—The Yoi" (1971:290–317) is one of the best I have read by an anthropologist who is a non-dance and movement specialist. Part of the reason it is so good is that Goodale does not attempt to describe the movements of the dance as they occur—an enterprise that is fraught with difficulties, producing results which are generally unsatisfactory either because the investigator is forced to use unsuitable metaphors, or because the process simply becomes unbearably tedious. So many parts of the body can move at the same time, that a verbal description (which by its very nature erases the simultaneity that is characteristic of danced movement) is rarely accurate in any case; hence, the need for a script which can handle human actions.

Instead, Goodale talks about the forms of dancing which occur in the *Pukamani* ceremony (the burial, the *ilanea* or final grave rituals) and the *kulama* ceremony. Her work yields many insights with regard to Tiwi dancing: "Songs and dances are not only forms of creative art among the Tiwi, but they are perhaps the most important for gaining prestige" (1971:290); "The culture hero, *Purakapali,* told the Tiwi 'to sing the things around them,' and so, like the *kulama* songs, the *pukamani* songs are about every subject imaginable to the Tiwi and are not traditional but individual compositions" (1971:292–3); "... but the singers and dancers were in fact 'marking' a particular animal because the associated dance was their *yoi,* their inherited dance form" (1971:296); and finally,

> The dances or *yoi* are as full of social implication as are the songs and are just as original and entertaining. I have in the preceding discussion of songs used the verb "to mark" in order to describe the symbolism of action or words referring to a particular subject. The Tiwi used this English word exclusively to describe what it was they were symbolizing in a song or dance, and I prefer to continue using this word (rather than "imitate" or "mimic") in order to emphasize the symbolic nature of these actions. What has been "marked" has been "emphasized," not merely imitated [1971:303].

Just one of the more puzzling features of Australian anthropology upon first encounter as an outsider is the varying usages of the terms *totem* and *totemic,* the meanings of which are, to say the least, elusive.[15] These terms crop up, as we have seen, with great regularity with regard to dances (see Burridge, 1973:176–187 for a thoughtful discussion). One of the more interesting and potentially significant doctoral theses which could be undertaken in an anthropology of dance and human movement consists of an analysis of the concept of *totem* in relation to the dances of one or more Aboriginal peoples.

The Notion of "Theory" Again

There are other significant topics that also await investigation. Some of them turn around obvious problems in the literature on dancing with the notion of "imitation" or "mimicry" regarding dances. The imitation theory of dancing has had a long life in the intellectual history of western civilization with reference to visual, graphic art and dancing. Attempts at real analysis and the teasing out of an ideology of creativity seems to be lacking,[16] yet we do not lack starting points, one of which might be found in the controversial writings of Ananda Coomeraswamy (1934, 1948 and 1956). Although he writes about the dances and arts of India, he nevertheless presents arguments that were meant to stimulate thought and research on the transformational processes involved in the creation of symbolic forms.

Is it perhaps the case that there is more similarity between Aboriginal creative processes and those of other historical periods in our own—or Indian—history? Maybe the painters of religious icons in pre-Renaissance times more closely approximated the kinds of processes involved in the development of dances and rituals from the basis of the Dreaming. It would be worth looking into, not because it would necessarily assist Aborigines in the short run in this case, but such an exercise might go some way towards assisting *us* better to understand (and therefore to appreciate and respect) what is uniquely a feature of their different orientations to cosmology and religion.

Western art has not always—or even for very long—been dominated by its present tendencies towards a cult of the individual, "pop" art and various forms of deconstructionism. I would venture to guess that it would be extremely difficult to comprehend the significance of much traditional art in Australia or in the rest of the world in terms of these itinerant, relatively superficial and generally short-lived schools of thought.

> ... a fifteenth century painting is the deposit of a social relationship. On the one side there was a painter who made the picture, or at least supervised its making. On the other side there was somebody else who asked him to make it, provided funds for him to make it and, after he had made it, reckoned on using it in some way or other. Both parties worked within institutions and conventions—commercial, religious, perceptual, in the widest sense social—that were different from ours and influenced the forms of what they together made [Baxandall, 1972:1].

The elements of body language—gestures, postures and such—that are depicted in the paintings Baxandall discusses are very different indeed from those to which we are accustomed. It requires equal efforts of understanding to comprehend these as it does to work out the elements of body language(s) of other cultural groups in whatever form they appear. Body language, in whatever form it may be depicted, is not a static, universally understood set of gestural or danced meanings which somehow remain constant while everything else in a culture moves and changes. Although it will come as a shock to some, there is no universally understood Esperanto of gesture and meaning.

> Since the fifteenth century in western cultures a large number of notation systems for movement have appeared and disappeared (over 87 notation systems for dance alone). Many of these have been little used because they were devised to meet the needs of one particular movement system, dance style, or research project and could not be generalised. It is only in the twentieth century that movement writing systems have emerged which can serve a great variety of applications. The problem has been one of developing a script that will preserve the identity of the movement, make possible accurate reproduction and maintain semantic content.

These observations, written by Farnell (1988) for an International Encyclopedia of Communications, indicate in a closely action-

oriented fashion, what some of the problems of notation, preservation and recording of dancing and sign languages amounts to. And
there is more: Farnell also says that "Definitions of human movement necessarily affect definitions of what being human amounts
to—and these have changed considerably in Western cultures
according to disciplinary and theoretical perspectives and as a result
of historical changes in general intellectual climate."

I cite the work above to draw attention to the fact that the
biggest single obstacle, if it can be so characterized, to the notion
of serious work in the field of an anthropology of dance and human
movement lies in the long-held premises about mind/body relationships in western cultures: the institutionalization of Christianity,
and even more important, the Cartesian split between mind and
body, and therefore, of the body and the movements it makes. Some
of the most deeply held prejudices in English-speaking cultures
about these matters manifest themselves in relation to the subject
of dancing and in the defining categories into which all dancing is
classified. A lesser, but no less aggravating problem for the serious
researcher, is the insistence by many on a final appeal to "commonsense" thinking about dancing. Yet, it is commonsense thinking
which labels Aboriginal dancing "stone-age dancing"; it is commonsense to see *all dancing* as a stronghold of uncontrolled emotion, sinful desires, corrupting appetites and private irrationalities
of an astonishing variety. The fact that these commonsensical
conclusions are based (maybe) on one or two kinds of dancing, or
that they stem from little exposure to the richness and variety of the
danced forms of body languages throughout the world is ignored.
It is from "commonsense" that the notion that dancing is "primitive" grew—and still grows.

If Stanner is to be believed, that "It would be helpful to stop
thinking of Aborigines as a 'primitive' people" (1979:59), then we
are also going to have to convince ourselves that it would be helpful
to stop thinking of dancing as "primitive" too: not just *their* dancing,
but *ours*. It would not be an exaggeration to say that the only form
of western dancing which has consistently escaped the primitive

stereotype is classical ballet. The relevant question is not *why* this is so, but *what* in the history of various segments of western civilization has caused this idiom of dancing to escape the classification that all other forms of western dancing and "ethnic" dancing have been subjected to.[17] A rather simplistic explanation but one which has some element of truth in it turns around the notions of an academy, a syllabus and a more or less universalized technique and practice structure for the idiom. Because other forms of dancing lack these, they are thought to be more "primitive," hence less "advanced" or "developed" than the ballet. Insufficient attention has been paid to the historical development of the ballet and the reasons why it holds the privileged status that it does in English-speaking societies.

There is a sense in which I am suggesting that our understanding of *the* dance is (and must be) relational; that is, what we think we know is always contingent upon that which we do *not* know. This raises several questions, some of which have been previously discussed, like the question of whether or not a choreologist who is solely trained in the idiom of ballet can adequately notate the dances of an unfamiliar idiom of dancing. There is no discussion of such questions in available literature at all. It has been my experience through the teaching of an anthropology of dance and human movement that we know very little about western forms of dancing or why we view *them* the way we do, thus the task of raising our collective consciousness about Aboriginal dancing or any other form of dancing other than our own, is necessarily going to involve considerable effort towards understanding our own forms of dancing as well. Without this dual, self-reflexive process, we are going to be in a poor position to make any generalizations that are worthy of attention about the act of dancing in any culture, far less the entire world. And "dance researchers" or "dance scholars," whether they are conscious of it or not, are going to continue to offer analyses or commentaries on the dances of other peoples solely in terms of the defining categories of the dominant culture, simply because without eduction and training, they cannot do anything else.

Questions

Familiarity, gained through a life-time's reading of most of the significant writings about the dance in English-speaking societies (which represents merely a segment of a notional world literature on the subject), has yielded evidence that there are a set of stock answers to the often-asked question, Why do people dance? Stated in minimal terms they are these:

1. They dance because they want to have fun and relax—the dance is basically a vehicle for leisure and entertainment;
2. They dance because of biological, organic or instinctive needs of some kind—the dance as a precursor to spoken language, or as an atavistic, primitive expression of the animal side of human nature;
3. They dance because they want to express themselves— the dance as a symbolic activity divorced from real life;
4. They dance because they feel sexy, happy or sad or something—the dance as a prime repository of emotions (and in a world of logical positivism, these emotions have very little to do with rationality or with the human capacity for language-use);
5. They dance to show off or to relieve their overburdened feelings—the dance as catharsis or as one of the governors on a stem-valve theory of human emotions;
6. They dance because it is an innate, genetically programmed activity and because they refuse to give up that which represents a throw-back to their ape-like ancestors;
7. They dance because they cannot speak or write very well—the dance as a pre-literate phenomenon which carries the implication that learning to speak and write is going to put a stop to the dancing;
8. They dance because they are dedicated to some notion of *bodily* praxis as against a dedication to some notion of *verbal* praxis—the dance as a more truthful, more integrated, more honest way of life:

9. They dance because dancing is really a form of play—the dance as an activity belonging to the species *homo ludens;*
10. They dance because they are performing some social function which contributes to the larger society (although just what this is, is rarely ever explained except in terms like *harmony* or some other term);
11. They dance because they are really magicians or escapists of some kind—the dance as illusion, along with the rest of the theatrical professions;
12. They dance because a spirit has possessed them, whether good or evil—the dance as an hysterical, neurotic or quasi-religious manifestation;
13. They dance because of an over-accumulation of sex hormones.

All of the above are documented in the text to which this Appendix is attached and the list I have given is by no means complete. However, a baker's dozen of them by way of illustration is enough to permit us to get on with the discussion.

To that end, it is necessary to examine two difficulties with the old printed record. All of the answers above are inadequate, not only with reference to the nature of something as mind-boggling as the notion of "the dance" on a global scale, but with reference the extent to which *local* definitions, reasons, motivations and such are applied in the literature to the notion of "the dance" on a worldwide scale. The fact is that "why do people dance?" as a viable question at this point in history is an exhausted question because it has prevented us from finding out about other aspects of the subject. If it is true that a legitimate response to the Kantian challenge of "what can we know?" lies in the prior question, "what can we ask?", then what can be known by any of us about the dance has an intimate relation with what is asked.

There are so many unanswered questions: What are people doing when they dance?; How is that dance put together so that it accomplishes the teleological ends for which it is designed?; What is the conceptual space of that dance and how far does it compare with the conceptual spaces of "X" dance (sign system or whatever)?; How far is gesture and human action influenced by taxonomies of the body, whether it is danced or non-danced human action?; What is the relationship of the danced actions of "X" people with the pronominal systems of reference and the gestures of greeting in the same society?; What are the implications and consequences of the proposition, "movement is a literate medium of human expression"?; Is there a difference between actions described as "signal," those described as "symbolic" and those described as "symptomatic"?; What are the effects of the tourist industry on traditional dancing?; What is meant by "artifactualizing" a dance if the people who own the dance do not have a defining category of "art"?

As I have said elsewhere (Williams, 1980), the difficulty is that where we pre-suppose a *real level of "language"* with regard to speaking, we do *not* tend to pre-suppose a similar level of abstraction when we speak of dancing or any other system of body language. The result is that the whole area of movement study is vitiated by generalizations that stem from comparatively limited notions about *specific and minor uses of the medium of movement.* Then too, we often seem to be the unconscious victims of our own defining categories, definitions and models of the role of movement in human societies. We divide actions (but not words) into "symbolic" and "instrumental" categories. Where we are familar with polysemy, homonymy and synonymy with reference to words, we seem to want to regard gestures as if they are in some sense semantically universal, even in the face of evidence that this is not at all the case. But it is to some different questions about dances and human movement that we will now turn, because there are examples in the Australian literature of attempts to enlarge the theoretical and methodological horizons of the field somewhat—or to undertake a different model of analysis entirely.

Different Questions

Boorsboom (1978) was concerned with the apparent shift of a major rite of passage, the *Maradjiri,* in Arnhem Land. The ceremony he investigated looked as if it had brought about a break with former *Maradjiri* rites, causing the new rite to be an exact opposite of the old one (Boorsboom, 1978:172). Through extended fieldwork, this was proved not to be the case. Instead, it was found that (1) the internal structures of the rite remained, and (2) elaborations were introduced of already existing features of the rite. There was also evidence of a rearrangement of existing symbolic elements of the rite, i.e., the Dreaming "cluster" to which it belonged (1978:172).

The refreshing thing about Boorsboom's work is that we see dances discussed in an overall context of a total Aboriginal cycle of life in the area; a singularly van Gennepian approach which in my view is a definite "plus." The major positive contribution of Boorsboom's work, specifically with regard to dances, is the attention paid to overall patterns of the dances (1978:90-129). These insights are offered: (1) "By means of traditionally stylized dances the actors re-enact the important Dreamtime exploits of their clan heroes, thus following up the instructions of what they usually call 'our Dreaming' (Sugar Bag). This Being showed how to sing and dance and in this way created the natural species and phenomena which now belong to the *Wurgigandijar* clan" (1978:90); (2) "A series of dances of a particular *Wurgigandjar* ceremony, however, does not comprise all the dreamings of the cluster but consist of a carefully selected group of dreamings which differs for every ceremony, and it is from such a selection of a certain number of dreamings—and the omission of others—that a clan ceremony such as the *Maradjiri* derives its definite character" (Ibid).

There are eight dreamings danced in the *Maradjiri* ceremony, and instead of falling into the trap of trying to give a blow-by-blow description of the movements done by the dancers, Boorsboom gives a detailed analysis of the spatial patterns thereof, the kin relations involved and such. The author is straightforward about his own limitations—a feature of his work that is greatly to be admire He says, for example, "No special attention will be paid to dancing patterns of the women as I have found it impossi observe properly their complicated and very stylized mo of feet, legs, arms, hands and head. They perform certa variations for every dreaming, which will be mentioned possible ... (1978:95).

Boorsboom's conclusions are interesting: rite and myth, he tells us, "have the capacity to absorb history, but at the same time history intrudes upon rite and myth and brings about changes in composition and content" (1978:183). He quotes Pouwer, whose article on signification and fieldwork (1973) is a standard reference for anthropologists of human movement. His work might have benefited by consulting Pocock (1967), as he is concerned with apperceptions of time. His work offers an intriguing and well-documented basis for further work by a trained anthropologist of human movement who might well begin by asking, What is the relation of the missing women's movements to the *Maradjiri* dance cycle as a whole? It would be useful to possess notated scores of this dance cycle as well (both men's and women's parts), but that must await developments in the field of study to which I alluded at the beginning of this essay.

Very different questions are being asked by two other researchers with regard to field studies already carried out in Arnhem Land: Stephen Wild and Margaret Clunies-Ross. Their current research seeks to answer the following questions:

1. What are the rules governing the sequences of melodic and textual phrases in *Djambidj* songs?
2. What are the rules governing the sequences of dance movement performed with the *Djambidj* songs?
3. What effect does the presence or absence of dancing have on the rules for melodic and textual elements of performances?

   How are all of these elements (melody, text, dancing, stick ~rns, didjeridu patterns and dance calls) coordinated in ~ce?

   ~t are the dreaming subjects of *Djambidj* the elements of performance?

   the contexts of occasions of performance ture of performance?

   s-Ross's research is being conducted by ments of a performance, classifying and coding the musical and textual phrases, danced movements, homogeneous stretches of stick beats and didjeridu sounds and discrete "bands" of ritual calls, and entering these coded sequences into a computer for analysis of syntagmatic and paradigmatic patterns. Notations are being made from audio and video recordings of performances spanning about twenty-five years. The recorded data are complemented by extensive field observations and discussions with performers.

The specific results that may be obtained from this research are not predictable at this stage, but whatever results may accrue, the project will be invaluable, especially from a kinological point of view, for no work of this kind has been undertaken before in Australia. Answers to the questions above will establish that *Djambidj* songs and dances *have* rules for a start. I think that the research will help to implant the idea, too, that the notion of "performance" is sufficiently complex that it demands a different approach to fieldwork than the traditional anthropological approach consisting of one ethnographer to one people. Any approach to the notion of a "performance" which is based on consideration of music *only,* dancing *only,* language *only* is a reductionist's approach which fails to see the notion of performance as an integrated whole. Clunies-Ross and Wild seek to reintegrate their data at a different level in the hope that doing so will make possible different kinds of generalizations.

There can be little doubt that different kinds of generalizations and fresh approaches to the Australian material are needed, both with regard to Aboriginal and non-Aboriginal dancing, sign languages and non-vocalized systems of human actions of all kinds. It has been argued that not enough attention has been (or is being) paid to performances (see von Sturmer, 1987:74) which go beyond conventional social scientific styles of analyses—an appeal, one assumes, for a recognition of dances as *le fait totale* in the classic Maussian sense. One can agree only that the meaning of any given performance of dancing cannot be reduced to the mechanical playing out of sign-systems, because one can exhaust the signs and yet know that there is something "over and above" (von Sturmer, 1987:74). But it is just this notion of "over and above" which has been very difficult to deal with in the past. Perhaps it is the case that excellent scholarship can only hope to point the finger (as in the Zen saying), restraining itself from the arrogance of confusing the pointing finger and the moon and accepting the fact of mysteries and beauties that cannot be captured in words in any case, but only in silence.

On a more mundane level, it can be said that Behaviorism, for example, has demonstrably failed to produce insights into dances considered as "behaviors"; phenomenology (as welcome as it was as a reaction against radical Behaviorism and hardcore empiricism) still denies the dance any ontological existence in time (see Sheets, 1966). The existence of "spirit" can be no more successfully proved than the existence of "psyche" in the tradition of post-Kantian metaphysics, thus it has been to off-shoots of the recent linguistic revolution in the sciences to which some modern researchers have turned—with precisely what results it is as yet too early to say. At least the shift in philosophical thinking, best represented in the work of Best (1978 and 1985), and the shift in British anthropology from function to meaning (see Crick, 1975) have opened new possibilities of theoretical and methodological approach, just as ethnoscience did in the American anthropological tradition (see Kaeppler, 1972, 1985 and 1986).

Conclusion

I should like to finish this essay by making three things about the scholarly study of dancing in Australia as plain as possible. Up to now, it is *not* the case that people have looked at dancing, Aboriginal or otherwise, without being able to see it. As I have tried to illustrate, through a balanced presentation of criticism and commendation, there are several writers who *have* "seen" and they have described, analyzed and discussed their particular areas of interest very well. There are also those who have seen the need in a multicultural context for establishing scholarly studies of the dance in an hospitable academic atmosphere making out of such study a legitimate area of serious research. Many friends of the subject have worked for many years, both within and outside of universities, to change the perspective on the subject in several different ways.

Internationally, the printed record, with regard to the anthropology of the dance and human movement, has improved remarkably in the past two decades. Australia has a unique contribution to make, but cannot make it unless the subject is able to take its place along with music, theater and the visual arts in higher educational institutions. No one seems adequately to be able to explain the obvious disparities between the lack of available university qualifications in this country for the subject of the dance and the richness of opportunities of this kind available in connection with other art forms. It has been tentatively suggested that there is not sufficient literature to bear the weight of full-scale intellectual scrutiny. I hope that I have indicated by this writing that this is not the case.

Second, it is as clear to me now as it was in 1970, when I commenced the study of social anthropology, that intimate knowledge of one, two, three or more idioms of dancing does not automatically produce the ability to write about (or notate) the *known* idioms of dancing, far less those which may be *unknown* (see Williams, 1976). If any of us who have persisted with the subject through doctoral levels of study could have foreseen the extraordinary confusions which existed (and still do exist) about the subject of dancing in English-speaking societies, we might have felt despair and have never undertaken further study at all. Our personal odysseys, taken together, seem somewhat less radical now than they did, because the issues that were so vital then (*circa* 1965) have been replaced by others. The real problems to which I alluded at the beginning of this essay pertain not to whether the subject is viable, but how the subject is to be incorporated into a university context in Australia. Nearly a decade has passed since the idea of a graduate degree in the anthropology of dance and human movement came into anyone's mind and began to be implemented through A.I.A.S. "Real" problems now consist of educating and training young Australians of Aboriginal and non-Aboriginal descent to the task of coping with the literature, the theoretical and methodological problems that they inherit in an Australian context, and of encouraging them to contribute to the field at local, national and international levels.

Third, a new volume of essays on *Songs of Aboriginal Australia* (1987) has just been released which contains discussions about dancing, because the two phenomena of singing and dancing are very closely if not irrevocably linked in that context. In this collection of works by reputable scholars, I have already found clues to some possible answers to the question, What is a reasonable estimate of the present theoretical position(s) concerning the subject of dancing in Aboriginal Australia? Whatever else may be said of this book by its future reviewers, it represents a significant contribution to the Australian literature on dancing because of its theoretical content and the clarity with which its authors and editors address some of these issues. It is a provocative and interesting set of essays which will provide future students with an invaluable intellectual foil as they attempt to sharpen their wits in preparation for their entry into an arena of discourse that is often contentious, certainly stimulating and rarely without genuine interest and satisfying rewards.

Drid Williams
September 5, 1987
University of Sydney

Notes

1. For more up-to-date approaches to the subject and work which would be usable by present-day anthropologists and linguists, see Durr (1984), Farnell (1984), Freedman (1986), Dixon-Stowell (1986), Friedland (1986), Hart-Johnson (1983), Fairbank (1985), Novack (1986), Adra (1986), Puri (1983), Volland (1986), Jablonko (1986), Blakely (1986), Grau (1983) and Dail-Jones (1984).

2. Those who for several years worked at, and finally succeeded in getting a dance lectureship in Australia were Drs. Stephen Wild, Margaret Clunies-Ross and Allen Marett.

3. For further bibliographic information of a more general anthropological nature see Burridge, 1973:56–57.

4. The citation is of a published work of Grau's. Restrictions placed on her Doctoral thesis, available for reading in Australia only at A.I.A.S., prevent more than the most general of comments.

5. Dail-Jones's work is seriously flawed because of the heavy Behavioristic overtones of the theoretical models she imposed, but if those can be disregarded, there are sections of great value.

6. See Williams (1986) for further discussion.

7. Quote marks and a capital *C* are meant to mark the differences between a technical definition of the term *culture* in anthropology (which stemmed from Tylor) and a popular misconception of "Culture," which tends towards ethnocentric bias, elitism and connotations of "superior" and "inferior" cultural behaviors and artifacts.

8. Quisenberry's fieldwork was carried out in Australia, but the thesis was written in the United States and the degree was granted at Southern Methodist University. Although she consulted several Australian anthropologists, their work seemed to have little or no impact on her study seen as a theoretical or methodological work. The anthropologists enter into the discussion only with regard to "ethnographic" matters. The point is this: Quisenberry's work is a classic example of the notion that theory and description (or ethnography) are somehow separable. Furthermore, her work displays extraordinary epistemological confusions, i.e., she seemed to have no clear idea of the parameters of that which she could comment upon. This could be simply the result of poor supervision; one does not know. Unfortunately, there is only the completed document to consult. Lest I appear to be biased, see Kaeppler, 1978:33, for further criticism of Curt Sachs.

9. It is a well-known fact that political and national boundaries do not often coincide well with the linguistic realities of usage among a people, thus it becomes necessary to stress the point here: Terms of national or political reference rarely do justice to the cultural realities that they attempt to encompass, including, for example, the present mixtures of traditions, even on one aboriginal reserve where one finds (for example) the Wanam and Apalech traditions co-existing in Aurukun.

10. I have tried, using von Sturmer's words, to illustrate exactly what is meant here: This anthropologist's "description" is an *informed* description, one which rests not only on intuition and experience of dancing with his informants in the field, but on years of scholarly study as well. This is why he can form the sentences in his description the way he does. He understands what the dancing *means*. His locutions are not simply "accidents" or the result of a better knowledge of the English language. Should colleagues think that I overstress the relation of theory and description, I would ask that they consult Williams (1986) and then reflect on the value of tutored as against untutored field observations.

11. The term *semasiology* is from a Greek source and can be defined as "signification" in the sense of "meaning" + "logy." In the late

nineteenth century, the word was used to refer to that branch of philology which dealt with the meanings of words. It was used by R. Martineau in 1877 with reference to "the semasiology of Arabic words." In 1884, a reference appeared in the *Athenaeum, 27* September 395/1, as follows:

> Philology is now advancing towards a new branch having intimate relations with psychology, the so-called semasiology of Abel and others.

The next recorded use of the term occurs in 1889, where F. Haverfield (Academy 7 Dec. 374/2) uses it to raise doubt about the phonetic connections of words. That is, where two words may seem to be phonetically linked, semasiologically their connection might be improbable. In 1880, a linguistic entity, the "semasiological solecism" was apparently known and understood, as the phrase occurs in the *Athenaeum*. In that publication (5 Aug./185) this phrase occurs:

> The semasiologist ... has to trace the vicissitudes which the history of forms, words and phrases presents with respect to signification.

Usage of this term has consistently pointed towards the semantic aspects of linguistic signification and the term is used throughout the texts of my work and that of my students in that sense, only, as it applies to human action sign signification. In anthropology, it is a neologism, and for the reasons why it arose, see Williams (1986b).

12. I have used a term *semantic primitives* here which is well-known in linguistic literature through the work of Anna Wierzbicka (1980, 1985). I first encountered the phrase, not in her books, but in Haviland (1986), where he does an extensive analysis of deictic categories, words and roots with reference to Guugu Ymidihirr (a local Paman language of the Hopevale people) in the southeastern part of the Cape York peninsula. My understanding of the notion of semantic primitives is closer to Haviland's usage than it is to its originator's usage.

13. By this, I mean that the only references to theorists of anthropology and the dance that are present in Grau's work are Kaeppler, Keali'inohomoku and Blacking. This would be all right if we were offered an explanation of the "muted group," i.e., Birdwhistell, Kendon, Williams, Royce, Hall and others. As it is, the one theoretical framework that includes the notion of universals—worked out in great detail—is ignored: semasiology.

14. There is no available space to spell out what is meant here, as the problem would require at least one lecture. Suffice it to say that an anthropologist's relation to his or her informants, to the data, to colleagues and to the folk-model of events is complex and quite unlike the relations between a so-called "hard" scientist and his or her work. One starts by teasing out the differences by studying Winch (1958), who stressed these relations and discussed the differences in detail and with great sagacity.

15. One is aware of the history of—and current debates over—this term in anthropology. Elsewhere, I have expressed perplexity over Kurath's statement, for example, that " ... clan totemism produces complex rituals, as in Australia ... " (1960:237). There are those who are convinced that "totemism" in the late 1950's and early 1960's was suffering from its death throes as a major explanatory category in social anthropology, but fuller discussion is impossible here. The term *totem* is commonly used with regard to dances, and stringent and critical examination needs to be made of such usages, as there is virtually no agreement among writers as to the reality to which the term is supposed to refer.

16. I here refer to collections of essays like those of Otten (1971) and Belo (1970), where a good deal of ethnographic fact is elucidated, but these facts are unaccompanied by discussions of what the *processes* are which generate the facts.

17. The ideological basis for the label "primitive" in connection with Aboriginal peoples has existed in Australia since the mid-eighteenth century at least. It still exists today. Mere mention of the matter is all that is possible here; however, the subject is dealt with in greater detail in Williams (1988), where the notion of "primitiveness" is connected with a concept of "Terra Nullius," which was accompanied by the idea that there were peoples who had not advanced beyond "a state of nature" (see Frost, 1981, for more thorough discussion).

Appendix A

Excerpts from *Review of Arts Education and Training,* October 1985, Australian Government Publication Service, Canberra, pp. 67–68.

PROVISION IN DANCE

6.9   There is comparatively little tertiary provision in dance. Table 3 sets out the distribution of institutions with offerings in dance by State, level, and type of institution.

Table 3: DANCE—Distribution by State, Level of Course, and Type of Institution in 1984

State	Higher Degree		Post graduate		Bachelor Degree		Diploma		Associate Diploma	
	CAE	UNI	CAE	UNI	CAE	UNI	CAE	UNI	CAE	UNI
NSW	-	-	-	-	1**	-	-	-	3	1**
VICTORIA	-	1*	-	-	1	1#	1	-	-	-

Table 3: DANCE—Distribution by State, Level of Course,
and Type of Institution in 1984

State	Higher Degree		Post graduate		Bachelor Degree		Diploma		Associate Diploma	
	CAE	UNI	CAE	UNI	CAE	UNI	CAE	UNI	CAE	UNI
QUEENSLAND	-	-	-	-	-	-	-	-	1	-
WA	-	-	-	-	-	-	-	-	1	-
SA	-	-	-	-	1	-	-	-	1	-
TASMANIA	-	-	-	-	-	-	-	-	-	-
ACT	-	-	-	-	-	-	-	-	-	-
NT	￢	-	-	-	-	-	-	-	-	-
TOTAL	-	1	-	-	3	1	1	-	6	1

*This is a research based Masters degree in the Performing Arts. It is not a discrete dance course, nor is the degree course marked #.
**Minor strand only offered

6.9   There is only one course in dance at diploma level and four at degee level although in one only a minor strand is offered. For the most part courses are only available at the associate diploma level. Courses are offered by a total of six colleges of advanced education: two in New South Wales and one each in Victoria, Queensland, Western Australia and South Australia. Dance is available as a minor study within an associate diploma course offered by the University of Wollongong and as an element within courses in the performing arts offered by Deakin University.

6.10   A number of institutions are proposing to expand their offerings in dance during the next few years. The Victorian College of the Arts proposes to introduce a post-graduate diploma course in 1986 and degree courses are planned for introduction in Queensland, Western Australia and New South Wales.

Appendix B

From: Wild, S. 1986. Australian Aboriginal Theatrical Movement. *Theatrical Movement: A Bibliographical Anthology*

(Ed. B. Fleshman) Metuchen, NJ: Scarecrow Press, Chapter 27, pp.610–620.

ALLEN, Elphine
1973. "Australian Aboriginal Dance." In Ronald M. Berndt and E.S. Phillips, eds. *The Australian Aboriginal Heritage, an Introduction Through the Arts.* Sydney: Australian Society for Education Through the Arts, in association with Ure Smith. Pp.275–90.

ANGAS, George F.
1967 [1847]a. "Savage Life and Scenes in Australia and New Zealand." *Landmarks in Anthropology,* Weston LaBarre, general editor. New York, London: Johnson Reprint Corp. Originally published by Smith, Elder, and Co., London.
1967 [1847]b. *South Australia: Illustrated.* Facsimile edition, Sydney: A.H. and A.W. Reed. Originally published by Thomas McLean, London.

ANONYMOUS
1971. "Mowanjum Dance Group." *Department of Native Welfare Newsletter* 1(10): 28–39.
1972. "The Yelangi and Waiben Dancers." *Identity* 1(5): 18–23.
1975. "Cairns Festival." *Identity* 2(6): 19–22.

BARLOW, Alex
1980. *Aboriginal Studies Resource List.* Canberra: AIAS.

BASEDOW, Herbert
1925. *The Australian Aboriginal.* Adelaide: Preece.

BATES, Daisy M.
1905–6. "The Marriage Laws and Some Customs of the West Australian Aborigines." *Victorian Geographical Journal* 13–14: 36–60.
n.d. "Songs, Dances, etc.—Corroborees and Songs, Murchison." Unpublished ms. deposited in National Library of Australia, Canberra; copy deposited in AIAS, Canberra.

BELL, Diane.
1980. *Daughters of the Dreaming.* Australian National University, Canberra: Ph.D. Thesis.

BERNDT, Catherine H.
1950. *Women's Changing Ceremonies in Northern Australia. L'Homme 1.* Paris: Hermann et Cie.

1962. "A Drama of North-Eastern Arnhem Land." *Oceania* 22: 216–39, 275–89.

1962. "The Arts of Life: An Australian Aboriginal Perspective." *Westerly* 1(2–3): 82–8.

1963. "Art and Aesthetic Expression." In Helen Sheils, ed. *Australian Aboriginal Studies.* A symposium of papers presented at the 1961 research conference. Melbourne: OUP. Pp.256–77.

1965. "Women and the 'Secret Life.'" In R.M. and C.H. Berndt, eds. *Aboriginal Man in Australia, Essays in Honour of Emeritus Professor A.P. Elkin.* Sydney, Melbourne, London: Angus and Robertson. Pp.238–82.

BERNDT, Ronald M.
1951. *Kunapipi.* Melbourne: Cheshire.

1952. *Djanggawul.* London: Routledge and Kegan Paul.

1974. "Australian Aboriginal Religion." In Th.P. van Baaren, L. Leertouwer and H. Buning, eds. *Iconography of Religions,* Section V. Leiden: E.J. Brill.

BERNDT, Ronald M., and Catherine H. Berndt
1942–45. "A Preliminary Report of Field Work in the Ooldea Region, Western Southern Australia." *Oceania 12–15.*

1951. *Sexual Behaviour in Western Arnhem Land.* New York: Viking Fund Publications in Anthropology no. 16.

1962. "Aborigines: Dancing." In *Australian Encyclopaedia,* second edition. Sydney: Grolier Society. Vol 1: 62–4.

1970. *Man, Land and Myth in North Australia: The Gunwinggu People.* Sydney: Ure Smith.

1977 [1964]. *The World of the First Australians.* Second edition. Sydney: Ure Smith.

BLACK, L.
1944. *The Bora Ground.* Sydney: Booth.

BOORSBOOM, Adrianus P.
1978. *Maradjiri: A Modern Ritual Complex in Arnhem Land, North Australia.* Nijmegan, Katholieke Universiteit, Central Reprographie, Directoraat A-Facultieten.

CAMPBELL, Tomas D.
1940. "The Drama and Theatre Arts of the Aborigines." *Mankind* 2(9): 329–30.

CHASE, Athol
1980. *Which Way Now?: Tradition, Continuity and Change in a North Queensland Aboriginal Community* [Lockhart River]. University of Queensland: Ph.D. Thesis.

CHURCH, A.E.
1945. "Ballet at Badu." *Walkabout* 11(9): 33–4.

CLUNIES ROSS, Margaret, and Stephen A. Wild
1981. "The Relations of Music, Text and Dance in Arnhem Land Clan Songs." Unpublished paper presented at the Conference on Transmission in Oral and Written Traditions, Humanities Research Centre, Australian National University, Canberra, August 1981.

COPPELL, W.G.
1978. *Audio-Visual Resource Material Relating to the Aboriginal Australians.* Canberra: Curriculum Development Centre.

CURR, Edward M.
1883. *Recollections of Squatting in Victoria: Then Called the Port Phillip District (From 1841–1851).* Melbourne: Robertson.
1886–87. *The Australian Race.* Melbourne: Ferres. (4 vols).

DALEY, Charles
1925. "Reminiscences from 1841 of William Kyle, a Pioneer." *Victorian Historical Magazine* 10(3): 158–72.

DAWSON, James
1981 [1881]. *Australian Aborigines: The Language and Customs of Several Tribes of Aborigines in the Western District of Victoria, Australia.* Canberra: AIAS. Originally published by George Robertson, Melbourne, Sydney, Adelaide.

DEAN, Beth
1955. "In Search of Stone-Age Dance." *Walkabout* 21(5): 15–20.

DEAN, Beth, and Victor Carell
1955. *Dust for the Dancers.* Sydney: Ure Smith.

DURACK, Mary
1971. "No Longer Just a Dream: The Aboriginal Theatre Foundation Gets to Work." *Identity* 1(2): 17–22.

EDWARDS, Gregson
1971. "Dancing for the Future." *Northern Territory Affairs* 2: 14–16.

ELKIN, A.P.
1972. "Two Rituals in South and Central Arnhem Land" [Yabuduruwa and Maraian]. Sydney: University of Sydney. Oceania Monographs no.19. Originally published in *Oceania* 31–2, 42.
1974 [1938]. *The Australian Aborigines*. Fifth edition. Sydney: Angus and Robertson.

ELLIS, Catherine
1970. "The Role of the Ethnomusicologist in the Study of Andagarinja Women's Ceremonies." *Miscellanea Musicologica* 5: 76–208.

EWERS, John K.
1954 [1953]. *With the Sun on My Back*. Second revised edition. Sydney: Angus and Robertson.
1964 [1947]. "Aboriginal Ballet." In A.T. Bolton, ed. *Walkabout's Australia: An Anthology of Articles and Photographs from Walkabout Magazine*. Sydney: Ure Smith in association with the Australian National Travel Association. Pp.62–75. Reprinted from *Walkabout* 14(2): 29–34.

EYRE, Edward J.
1964 [1845]. "Manners and Customs of the Aborigines of Australia." *In* his *Journals of Expeditions of Discovery into Central Australia*. Australiana Facsimile Editions no.7. Adelaide: Libraries Board of South Australia. Vol. II: 145–507. Originally published by T. & W. Boone, London.

FINK, Ruth A.
1960. *The Changing Status and Cultural Identity of Western Australian Aborigines: A Field Study of Aborigines in the Murchison District, Western Australia, 1955–1957*. Columbia University, New York: Ph.D. Thesis.

GOODALE, Jane C.
1971. *Tiwi Wives: A Study of Women of Melville Island, Northern Australia*. Seattle: University of Washington Press.

GOODALE, Jane, and J.D. Koss
1966. "The Cultural Context of Creativity Among Tiwi." *American Ethnological Society Proceedings*, 1966: 175–91.

HADDON, Alfred C.
1893. "The Secular and Ceremonial Dances of Torres Straits." *Internationales Archive für Ethnographic* 6: 131–62.

HASSELL, Ethel
1975. *My Dusky Friends: Aboriginal Life, Customs and Legends and Glimpses of Life at Jarramungup in the 1880s; With an Introduction by Sara Meagher.* Fremantle, Western Australia: C.W. Hassell.

HIATT, Betty
1966. "Report on the Female Aboriginal Dancing Associated with the Bora Ceremony at Lockhart River Mission in the Cape York Peninsula." Unpublished ms. deposited in AIAS, Canberra.

HIATT, L.R.
1965. "Kingship and Conflict: A Study of an Aboriginal Community in Northeast Arnhem Land. Canberra: Australian National University Press.

HODGKINSON, Clement
1845. *Australia from Port MacQuarie to Moreton Bay.* London: T. & W. Boone.

HOWITT, Alfred W.
1844. "On Some Australian Ceremonies of Initiation." *Royal Anthropological Institute Journal* 13: 432–59.
1855. "The Jeraeil or Initiation Ceremonies of the Kurnai Tribes." *Royal Anthropological Institute Journal* 14: 302–25.
1904. *The Native Tribes of South-East Australia.* London: Macmillan & Co.

JONES, Mary
1979. "Dancing Feet?: The History of Sacred Dance." *Zadoc Central News,* October 1979: 13–25.
1980. "The History of Sacred and Biblically-Inspired Dance in Australia." *Nelen Yubu* 6: 3–18.

KABERRY, Phyllis M.
1939. *Aboriginal Woman, Sacred and Profane.* London: Routledge.

KARTOMI, Margaret
1970. "Tjitji Inma at Yalata." *Hemisphere* 14(6): 33–7.

KEEN, Ian
1978. *One Ceremony, One Song: An Economy of Religious Knowledge Among the Yolngu of North-East Arnhem Land.* Australian National University, Canberra: Ph.D. Thesis.

KEMP, Thérèse B.
1968–69. "A Propos de Certaines Danses des Aborigènes de la Tasmanie." *Ethnographie,* Paris 63(3): 156–9.

KENNEDY, Peter (ed.)
1970. *Films on Traditional Music and Dance, a First International Catalogue.* Paris: UNESCO for International Folk Music Council.

LAADE, Walfgang
1968. "Etwas über Musik and Tanz bei den Insulanern der Torres-Strasse." *Kontakte* 4: 121–5.

LOCKWOOD, Douglas W.
1963. *Crocodiles and Other People.* Adelaide: Rigby.

LONG, G. MacDonald
1937. "Corroboree." *Walkabout,* September 1937: 49, 51, 53, 55.

MacFARLANE, Philip H.
1950. "The Wild-Fowl and the Devil: A Legend of the Torres Strait." *Walkabout* 16(1): 46–8.

MADDOCK, Kenneth
1972. *The Australian Aborigines: A Portrait of Their Society.* Penguin Books.
n.d. "Report on Field Work in the Northern Territory 1964–65." Unpublished ms. deposited in AIAS, Canberra.

MAJOR, Thomas
1900. *Leaves from a Squatter's Notebook.* London: Sands.

MASSOLA, Aldo
1971. *The Aborigines of South-Eastern Australia as They Were.* Melbourne: Heinemann.

MATHEW, John
1887. "Mary River and Bunya Bunya Country." In E.M. Curr. *The Australian Race.* Melbourne: Ferres. Vol.3: 125–209.

1889. "The Australian Aborigines." *In Royal Society of New South Wales Journal and Proceedings* 23: 335–449.
1899. *Eaglehawk and Crow: A Study of the Australian Aborigines Including an Inquiry into their Origin and a Survey of Australian Languages.* Melbourne: Melville, Mullen and Slade.

MATHEWS, Robert H.
1898. "Initiation Ceremonies of Australian Tribes." *American Philosophical Society Proceedings* 37: 54–73.

McCARTHY, Frederick D.
1957. *Australia's Aborigines: Their Life and Culture.* Melbourne: Colorgravure Publishers.
1964. "The Dancers of Aurukun." *Australian Natural History* 14(9): 296–300.
1978. "Aurukun Dances." Northbridge, NSW. Unpublished ms. deposited in AIAS, Canberra.

McCONNEL, Ursula H.
1930–34. "The Wik-munkan Tribe of Cape York Peninsula." *Oceania* 1(1): 97–194; 1(2): 181–205; 4(3): 310–67.

MEGGITT, M.J.
1955. "Djanba Among the Walbiri, Central Australia." *Anthropos 50:* 375–403.
1965 [1962]. *Desert People: A Study of the Walbiri Aborigines of Central Australia.* Chicago and London: The University of Chicago Press. Originally published by Angus and Robertson, Sydney.
1966. "Gadjari Among the Walbiri of Central Australia." Sydney: The University of Sydney. The Oceania Monographs no.14. Originally published in *Oceania* 36–7.

MORPHY, Howard
1977. *"Too Many Meanings": An Analysis of the Artistic System of the Yongu of North-East Arnhem Land.* Australian National University, Canberra: Ph.D. Thesis. (2 vols)

MORSE, Babette
1968. "Dance Notation and Aboriginal Culture." *Hemisphere* 12(11): 2–6

MOUNTFORD, Charles P.
1956. "Expedition to the Land of the Tiwi." *National Geographic Magazine* 109: 417–40.
1958. *The Tiwi, Their Art, Myth and Ceremony.* London: Phoenix House; Melbourne: Georgian House.

1962. *Brown Men and Red Sand: Journeying in Wild Australia.* Sydney: Angus and Robertson.
1976. *Nomads of the Australian Desert.* Adelaide: Rigby.

MOYLE, Alice M.
1972. "Sound Films for Combined Notation: The Groote Eylandt Field Project, 1969." *International Folk Music Council Yearbook* 4: 104–18.
1977a. "Aborigines: Music, Song and Dance." In *The Australian Encyclopaedia,* third edition. Sydney: Grolier Society of Australia. Vol.1: 37–40.
1977b. "Music and Dance: Mastersingers of the Bush." In P. Stanbury, ed. *The Moving Frontier: Aspects of Aboriginal-European Interaction in Australia.* Sydney: Reed.
1978. "Song and Dance." In M.C. Hill and A.P.C. Barlow, comps. *Black Australia: An Annotated Bibliography and Teachers' Guide to Resources on Aborigines and Torres Strait Islanders.* Canberra: AIAS; Atlantic Highlands, NJ: Humanities Press. Pp.63–6.

MOYLE, Richard M.
1979. *Songs of the Pintupi: Musical Life in a Central Australian Society.* Canberra: AIAS.

MUNN, Nancy D.
1973. *Walbiri Iconography: Graphic Representations and Cultural Symbolism in a Central Australian Society.* Ithaca and London: Cornell University Press.

PETERSON, Nicolas
1970. "Buluwandi: A Central Australian Ceremony for the Resolution of Conflict." In R.M. Berndt, ed. *Australian Aboriginal Anthropology.* Nedlands, Western Australia: University of Western Australia Press for AIAS. Pp.200–15.

PLOMLEY, N.J.B. (ed.)
[1966]. *Friendly Mission: The Tasmanian Journals and Papers of George Augustus Robinson, 1829–1834.* Hobart: Tasmanian Historical Research Association.

QUISENBERRY, Kay
1973. *Dance in Arnhem Land: A Field Study Project 1970–72.* Southern Methodist University, Dallas: M.F.A. Thesis.

RAVEN-HART, R.
1948. "Islands of Torres Strait." *Walkbout* 14(12): 14–16.
1949. *The Happy Isles.* Melbourne: Georgian House.

RICHARD, Francis
1925. "Customs and Language of the Western Hodgkinson Aboriginals."
    Queensland Museum Memoirs 8(3): 249–65.

ROHEIM, Géza
1933. "Women and Their Life in Central Australia." *Royal Anthropolog-
    ical Institute Journal* 63: 207–65.
1943. *The Eternal Ones of the Dream.* New York: International Univer-
    sities Press.

ROTH, Walter
1897. *Ethnological Studies Among the North-West Central Queensland
    Aborigines.* Brisbane: Government Printer.
1902. "Games, Sports and Amusements." *North Queensland Ethnogra-
    phy: Bulletin no.4.* Brisbane: Government Printer.

SALVADO, Rosendo
1977 [1851]. *The Salvado Memoirs: Historical Memoirs of Australia and
    Particularly of the Benedictine Mission of New Norcia and of the
    Habits and Customs of the Australian Natives.* Translated and
    edited by E.J. Storman. Nedlands, Western Australia: University
    of Western Australia Press. Originally published by Society for
    the Propagation of the Faith, Rome.

SANSOM, Basil
1980. *The Camp at Wallaby Cross.* Canberra: AIAS.

SHANNON, Cynthia.
1971. *Walpiri Women's Music.* Monash University, Clayton, Victoria:
    B.A. Honours Thesis.

SIMPSON, Colin
1971. "The Balnooknook Corroboree." In Reader's Digest Association
    Australia. *This Land—These People.* Sydney.

SMYTH, Robert B.
1878. *The Aborigines of Victoria.* Melbourne: Government Printer.

SPENCER, Sir Walter Baldwin
1896. "Through Larapinta Land: A Narrative of the Expedition." *In*

Report on the Work of the Horn Scientific Expedition ... , Vol.1: 1–136.

1914. *Native Tribes of the Northern Territory of Australia.* London: Macmillan.

1928. *Wanderings in Wild Australia.* London: Macmillan. (2 vols).

SPENCER, Sir Walter Baldwin, and F.J. Gillen

1899. *The Native Tribes of Central Australia.* London: Macmillan.

1904. *The Northern Tribes of Central Australia.* London: Macmillan.

1927. *The Arunta: A Study of a Stone Age People.* London: Macmillan. (2 vols.)

STANNER, W.E.H.

1966. *On Aboriginal Religion.* Sydney: The University of Sydney. The Oceania Monographs no.11. Originally published in *Oceania* 30–4.

STIRLING, Edward C.

1896. "Anthropology." In Report on the Work of the Horn Scientific Expedition ... , Vol. 4: 1–157.

STREHLOW, T.G.H.

1971. *Songs of Central Australia.* Sydney: Angus and Robertson.

STUBINGTON, Jill

1977. "Songs to Live By." *Hemisphere* 21(8): 25–30.

1979. "North Australian Aboriginal Music." In Jennifer Isaacs, ed. *Australian Aboriginal Music.* Sydney: Aboriginal Artists Agency.

TAPLIN, G.

1879. *The Folklore, Manners, Customs, and Languages of the South Australian Aborigines.* Adelaide: Government Printer.

THOMAS, N.W.

1906. *Natives of Australia.* London: Archibald Constable & Company.

THOMSON, Donald

1934. "Notes on a Hero Cult from the Gulf of Carpentaria, North Queensland." *Royal Anthropological Institute Journal* 64: 217–35.

THORNE, Jessie C.

1939. "'Playabout' Corroboree." *Wildlife* 1(14): 12–13.

TONKINSON, Robert
1970. "Aboriginal Dream-Spirit Beliefs in a Contact Situation: Jigalong, Western Australia." In R.M. Berndt, ed. *Australian Aboriginal Anthropology*. Nedlands, Western Australia: University of Western Australia Press for AIAS. Pp.277–91.

TRAVERS, Robert
1968. *The Tasmanians: The Story of a Doomed Race*. Melbourne: Cassell.

TURNER, David H.
1974. *Tradition and Transformation: A Study of the Groote Eylandt Area Aborigines of Northern Australia*. Canberra: AIAS.

VON STURMER, John R.
1980. "Notes on Dancing at Cannon Hill, Thursday 18 December 1980: A Demonstration of the Character of *Mulil* Before the Aboriginal Land Commissioner, Mr. JusticeToohey, at the Alligator Rivers Stage 2 Land Claim Hearing." Unpublished ms. deposited in AIAS, Canberra.

WARNER, W. Lloyd
1958 [1937]. *A Black Civilization*. New York: Harper & Row.

WEST, Lamont
1964. "Notes on Tapes in AIAS Archives." Unpublished ms. deposited in AIAS, Canberra.

WILD, Stephen A.
1975. *Warlbiri Music and Dance in Their Social and Cultural Nexus*. Indiana University, Bloomington: Ph.D. Thesis.
1977. "Australian Ritual as Performance: Structure of Communication in Men's Mimetic Dance Among Walbiri Aborigines of Central Australia." Paper presented at Conference on Culture and Communication, Temple University, March 1977. Unpublished ms. deposited at AIAS, Canberra.
1977–78. "Men as Women: Female Dance Symbolism in Walbiri Men's Rituals." *Dance Research Journal* 10(1): 14–22.
1980. "Australian Aboriginal Performances, Past and Present." In Souvenir Programme Book, The Festival of Asian Arts, Hong Kong.
1981. "Aboriginal Music and the Australian Institute of Aboriginal Studies." *The Australian Journal of Music Education* 28: 33–8.

WOLFF, H.
1938. "Nachrichten von der 2 Frobenius—Expedition in Nordwest-Aus-
    tralien." [Communications from the Second Frobenius Expedition in
    North-West Australia, Collated from the Journals of H. Wolff.]
    Paideuma bd. 1: 89–99.

GLOSSARY OF TERMS

This glossary is compiled from several sources. On the whole, the explanations given are those which have been given in beginning classes and lectures in answer to terminological questions, thus it is best to consider most of the definitions in context; that is, with reference to their usage in the texts of the lectures. *Apotheosis* is a good example: in context, the term is used facetiously. Readers are not meant to conclude that Segy constructed an "apotheosis" of a dancer himself in the text of his article (see page 46 for reference).

When I teach a course like this, students are required to purchase a reference book to use throughout: *A Dictionary of Philosophy*, by Peter A. Angeles (Harper & Row, New York, 1981). Where possible, I have taken definitions from that dictionary, but they are sometimes amended, and students must be aware at all times, especially for words like *connote*, *denote, hermeneutic* and several others, that such words are semantically *very* dense, and that a simple "definition," while providing something to get on with, will not suffice for prolonged or in-depth study. Moreover, from the outset, students are encouraged to develop a more sophisticated view of language, starting with a careful reading of Saussure's chapter entitled, "Nature of the Linguistic Sign" (1966:65ff).

ACEPHALOUS: used by anthropologists to refer to tribes who, like the Nuer, do not have a "head," a "chief" or someone who is designated ruler. Literally: "without a head."

AETIOLOGICAL: inquiring into (giving an account of, or reasons for) why a thing is what it is (see Angeles, p. 5).

AGONISTIC: used to designate a type of model of events, specifically of games or events where the upshot is winning or losing. For further explanation, consult the index of Harré and Secord (1972), cited in the bibliography.

ANALOGY (ANALOG):   "The Greek term came later to mean the [usually] linguistic comparison of similarities, concepts or things" (see Angeles, p. 8). The notion of analogy is very important with regard to semasiology and also to the understanding of Kaeppler's approach. For more discussion of its usage, see Kaeppler (1986), cited in bibliography.

APOTHEOSIS: to deify; to exalt or glorify to an ideal.

APPERCEPTION: the deliberate assimilation and reorganization of ideas by an act of intellectual will. The mental activity which (a) brings faint items of knowledge (indistinct impressions, vague notions or feelings) out of the subconscious to the level of conscious attention and which (b) puts them into intellectual patterns, thereby making sense of them (see Angeles, p. 16).

A PRIORI: (L., "that which precedes," for a, ab, "from," "out of," and "prior," i.e., "former," "before," "prior"). Prior to and independent of sense experience. Opposite to *a posteriori.* Used in the context of concepts such as "necessary," "certain," "definitional," "deductive," "universally true," "innate," "intuitive" (see Angeles, p. 16).

CONNOTE: additional associations, suggestions or meanings; different from "connotation" (intension), which is the collection of characteristics (properties or qualities) common to all (and only to those) things referred to by a word. Those characteristics intended by the use of the word (see Angeles, p. 16).

CYBERNETICS: the study of feedback systems, mechanisms, and controls found in machines and in living organisms. The theory of cybernetics originated with an American mathematician, Norbert Weiner, and there is a book entitled *Cybernetics,* for those who care to look into the subject more deeply (see Angeles, p. 52).

DENOTATIVE (DENOTE):   the application of the meaning of a word; the naming of instances that a word has—giving examples (see Angeles, p. 60).

DICHOTOMY: the division of things into two basic parts that are regarded as fundamentally or irreducibly different. Refers to *a mutually exclusive relationship of two things.* It presents a real problem in anthropological discourse, where particularly with regard to classificatory and categorical systems, there are a number of kinds of oppositions and oppositional contrasts used. In fact, there are very few things, classes, etc., which are true dichotomies. A good example is that of up/down (the spatial dimension), which is a contrary opposition that admits of many degrees and points in between, although it is often (wrongly) *treated like* a dichotomy. A good reference for further understanding of the nature of oppositions is C.K. Ogden, 1932, *Opposition* (Indiana University Press, Bloomington, Indiana). Also see Angeles, p. 63, and p. 215 for a related term, *polarities*.

DIDACTIC: expository, usually to an excess; pedantic. Often used pejoratively.

DRAMATURGICAL: Like *agonistic,* it is used to refer to a kind of model of events which is based in its major aspects on the theater or some dramatic form. Further discussion is available in Harré and Secord (1972), cited in the bibliography.

EMPIRICAL: referring to knowledge founded on experience, observation, facts, sensation, practice, concrete situations, and real events; connotes *a posteriori* knowledge, and is usually contrasted with *experiential. Empiricism* denotes the view that all ideas are abstractions formed by compounding (combining, recombining) what is experienced (observed, immediately given in sensation), and "hard core empiricism" (a phrase used in the text), refers to the notion that experience is the *sole* source of knowledge; that ultimately all that we know is directly derived or indirectly inferred from sense data (excepting some definitional truths of logic and mathetmatics). See Angeles, pp. 74–75.

EPISTEMOLOGY: ("epistemological paradigm," "episteme," etc.): theory of knowlege or pertaining to a theory of knowledge. Includes [in philosophy] the study of the origins, the presuppositions, the nature, extent, and veracity of knowledge (see Angeles, p. 78). The best succinct discussion that I know of is in Harré, 1972, *The Philosophies of Science* (Oxford University Press), in a subsection entitled "Epistemology."

ETIOLOGICAL: *see* AETIOLOGICAL

EXEGESIS: a critical explanation or analysis.

HEISENBERG'S PRINCIPLE OF UNCERTAINTY: for subatomic particles, both the exact *position* and the exact *momentum* (motion or velocity) of a particle cannot be known at the same time (see Angeles, p. 301). This principle is relevant to the study of dancing because an *analogous* situation applies to the dancers in a dance while it is being performed: If one stops the dancer to determine his or her *position,* then the motion (the "gesture," the movement) is altered. If one leaves the motion unaltered then the *position*(s) both of the dancer in space and the position(s) of the body parts in relation to one another are often indeterminate.

HERMENEUTIC: interpretive or explanatory. For modern applications, arguments and problems in modern philosophy, please see Bernstein (1983) for further discussion, especially pp. 31–32, 132ff, and p. 142. Full citation to be found in bibliography.

HEURISTIC: providing assistance in discovering or presenting a truth or solving a problem, thus one can speak of an heuristic device, or of the heuristic value of something. Also used to designate an educational method where the student is encouraged to learn through his or her own investigation (see Angeles, p. 115).

HOMOLOGUE (HOMOLOGOUS): refers to that whose meaning characterizes or applies to, itself. Example: the world *polysyllabic* is itself a polysyllabic word. It is also sometimes used to indicate a thing or concept that is exactly like another thing or concept: in context—is a dog wagging its tail homologous to a human being giving thanks to a divinity?

MODEL: Two common usages of the word *model* are ignored, i.e., "to wear in an exemplary fashion" and "to make something with the fingers out of some plastic material." Some reference is made to the use of the word *model* to designate a type. In mathematics, the word *model* is used in two ways: for a set of sentences (a sentential model), and for a set of objects, real or imaginary, statements about which are made by means of sentences, and thus constitute types of sentential models. For a complete understanding of the way *model* is used in semasiology and what is meant when models are referred to in the text, see Harré (1970), Chapter 2 "Models in Theories," pp. 35–62. Harré's Taxonomy of Models is reproduced under the term *paramorph* below. Probably the most important feature to understand for beginners is that the concept of *model* is based on the relation between subject and source.

MONISM: (from the Greek *monos,* or "single"). 1) The theory that all things in the universe can be reduced to or explained in terms of the activity of one fundamental constituent (God, mind, matter, form, etc.). 2) The theory that all things are derived from one single ultimate source. 3) The belief that reality is One, and everything else is illusion. Contrasted with dualism and pluralism (see Angeles, p. 178).

ONTOLOGY, ONTOLOGICAL: (from the Greek, *onta,* "the really existing things," "true reality," and *logos,* "the study of," "the theory which accounts for"). 1) The study of essential characteristics of Being in itself apart from the study of particular existing things. In studying Being in its most abstract form, it asks questions such as "What is Being-in-itself?" "What is the nature of Being-as-Being?" 2) That branch of philosophy which deals with the order and structure of reality in the broadest sense possible, using categories such as being/becoming, actuality/potentiality, real/apparent, change, time, existence/nonexistence, essence, necessity, being-as-being, self-dependency, self-sufficiency, ultimate, and ground. There is much more, but, in context, the usage generally refers to the definition (2) above (see Angeles, pp. 197–199.)

ORTHOGENESIS *see* PHYLOGENESIS

PARADIGM: (from the Greek, *paradeigma,* from *para,* "bedside," and *dekynai,* "to show," meaning "model," "exemplar," "archtype," "ideal"). 1) A way of looking at something. 2) In science, a model, pattern, or ideal theory from which perspective phenomena are explained (see Angeles, p. 203). There is a sense in which this book on the dance could be entitled *Paradigms of the Dance* because, on the whole, what has been explicated is really "ways of looking" at the dance, rather than "theories" in any precise sense.

PARAMORPH: (taken from Harré, 1970:33).

TAXONOMY OF MODELS

A. Subject = Source; homeomorphs

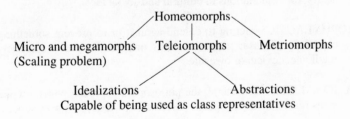

Homeomorphs

Micro and megamorphs   Teleiomorphs   Metriomorphs
(Scaling problem)

Idealizations   Abstractions
Capable of being used as class representatives

B. Subject ≠ Source; paramorphs

(a)	(b)
in relation to subject	in relation to source
partial analogue	semi-connected
complete analogue	singly connected
partial homologue	multiple connected

Step 1 in theory construction involves the creation of a paramorph.
Step 2 in theory construction involves the hypothesis of the
    paramorph as a hypothetical mechanism.

Thus a theory generates existential hypotheses.

PARS PRO TOTO: one of the many kinds of fallacies to be found in
    argument or debate—or in thinking generally. Usually, it is taken to
    mean putting the part before the whole, or failing to see the whole
    because of focus on one or more parts. For an excellent study, consult
    Angeles, pp. 95–100, for the many kinds of informal fallacy that
    exist.

PHYLOGENESIS (PHYLOGENY, PHYLOGENETIC):   The evolu-
    tionary development of any species of plant or animal. Usually
    contrasted with ontogeny, which denotes the course of development
    of any single organism. *Phylogeny* is sometimes understood to refer
    to the historical development of a tribe or racial group. However, the
    term *orthogenesis* is more commonly used in the social sciences. In
    the field of biology, *Orthogenesis* means progressive evolution in a
    certain direction, seen in successive generations and leading towards
    a definite new form; determinate evolution, in other words. In
    sociology, *orthogenesis* connotes a theory that every culture in
    society follows the same fixed course of evolution, uninfluenced by
    differing environments or other factors of human life. Among others,
    Franz Boas opposed a simple to complex orthogenetic continuum for
    explanation of culture and he opposed history to orthogenesis in his
    search for explanations of cultural and social facts.

PROPHYLACTIC: acting to defend against or to prevent something,
    especially disease; protective, thus one can have a prophylactic
    medicine, device, or measure.

RATIONALISM: In general, the philosophic approach which empha-
    sizes reason as the primary source of knowledge, prior or superior

to, and independent of, sense perceptions. For the main tenets of rationalism, see Angeles, p. 236.

REFLEX, REFLEXIVE: (Latin: *reflectere*, "to tend back"). 1) Referring to that which is, or can be directed (reflected) back to the subject or to a thing. 2) Referring to any expression whose meaning can be applied to any of its terms. In language, common English sentences which are self-reflexive are, "I didn't know what I was doing," "I was beside myself," etc. (*N.B.:* the use of double pronouns.) See Angeles, p. 243 for *reflexive, reflect, and reflection.* It may be of interest to consider how an author might use the term in social scientific writing:

> Although the matter of reflexivity will be discussed later in the text, and at some length, a preliminary treatment at this point may be helpful. The idea is fundamental to all of the three social scientists under consideration. Reflexivity is to be distinguished from reflection in the following way: to think about the *other* is to be *reflective,* to think about one's *self* is to be *reflexive.* To think about the self, one can focus on the *psychological* dimension, i.e., personality—the subjective. To think about the self, one may also focus on the *sociological* dimension, i.e., person—the objective. Reflexivity in the context of the work discussed here is a sociological activity concerning itself with the tacit commitment of a person to a framework of meaning which authorizes claims to and achievements of knowledge. To be reflexive, then, is to think about one's commitment critically and responsibly: an objective interest in the relation between the person and his role of knowledge (Varela, 1984:71).

SEGMENTARY: a technical term in social anthropology, used to designate socio-political and/or geographical segments of a tribe or clan. See Evans-Pritchard (1940) for a thorough discussion of Nuer political life as a segmentary system.

SYNCHRONIC (SYNCHRONY):   descriptive, as in linguistics, which is contrasted to *diachronic,* which is to consider phenomena as they develop over time. Pertains to the study of language(s) as it develops over time (DIACHRONIC) in contrast to the kind of study (SYNCHRONIC) which describes the state of a language at any one "slice" or "point" of time. The terms are used extensively in Saussurian linguistics, and for a beginning understanding, it is useful to read carefully the material under these terminological headings in Saussure (1966).

SYNCRETISM: (Greek, *syngkrasis,* "a blending," "a tempering," "a mixing together" "uniting"). The bringing together of, or the attempt to bring together, conflicting ideologies into a unity of thought and/or into a cooperating, harmonious social relationship (see Angeles, p. 286). The term used pejoratively connotes a mixture of dubious sorts of things, usually in order to please everyone concerned.

TAUTOLOGY: (Greek; *tautologia,* "the selfsame" and *logos,* "word" or "meaning"). 1) The repetition of the same meaning but using different words. Example: "audible to the ear." 2) Restating the same idea but in different words. Example: "That bachelor is unmarried." 3) In categorical logic, expressing a quality or meaning in the predicate which is already contained implicitly or explicitly in the subject. Examples: "All women are human." "All bachelors are unmarried," etc. 4) Any statement which is necessarily true because of its meaning. Example: "All black horses are black," "Every effect has a cause," "Today is tomorrow's yesterday and today is yesterday's tomorrow," etc. Angeles (p. 289) gives an excellent list of points which apply to tautologies.

TAXONOMY: The science, laws or principles of classification. A "taxon" is understood somewhat differently in linguistics and anthropology than it is in biology. The root *(taxo-, tax-,* and *taxi-)* indicates arrangement or order, from the Greek term *taxis* (not to be confused with the hired motor vehicle).

TELEOLOGY: (Greek, *telos,* "end," "purpose," "completed state," and *logos,* "the study of"). The study of phenomena exhibiting order, design, purposes, ends, goals, tendencies, aims, direction, and how these are achieved in a process of development (see Angeles, p. 290).

THEORY: (Greek, *theoria,* "a beholding," "a looking at," "viewing"). An apprehension of things in their universal and ideal relationships to one another. Usually considered to be the opposite of practice and/or factual existence. An abstract or general principle within a body of knowledge that presents a clear and systematic view of some of its subject matter, as in a "theory" of art (or the dance), or atomic "theory." In the text, this term is used in several different ways, including the notion that a "theory" is a general principle or model used to *explain* phenomena. Often, the term is used to indicate a *theoretical construct,* i.e., an inferred, nonobservable entity, or an entity or process whose existence is postulated (assumed, hypothesized, supposed) and used within a system of explanation to explain observable phenomena. See Angeles, p. 47 and p. 293. It is strongly suggested that students acquaint themselves with the notion of "scientific theory" (Angeles, p. 293), for an additional understanding of the semantic field of the term.

BIBLIOGRAPHY

ADRA, N. 1986. "Replicating Culture: Dancing in the Yemen Arab Republic." Paper for A.A.A. Conference, Philadelphia, (available, American Institute for Yemeni Studies, N.Y.).

ALLEN, E. 1973. "Australian Aboriginal Dance." *The Australian Aboriginal Heritage: An Introduction Through the Arts.* (Eds. Berndt, R.M., and Phillips, E.S.), Australian Society for Education Through the Arts, in association with Ure Smith, Sydney.

ARBEAU, T. 1588/1925. *Orchesography.* (Trans. Beaumont). Dance Horizons, New York.

ARDENER, E.W. (Ed.). 1971. "Introductory Essay." *Social Anthropology and Language.* (ASA 10), Tavistock, London.

ARDENER, E.W. 1973. "Behaviour: A Social Anthropological Criticism." *JASO* (Journal of the Anthropological Society of Oxford), 4(3):153–155.

———. 1975. "The Voice of Prophecy: Further Problems in the Analysis of Events." *The Munroe Lecture,* Edinburgh University, Edinburgh, Scotland.

———. 1977. "Language and the Social Anthropologist as Translator of Culture." Paper delivered to the Wenner-Gren Symposium on *Focus on Linguistics.* Burg-Wartenstein, Austria.

———. 1980. "Some Outstanding Problems in the Analysis of Events." *Symbol as Sense.* (Eds. Foster and Brandes), Academic Press, London. (Paper first given for Decennial Conference of the ASA, Oxford University, 1973.)

———. 1982. "Social Anthropology Language and Reality." *Semantic Anthropology, ASA* 22 (Ed. Parkin, D.), Academic Press, London.

ARDENER, S. 1975/1977. "Sexual Insult and Female Militancy." *Perceiving Women.* (Ed. S. Ardener), Halsted Press, New York. (Paperback edition).

ARGYLE, M. 1975. *Bodily Communication.* Methuen, London.

ARTAUD, A. 1958. *The Theatre and Its Double.* (Trans. Richards), Grove Press, New York.

ASHLEY-MONTAGUE, M.F. 1937. *Coming into Being Among the Australian Aborigines.* Routledge and Sons, London.

BARAKAT, R.A. 1979. *The Cistercian Sign Language. A Study in Non-Verbal Communication.* Cistercian Publications, Kalamazoo, Michigan.

BARISH, J. 1981. *The Antitheatrical Prejudice.* University of California Press, Berkeley.

BARTENIEFF, I. 1967. "Research in Anthropology: A Study of Dance Styles in Primitive Culture." *CORD Research Annual,* May, p. 103.

BARTHES, R. 1967. *Elements of Semiology.* (Trans. Lavers & Smith), Jonathan Cape, London.

BASTIEN, J.W. 1985. "Qollahuaya-Andean Body Concepts: A Topographical-Hydrolic Model of Physiology" *American Anthropologist,* 87:595–611.

BATESON, G. and C. Holt. 1944 "Form and Function of the Dance in Bali." *The Function of Dance in Human Society,* (Ed. Fka. Boas), Boas Publications, New York.

BAXANDALL, M. 1972. *Painting and Experience in Fifteenth Century Italy.* Oxford University Press, London.

BEATTIE, J. 1964. *Other Cultures.* Routledge & Kegan Paul, London.

BEAUMONT, C. 1941. *Complete Book of Ballets.* Garden City Pub., New York.

———. 1955. *Ballets Past and Present.* Putnam, London.

BELL, D. 1982. "Aboriginal Women and the Religious Experience." *Australian Association for the Study of Religion,* for the Charles Strong Trust, Bedford Park, S.A.

———. 1983. *Daughters of the Dreaming.* McPhee Gribble/Allen & Unwin, Melbourne.

———. 1983/4. "Going It Alone: Practicising Applied Anthropology." *Anthropological Forum,* 5(2):176–181.

BELO, J. (Ed.). 1970. *Traditional Balinese Culture.* Columbia University Press, New York.

BENTHALL, J., and T. Polhemus. (Eds.) 1975. *The Body as a Medium of Expression.* The Institute of Contemporary Arts, London. (*N.B.*: Includes Cicourel, MacRae and others).

BERNDT, R.M., and E.S. Phillips. (Eds.). 1973. *The Australian Aboriginal Heritage; An Introduction Through the Arts.* Australian Society for Education Through the Arts, in association with Ure Smith, Sydney.

BERNSTEIN, R.J. 1983. *Beyond Objectivism and Relativism: Science, Hermeneutics and Praxis.* University of Pennsylvania Press, Philadelphia.

BERREMAN, G. 1982. *The Politics of Truth.* Humanities Press, Atlantic Highlands, New Jersey.

BEST, D. 1974. *Expression in Movement and the Arts*. Lepus, London.

———. 1978. *Philosophy and Human Movement*. Allen & Unwin, New York.

———. 1982. "Free Expression, or the Teaching of Techniques?" *JASHM (Journal for the Anthropological Study of Human Movement)*, 21(2):89–98. (Reprinted from the *British Journal of Educational Studies*, 24(3), October 1979).

———. 1985. *Feeling and Reason in the Arts*. Allen & Unwin, New York.

BIRDWHISTELL, R. 1970. *Kinesics and Context: Essays in Body Motion Communication*. University of Pennsylvania Press, Philadelphia.

BLACKING, J. (Ed.). 1977. *The Anthropology of the Body*. (ASA 15), Academic Press, London.

BLACKING, J., and J.W. Keali'inohomoku. (Eds.). 1979. *The Performing Arts*. Academic Press, London and New York.

BLAKELY, T. 1986. "Communicative Resources in Hemba Women's Funerary Dance Performance." Paper for A.A.A. Conference, Philadelphia. (Available: Brigham Young University, Utah).

BLASIS, C. 1830. *Code of Terpsichore*. Bull, London.

BOAS, F(ranz). 1938. *General Anthropology*. D.C. Heath, Boston.

———. 1944. "Dance and Music in the Life of the Northwest Coast Indians of North America (Kwakiutl)." *The Function of Dance in Human Society*. Boas Publication, New York.

BOAS, F(ranziska). (Ed.). 1944. *The Function of Dance in Human Society*. Boas Publication, New York. (Republication by Dance Horizons in 1972.)

BOORSBOOM, A.P. 1978. "Maradjiri: A Modern Ritual Complex in Arnhem Land, North Australia." Doctoral Thesis, Katholieke Universiteit, Nijmegan, The Netherlands (available: AIAS Library).

BOUISSAC, P. 1976. *Circus and Culture: A Semiotic Approach*. Indiana University Press, Bloomington.

BRAINARD, I. 1969. "Bassedanse, Bassedanza and Ballo in the 15th Century." *CORD Dance History Research: Perspectives from Related Arts and Disciplines*. (Ed. Keali'inohomoku). Proceedings of the 2nd Conference on Research in Dance, Part 3, pp. 64–79.

BROWN, C.M. 1907. *Maori and Polynesian, Their Origin, History and Culture*. Hutchinson, London.

BURRIDGE, K. 1973. *Encountering Aborigines: A Case Study, Anthropology and the Australian Aboriginal*. Pergamon Press, New York.

CALLAN, H. 1970. *Ethology and Society: Towards an Anthropological View*. Oxford University Press, Clarendon.

CASSIRER, E. 1953. *Substance and Function & Einstein's Theory of Relativity*. (Trans. Swabey, Wm. and Marie), Dover, New York.

CHAPMAN, M. 1982. "'Semantics' and the Celt.'" *Semantic Anthropology.* (ASA 22), (Ed. Parkin). Academic Press, London.

CHUJOY, A., and P. Manchester. 1967. *The Encyclopedia of Dance.* Simon & Schuster, New York.

CLUNIES-ROSS, M., and S. Wild. 1981. "The Relations of Music, Text and Dance in Arnhem Land Clan Songs." Unpublished paper presented at the Conference on Transmission in Oral and Written Traditions, Humanities Research Centre, Australian National University, Canberra, August.

COHEN, L.R. 1978. "Labanalysis for the Social Scientist with a General Systems Perspective." *Essays in Dance Research,* Dance Research Annual #9, Concord, New York University, pp.145–154.

COLLIER, J. 1882. *A Primer of Art.* Macmillan, London.

COOMERASWAMY, A. 1934. *The Transformation of Nature in Art.* Harvard University Press, Cambridge, Massachusetts.

———. 1948. "The Dance of Shiva." *Fourteen Indian Essays.* Asian Publishing House, Bombay, India.

———. 1956. *Christian and Oriental Philosophy of Art.* Dover, New York.

COURLANDER, H. 1944. "Dance and Drama in Haiti." *The Function of Dance in Human Society,* (Ed. Fka. Boas). Boas Publication, New York.

CRAWLEY, J. 1911. "Processions and Dances." *Encyclopaedia of Religion and Art* (Hastings). T. & T. Clark, Edinburgh, Scotland.

CRICK, M. 1975. *Explorations in Language and Meaning: Towards a Semantic Anthropology.* Halsted Press, New York.

———. 1982. "Anthropological Field Research, Meaning Creation and Construction." *Semantic Anthropology* (ASA 22), (Ed. Parkin), Academic Press, London.

DAIL-JONES, M. 1984. "A Culture in Motion: A Study of the Interrelationship of Dancing, Sorrowing, Hunting and Fighting as Performed by the Walpiri Women of Central Australia." M.A. Thesis, University of Hawaii.

DAMON, S.J. 1957. *The History of Square Dancing.* Barre Gazette, Barre, Massachusetts.

DARWIN, C. 1899. *The Descent of Man, and Selection in Relation to Sex.* Two volumes, second edition. J. Murray, London.

DAVIS, M. 1972. *Understanding Body Movement. An Annotated Bibliography.* Indiana University Press, Bloomington. (Reprinted, 1982).

DAVIS, M., and M. Skupian. (Eds.). 1982. *Nonverbal Communication and Body Movement (1971–1981), An Annotated Bibliography.* Indiana University Press, Bloomington.

DEAN, B. 1955. "In Search of Stone Age Dance." *Walkabout,* 21(5):15–20.

———. 1955a. *Dust for the Dancers*. Ure Smith, Sydney.

DeMILLE, A. 1963. *The Book of the Dance*. Golden Press, New York.

DEUTSCH, C.W. 1952. "Communication Models in the Social Sciences." *Public Opinion Quarterly*, 16:356–380.

DEUTSCH, F.W. 1947. "Analysis of Postural Behavior" (Thus Speaks the Body, I). *Psychoanalytic Quarterly*, 16:195–213.

———. 1949. "Thus Speaks the Body." *Transactions of the New York Academy of the Sciences*, Series 2, Vol. 12.

———. 1952. "Thus Speaks the Body (Analytical Posturology)." *Psychoanalytic Quarterly, 16:356–380*.

DIESING, P. 1971. *Patterns of Discovery in the Social Sciences*. Aldine, New York.

DIXON-STOWELL, B. 1986. "Survival of the Fittest: An Oral History of Selected Aspects of Black Dance in Philadelphia." Paper for A.A.A. Conference, Philadelphia (available: Temple University, Philadelphia).

DOLGIN, J., *et al.* (Eds.). 1977. *Symbolic Anthropology. A Reader in the Study of Symbols and Meanings*. Columbia University Press, New York. (Kemnitzer and Schneider are also editors.)

DUNCAN, I. 1933. *My Life*. Liveright, New York.

DURR, D. 1981. "Labanotation: Language or Script?" *JASHM*, 1(3):132–138.

———. 1984. "The Structure of Ballet-Dancing, with Special Emphasis on Roles, Rules, Norms and Status." Unpublished MA. Thesis, Anthropology of Human Movement, New York University.

———. 1986. "On the Ethnicity of the Ballet and Ballet-Dancing." *JASHM*, 4(1):1–13.

DUTTON, D. 1979. "Aspects of Environmental Explanation in Anthropology and Criticism." *Experience Forms*. Mouton, The Hague.

EBERLE, O. 1955. *Cenelora: Leben, Glaube, Tanz und Theatre der Urvolker*. Verlag, Switzerland (cited in Kurath, 1960).

EFRON, D. 1942. *Gesture and Environment*. King's Crown Press, New York.

ELAM, K. 1980 *The Semiotics of Theatre and Drama*. Methuen, London.

ELKIN, A.P. 1972. "Two Rituals in South and Central Arnhem Land" (Yabuduruwa and Maraian). *Oceania*, 31(2):42.

———. 1974. *The Australian Aborigines*. Angus and Robertson, Sydney (first published in 1938).

ELLEN, R.F. 1977. "Anatomical Classification and the Semiotics of the Body." *The Anthropology of the Body*. (Ed. Blacking). Academic Press, London, pp.343–374.

ELLIS, C. 1970. "The Role of Ethnomusicologist in the Study of Andagarinja Women's Ceremonies." *Miscellania Musicologica,* 5:76–208.

ELLIS, H. 1914. "The Philosophy of Dance." *Atlantic Monthly,* May, New York.

———. 1920. *Studies in the Psychology of Sex.* F.A. Davis Co., Philadelphia.

———. 1923. *The Dance of Life.* Houghton Mifflin, Boston.

EVANS-PRITCHARD, E.E. 1928. "The Dance (Azande)." *Africa,* 1(1):446–462.

———. 1940. *The Nuer.* Oxford University Press, Clarendon.

———. 1962. *Essays in Social Anthropology.* Faber & Faber, London. (With special reference to "Anthropology and History.")

———. 1965. *Theories of Primitive Religion.* Oxford University Press, Clarendon.

FAIRBANK, H. 1985. "Chinese Minority Dances: Processors and Preservationists—Part I." *Journal for the Anthropological Study of Human Movement,* 3(4):168–189.

———. 1986. "Chinese Minority Dances: Processors and Preservationists—Part II." *Journal for the Anthropological Study of Human Movement,* 4(1):1–19.

FARNELL, B. 1984. "Visual Communication and Literacy: An Anthropological Enquiry into Plains Indian and American Sign Language." Unpublished M.A. Thesis Anthropology of Human Movement, New York University.

———. 1984a. "Two Sign Languages: A Report on Work in Progress." *Journal for the Anthropological Study of Human Movement,* 3(1):8–34.

———. 1984b. "Report on the First International Congress on Movement Notation." Tel Aviv University, August 12–22, 1984. *Journal for the Anthropological Study of Human Movement,* 3(2):84–93.

———. 1985. "The Hands of Time: An Exploration into Some Features of Deixis in American Sign Language." *Journal for the Anthropological Study of Human Movement,* 3(3):100–116.

———. 1988. *International Encyclopedia of Communications.* Univ. of Pennsylvania and Oxford University Press, U.K.

FAST, J. 1970. *Body Language.* Evans, New York.

FIELD, M. 1937. *Religion and Medicine Among Ga People.* Accra Presbyterian Book Depot, Ghana, West Africa. (1961 edition, Oxford University Press).

FILLMORE, C. 1983. "Commentary on Papers of Talmy and Klein." *Spatial Orientation: Theory, Research and Application.* (Eds. Pick, H., and L. Acredolo), Plenum Press, New York.

FIRTH, R. 1936/1965. *We, the Tikopia.* Beacon Press, Boston.

———. 1970. "Postures and Gestures of Respect." *Echanges et Communications;* Mélanges offerts à Claude Lévi-Strauss l'Occasion de son 60ème anniversaire. Collected by J. Pouillon and F. Maranda. Mouton, The Hague, pp.188–209.

FISHER, S., and S.E. Cleveland. 1958. *Body Image and Personality.* Van Nostrand, Princeton, New Jersey.

FISHER, S. 1973. *Body Consciousness.* Prentice-Hall, Englewood Cliffs, New Jersey.

FLESHMAN, B. (Ed.). 1986. *Theatrical Movement: A Bibliographical Anthology.* Scarecrow Press, Metuchen, New Jersey.

FLITCH, J.E.C. 1912. *Modern Dancing and Dancers.* Grant Richards, Ltd., London.

FRAZER, J.G. 1911. *The Magic Art and the Evolution of Kings.* Macmillan, London.

———. 1912. *The Golden Bough.* Macmillan, London.

FREEDMAN, D. 1986. "Dance Code and Gender Role in a Transylvanian Village." Paper for A.A.A. Conference, Philadelphia (available: Temple University, Philadelphia).

FRENCH, D. 1963. "The Relationship of Anthropology to Studies in Perception and Cognition." *Psychology: A Study of a Science,* (Ed. Koch), Vol. 6, McGraw-Hill, New York, pp.388–428.

FRIEDLAND, L. 1986. "Kinesic Genres and Artistic Performance in Afro-American Culture." Paper for A.A.A. Conference, Philadelphia (available: Annenberg School of Communication, Philadelphia).

FRISHBERG, N. 1983. "Writing Systems and Problems for Sign Language Notation." *JASHM,* 2(4):169–195.

FROBENIUS, L. 1908. *The Childhood of Man.* Seeley, London.

FROST, A. 1981. "New South Wales as Terra Nullius: The British Denial of Aboriginal Land Rights." *Historical Studies,* 19(77):513–523.

GATES, A. 1965. *A New Look at Movement—A Dancer's View.* Burgess, Minneapolis, Minnesota.

GAUTHIER, M. 1775. *Traite Contre les Danses et les Mauvaises Chansons ...* (etc.). (Treatise Against Dancing and Dirty Songs). (2nd edition). Chez Antoine, Boudet, Paris.

GELL, A. 1985. "Style and Meaning in Umeda Dance." *Society and the Dance: The Social Anthropology of Process and Performance.* (Ed. Spencer), Cambridge University Press, Cambridge, U.K.

GLUCKMAN, M. 1959. *Culture and Conflict in Africa.* Free Press, Glencoe, Illinois.

GOETHE, J.W. von. 1906. *The Maxims and Reflections of Goethe.* (Trans. Saunders), Macmillan, London.

GOFFMAN, E. 1959. *The Presentation of Self in Everyday Life.* Doubleday, New York.

———. 1961. *Interaction Ritual.* Doubleday, New York.

GOLDFRANK, E. 1945. "Socialization, Personality and the Structure of Pueblo Society (with Particular Reference to Hopi and Zuni)." *American Anthropologist,* 47:516–539.

GOODALE, J. 1971. *Tiwi Wives: A Study of Women of Melville Island, Northern Australia.* University of Washington Press, Seattle.

GORER, G. 1944. "Function of Dance Forms in Primitive Africa Communities." *The Function of Dance in Human Society.* (Ed. Fka. Boas), Boas Publication, New York.

———. 1949. *Africa Dances.* J. Lehman, London.

GOULD, S.J. 1971. *The Mismeasure of Man.* W.W. Norton, London.

GOULDNER, A.W. 1973. "Anti-Minotaur: The Myth of a Value-Free Sociology." *For Sociology,* (Ed. Gouldner), Basic Books, New York.

GRAU, A. 1983. "Sing a Dance: Dance a Song." *Dance Research,* 1(2):32-44, U.K.

GRENE, M. (Ed.). 1971. *Interpretations of Life and Mind. Essays Around the Problem of Reduction.* Humanities Press, New York.

GROVE, L. 1895. *Dancing.* Longman, Green & Co., London (Badminton Library Edition). [*N.B.*: Lilly Grove is the pen-name for Lady Frazer, i.e., Sir James Frazer's wife. The fact of the pen-name is recorded in Downie, Angus. 1967. *Frazer and the Golden Bough.* Victor Gollancz, London.]

GUYAU, J.M. 1884. *Les Problemes de Aesthetique Contemporaine.* Paris.

HADDON, A.C. 1895. *Evolution in Art.* W. Scott, London.

HALL, E.T. 1966. *The Silent Language.* Doubleday, New York.

———. 1966a. *The Hidden Dimension.* Doubleday, New York.

———. 1977. *Beyond Culture.* Anchor Press (Doubleday), New York.

———. 1983. *The Dance of Life: The Other Dimension of Time.* Anchor Press (Doubleday), New York.

HAMBLY, W.D. 1926, *Tribal Dancing and Social Development.* Witherby, London.

HAMPSHIRE, S. 1959. *Thought and Action.* Chatto & Windus, London.

HANNA, J.L. 1965a. "Africa's New Traditional Dance." *Ethno-musicology, 9(1):132.*

———. 1965a. "Dance Plays of the Ubakala." *Presence Africaine,* 65:13–37 (First Quarter).

———. 1976. *Anthropology of the Dance: A Selected Bibliography.* Columbia University, New York.

_____. 1979. *To Dance Is Human. A Theory of Non-verbal Communication.* University of Texas Press, Austin.

HARDY, B. 1968. "Towards a Poetics of Fiction." *Novel,* 2:15–14.

HARPER, N. 1967. "Dance in a Changing Society." *African Arts/Arts d'Afrique,* University of California, Los Angeles.

HARRE, R. 1970. *The Principles of Scientific Thinking.* Macmillan, London.

_____. 1971. "The Shift to an Anthropomorphic Model of Man." *JASO,* 2(1), Hilary Term, Oxford University, U.K.

_____. 1972. *The Philosophies of Science.* Oxford University Press, London.

_____, and P. Secord. 1972a. *The Explanation of Social Behaviour.* Blackwell, Oxford.

HARRISON, J.E. 1913/1948. *Ancient Art and Ritual.* Oxford University Press, London.

HARRISON, R. 1986. "Body Language and Nonverbal Communication." *Theatrical Movement: A Bibliographical Anthology,* (Ed. B. Fleshman), Scarecrow Press, Metuchen, New Jersey.

HART-JOHNSON, D. 1983. "On Structure in Martha Graham Technique with Comparisons to American Sign Language." *Journal for the Anthropological Study of Human Movement,* 2(4):196–210.

_____. 1984. "The Notion of Code in Body Language: A Comparative Approach to Martha Graham Technique and American Sign Language." Unpublished M.A. Thesis Anthropology of Human Movement, New York University.

HASKELL, A. 1960. *The Story of Dance.* Rathbone, London.

_____. 1969. *The Wonderful World of Dance.* Doubleday, Garden City, New York.

HAVEMEYER, L. 1916. *The Drama of Savage Peoples.* Oxford University Press, London.

HAVILAND, J.B. 1986. "Complex Referential Gestures." (Draft). *Center for Advanced Study in the Behavioral Sciences,* Stanford University, California.

H'DOUBLER, M. 1962. *Dance: A Creative Art Experience.* University of Wisconsin Press, Madison.

HEISENBERG, W. 1958. *Physics and Philosophy.* [Allen &] Unwin University Books, London.

HELLER, E. 1969. "Yeats and Nietzsche." *Encounter,* 33(6).

HEMPEL, C.G. 1959. "The Logic of Functional Analysis." *Symposium on Sociological Theory.* (Ed. Gross), Harper & Row, New York.

HENSON, H. 1974. *British Social Anthropologists and Language: A History of Separate Development.* Oxford University Press, London.

HERSKOVITZ, M. *Man and His Works: The Science of Cultural Anthropology.* Knopf, New York.

HEWES, G. 1955. "World Distribution of Certain Postural Habits." *American Anthropologist*, 57(2):231–244.

———. 1961. "Food Transport and the Origin of Hominid Bi-Pedalism." *American Anthropologist*, 63(4):687–710.

HINDE, E. (Ed.) 1972. *Non-verbal Communication*. (Non-verbal Communication and the Ethology of Human Behaviour). Cambridge University Press, Cambridge, U.K.

HIRN, Y. 1900. *The Origins of Art*. Macmillan, London.

HORST, L. 1937. *Pre-classical Dance Forms*. Dance Observer, New York.

HUIZINGA, J., and A.E. Jensen. 1949. *Homo Ludens: A Story of the Play Element in Culture*. Routledge & Kegan Paul, London.

HUNT, M. 1982. *The Universe Within: A New Science Explores the Human Mind*. Simon & Schuster, New York.

HYMES, D. (Ed.). 1964. *Culture and Society*. Harper & Row, New York.

———. 1983. *Essays in the History of Linguistic Anthropology*. Benjamins, Philadelphia.

———, and J. Gumperz. 1986. *Directions in Sociolinguistics: The Ethnography of Communication*. Blackwell, Oxford.

INTERNATIONAL Encyclopedia of the Dance. (Forthcoming). Charles Scribner's Sons, New York

ITEANU, A. 1984. "The Ritual Body." Paper presented for SASHM (Society for the Anthropological Study of Human Movement) seminar, December 2, New York University.

JABLONKO, A. 1980. "Patterns of Daily Life in the Dance of the Maring of New Guinea: From Microanalysis to Macroanalysis." Paper for the A.A.A. Conference, Philadelphia (available: Human Studies Film Archives, Smithsonian Institution, Washington, D.C.).

JACKSON, A. (Ed.). 1987. *The Anthropologist At Home* (ASA 25). Tavistock, London.

JACKSON, M. 1983. "Knowledge of the Body." *Man* (N.S.), 18:327–345.

JAIRAZBHOY, N.A. 1971. *The Rāgs of North Indian Music*. Faber & Faber, London.

JEFFREYS, M.D.W. 1952–3. "African Tarantula or Dancing Mania." *Eastern Anthropologist*, 6(2), Lucknow, India.

JONES, M. 1980. "The History of Sacred and Biblically-Inspired Dance in Australia." *Neben Yabu*, 6:3–18, Australia.

JONES, R. 1967. *The Functional Analysis of Politics*. Routledge & Kegan Paul, London.

KAEPPLER, A. 1972. "Method and Theory in Analyzing Dance Structure with an Analysis of Tongan Dance." *Ethno-musicology,* 16(2):173–217.

———. 1978. "The Dance in Anthropological Perspective." *Annual Review of Anthropology,* 7:31–39.

———. 1985. "Structured Movement Systems in Tonga." *Society and the Dance.* (Ed. Spencer), Cambridge University Press, U.K., pp.92–118.

———. 1986. "Cultural Analysis, Linguistic Analogies and the Study of Dance in Anthropological Perspective." *Explorations in Ethnomusicology: Essays in Honor of David P. McAllester.* (Ed. Frisbie), Detroit Monographs on Musicology, #9, Detroit, Michigan, pp.25–33.

KAYBERRY, P. 1939. *Aboriginal Woman, Sacred and Profane.* Routledge, London.

KEALI'INOHOMOKU, J.W. 1970. "Perspective 5: Ethnic Historical Study." *CORD Proceedings of the 2nd Conference on Research in Dance,* New York University, July 4–6, 1969, pp.86–97.

———. 1976. "Caveat on Causes and Correlations." *CORD News,* New York University, 6(2):20–24.

———. 1979. "Review Essay" (Dance and Human History: A Film by Alan Lomax). *Ethno-musicology,* 25(1):169–176.

———. 1980. "The Non-Art of the Dance." *Journal for the Anthropological Study of Human Movement,* New York University, 1(2):83–97. [First published in *Impulse* Magazine, in 1969].

———. 1980a. "An Anthropologist Looks at Ballet as an Ethnic Form of Dance." *Journal for the Anthropological Study of Human Movement,* 1(2):83–97. [First printed in *Impulse* in 1969.]

———, and F. Gillis. 1970a. "Special Bibliography: Gertrude Prokosch Kurath." *Ethnomusicology,* January, 14(1):114–128.

KENDON, A. 1983. "Gesture and Speech: How They Interact." *Nonverbal Interaction.* (Eds. Wiemann and Harrison), Sage Publications, Beverly Hills, California, pp.13–45.

KINGSLEY, M. 1899. *West African Studies.* Macmillan, London.

———. 1899. *Travels in West Africa.* Macmillan, London.

KIRSTEIN, L. 1924. *Dance.* F.A. Stokes & Co., New York.

KRIS, E. 1952. *Psycho-Analytic Explanations in Art.* International University Press, New York.

KURATH, G.P. 1960. "Panorama of Dance Ethnology." *Current Anthropology,* May, 1(3):233–254.

KURTI, L. 1980. Review of *The Performing Arts.* (Eds. Blacking and Keali'inohomoku), Journal for the Anthropological Study of Human Movement, 1(2):123–128.

———. 1980a. "The Structure of Hungarian Dance: A Linguistic Approach." *Journal for the Anthropological Study of Human Movement,* New York University, 1(1):45–72.

LABAN, R. von. 1966. *Choreutics*. MacDonald & Evans, London.

LA BARRE, W. 1947. "The Cultural Basis of Emotions and Gestures." *Journal of Personality*, 16:49–68.

LAIR, N. 1984. "Syllabus, Course Outline and Instructions for Papers, L525." *School of Library and Information Science*. Indiana University, Bloomington.

LANG, A. 1887. *Myth, Ritual and Religion*. Longman, Green & Co., London.

LANGE, R. 1970. "The Traditional Dances of Poland." *Viltis*, 29(1):4–14.

———. 1975. *The Nature of Dance. An Anthropological View*. Mac-Donald & Evans, London.

LANGER, S. 1942/1951. *Philosophy in a New Key*. Mentor, New York.

———. 1953. *Feeling and Form*. Routledge & Kegan Paul, London.

———. 1957. *Problems of Art*. Scribner, New York.

LAUZE, F. de. 1623/1952. *Apologie de la Danse*. (Trans. Wildeblood), F. Muller, London.

LAWLER, L. 1964. *The Dance in Ancient Greece*. Adam & Charles Black, London.

LEACH, E. 1961/1966. *Rethinking Anthropology*. L.S.E. Monographs, Athlone Press, University of London.

———. 1966. "Ritualization in Man in Relation to Conceptual and Social Development." *Ritualization in Animals and Man*. (Ed. Hurley), The Philosophical Transactions of the Royal Society, London.

LEEUW, G. van der. 1963. *Sacred and Profane Beauty. The Holy in Art*. (Trans. Green), Holt, Rinehart & Winston, New York.

LEVI-STRAUSS, C. 1966. *Structural Anthropology*. Basic Books, New York.

———. 1966a. *The Savage Mind*. Weidenfeld & Nicholson, London.

———. 1973. *Totemism*, Penguin, London. [*N.B.*: Edition with Introduction by Roger Poole.]

LIENHARDT, G. 1957/1958. "Anuak Village Headmen." Part I: "Headmen and Village Culture," *Africa*, 27. Part II: "Village Structure and Rebellion," *Africa*, 28.

———. 1968. *Social Anthropology*. Oxford University Press, London.

———. 1969. "Edward Tylor." *The Founding Fathers of Social Science*. (Ed. Raison), Penguin, London. [Out of print.]

LIPS, J. 1937. *The Savage Hits Back*. (Trans. Benson), Lovatt Dickson, London.

LOMAX, A. 1968–69. *Folk Song Style and Culture*. A.A.A.S. Publication #88, Washington, D.C.

———. 1971. "Choreometrics and Ethnographic Film-Making." *The Film-maker's Newsletter*, 4(4), February.

LOWIE R. 1925. *Primitive Religion*. Routledge & Sons, London.

MALINOWSKI, B. 1922. *Argonauts of the Western Pacific.* Routledge & Kegan Paul, London.

———. 1937. "Introduction." *Coming into Being Among the Australian Aborigines,* by Ashley-Montague. Routledge & Sons, London.

MALLERY, G. 1880. *A Collection of Gesture-Signs and Signals of the North American Indians, With Some Comparisons.* Bureau of Ethnology, Smithsonian Institution, Superintendent of Documents, Washington, D.C.

———. 1893. *Picture-Writing of the American Indians.* Bureau of Ethnology, Smithsonian Institution, Superintendent of Documents, Washington, D.C.

MANNERS, R., and D. Kaplan. (Eds.). 1968. *Theory in Anthropology.* Aldine, Chicago.

MANSFIELD, P. 1952. "The Conchero Dancers of Mexico." Unpublished Ph.D. Dissertation New York University, New York. (Music by Raoul Guerro).

MARETT, R.R. 1914. *The Threshold of Religion.* Methuen, London.

———. 1932. *Faith, Hope and Charity in Primitive Religion.* Oxford University Press, London.

MARTIN, G., and E. Pesovar. 1961. "A Structural Analysis of the Hungarian Folk Dance." *Acta Ethnographica,* 10, pp.1–40.

MARTIN, J. 1939. *Introduction to the Dance.* Norton, New York.

———. 1963. *Book of the Dance.* Tudor, New York. (First published as *The Dance,* Tudor, New York, 1947.)

McCARTHY, F.D. 1957 *Australia's Aborigines: Their Life and Culture.* Colorgravure Publishers, Melbourne.

———. 1964. "The Dancers of Aurukun," *Australian Natural History,* 14(9):296–300.

———. 1978. "Aurukun Dances." Unpublished ms. deposited at AIAS, Canberra.

McNEILL, D. 1979. *The Conceptual Basis of Language.* Lawrence Erlbaum Associates, Hillsdale, New Jersey.

———, and E. Levy. 1982. "Conceptual Representations in Language Activity and Gesture." *Speech, Place and Action.* (Eds. Jarvella, R. and Klein, W.), Wiley, Chichester.

McPHEE, C. 1970. "Dance in Bali." *Traditional Balinese Culture.* (Ed. Belo), Columbia University Press, New York.

MEAD, M. 1931. *Growing Up in New Guinea.* Routledge & Sons, London.

———. 1959. *Coming of Age in Samoa.* Mentor Books, New York. (First published in 1928; cited in Kurath [1960] dated 1949, p.122).

———, and G. Bateson. 1942. *Balinese Character: A Photographic*

Analysis. New York Academy of Sciences, New York.

MEERLOO, J.A.M. 1961. *Dance Craze and Sacred Dance.* Peter Owen, London.

MINK, L. 1970. "History and Fiction as Modes of Comprehension." *New Literary History,* 1, pp.541–558.

MITCHELL, C. 1956. "The Kalela Dance." The Rhodes Livingston Institute Papers, No. 27, Manchester University Press, Manchester, U.K.

MORRIS, D.; P. Collett; *et al.* 1979. *Gestures: Their Origins and Distribution,* Stein & Day, New York.

MORSE, B. 1979. "Dance Notation and Aboriginal Culture," *Hemisphere,* 12(11):2–6.

MOYLE, A. 1977. "Aborigines: Music, Song and Dance." *The Australian Encyclopaedia,* 3rd edition. Grolier Society of Australia, Sydney, Vol. I:37–40.

———. 1977a. "Music and Dance: Mastersingers of the Bush." *The Moving Frontier: Aspects of Aboriginal-European Interaction in Australia.* (Ed. Stanbury, P.), Reed, Sydney.

———. 1978. "Song and Dance." *Black Australia: An Annotated Bibliography and Teacher's Guide to Resources on Aborigines and Torres Strait Islanders,* AIAS, Canberra; Humanities Press, Atlantic Highlands, New Jersey, pp.63–66.

MOYLE, R. 1984. "Jumping to Conclusions." *Problems and Solutions: Occasional Essays in Musicology.* Presented to Alice M. Moyle. (Eds. Kassler, J. and Stubington, J.), Hale & Iremonger, Sydney.

MUKERJEE, R. 1957. *The Lord of the Autumn Moons.* Asia Publishing House, Bombay, India.

MYERS, E. 1981. "A Phrase-Structural Analysis of the Foxtrot, with Tranformational Rules." *Journal for the Anthropological Study of Human Movement,* 1(4):246–268.

NAGEL, E. 1960. *The Structure of Science: Problems in the Logic of Scientific Explanation.* Harcourt, Brace & World, New York.

NEEDHAM, R. 1958. "A Structural Analysis of Purum Society." *American Anthropologist,* 60:75–101.

———. 1960. "Alliance and Classification Among the Lamet." *Sociologus,* 10(2).

———. (Ed.). 1973. *Right and Left. Essays on Dual Symbolic Classification.* University of Chicago Press, Chicago.

NORTH, M. 1966. *An Introduction to Movement Study and Teaching.* MacDonald & Evans, London.

NOVACK, C. 1986. "Dance As Social Text." Paper for A.A.A. Conference, Philadelphia. (Available: Barnard College, New York.)

NOVERRE, J.G. 1760/1930. *Lettres sur la Danse et sur les Ballets.* (Trans. Beaumont), C.W. Beaumont Publications, London.

OESTERLEY, W.O.E. 1923. *The Sacred Dance*. Cambridge University Press, Cambridge, U.K.

OGDEN, C.K. 1932. *Opposition*. Indiana University Press, Bloomington.

ORTUTAY, G. (Ed.). 1974. *Hungarian Folk Dances*. Corvina Press, New York. [Authorship attributed to G. Martin.]

OTTEN, C. (Ed.). 1971. *Anthropology and Art. Readings in Cross-Cultural Aesthetics*. Natural History Press, Garden City, New York.

PADEN, J. and E. Soja. 1970. *The African Experience*. Northwestern University Press, Evanston, Illinois, [with particular reference to Volume III].

PATER, W. 1892. *Marius, the Epicurean*. Macmillan, London. [*N.B.*: This writer also refers specifically to dancing in an article on Lacedaemon in an issue (1892) of the *Contemporary Review.*]

PENG, F.C.C. 1978. *Sign Language and Language Acquisition in Man and Ape: New Dimensions in Comparative Pedo-Linguistics*. A.A.A.S. with Westview Press, Boulder, Colorado.

PFORSICH, J. 1978. "Labanalysis and Dance Style Research: An Historical Survey and Report of the 1976 Ohio State University Research Workshop." *Essays in Dance Research,* Dance Research Annual #9, CORD, New York University, pp.59–74.

PIKE, K. 1954. "Emic and Etic Standpoints for the Description of Behaviour." *Language in Relation to a Unified Theory of the Structure of Human Behavior, Part I* (Preliminary Edition), Summer Institute of Linguistics, Glendale, California, pp.8–28.

POCOCK, D. 1967. "The Anthropology of Time-Reckoning." *Myth and Cosmos*. (Ed. Middleton, J.), Natural History Press, Garden City, New York, pp.303–314.

———. 1973. "The Idea of a Personal Anthropology." Paper given for the Decennial Conference of the Association of Social Anthropologists (ASA), Oxford, July.

———. 1975. *Understanding Social Anthropology*. Hodder & Stoughton, London.

———. 1977. *Social Anthropology*. 2nd edition. Sheed & Ward, London. [First printed in 1961.]

POLANYI, M. 1962. *Personal Knowledge: Towards a Post-Critical Philosophy*. Routledge & Kegan Paul, London.

———. 1959. *The Study of Man*. (Lindsay Memorial Lecture), University of Chicago Press, Chicago.

POLHEMUS, T. (Ed.). 1978. *The Body Reader. Social Aspects of the Human Body*. Pantheon, New York.

POOLE, R. 1973. "Introduction." *Totemism,* by Lévi-Strauss. Penguin, London.

POUWER, J. 1973. "Signification and Fieldwork." *Journal of Symbolic*

Anthropology, 1, Mouton, The Hague.

POWERS, W. 1983. "Review. [J.L. Hanna, *To Dance Is Human,* 1979]." *Journal for the Anthropological Study of Human Movement,* 3(4). (Reprinted from *American Anthropologist,* 1983, 85(3):687–689.

PURI, R. 1981. "Review of D. Morris, P. Collett, *et al.* (*Gestures,* 1979)." *Journal for the Anthropological Study of Human Movement,* 1(3):189–194.

———. 1981a. "Polysemy and Homonymy, and the Mudra, 'Shikara': Multiple Meaning and the Use of Gesture." *Journal for the Anthropological Study of Human Movement,* 1(4):269–287.

———. 1983. "A Structural Analysis of Meaning in Movement: The Hand Gestures of Indian Classical Dance." Unpublished M.A. Thesis, Anthropology of Human Movement, New York University.

QUISENBERRY, K. 1973. "Dance in Arnhem Land: A Field Study Project, 1970–72." MFA Thesis, Southern Methodist University, Dallas, Texas.

RADCLIFFE-BROWN, A.R. 1913/1964. *The Andaman Islanders.* Free Press, Glencoe, Illinois.

RADIN, P. 1932. *Social Anthropology.* McGraw-Hill, New York.

RAFFEE, W.G. 1964. *Dictionary of the Dance.* A.S. Barnes, New York.

RAISON, Timothy (Ed.). 1969. *The Founding of Social Science.* Penguin, London. [Out of print.]

RAMSEY, I.T. (Ed.). 1961. "On the Possibility and Purpose of a Metaphysical Theology." *Prospect for Metaphysics; Essays in Metaphysical Exploration.* Allen & Unwin, New York.

RATTRAY, R.S. 1923. *Ashanti.* Oxford University Press, Clarendon.

RIDGEWAY, W. 1915. *Dramas and Dramatic Dances of Non-European Peoples.* Cambridge University Press, Cambridge, U.K.

RORTY, R. 1979. *Philosophy and the Mirror of Nature.* Princeton University Press, Princeton, New Jersey.

ROYCE, A. 1977. *The Anthropology of Dance.* Indiana University Press, Bloomington.

RUST, F. 1969. *Dance in Society.* Routledge & Kegan Paul, London.

SACHS, C. 1933. *Eine Weltegeschichte des Tanzes.* Reiment, Berlin. [Cited in Kurath, 1960.]

———. 1937. *The World History of the Dance.* (Trans. Schöenberg), Allen & Unwin, London.

SAPIR, E. 1949. "Communication." *Selected Writings of Edward Sapir in Language, Culture and Personality.* (Ed. Mandelbaum), University of California Press, Berkeley.

SAUSSURE, F. de. 1966. *Course in General Linguistics.* (Eds. Bally, Sechehaye and Reidlinger; Trans. Baskin), McGraw-Hill, New York.

SAYCE, A.H. 1880. *Introduction to the Science of Language.* C.K. Paul Co., London.

SCHIEFFELIN, E. 1976. *The Sorrow of the Lonely and the Burning of the Dancers.* St. Martin's Press, New York.

SCOTT, E. 1899. *Dancing in All Ages.* Swan Sonnerschein & Co., London.

SEBEOK, T. 1979. "Prefigurements of Art." *Semiotica,* 27(1/3): 3–74.

SEGY, L. 1953. "The Mask in African Dance." *The Negro History Bulletin,* 14.

SHARP, E. 1928. *Here We Go Round.* Gerald Howe, London.

SHEEHY, G. 1976. *Guide to Reference Books.* (Ninth edition), ALA, Chicago.

SHEETS, M. 1966. *The Phenomenology of Dance.* University of Wisconsin Press, Madison.

SHEETS-JOHNSTONE, M. 1983. "Interdisciplinary Travel: From Dance to Philosophical Anthropology." *Journal for the Anthropological Study of Human Movement,* 2(3):129–142.

SHERZER, J., and R. Bauman. 1982. *Case Studies in the Ethnography of Speaking: A Compilation of Papers in Socio-linguistics.* Southwest Educational Development Laboratory, Austin, Texas.

———. 1983. *Kuna Ways of Speaking: An Ethnographic Perspective.* University of Texas Press, Austin.

SIMMONS, J. 1983. "A Matter of Interpretation." *American Way,* April, pp.106–111.

SINGER, A. 1970. "Holiday Dancing in a Greek-Macedonian Village." Unpublished paper, Department of Dance Ethnology, University of California, Los Angeles.

SINGHA, R., and R. Massey. 1967. *Indian Dances.* Faber & Faber, New York.

SONGS of Aboriginal Australia. 1987. Eds: Clunies-Ross, M.; Donaldson, T,; and Wild, S. Oceania Monograph, #32, University of Sydney.

SORELL, W. 1960. *Dance Throughout the Ages.* Thames & Hudson, London.

SPECK, F., and L. Broom. 1951. *Cherokee Dance and Drama.* University of California Press, Berkeley.

SPENCER, P. (Ed.). 1985. *Society and the Dance.* Cambridge University Press, Cambridge, U.K.

STANNER, W.E.H. 1979. *White Man Got No Dreaming: Essays 1938–1973.* Australia National University Press, Canberra.

STOKOE, W. 1960. "Sign Language Structure." *Studies in Linguistics:*

Occasional Papers. University of Buffalo, reprinted by Linstok Press.

―――. 1980. "Sign Language Structure." *Annual Review of Anthropology,* 9, pp.365–390.

STREET, B. 1975. *The Savage in Literature: Representations of Primitive Societies in English Fiction, 1858–1920.* Routledge & Kegan Paul, London.

STURTEVANT, W. 1968. "Studies in Ethnoscience." *American Anthropologist,* Special Issue on Transcultural Studies in Cognition, 66(2):99–131. [Reprinted in Manners and Kaplan, *Theory in Anthropology,* pp.475–499.]

SWEIGARD, L. 1974. *Human Movement Potential: Its Ideokinetic Facilitation,* Dodd-Mead, New York.

TERRY, W. 1956. *The Dance in America.* Harper Bros., New York.

―――. 1967. "Dance, History of," in *The Dance Encyclopedia.* (Eds. Chujoy, A., and Manchester, P.), Simon and Schuster, New York.

THOMPSON, R.F. 1966. "An Aesthetic of the Cool: West African Dance." *Africa Forum,* (AMSAC), 2(2), New York.

TITIEV, M. 1944, "Old Oraibi." *Papers of the Peabody Museum of American Archaeology and Ethnology 22.* Harvard University, Cambridge, Massachusetts.

TOULMIN, S. 1953. *The Philosophy of Science. An Introduction.* Hutchinson, London.

―――. 1961. *Foresight and Understanding.* Hutchinson, London.

TYLER, S. (Ed.). 1969. *Cognitive Anthropology.* Holt, Rinehart & Winston, New York.

TYLOR, E.B. 1878. *The Early History of Mankind.* J. Murray, London; 3rd Edition, Henry Holt, New York.

―――. 1895-1930. *Anthropology.* Watts, London. (The Thinker's Library, Volume II.)

VARELA, C. 1983. "Cartesianism Revisited: The Ghost in the Moving Machine." *Journal for the Anthropological Study of Human Movement,* 2(3):143–157.

―――. 1984. "Pocock, Williams, Gouldner: Initial Reactions of Three Social Scientists to the Problem of Objectivity." *Journal for the Anthropological Study of Human Movement,* 3(2):53–73.

VOLLAND, A. 1986. "Movement and Metaphor in a South Indian Dance-Form." Paper for A.A.A. Conference, Philadelphia. (Available: Wagner College, New York.)

VON STURMER, J. 1987. "Aboriginal Singing and Notions of Power." *Songs of Aboriginal Australia.* (Eds. Wild, S.; Clunies-Ross, M.; and Donaldson, T.), Oceania Monograph #32, University of Sydney, pp.63–76.

————. (forthcoming). "Australian Aboriginal Dances—The Cape York Peninsula." *International Encyclopedia of the Dance,* Charles Scribner's Sons, New York.

VOSS, R. 1869(?) *Der Tanz und seine Geschichte. Eine kulturhistorische-choregraphische Studie. Mit einem Lexicon der Tanze.* (The Dance and Its History. A Cultural-Historical Choreographic Study, With a Lexicon of Dances). Berlin. [There is some disagreement over the date of this work between London Library and British Museum Library. There is also disagreement over whether it is dated at all.]

WAYLEY, A. 1938. "Introduction." *Drama and Dance in Bali,* by de Zöete and Spies. Faber and Faber, London.

WEAVER, T. (Ed.). 1973. *To See Ourselves: Anthropology and Modern Social Issues.* Scott, Foresman & Co., Glenview, Illinois.

WIERZBICKA, A. 1980. *Lingua Mentalis: The Semantics of Natural Language.* Academic Press, Sydney.

WILD, S. 1977. "Men as Women: Female Dance Symbolism in Walbiri Men's Rituals," *Dance Research Journal* (CORD), 10(1):14–22. (Reprinted in *Journal for the Anthropological Study of Human Movement,* 4(3):166–183, 1986.)

————. 1986. "Australian Aboriginal Theatrical Movement." *Theatrical Movement: A Bibliographical Anthology.* (Ed. Fleshman, B.), Scarecrow Press, Metuchen, New Jersey.

————. (forthcoming). "Australian Aboriginal Dances: The Walpiri." *International Encyclopedia of the Dance.* Charles Scribner's Sons, New York.

WILLIAMS, D. 1967. "The Ghanaian Dancer's Environment." *Impulse,* San Francisco.

————. 1968. "The Dance of the Bedu Moon." *African Arts/Arts d'Afrique,* University of California, Los Angeles.

————. 1972. "Signs, Symptoms and Symbols." *JASO,* 3(1):24–32.

————. 1972a. "Review of Lomax, *et al.,* Choreometrics." *Dance Research Journal,* 6(2), New York University (CORD).

————. 1972b. "Social Anthropology and Dance." Unpublished B. Litt. Thesis, Oxford University, U.K.

————. 1974. Review of F. Rust, *Dance in Society (An Analysis of the Relationship Between the Social Dance and Society in England from the Middle Ages to the Present Day). Dance Research Journal,* 6(2), July (CORD).

————. 1975. "The Role of Movement in Selected Symbolic Systems." Unpublished D. Phil. Thesis, Oxford University, U.K.

————. 1976. "An Exercise in Applied Personal Anthropology." *DRJ* (CORD), 11(1), New York University.

————. 1976a. "Deep Structures of the Dance." Part I: Constituent Syntagmatic Analysis, *Journal of Human Movement Studies (JHMS)*. (Ed. Whiting), 2(2):123–144.

————. 1976b. "Deep Structures of the Dance." Part II: The Conceptual Space of the Dance, *JHMS*, 2(3):155–171.

————. 1976c. Review of R. Lange, *The Nature of Dance: An Anthropological Perspective. DRJ*, 1. (CORD).

————. 1978. "Sacred Spaces: A Preliminary Enquiry into the Latin Post-Tridentine Mass." Paper given for the Canadian Sociology and Anthropology Association, London, Ontario, May.

————. 1979. "The Human Action Sign and Semasiology." *CORD Research Annual No. X*, New York University.

————. 1980. "Taxonomies of the Body, With Special Reference to the Ballet, Part I." *Journal for the Anthropological Study of Human Movement*, 1(1):1–19.

————. 1980a. "Taxonomies of the Body, With Special Reference to the Ballet, Part II." *Journal for the Anthropological Study of Human Movement*, 1(2):98–122.

————. 1980b. "On Structures of Human Movement: A Reply to Gell." *Journal of Human Movement Sciences*, 6(4):303–322.

————. 1980c. "Anthropology and Art." Paper for S.E.H.N.A.P. Symposium on Qualitative Evaluation in the Arts, July, New York University.

————. 1981. "Introduction." Special Issue on Semasiology, *Journal for the Anthropological Study of Human Movement*, 1(4):207–225.

————. 1982. "Semasiology: A Semantic Anthropologist's View of Human Movements and Actions." *Semantic Anthropology (ASA 22)*. (Ed. Parkin), Academic Press, London.

————. 1983. "A New Paradigm in Movement Research." *Journal of the Association of Graduate Ethnologists*, 7, University of California, Los Angeles.

————. 1986. "(Non)Anthropologists, the Dance and Human Movement." *Theatrical Movement: A Bibliographical Anthology*, (Ed. B. Fleshman), Scarecrow Press, Metuchen, New Jersey.

————. 1986a. Review Article: *The Dance of Life...*, by E.T. Hall. *Journal for the Anthropological Study of Human Movement*, 3(4):218–226.

————. 1986b. "Prefigurements of Art: A Reply to Sebeok." *Journal for the Anthropological Study of Human Movement*, 4(2):68–80.

————. 1988. "Homo Nullius: The Status of Traditional Dancing in Northern Queensland." Paper for International Conference on Hunters and Gatherers (Anthropology), Darwin, N.T., August 31.

WILSON, B. (Ed.). 1970. *Rationality*. Blackwell, Oxford.

WINCH, P. 1958. *The Idea of a Social Science and Its Relation to Philosophy*. Routledge & Kegan Paul, London.

WIRZ, P. 1954. *Exorcism and the Art Healing in Ceylon*. Brill, Leiden, The Netherlands.

WITTGENSTEIN, L. 1958. *Philosophical Investigations*. Blackwell, Oxford.

————. 1967. *Remarks on the Foundations of Mathematics*. Blackwell, Oxford.

WOLF, F. 1981. *Taking the Quantum Leap*. Harper & Row, New York.

WORTH, S., and J. Adair. 1972. *Through Navajo Eyes. An Exploration in Film Communication and Anthropology*. Indiana University Press, Bloomington.

WUNDT, W. 1973. *The Language of Gestures*. (Introduction by Blumenthal, and additional essays by Mead and Buhler), Mouton, The Hague.

WYNNE, S. 1969. "Reconstruction of a Dance from 1700." *CORD Dance History Research: Perspectives from Related Arts and Disciplines*. (Ed. Keali'inohomoku), Proceedings of the 2nd conference on Research in Dance, Part I, pp.64–79.

YOUNGERMAN, S. 1974. "Curt Sachs and His Heritage: A Critical Review of World History of the Dance with a Survery of Recent Studies That Perpetuate His Ideas." *CORD News*, 6(2), pp.6–19.

ZANER, R. 1971. *The Problem of Embodiment: Some Contributions to a Phenomenology of the Body*. Martinus Nijoff, The Hague.

ZOETE, B. de, and W. SPIES, 1938. *Dance and Drama in Bali*. Faber & Faber, London.

SUBJECT INDEX

AUTHOR INDEX